Anu

msdn training

C0-AZT-496

2609A: Introduction to C# Programming with Microsoft® .NET

Books

Dino Esposito — author.
   Building web Solutions for Asp. net & ADO. net

Microsoft®

END-USER LICENSE AGREEMENT FOR MICROSOFT OFFICIAL CURRICULUM COURSEWARE –STUDENT EDITION

PLEASE READ THIS END-USER LICENSE AGREEMENT ("EULA") CAREFULLY. BY USING THE MATERIALS AND/OR USING OR INSTALLING THE SOFTWARE THAT ACCOMPANIES THIS EULA (COLLECTIVELY, THE "LICENSED CONTENT"), YOU AGREE TO THE TERMS OF THIS EULA. IF YOU DO NOT AGREE, DO NOT USE THE LICENSED CONTENT.

1.   **GENERAL.** This EULA is a legal agreement between you (either an individual or a single entity) and Microsoft Corporation ("Microsoft"). This EULA governs the Licensed Content, which includes computer software (including online and electronic documentation), training materials, and any other associated media and printed materials. This EULA applies to updates, supplements, add-on components, and Internet-based services components of the Licensed Content that Microsoft may provide or make available to you unless Microsoft provides other terms with the update, supplement, add-on component, or Internet-based services component. Microsoft reserves the right to discontinue any Internet-based services provided to you or made available to you through the use of the Licensed Content. This EULA also governs any product support services relating to the Licensed Content except as may be included in another agreement between you and Microsoft. An amendment or addendum to this EULA may accompany the Licensed Content.

2.   **GENERAL GRANT OF LICENSE.** Microsoft grants you the following rights, conditioned on your compliance with all the terms and conditions of this EULA. Microsoft grants you a limited, non-exclusive, royalty-free license to install and use the Licensed Content solely in conjunction with your participation as a student in an Authorized Training Session (as defined below). You may install and use one copy of the software on a single computer, device, workstation, terminal, or other digital electronic or analog device ("Device"). You may make a second copy of the software and install it on a portable Device for the exclusive use of the person who is the primary user of the first copy of the software. A license for the software may not be shared for use by multiple end users. An "Authorized Training Session" means a training session conducted at a Microsoft Certified Technical Education Center, an IT Academy, via a Microsoft Certified Partner, or such other entity as Microsoft may designate from time to time in writing, by a Microsoft Certified Trainer (for more information on these entities, please visit www.microsoft.com). WITHOUT LIMITING THE FOREGOING, COPYING OR REPRODUCTION OF THE LICENSED CONTENT TO ANY SERVER OR LOCATION FOR FURTHER REPRODUCTION OR REDISTRIBUTION IS EXPRESSLY PROHIBITED.

3.   **DESCRIPTION OF OTHER RIGHTS AND LICENSE LIMITATIONS**

    3.1   *Use of Documentation and Printed Training Materials.*

        3.1.1   The documents and related graphics included in the Licensed Content may include technical inaccuracies or typographical errors. Changes are periodically made to the content. Microsoft may make improvements and/or changes in any of the components of the Licensed Content at any time without notice. The names of companies, products, people, characters and/or data mentioned in the Licensed Content may be fictitious and are in no way intended to represent any real individual, company, product or event, unless otherwise noted.

        3.1.2   Microsoft grants you the right to reproduce portions of documents (such as student workbooks, white papers, press releases, datasheets and FAQs) (the "Documents") provided with the Licensed Content. You may not print any book (either electronic or print version) in its entirety. If you choose to reproduce Documents, you agree that: (a) use of such printed Documents will be solely in conjunction with your personal training use; (b) the Documents will not republished or posted on any network computer or broadcast in any media; (c) any reproduction will include either the Document's original copyright notice or a copyright notice to Microsoft's benefit substantially in the format provided below; and (d) to comply with all terms and conditions of this EULA. In addition, no modifications may made to any Document.

        Form of Notice:

        © 2002. Reprinted with permission by Microsoft Corporation. All rights reserved.

        Microsoft and Windows are either registered trademarks or trademarks of Microsoft Corporation in the US and/or other countries. Other product and company names mentioned herein may be the trademarks of their respective owners.

    3.2   *Use of Media Elements.* The Licensed Content may include certain photographs, clip art, animations, sounds, music, and video clips (together "Media Elements"). You may not modify these Media Elements.

    3.3   *Use of Sample Code.* In the event that the Licensed Content includes sample code in source or object format ("Sample Code"), Microsoft grants you a limited, non-exclusive, royalty-free license to use, copy and modify the Sample Code; if you elect to exercise the foregoing rights, you agree to comply with all other terms and conditions of this EULA, including without limitation Sections 3.4, 3.5, and 6.

    3.4   *Permitted Modifications.* In the event that you exercise any rights provided under this EULA to create modifications of the Licensed Content, you agree that any such modifications: (a) will not be used for providing training where a fee is charged in public or private classes; (b) indemnify, hold harmless, and defend Microsoft from and against any claims or lawsuits, including attorneys' fees, which arise from or result from your use of any modified version of the Licensed Content; and (c) not to transfer or assign any rights to any modified version of the Licensed Content to any third party without the express written permission of Microsoft.

3.5   *Reproduction/Redistribution Licensed Content.* Except as expressly provided in this EULA, you may not reproduce or distribute the Licensed Content or any portion thereof (including any permitted modifications) to any third parties without the express written permission of Microsoft.

4.   **RESERVATION OF RIGHTS AND OWNERSHIP.** Microsoft reserves all rights not expressly granted to you in this EULA. The Licensed Content is protected by copyright and other intellectual property laws and treaties. Microsoft or its suppliers own the title, copyright, and other intellectual property rights in the Licensed Content. You may not remove or obscure any copyright, trademark or patent notices that appear on the Licensed Content, or any components thereof, as delivered to you. **The Licensed Content is licensed, not sold.**

5.   **LIMITATIONS ON REVERSE ENGINEERING, DECOMPILATION, AND DISASSEMBLY.** You may not reverse engineer, decompile, or disassemble the Software or Media Elements, except and only to the extent that such activity is expressly permitted by applicable law notwithstanding this limitation.

6.   **LIMITATIONS ON SALE, RENTAL, ETC. AND CERTAIN ASSIGNMENTS.** You may not provide commercial hosting services with, sell, rent, lease, lend, sublicense, or assign copies of the Licensed Content, or any portion thereof (including any permitted modifications thereof) on a stand-alone basis or as part of any collection, product or service.

7.   **CONSENT TO USE OF DATA.** You agree that Microsoft and its affiliates may collect and use technical information gathered as part of the product support services provided to you, if any, related to the Licensed Content. Microsoft may use this information solely to improve our products or to provide customized services or technologies to you and will not disclose this information in a form that personally identifies you.

8.   **LINKS TO THIRD PARTY SITES.** You may link to third party sites through the use of the Licensed Content. The third party sites are not under the control of Microsoft, and Microsoft is not responsible for the contents of any third party sites, any links contained in third party sites, or any changes or updates to third party sites. Microsoft is not responsible for webcasting or any other form of transmission received from any third party sites. Microsoft is providing these links to third party sites to you only as a convenience, and the inclusion of any link does not imply an endorsement by Microsoft of the third party site.

9.   **ADDITIONAL LICENSED CONTENT/SERVICES.** This EULA applies to updates, supplements, add-on components, or Internet-based services components, of the Licensed Content that Microsoft may provide to you or make available to you after the date you obtain your initial copy of the Licensed Content, unless we provide other terms along with the update, supplement, add-on component, or Internet-based services component. Microsoft reserves the right to discontinue any Internet-based services provided to you or made available to you through the use of the Licensed Content.

10.   **U.S. GOVERNMENT LICENSE RIGHTS**. All software provided to the U.S. Government pursuant to solicitations issued on or after December 1, 1995 is provided with the commercial license rights and restrictions described elsewhere herein. All software provided to the U.S. Government pursuant to solicitations issued prior to December 1, 1995 is provided with "Restricted Rights" as provided for in FAR, 48 CFR 52.227-14 (JUNE 1987) or DFAR, 48 CFR 252.227-7013 (OCT 1988), as applicable.

11.   **EXPORT RESTRICTIONS**. You acknowledge that the Licensed Content is subject to U.S. export jurisdiction. You agree to comply with all applicable international and national laws that apply to the Licensed Content, including the U.S. Export Administration Regulations, as well as end-user, end-use, and destination restrictions issued by U.S. and other governments. For additional information see <http://www.microsoft.com/exporting/>.

12.   **TRANSFER.** The initial user of the Licensed Content may make a one-time permanent transfer of this EULA and Licensed Content to another end user, provided the initial user retains no copies of the Licensed Content. The transfer may not be an indirect transfer, such as a consignment. Prior to the transfer, the end user receiving the Licensed Content must agree to all the EULA terms.

13.   **"NOT FOR RESALE" LICENSED CONTENT.** Licensed Content identified as "Not For Resale" or "NFR," may not be sold or otherwise transferred for value, or used for any purpose other than demonstration, test or evaluation.

14.   **TERMINATION.** Without prejudice to any other rights, Microsoft may terminate this EULA if you fail to comply with the terms and conditions of this EULA. In such event, you must destroy all copies of the Licensed Content and all of its component parts.

15.   <u>**DISCLAIMER OF WARRANTIES.**</u> **TO THE MAXIMUM EXTENT PERMITTED BY APPLICABLE LAW, MICROSOFT AND ITS SUPPLIERS PROVIDE THE LICENSED CONTENT AND SUPPORT SERVICES (IF ANY)** *AS IS AND WITH ALL FAULTS,* **AND MICROSOFT AND ITS SUPPLIERS HEREBY DISCLAIM ALL OTHER WARRANTIES AND CONDITIONS, WHETHER EXPRESS, IMPLIED OR STATUTORY, INCLUDING, BUT NOT LIMITED TO, ANY (IF ANY) IMPLIED WARRANTIES, DUTIES OR CONDITIONS OF MERCHANTABILITY, OF FITNESS FOR A PARTICULAR PURPOSE, OF RELIABILITY OR AVAILABILITY, OF ACCURACY OR COMPLETENESS OF RESPONSES, OF RESULTS, OF WORKMANLIKE EFFORT, OF LACK OF VIRUSES, AND OF LACK OF NEGLIGENCE, ALL WITH REGARD TO THE LICENSED CONTENT, AND THE PROVISION OF OR FAILURE TO PROVIDE SUPPORT OR OTHER SERVICES, INFORMATION, SOFTWARE, AND RELATED CONTENT THROUGH THE LICENSED CONTENT, OR OTHERWISE ARISING OUT OF THE USE OF THE LICENSED CONTENT. ALSO, THERE IS NO WARRANTY OR CONDITION OF TITLE, QUIET ENJOYMENT, QUIET POSSESSION, CORRESPONDENCE TO DESCRIPTION OR NON-INFRINGEMENT WITH REGARD TO THE LICENSED CONTENT. THE ENTIRE RISK AS TO THE QUALITY, OR ARISING OUT OF THE USE OR PERFORMANCE OF THE LICENSED CONTENT, AND ANY SUPPORT SERVICES, REMAINS WITH YOU.**

16.   <u>**EXCLUSION OF INCIDENTAL, CONSEQUENTIAL AND CERTAIN OTHER DAMAGES.**</u> **TO THE MAXIMUM EXTENT PERMITTED BY APPLICABLE LAW, IN NO EVENT SHALL MICROSOFT OR ITS SUPPLIERS BE LIABLE FOR ANY SPECIAL, INCIDENTAL, PUNITIVE, INDIRECT, OR CONSEQUENTIAL DAMAGES WHATSOEVER (INCLUDING, BUT NOT**

LIMITED TO, DAMAGES FOR LOSS OF PROFITS OR CONFIDENTIAL OR OTHER INFORMATION, FOR BUSINESS INTERRUPTION, FOR PERSONAL INJURY, FOR LOSS OF PRIVACY, FOR FAILURE TO MEET ANY DUTY INCLUDING OF GOOD FAITH OR OF REASONABLE CARE, FOR NEGLIGENCE, AND FOR ANY OTHER PECUNIARY OR OTHER LOSS WHATSOEVER) ARISING OUT OF OR IN ANY WAY RELATED TO THE USE OF OR INABILITY TO USE THE LICENSED CONTENT, THE PROVISION OF OR FAILURE TO PROVIDE SUPPORT OR OTHER SERVICES, INFORMATION, SOFTWARE, AND RELATED CONTENT THROUGH THE LICENSED CONTENT, OR OTHERWISE ARISING OUT OF THE USE OF THE LICENSED CONTENT, OR OTHERWISE UNDER OR IN CONNECTION WITH ANY PROVISION OF THIS EULA, EVEN IN THE EVENT OF THE FAULT, TORT (INCLUDING NEGLIGENCE), MISREPRESENTATION, STRICT LIABILITY, BREACH OF CONTRACT OR BREACH OF WARRANTY OF MICROSOFT OR ANY SUPPLIER, AND EVEN IF MICROSOFT OR ANY SUPPLIER HAS BEEN ADVISED OF THE POSSIBILITY OF SUCH DAMAGES. BECAUSE SOME STATES/JURISDICTIONS DO NOT ALLOW THE EXCLUSION OR LIMITATION OF LIABILITY FOR CONSEQUENTIAL OR INCIDENTAL DAMAGES, THE ABOVE LIMITATION MAY NOT APPLY TO YOU.

17.   LIMITATION OF LIABILITY AND REMEDIES. NOTWITHSTANDING ANY DAMAGES THAT YOU MIGHT INCUR FOR ANY REASON WHATSOEVER (INCLUDING, WITHOUT LIMITATION, ALL DAMAGES REFERENCED HEREIN AND ALL DIRECT OR GENERAL DAMAGES IN CONTRACT OR ANYTHING ELSE), THE ENTIRE LIABILITY OF MICROSOFT AND ANY OF ITS SUPPLIERS UNDER ANY PROVISION OF THIS EULA AND YOUR EXCLUSIVE REMEDY HEREUNDER SHALL BE LIMITED TO THE GREATER OF THE ACTUAL DAMAGES YOU INCUR IN REASONABLE RELIANCE ON THE LICENSED CONTENT UP TO THE AMOUNT ACTUALLY PAID BY YOU FOR THE LICENSED CONTENT OR US$5.00. THE FOREGOING LIMITATIONS, EXCLUSIONS AND DISCLAIMERS SHALL APPLY TO THE MAXIMUM EXTENT PERMITTED BY APPLICABLE LAW, EVEN IF ANY REMEDY FAILS ITS ESSENTIAL PURPOSE.

18.   APPLICABLE LAW. If you acquired this Licensed Content in the United States, this EULA is governed by the laws of the State of Washington. If you acquired this Licensed Content in Canada, unless expressly prohibited by local law, this EULA is governed by the laws in force in the Province of Ontario, Canada; and, in respect of any dispute which may arise hereunder, you consent to the jurisdiction of the federal and provincial courts sitting in Toronto, Ontario. If you acquired this Licensed Content in the European Union, Iceland, Norway, or Switzerland, then local law applies. If you acquired this Licensed Content in any other country, then local law may apply.

19.   ENTIRE AGREEMENT; SEVERABILITY. This EULA (including any addendum or amendment to this EULA which is included with the Licensed Content) are the entire agreement between you and Microsoft relating to the Licensed Content and the support services (if any) and they supersede all prior or contemporaneous oral or written communications, proposals and representations with respect to the Licensed Content or any other subject matter covered by this EULA. To the extent the terms of any Microsoft policies or programs for support services conflict with the terms of this EULA, the terms of this EULA shall control. If any provision of this EULA is held to be void, invalid, unenforceable or illegal, the other provisions shall continue in full force and effect.

Should you have any questions concerning this EULA, or if you desire to contact Microsoft for any reason, please use the address information enclosed in this Licensed Content to contact the Microsoft subsidiary serving your country or visit Microsoft on the World Wide Web at http://www.microsoft.com.

Si vous avez acquis votre Contenu Sous Licence Microsoft au CANADA :

DÉNI DE GARANTIES. Dans la mesure maximale permise par les lois applicables, le Contenu Sous Licence et les services de soutien technique (le cas échéant) sont fournis *TELS QUELS ET AVEC TOUS LES DÉFAUTS* par Microsoft et ses fournisseurs, lesquels par les présentes dénient toutes autres garanties et conditions expresses, implicites ou en vertu de la loi, notamment, mais sans limitation, (le cas échéant) les garanties, devoirs ou conditions implicites de qualité marchande, d'adaptation à une fin usage particulière, de fiabilité ou de disponibilité, d'exactitude ou d'exhaustivité des réponses, des résultats, des efforts déployés selon les règles de l'art, d'absence de virus et d'absence de négligence, le tout à l'égard du Contenu Sous Licence et de la prestation des services de soutien technique ou de l'omission de la 'une telle prestation des services de soutien technique ou à l'égard de la fourniture ou de l'omission de la fourniture de tous autres services, renseignements, Contenus Sous Licence, et contenu qui s'y rapporte grâce au Contenu Sous Licence ou provenant autrement de l'utilisation du Contenu Sous Licence. PAR AILLEURS, IL N'Y A AUCUNE GARANTIE OU CONDITION QUANT AU TITRE DE PROPRIÉTÉ, À LA JOUISSANCE OU LA POSSESSION PAISIBLE, À LA CONCORDANCE À UNE DESCRIPTION NI QUANT À UNE ABSENCE DE CONTREFAÇON CONCERNANT LE CONTENU SOUS LICENCE.

EXCLUSION DES DOMMAGES ACCESSOIRES, INDIRECTS ET DE CERTAINS AUTRES DOMMAGES. DANS LA MESURE MAXIMALE PERMISE PAR LES LOIS APPLICABLES, EN AUCUN CAS MICROSOFT OU SES FOURNISSEURS NE SERONT RESPONSABLES DES DOMMAGES SPÉCIAUX, CONSÉCUTIFS, ACCESSOIRES OU INDIRECTS DE QUELQUE NATURE QUE CE SOIT (NOTAMMENT, LES DOMMAGES À L'ÉGARD DU MANQUE À GAGNER OU DE LA DIVULGATION DE RENSEIGNEMENTS CONFIDENTIELS OU AUTRES, DE LA PERTE D'EXPLOITATION, DE BLESSURES CORPORELLES, DE LA VIOLATION DE LA VIE PRIVÉE, DE L'OMISSION DE REMPLIR TOUT DEVOIR, Y COMPRIS D'AGIR DE BONNE FOI OU D'EXERCER UN SOIN RAISONNABLE, DE LA NÉGLIGENCE ET DE TOUTE AUTRE PERTE PÉCUNIAIRE OU AUTRE PERTE

DE QUELQUE NATURE QUE CE SOIT) SE RAPPORTANT DE QUELQUE MANIÈRE QUE CE SOIT À L'UTILISATION DU CONTENU SOUS LICENCE OU À L'INCAPACITÉ DE S'EN SERVIR, À LA PRESTATION OU À L'OMISSION DE LA 'UNE TELLE PRESTATION DE SERVICES DE SOUTIEN TECHNIQUE OU À LA FOURNITURE OU À L'OMISSION DE LA FOURNITURE DE TOUS AUTRES SERVICES, RENSEIGNEMENTS, CONTENUS SOUS LICENCE, ET CONTENU QUI S'Y RAPPORTE GRÂCE AU CONTENU SOUS LICENCE OU PROVENANT AUTREMENT DE L'UTILISATION DU CONTENU SOUS LICENCE OU AUTREMENT AUX TERMES DE TOUTE DISPOSITION DE LA U PRÉSENTE CONVENTION EULA OU RELATIVEMENT À UNE TELLE DISPOSITION, MÊME EN CAS DE FAUTE, DE DÉLIT CIVIL (Y COMPRIS LA NÉGLIGENCE), DE RESPONSABILITÉ STRICTE, DE VIOLATION DE CONTRAT OU DE VIOLATION DE GARANTIE DE MICROSOFT OU DE TOUT FOURNISSEUR ET MÊME SI MICROSOFT OU TOUT FOURNISSEUR A ÉTÉ AVISÉ DE LA POSSIBILITÉ DE TELS DOMMAGES.

LIMITATION DE RESPONSABILITÉ ET RECOURS. MALGRÉ LES DOMMAGES QUE VOUS PUISSIEZ SUBIR POUR QUELQUE MOTIF QUE CE SOIT (NOTAMMENT, MAIS SANS LIMITATION, TOUS LES DOMMAGES SUSMENTIONNÉS ET TOUS LES DOMMAGES DIRECTS OU GÉNÉRAUX OU AUTRES), LA SEULE RESPONSABILITÉ 'OBLIGATION INTÉGRALE DE MICROSOFT ET DE L'UN OU L'AUTRE DE SES FOURNISSEURS AUX TERMES DE TOUTE DISPOSITION DEU LA PRÉSENTE CONVENTION EULA ET VOTRE RECOURS EXCLUSIF À L'ÉGARD DE TOUT CE QUI PRÉCÈDE SE LIMITE AU PLUS ÉLEVÉ ENTRE LES MONTANTS SUIVÀNTS : LE MONTANT QUE VOUS AVEZ RÉELLEMENT PAYÉ POUR LE CONTENU SOUS LICENCE OU 5,00 $US. LES LIMITES, EXCLUSIONS ET DÉNIS QUI PRÉCÈDENT (Y COMPRIS LES CLAUSES CI-DESSUS), S'APPLIQUENT DANS LA MESURE MAXIMALE PERMISE PAR LES LOIS APPLICABLES, MÊME SI TOUT RECOURS N'ATTEINT PAS SON BUT ESSENTIEL.

À moins que cela ne soit prohibé par le droit local applicable, la présente Convention est régie par les lois de la province d'Ontario, Canada. Vous consentez Chacune des parties à la présente reconnaît irrévocablement à la compétence des tribunaux fédéraux et provinciaux siégeant à Toronto, dans de la province d'Ontario et consent à instituer tout litige qui pourrait découler de la présente auprès des tribunaux situés dans le district judiciaire de York, province d'Ontario.

Au cas où vous auriez des questions concernant cette licence ou que vous désiriez vous mettre en rapport avec Microsoft pour quelque raison que ce soit, veuillez utiliser l'information contenue dans le Contenu Sous Licence pour contacter la filiale de succursale Microsoft desservant votre pays, dont l'adresse est fournie dans ce produit, ou visitez écrivez à : Microsoft sur le World Wide Web à http://www.microsoft.com

Contents

Module 10: Creating a Web Application with Web Forms

Module 11: Application Settings and Deployment

Module 12: Exploring Future Learning

Appendix A: Key Concepts Guide

Appendix B: Advanced Topics

About This Course

This section provides you with a brief description of the course, audience, suggested prerequisites, and course objectives.

Description

This 5-day instructor-led course provides developers with the opportunity to learn the fundamental skills that are required to use C#, the Microsoft® .NET Framework, and the Microsoft Visual Studio® .NET development environment to build graphical object-oriented Web applications and applications based on Microsoft Windows®. This course teaches the concepts of development from a C# perspective and introduces C# programming language fundamentals.

This course is designed to be a hands-on, performance-based learning experience. Fifty percent of the students' time, therefore, is allocated to practices, which follow each lesson, and one or more labs at the conclusion of each module.

Note   See Appendix A: Key Concepts Guide for an alphabetical listing of key concepts in this course.

All the applications that the students develop and use in the practices and labs are graphical, based either on Web Forms or Windows Forms. However, to provide enough room for complete code samples in the Student Workbook, some of the sample code is console based. Console-based code is also used in slides to save space.

Important   This course offers optional practices and labs, in addition to optional tasks in each practice or lab, to provide a successful learning experience, allow instructional flexibility, and accommodate advanced learners.

The practices and labs in this course are categorized as follows:

- *Matching Practices.* Students independently match questions with available answers.

- *Hands-on Practices.* Students independently complete the assigned tasks.

- *Guided Practices.* The instructor allows the students a few minutes to begin working on their tasks and then guides the students through the practice by performing the tasks on the board or on the screen.

- *Optional* or *Advanced Labs.* The instructor or students choose a lab from the available options.

In addition, several advanced topics have been included in Appendix B: Advanced Topics.

Please also note that the students' install_folder is located at C:\Program Files\Msdntrain\2609.

Audience

This course is intended for developers who understand computer programming but may have learned programming by using a non-graphical language.

This course is also intended for developers of corporate applications who want to build applications by using C#; use the .NET Framework and C#, in addition to Microsoft Visual Basic® and Managed Extensions for C++; and eventually write highly functional Windows-based applications, Web applications, and XML Web services.

Student prerequisites

This course requires that students meet the following prerequisites:

- Be familiar and comfortable with basic operating system functions such as file manipulation.

- Understand the basics of structured programming, including concepts such as flow control, variables and parameters, and function calls.

  Course 1587, *Introduction to Programming with Microsoft Visual Basic 6*, may help students gain basic skills in programming techniques.

- Have at least three months of experience developing applications in either a graphical or non-graphical environment, or equivalent knowledge.

- Experience in object-oriented programming and concepts is not required.

Course objectives

After completing this course, the student will be able to:

- Configure and use the Visual Studio .NET integrated development environment (IDE).

- Create a Windows Forms project, by using the Windows Application template, with controls and code to respond to events.

- Use and create methods.

- Test and debug an application.

- Use object-oriented design techniques to design a .NET-based application.

- Create classes.

- Use C# techniques to enhance methods and classes.

- Use Microsoft ADO.NET to access and manipulate data in a database.

- Create a Web application by using Web Forms.

- Use an XML Web service in a C# application.

- Create a Windows-based application with multiple forms.

- Explore future learning.

Student Materials Compact Disc Contents

The Student Materials compact disc contains the following files and folders:

- *Autorun.exe*. When the compact disc is inserted into the CD-ROM drive, or when you double-click the **Autorun.exe** file, this file opens the compact disc and allows you to browse the Student Materials compact disc.

- *Autorun.inf*. When the compact disc is inserted into the compact disc drive, this file opens Autorun.exe.

- *Default.htm*. This file opens the Student Materials Web page. It provides you with resources pertaining to this course, including additional reading, review and lab answers, lab files, multimedia presentations, and course-related Web sites.

- *Readme.txt*. This file explains how to install the software for viewing the Student Materials compact disc and its contents and how to open the Student Materials Web page.

- *2609A_ms.doc*. This file is the Manual Classroom Setup Guide. It contains a description of classroom requirements, classroom setup instructions, and the classroom configuration.

- *Flash*. This folder contains the installer for the Macromedia Flash 5.0 browser plug-in.

- *Fonts*. This folder contains fonts that may be required to view Microsoft Word documents that are included with this course.

- *Labfiles*. This folder contains files that are used in the hands-on labs. These files may be used to prepare the student computers for the hands-on labs.

- *Media*. This folder contains files that are used in multimedia presentations for this course.

- *Mplayer*. This folder contains the setup file to install Microsoft Windows Media™ Player.

- *Practices*. This folder contains files that are used in the hands-on practices.

- *Samples*. This folder contains code samples that are associated with this course.

- *Webfiles*. This folder contains the files that are required to view the course Web page. To open the Web page, open Windows Explorer, and in the root directory of the compact disc, double-click **Default.htm** or **Autorun.exe**.

- *Wordview*. This folder contains the Word Viewer that is used to view any Word document (.doc) files that are included on the compact disc.

Document Conventions

The following conventions are used in course materials to distinguish elements of the text.

Convention	Use
Bold	Represents commands, command options, and syntax that must be typed exactly as shown. It also indicates commands on menus and buttons, dialog box titles and options, and icon and menu names.
Italic	In syntax statements or descriptive text, indicates argument names or placeholders for variable information. Italic is also used for introducing new terms, for book titles, and for emphasis in the text.
Title Capitals	Indicate domain names, user names, computer names, directory names, and folder and file names, except when specifically referring to case-sensitive names. Unless otherwise indicated, you can use lowercase letters when you type a directory name or file name in a dialog box or at a command prompt.
ALL CAPITALS	Indicate the names of keys, key sequences, and key combinations—for example, ALT+SPACEBAR.
`monospace`	Represents code samples or examples of screen text.
[ ]	In syntax statements, enclose optional items. For example, [*filename*] in command syntax indicates that you can choose to type a file name with the command. Type only the information within the brackets, not the brackets themselves.
{ }	In syntax statements, enclose required items. Type only the information within the braces, not the braces themselves.
|	In syntax statements, separates an either/or choice.
▶	Indicates a procedure with sequential steps.
...	In syntax statements, specifies that the preceding item may be repeated.
. . .	Represents an omitted portion of a code sample.

msdn training

Introduction

Contents

Introduction

- **Name**
- **Company affiliation**
- **Title/function**
- **Job responsibility**
- **Programming, networking, database experience**
- **Product experience**
- **Expectations for the course**

Introduction   Your instructor will ask you to introduce yourself and provide a brief overview of your background, addressing the bulleted items on the slide as appropriate.

Course Materials

- ■ **Name card**
- ■ **Student workbook**
- ■ **Student Materials compact disc**
- ■ **Course evaluation**

The following materials are included with your kit:

- ■ *Name card.* Write your name on both sides of the name card.
- ■ *Student workbook.* The student workbook contains the material covered in class, in addition to the hands-on lab exercises.
- ■ *Student Materials compact disc.* The Student Materials compact disc contains the Web page that provides you with links to resources pertaining to this course, including additional readings, review and lab answers, lab files, multimedia presentations, and course-related Web sites.

> **Note** To open the Web page, insert the Student Materials compact disc into the CD-ROM drive, and then in the root directory of the compact disc, double-click **Autorun.exe** or **Default.htm**.

- ■ *Course evaluation.* To provide feedback on the course, training facility, and instructor, you will have the opportunity to complete an online evaluation near the end of the course.

To provide additional comments or inquire about the Microsoft Certified Professional program, send e-mail to mcphelp@microsoft.com.

Prerequisites

- **Familiarity with basic operating system functions**
- **Understanding of the basics of structured programming**
- **At least three months of experience developing applications**

This course requires that you meet the following prerequisites:

- Be familiar with basic operating system functions such as file manipulation.
- Understand basics of structured programming, including concepts such as flow control, variables and parameters, and function calls.
- At least three months of experience developing applications in either a graphical or non-graphical environment, or equivalent knowledge.

Course Outline

- **Module 1: Getting Started**

- **Module 2: Understanding C# Language Fundamentals**

- **Module 3: Creating Objects in C#**

- **Module 4: Implementing Object-Oriented Programming Techniques in C#**

- **Module 5: Programming with C#**

- **Module 6: Building .NET–based Applications with C#**

Module 1, "Getting Started," introduces the Microsoft® .NET platform and Microsoft Visual Studio® .NET, and explains how to use the programming tools in Visual Studio .NET.

Module 2, "Understanding C# Language Fundamentals," introduces the basic syntax and structure of the C# language. It describes C# data types, describes the .NET common type system, and discusses code style guidelines.

Module 3, "Creating Objects in C#," introduces the fundamentals of object-oriented programming, including the concepts of objects, classes, and methods.

Module 4, "Implementing Object-Oriented Programming Techniques in C#," describes in detail the object-oriented principles of encapsulation, inheritance, and polymorphism.

Module 5, "Programming with C#," covers data structures, exception handling, interfaces, delegates, and events. It introduces various data structures, including arrays, including the **System.Array** class, and collections. This module also covers interfaces, introduces the concepts and syntax of exception handling, and explains delegates and their use in event handling.

Module 6, "Building .NET–based Applications with C#," introduces the .NET Framework class library, focusing on the **System.Object** class and several of the most useful derived classes. This module also examines classes in the **System.Windows.Forms** namespace and discusses the handling of events in Microsoft Windows® Forms.

Course Outline *(continued)*

- Module 7: Using ADO.NET to Access Data
- Module 8: Creating Windows-based Applications
- Module 9: Using XML Web Services in a C# Application
- Module 10: Creating a Web Application with Web Forms
- Module 11: Application Settings and Deployment
- Module 12: Exploring Future Learning

Module 7, "Using ADO.NET to Access Data," explains how to use the **System.Data** namespace and Microsoft ADO.NET to access data in a database. It describes how to create a Windows-based application that uses ADO.NET and then use the application to connect to a database, create a query, populate a **DataSet** object, bind data to controls, and update a database.

Module 8, "Creating Windows-based Applications," describes how to create menus, common and custom dialog boxes, status bars, and toolbars to enhance the usability of an application.

Module 9, "Using XML Web Services in a C# Application," introduces the **System.Web.Services** namespace and the process of building and using XML Web services in a C# application.

Module 10, "Creating a Web Application with Web Forms," introduces the **System.Web.UI** namespace and describes how to create a Web application with a Web Form. The module explains how to create a Web Form, add controls to the Web Form, and then use the Web Form to submit data and respond to events.

Module 11, "Application Settings and Deployment," describes how to store user preferences and configure application settings. It also introduces the procedures that are involved in deploying a C# application by using Microsoft Visual Studio .NET. It explains how to deploy both Web-based applications and applications that are based on Microsoft Windows.

Module 12, "Exploring Future Learning," provides an opportunity for students to explore some of the additional and more advanced capabilities of C#, to practice the knowledge and skills they acquired during the course, and to ask questions.

Microsoft Official Curriculum

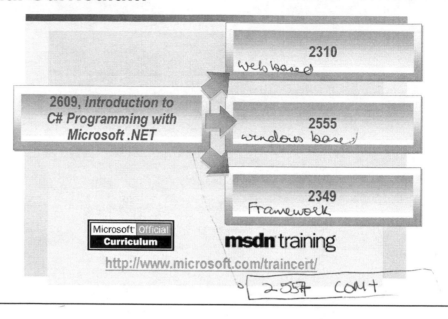

Introduction

Microsoft Training and Certification develops Microsoft Official Curriculum (MOC), including MSDN® Training, for computer professionals who design, develop, support, implement, or manage solutions using Microsoft products and technologies. These courses provide comprehensive skills-based training in instructor-led and online formats.

Additional recommended courses

Each course relates in some way to another course. A related course may be a prerequisite, a follow-up course in a recommended series, or a course that offers additional training.

After taking Course 2609, *Introduction to C# Programming with Microsoft .NET*, you can take the following courses in any order:

- 2310, *Developing Microsoft ASP.NET Web Applications Using Visual Studio .NET*

- 2555, *Developing Microsoft .NET Applications for Windows (Visual C#™ .NET)*

- 2349, *Programming with the Microsoft .NET Framework (Microsoft Visual C# .NET)*

Course	Title and description
2310	*Developing Microsoft ASP.NET Web Applications Using Visual Studio .NET* This course teaches the fundamentals of Web site implementation using ASP.NET and Microsoft Visual Basic® .NET with the Visual Studio .NET environment and the .NET platform.
2555	*Developing Microsoft .NET Applications for Windows (Visual C# .NET)* This course provides students with the skills required to build Windows Forms applications by using the Microsoft .NET Framework.
2349	*Programming with the Microsoft .NET Framework (Microsoft Visual C# .NET)* This course enables developers to build applications that use the .NET Framework.

Other related courses may become available in the future, so for up-to-date information about recommended courses, visit the Training and Certification Web site.

Microsoft Training and Certification information

For more information, visit the Microsoft Training and Certification Web site at http://www.microsoft.com/traincert/.

Microsoft Certified Professional Program

Introduction

Microsoft Training and Certification offers a variety of certification credentials for developers and IT professionals. The Microsoft Certified Professional program is the leading certification program for validating your experience and skills, keeping you competitive in today's changing business environment.

MCP certifications

The Microsoft Certified Professional program includes the following certifications.

- MCSA on Microsoft Windows 2000

  The Microsoft Certified Systems Administrator (MCSA) certification is designed for professionals who implement, manage, and troubleshoot existing network and system environments based on Microsoft Windows 2000 platforms, including the Windows .NET Server family. Implementation responsibilities include installing and configuring parts of the systems. Management responsibilities include administering and supporting the systems.

- MCSE on Microsoft Windows 2000

  The Microsoft Certified Systems Engineer (MCSE) credential is the premier certification for professionals who analyze the business requirements and design and implement the infrastructure for business solutions based on the Microsoft Windows 2000 platform and Microsoft server software, including the Windows .NET Server family. Implementation responsibilities include installing, configuring, and troubleshooting network systems.

- MCAD

  The Microsoft Certified Application Developer (MCAD) for Microsoft .NET credential is appropriate for professionals who use Microsoft technologies to develop and maintain department-level applications, components, Web or desktop clients, or back-end data services, and for those who work in teams that develop enterprise applications. The credential covers job tasks that include developing, deploying, and maintaining the solution.

- MCSD

  The Microsoft Certified Solution Developer (MCSD) credential is the premier certification for professionals who design and develop leading-edge business solutions with Microsoft development tools, technologies, platforms, and the Microsoft Windows DNA architecture. The types of applications MCSDs can develop include desktop applications and multi-user, Web-based, N-tier, and transaction-based applications. The credential covers job tasks ranging from analyzing business requirements to maintaining solutions.

- MCDBA on Microsoft SQL Server™ 2000

  The Microsoft Certified Database Administrator (MCDBA) credential is the premier certification for professionals who implement and administer Microsoft SQL Server databases. The certification is appropriate for individuals who derive physical database designs, develop logical data models, create physical databases, create data services by using Transact-SQL, manage and maintain databases, configure and manage security, monitor and optimize databases, and install and configure SQL Server.

- MCP

  The Microsoft Certified Professional (MCP) credential is for individuals who have the skills to successfully implement a Microsoft product or technology as part of a business solution in an organization. Hands-on experience with the product is necessary to successfully achieve certification.

- MCT

  Microsoft Certified Trainers (MCTs) demonstrate the instructional and technical skills that qualify them to deliver Microsoft Official Curriculum through Microsoft Certified Technical Education Centers (Microsoft CTECs).

Certification requirements

The certification requirements differ for each certification category and are specific to the products and job functions addressed by the certification. To become a Microsoft Certified Professional, you must pass rigorous certification exams that provide a valid and reliable measure of technical proficiency and expertise.

For More Information   See the Microsoft Training and Certification Web site at http://www.microsoft.com/traincert/.

You can also send e-mail to mcphelp@microsoft.com if you have specific certification questions.

Acquiring the skills tested by an MCP exam

Microsoft Official Curriculum (MOC) and MSDN Training can help you develop the skills that you need to do your job. They also complement the experience that you gain while working with Microsoft products and technologies. However, no one-to-one correlation exists between MOC and MSDN Training courses and MCP exams. Microsoft does not expect or intend for the courses to be the sole preparation method for passing MCP exams. Practical product knowledge and experience is also necessary to pass the MCP exams.

To help prepare for the MCP exams, use the preparation guides that are available for each exam. Each Exam Preparation Guide contains exam-specific information, such as a list of the topics on which you will be tested. These guides are available on the Microsoft Training and Certification Web site at http://www.microsoft.com/traincert/.

Facilities

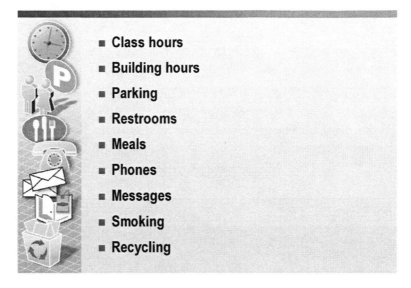

- Class hours
- Building hours
- Parking
- Restrooms
- Meals
- Phones
- Messages
- Smoking
- Recycling

msdn training

Module 1: Getting Started

Contents

Overview

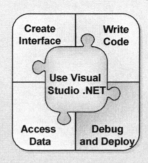

- **Introduction to .NET and the .NET Framework**
- **Exploring Visual Studio .NET**
- **Creating a Windows Application Project**

Introduction

This module presents the concepts that are central to the Microsoft® .NET Framework and platform and the Microsoft Visual Studio® .NET integrated development environment (IDE). This module also describes how to work in the development environment and explains how to use Visual Studio .NET to create and build applications based on Microsoft .NET.

Although you can use Microsoft Notepad to write applications and compile the applications separately by using the command line, the development environment increases your productivity by centralizing all application development tasks in one tool that provides you with many features, including Microsoft IntelliSense® and Dynamic Help.

Objectives

After completing this module, you will be able to:

- Identify components of the .NET platform and the .NET Framework by their function.
- Explore the Visual Studio development environment.
- Create an application based on Microsoft Windows®.

Lesson: Introduction to .NET and the .NET Framework

- **What Is the .NET Platform?**
- **What Is the .NET Framework?**
- **How the .NET Framework Works**

Introduction

In this lesson, a multimedia presentation introduces the concepts that are fundamental to your knowledge of the .NET platform and the .NET Framework.

Lesson objectives

After completing this lesson, you will be able to:

- Identify the components of the .NET platform and the .NET Framework by their functions.
- Explain the function of the NET Framework class library and the common language runtime.

Lesson agenda

This lesson includes the following topics and activities:

- What Is the .NET Platform?
- Multimedia: Introduction to .NET
- What Is the .NET Framework?
- How the .NET Framework Works
- Multimedia: Introduction to the .NET Framework
- Practice: Defining the Elements of .NET

What Is the .NET Platform?

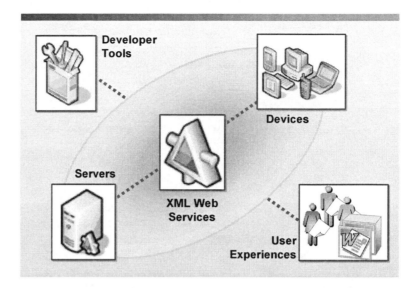

Introduction

The .NET platform provides several core technologies and services that simplify the development of Web-based applications.

.NET platform components

- Developer tools

  Microsoft Visual Studio .NET and the .NET Framework supply a complete solution for developers. Visual Studio .NET provides the development environment for building applications on the .NET Framework. The development environment provides tools that simplify the creation, deployment, and ongoing evolution of secure, scalable, highly available Web applications and XML Web services.

- Devices

  Devices are personal computers, laptops, workstations, phones, handheld computers, Tablet PCs, game consoles, and others. A *smart* device can access XML Web services and enable access to data regardless of the location, type, and number of devices in use.

- User experiences

  .NET experiences are applications that use XML Web services to allow users to access information across the Internet and from stand-alone applications in an integrated and efficient way.

■ Servers

The .NET Enterprise Server family accelerates the integration of systems, applications, and partners by supporting XML Web services. Support of XML allows enterprises to build on earlier systems rather than replacing them. For example, Microsoft Host Integration Server provides simple access to mainframes and Microsoft BizTalk® Server offers automatic conversions of existing data formats to and from XML.

Tip For information about the .NET Enterprise Server family, see http://www.microsoft.com/net/products/servers.asp.

■ XML Web services

By using XML Web services, applications can share data and invoke capabilities from other applications without regard to how those applications were built, what operating system or platform they run on, and what devices are used to access them.

.NET platform benefits for developers

The .NET platform provides several benefits for developers, including:

■ Faster application development

Developers can create applications by using one of many modern programming languages, greatly increasing the pool of available developer resources in addition to allowing developers the freedom to use the programming language that is most suitable for solving a specific problem.

■ Greater reliability

- The .NET platform takes advantage of the power of distributed computing.

- The common language runtime provides for a managed execution environment, which eliminates memory leaks, access violations, and versioning problems.

- The .NET Framework enforces type safety, explicit code sharing, and application isolation, guaranteeing that no application can affect or illegally call another.

■ Based on Web standards

The use of XML removes barriers to data sharing and software integration. The Simple Object Access Protocol, an XML-based messaging technology standardized by the World Wide Web Consortium (W3C), specifies all the necessary rules for using XML Web services, integrating them into applications and communicating between them.

- .NET has database access capabilities, allowing developers to bring open database connectivity (ODBC)-compliant data stores into their application architecture.

Multimedia: Introduction to Microsoft.NET

Introduction

This multimedia presentation introduces the concepts that are fundamental to the .NET platform and covers the following topics:

- Traditional client desktop and server communication
- .NET platform use of XML Web services
- .NET platform components
  - XML Web services
  - .NET experiences
  - .NET Devices
  - .NET Servers
  - .NET Developer Tools
    - Visual Studio .NET
    - .NET Framework

Note For your reference, the Introduction to Microsoft .NET.htm multimedia presentation file is located on your student compact disc in the Media folder.

What Is the .NET Framework?

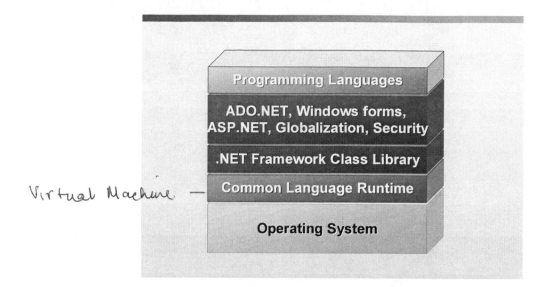

Virtual Machine —

Introduction	The .NET Framework provides the foundation for building and running .NET-based applications. The .NET Framework consists of two components, the common language runtime and the .NET Framework class library, which run on an operating system. Any language that conforms to the common language specification (CLS) can run on the common language runtime. In the .NET Framework, Microsoft provides support for Microsoft Visual Basic®, Microsoft Visual C++®, Microsoft Visual C#™ (pronounced C sharp), and Microsoft JScript®. Third parties can provide additional languages.

Note   Currently, the .NET Framework is built to run on the Microsoft Win32® operating systems.

The common language runtime	The common language runtime manages the execution of code and provides services to simplify the development process. The common language runtime provides a robust and secure execution environment, support for multiple languages, and a managed environment where common services, such as garbage collection and security, are automatically provided.

VS6 – VB6, C++ un managed
                        managed
VS-2002 – .NET 1.0
    2003   .NET 1.1
future 2005   .NET 2.0

SQL Server Stored procs will allow C# code in addition
to T-SQL.

The .NET Framework class library

The .NET Framework class library exposes features of the runtime and provides a library of classes that are accessed by all Web, Windows-based, and XML Web service applications.

In addition to base classes, the .NET Framework class library includes:

Element	Description
ADO.NET	Microsoft ADO.NET is the next generation of Microsoft ActiveX® Data Objects (ADO) technology. ADO.NET provides improved support for the disconnected programming model. It also provides rich XML support.
ASP.NET	Microsoft ASP.NET is a programming framework that is built on the common language runtime. ASP.NET can be used on a server to build Web applications. ASP.NET Web Forms provide an easy and powerful way to build dynamic Web user interfaces (UI).
XML Web services	XML Web services are programmable Web components that can be shared among applications on the Internet or the intranet. The .NET Framework provides tools and classes for building, testing, and distributing XML Web services.
User interfaces	The .NET Framework supports three types of user interfaces: • Web Forms, which work by using ASP.NET. • Windows Forms, which run on Win32 client computers. • Console applications.

How the .NET Framework Works

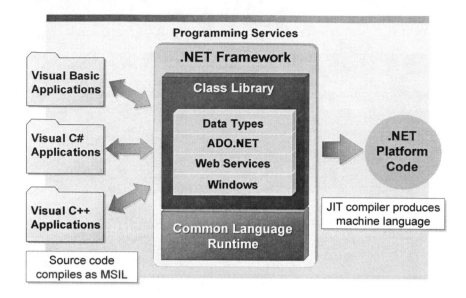

Introduction

The common language runtime is the foundation of the .NET Framework.

MSIL

When you compile an application in Visual Studio .NET, it is translated into the runtime's common language, Microsoft Intermediate Language (MSIL). After the application is compiled, the runtime manages the execution of the application.

JIT compilation

The runtime includes a feature called just-in-time (JIT) compilation that translates the MSIL code into the machine language of the system on which the application will run. When a client device on the .NET platform launches the .NET-based application, it starts running in the machine language of the client system and can fully integrate and interact with other .NET-based applications and services regardless of the language in which it was developed.

Multimedia: Introduction to the .NET Framework

Introduction

This multimedia presentation covers key concepts of the .NET Framework, including:

- .NET Framework components
  - .NET Framework class library
  - .NET Framework common language runtime
- Objects in the .NET Framework class library
  - XML Web services
  - User interface classes
  - ASP.NET
  - ADO.NET
- .NET Framework security
- The common language runtime manages the execution of code and provides services to simplify the development process. The multimedia presentation covers the function of the common language runtime in more depth, explaining how the .NET Framework works with the common language runtime.

Note For your reference, the Introduction to the .NET Framework.htm multimedia presentation file is located on your student compact disc in the Media folder.

Practice: Defining the Elements of .NET

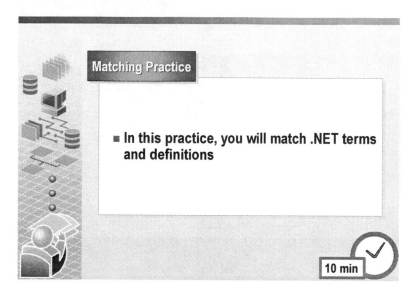

Match the following terms with the appropriate definition by drawing a line that connects the term and definition.

Term	Definition

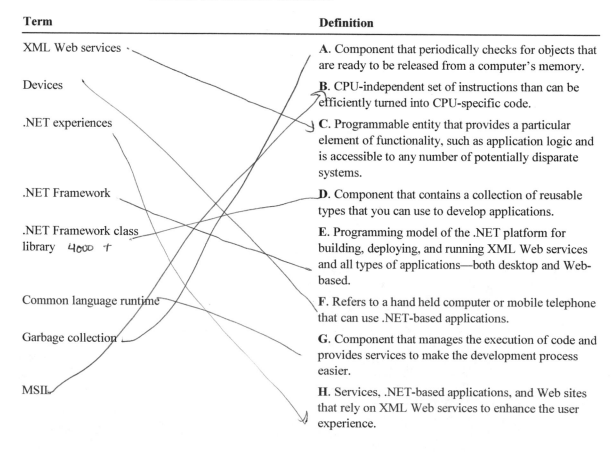

Term

XML Web services

Devices

.NET experiences

.NET Framework

.NET Framework class
library 4000 †

Common language runtime

Garbage collection

MSIL

Definition

A. Component that periodically checks for objects that are ready to be released from a computer's memory.

B. CPU-independent set of instructions than can be efficiently turned into CPU-specific code.

C. Programmable entity that provides a particular element of functionality, such as application logic and is accessible to any number of potentially disparate systems.

D. Component that contains a collection of reusable types that you can use to develop applications.

E. Programming model of the .NET platform for building, deploying, and running XML Web services and all types of applications—both desktop and Web-based.

F. Refers to a hand held computer or mobile telephone that can use .NET-based applications.

G. Component that manages the execution of code and provides services to make the development process easier.

H. Services, .NET-based applications, and Web sites that rely on XML Web services to enhance the user experience.

Lesson: Exploring Visual Studio .NET

- **Programming Features of Visual Studio .NET**
- **Structure of Visual Studio Solutions and Projects**
- **The Development Process**

Introduction

This lesson uses an instructor-led demonstration to present some of the most commonly performed tasks and features of the development environment of Visual Studio .NET and explains the file structure and development cycle of the development environment.

Lesson objectives

After completing this lesson, you will be able to:

- Identify the programming features of Visual Studio .NET by their functions.
- Describe the structure of solutions and projects in the development environment.
- Determine which programming feature to use to perform a development task.

Lesson agenda

This lesson includes the following topics and activity:

- Demonstration: Working in the Development Environment
- Programming Features of Visual Studio .NET
- Structure of Visual Studio Solutions and Projects
- The Development Process

Demonstration: Working in the Development Environment

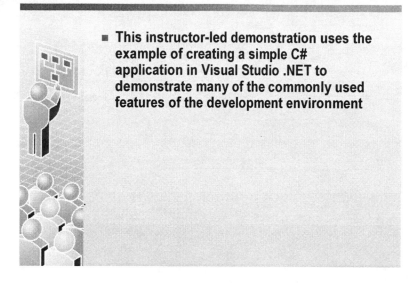

This instructor-led demonstration uses the example of creating a simple C# application in Visual Studio .NET to demonstrate many of the commonly used features of the development environment.

Your instructor will demonstrate the following procedures:

▶ **Open Visual Studio .NET and use the Start Page**

1. Start Visual Studio .NET.

2. Click **Online Community**.

3. Click **Search Online**.

4. Click **Get Started**.

▶ **Create a new project**

1. On the **Projects** tab, click **New Project**.

2. In the **New Project** dialog box, in the Templates pane, click **Windows Application**.

3. In the **Name** box, type **DemoApplication** and then click **OK**.

▶ **Examine Solution Explorer**

1. In Solution Explorer, click **Form1.cs**.

2. Right-click **Solution 'DemoApplication' (1 project)**.

3. Right-click **DemoApplication** under the Solution node.

▶ **Add a new class file to the project**

1. Right-click the project **DemoApplication,** point to **Add**, and then click **Add Class**.

2. In the **Add New Item** window, in the **Name** box, type **Animals.cs** and then click **Open**.

3. Close the Animals.cs Code Editor window.

▶ **Change the size of the form**

- Drag the bottom-right resize handle on the form to make the form rectangular.

▶ **Add buttons to the form**

1. In the Toolbox, click a **Button** control, and then use a drag-and-drop operation to place a button onto the form.

2. Place a second button onto the form.

▶ **Add code to a button**

1. Double-click **Button1** on the form.

2. In the Code Editor, between `Private Sub Button1_Click` and `End Sub`, where the pointer should be located, type the following code:

```
MessageBox.Show("Visual C# is awesome!");
```

▶ **Use Dynamic Help and IntelliSense**

1. On the **Help** menu, click **Dynamic Help**.

   This step ensures that the Dynamic Help window is visible.

2. Choose **Design** view for Form1.cs.

3. Double-click **Button2** on the form.

4. In the Code Editor, between `Private Sub Button2_Click` and `End Sub`, where the pointer should be located, type the following code, and observe the Dynamic Help window as you type:

```
MessageBox.Show ("Visual Studio .NET makes it all easy!");
```

   Notice that the Dynamic Help contents change as you type the line.

5. Delete the line of code that you entered in the preceding step and then enter the code again. This time, notice how IntelliSense functions as you type the code.

▶ **Run and test the application**

1. On the standard toolbar, click the **Start** button ▶.

2. In the **Form1** dialog box, click **Button1**.

3. In the message box, click **OK**.

4. In the **Form1** dialog box, click **Button2**.

5. In the message box, click **OK**.

6. Close Form1.

▶ **Use the Auto Hide feature**

• On the Output window title bar, click the pushpin icon.

▶ **Undock a window**

1. On the Toolbox title bar, click the pushpin icon.

2. Click the Toolbox title bar and drag the window into the middle of the screen.

▶ **Dock a window**

1. Click the title bar of the Toolbox, and then drag the window to the left side of the Visual Studio application window until the pointer is almost at the left edge of the screen.

2. Click the pushpin icon in the Toolbox title bar to enable the Auto Hide feature again.

▶ **Save a project**

• On the standard toolbar, click the **Save All** button.

Note   The location of the solution is set when the solution is created.

▶ **Close a solution**

• On the **File** menu, click **Close Solution**.

Note   The **Projects** tab of the Start Page will display **DemoApplication** in the list of recent projects when you restart Visual Studio .NET.

▶ **Quit Visual Studio**

• On the **File** menu, click **Exit**.

Programming Features of Visual Studio .NET

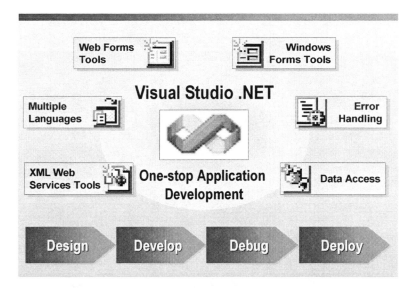

Introduction

Visual Studio .NET is an integrated development environment that helps you to quickly design, develop, debug, and deploy .NET-based applications. You can access a common set of tools, designers, and editors from any Visual Studio .NET programming language. You can create Windows Forms and Web Forms applications that integrate data and business logic.

Programming features

Visual Studio .NET includes the programming features described in the following table.

Feature	Description
Windows Forms Designer	A graphical design surface enables you to quickly create the user interface for an application. You can drag or draw controls onto this surface.
Tools for Windows Forms	A Windows Forms Designer, a Windows Application template, essential project references, and starter code are provided to help you create standard Windows Forms applications.
Tools for Web Forms	A Web Forms Designer, an ASP.NET Web Application template, essential project references, and starter code are provided to help you build Web Forms applications in which the primary user interface is a browser.

(continued)

Feature	Description
Tools for XML Web services	An ASP.NET Web services template is provided that constructs a Web application project structure on a development Web server and a Visual Studio solution file on your local computer.
Multiple language support	All of the .NET platform programming languages, including Visual C#, are integrated into the development environment.
Data access	Components for creating applications that share data, visual database tools for accessing data, and a robust set of ADO.NET classes make it easy to work with all types of data.
Error handling	Debugging tools with cross-language support help you to find and fix errors in your code, and you can use structured exception classes to build error handling into your application.
Wizards	Wizards help you to quickly complete common and perhaps complex tasks. Each page of a wizard helps you set options, configure settings, and customize projects.

Structure of Visual Studio Solutions and Projects

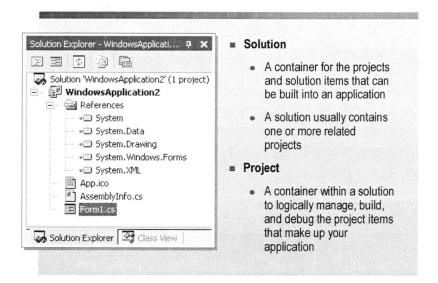

- **Solution**
  - A container for the projects and solution items that can be built into an application
  - A solution usually contains one or more related projects

- **Project**
  - A container within a solution to logically manage, build, and debug the project items that make up your application

Introduction

Solution Explorer allows you to view files and perform file management tasks in a solution or a project. A single Visual Basic .NET solution and its projects appear in a hierarchical list that provides updated information about the status of your solution, projects, and files.

Terms and definitions

When you create a project in Visual Studio .NET, project files are organized in a larger container called a *solution*. A solution usually contains one or more related projects.

A *project* is a container in a solution that you can use to logically manage, build, and debug the project items that make up your application.

Solution benefits

Solutions allow you to concentrate on the project or set of projects that are required to develop and deploy your application, instead of having to focus on the details of managing the objects and files that define them.

A solution allows you to:

- Work on multiple projects in the same instance of the development environment.

- Work on items, settings, and options that apply to a group of projects.

- Manage miscellaneous files that are opened outside the context of a solution or project.

- Use Solution Explorer, which is a graphical view of your solution, to organize and manage all of the projects and files that are required to design, develop, and deploy an application.

Solution and project files

Visual Studio .NET supports many file types and their associated file extensions. The following table describes some common file types that are specific to .NET-based applications.

Extension	Name	Description
.sln	Visual Studio solution	Organizes projects, project items, and solution items in the solution by giving the environment references to their locations on disk.
.suo	Solution user options	Records all of the options that you may associate with your solution so that each time you open the solution, it includes any customizations that you made.
.cs	Visual C# project	Represents forms, user controls, classes, and module files that belong to a single-project solution. Any files that are not based on a programming language have their own extension. For example, a Crystal Report file has the extension .rpt, and a text file has the extension .txt.
.csproj	Visual C# projects	Represents forms, user controls, classes, and module files that belong to a multiple-project solution. This extension allows you to differentiate between files written in Visual C# and other .NET-compatible languages.
.aspx .asmx .asax	Web project items	Web project items include Web-specific files such as .aspx for Web Forms, .asmx for XML Web services, and .asax for global application classes. Web projects also use the .cs file extension for classes and modules.

The Development Process

1	Create a design specification
2	Create the user interface
3	Set properties for the user interface objects
4	Write code to add functionality
5	Test and debug the application
6	Make an executable file
7	Create a setup application

Introduction

Visual Studio .NET contains everything you need to build your own applications from start to finish. To create the user interface, you place controls from the Toolbox on a form, then you customize the controls by setting properties. After that, you write code to define what your program will do. Finally, you can save, run, and compile your program so others can use it.

Creating an application in Visual Studio .NET

Creating an application in Visual Studio .NET involves seven basic steps:

1. Create a design specification.

   The design specification is the blueprint that you use when you create an application. Before writing any code, take time to design the application you will create. Although Visual Studio .NET provides tools to help you quickly develop an application, having a clear understanding of the user needs and initial feature set will help you be more efficient in your development efforts. Planning the design will also help you save time by minimizing the potential for rewriting code because of a poor or nonexistent design specification.

2. Create the user interface.

   To create the interface for your application, first place controls and objects on a form by drawing or painting them in the Windows Forms Designer. You can look at other applications, such as Microsoft Excel or Microsoft Word, for ideas on how to design the interface. For information about interface design, see *Microsoft Windows User Experience* published by Microsoft Press®.

3. Set properties for the user interface objects.

   After you add objects to a form, you can set their properties in the Properties window or in the Code Editor.

4. Write code to add functionality.

   After you set the initial properties for the form and its objects, you can add code that runs in response to events. Events occur when various actions are performed on a control or object. For example, the **Click** event of a command button occurs when the user clicks it with the mouse. For most applications, you must also write code to add business logic and to access data.

5. Test and debug the application.

   Testing and debugging is not a one-time step but something that you do iteratively throughout the development process. Each time you make a major change in steps 2, 3, or 4, you must run a debug build of the application and ensure that it is working as expected. Visual Studio .NET provides debugging tools for finding and fixing errors in your application.

6. Make an executable file.

   After completing the project, create a release build of the project. Creating a release build compiles the various files that make up the program into a stand-alone executable file called an *assembly*.

7. Create a setup application.

   To run your application, the user usually needs other files, such as any dynamic-link library (DLL) files that you used to create your application. Visual Studio provides the Setup Wizard, which automates the creation of the setup program and ensures that the user has all of the necessary files.

Lesson: Creating a Windows Application Project

- ■ **What Is an Application Template?**
- ■ **How to Use the Windows Forms Designer**
- ■ **How to Use the Properties Window**

Introduction

This lesson prepares you for creating your first basic Windows application.

Lesson objectives

After completing this lesson, you will be able to:

- ■ Start a Visual C# project based on the Windows Application template.
- ■ Explore Windows Forms Designer.
- ■ Explore the Properties window.
- ■ Create a basic Windows application.

Lesson agenda

This lesson includes the following topics and activity:

- ■ What Is an Application Template?
- ■ How to Use the Windows Forms Designer
- ■ How to Use the Properties Window
- ■ Practice: Creating a Basic Windows Application

What Is an Application Template?

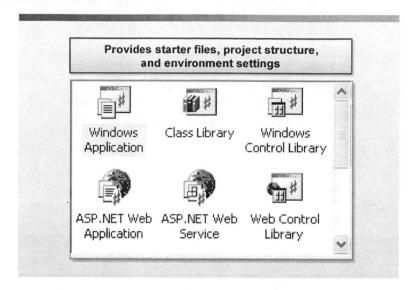

Introduction

Visual Studio .NET offers several application templates to support the development of different kinds of applications and components. Before you start a new project, you must choose the type of template that you want to use.

Definition

An *application template* provides starter files and a project structure and contains the basic project objects and the environment settings you need to create the type of application that you want to build.

Examples of application templates

Two of the most commonly used templates are the Windows Application and the ASP.NET Web Application templates.

- Windows Application template

  This template provides the tools, structure, and starter code for a standard Windows-based application. It automatically adds the essential project references and files to use as a starting point for your application.

- ASP.NET Web Application template

  This template is used to create an ASP.NET Web application on a computer that has Microsoft Internet Information Services (IIS) version 5.0 or later installed. The template creates the basic files that the server requires to help you start designing your application.

Creating a Windows Application project

When you start a new Microsoft Visual C# .NET project, one of the first steps is to choose an application template.

To create a Windows Application project in Visual Studio .NET:

1. Start Visual Studio .NET.

2. On the Get Started pane, click **New Project**.

   – or –

   On the **File** menu, point to **New**, and then click **Project**.

3. In the Project Types pane, click **Visual C# Projects**. In the Templates pane, click **Windows Application**.

4. In the **Name** field, type a unique project name that indicates the purpose of the application.

5. In the **Location** field, type the directory in which you want to save your project, or click the **Browse** button to browse to it.

6. Click **OK**.

   The Windows Forms Designer opens and displays Form1 of the project that you created.

How to Use the Windows Forms Designer

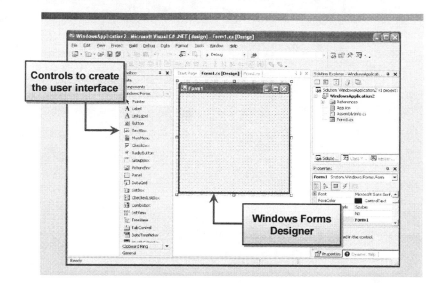

Introduction	When you start a project in Visual C# .NET, the Windows Forms Designer opens in Design view, showing Form1 of the project. You place controls from the Toolbox on the form to create the user interface for a window used in your application.
Elements of a form	The default form contains the basic elements that most forms use: a title bar, a control box, and **Minimize**, **Maximize**, and **Close** buttons.
Viewing a form	To view a form in Design view:

- In Solution Explorer, double-click the form.

  – or –

  In Solution Explorer, click the form, and then, on the toolbar, click **View Designer**.

Creating the user interface	You create the user interface objects for your application by adding controls from the Toolbox to a form. The Toolbox is initially located on the left side of the development environment. There are several tabs for different categories of controls, such as **Windows Forms** and **Data**.
Toolbox controls	The Toolbox contains a variety of controls that you can use to add images labels, buttons, list boxes, scroll bars, menus, and geometric shapes to a user interface. Each control that you add to a form becomes a programmable user interface object in your application. These objects are visible to the user when the application runs and operate like the standard objects in any Windows-based application.

Closing and opening the Toolbox

To close and open the Toolbox:

1. To close the Toolbox, in the upper-right corner of the Toolbox, click **Close**.
2. To open the Toolbox, on the **View** menu, click **Toolbox**.
3. To keep the Toolbox open, on the Toolbox title bar, click the pushpin.

Hiding and reopening the Toolbox

To hide and reopen the Toolbox:

1. To hide the Toolbox, on the Toolbox title bar, click the pushpin.
2. To reopen the Toolbox when it is hidden, on the **View** menu, click **Toolbox**.

Moving the Toolbox

To move the Toolbox:

1. Right-click the Toolbox title bar, and then click **Floating**.
2. Drag the Toolbox to the desired location.

How to Use the Properties Window

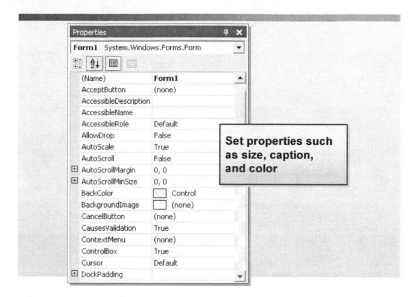

Set properties such as size, caption, and color

| Introduction | The Properties window lists the property settings for the selected form or control that you can modify while you create or edit the application. A property describes a characteristic of an object, such as size, caption, or color. |

Introduction

The Properties window lists the property settings for the selected form or control that you can modify while you create or edit the application. A property describes a characteristic of an object, such as size, caption, or color.

Terms and definitions

A *form* is made up of various controls. You can modify the style and function of forms and controls by changing various attributes of these controls. These attributes are referred to as *properties*.

Opening the Properties window

To open the Properties window:

- If the Properties window is not visible, click **Properties Window** on the **View** menu, or press F4.

Viewing properties

Some controls, documents, and forms display a large number of properties in the Properties window. This can make it difficult to locate the property that you want to set. The Properties window allows you to view the properties for a form or control in a categorized view instead of an alphabetic view.

To view properties:

1. To view the properties by category, click the **Categorized** button in the Properties window.

   The properties for the selected form or control will be separated into the categories that are defined by the control.

2. To view the properties in a category, expand the category node. To hide the properties in a category, collapse the category node.

3. To view the properties alphabetically, click the **Alphabetic** button in the Properties window.

Practice: Creating a Basic Windows Application

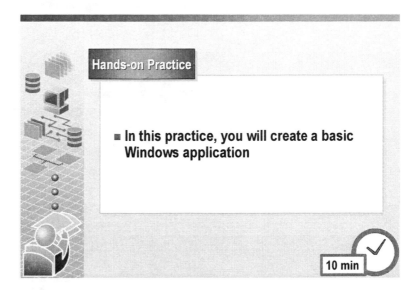

In this practice, you will create a basic Windows application.

Tasks	Detailed steps
1. Start Visual Studio .NET.	▪ Start a new instance of Visual Studio .NET.
2. Create a new project. Project Type: **Visual C#** Template: **Windows Application** Name: **SimpleWindowsApplication**	a. On the **Start Page**, click **New Project**. b. In the **New Project** window, under **Project Types**, click **Visual C# Projects**. c. Under **Templates**, click **Windows Application**. d. In the **Name** box, type **SimpleWindowsApplication** and then click **OK**.
3. Change the Text property of Form1 to **SimpleApplication** and then change the size of the form. Width = **400 pixels** Height = **200 pixels**	a. On the **View** menu, click **Properties Window**. b. In the Properties window, in the **Text** property box, type **SimpleApplication** c. In the **Size** property box, type **400,200** and then press ENTER.
4. Add a Label control to Form1. Locate this label on the form at position **20,20**. Change this label to be **350** pixels wide and **130** pixels high.	a. Click the **Toolbox**. b. Drag a **Label** control from the Toolbox to the Form. c. In the Properties window, in the **Location** property box type **20,20** and then press ENTER. d. In the **Size** box, type **350,130** and then press ENTER.

Tasks	Detailed steps
5. Change the **Text** property of the label to **Hello World** and then change the font size to **40 points**.	a. In the **Text** property field, type **Hello World** b. Expand the **Font** property, in the **Size** field type **40** and then press ENTER.
6. Change the **TextAlign** property of the label to **MiddleCenter**.	▪ Change the **TextAlign** property to **MiddleCenter**.
7. Run the application.	▪ On the standard toolbar, click the **Start** button.
8. Close the application, save all changes, and then quit Visual Studio .NET.	a. Close the SimpleApplication window. b. On the standard toolbar, click the **Save All** button. c. On the **File** menu, click **Exit**.

Review

- **Introduction to .NET and the .NET Framework**
- **Exploring Visual Studio .NET**
- **Creating a Windows Application Project**

1. Complete the following statement:

   When you create a project in Visual Studio .NET, _Project/Source_ files are organized in a larger container called a _Solution_.

2. Draw a line to match the following file extensions with the correct description.

Extension	Description
.cs	**A.** Organizes projects, project items, and solution items in the solution.
.sln	**B.** Records all of the options that you may associate with your solution.
.aspx	**C.** Represents forms, user controls, classes, and module files that belong to a single-project solution.
.suo	**D.** Represents forms, user controls, classes, and module files that belong to a multiple-project solution.
.csproj	**E.** Represents a Web project item.

3. Complete the following statement:

An _application template_ provides starter files and a project structure and contains the basic project objects and the environment settings that you need to create the type of application that you want to build.

framework + CLR

4. What must be installed on a client computer to run .NET-based applications?

5. What is one advantage of programming by using the .NET Framework versus using a traditional development environment?

msdn training

Module 2: Understanding C# Language Fundamentals

Contents

Microsoft

Overview

- ■ **Understanding the Fundamentals of a C# Program**
- ■ **Using C# Predefined Types**
- ■ **Writing Expressions**
- ■ **Creating Conditional Statements**
- ■ **Creating Iteration Statements**

Introduction

This module introduces you to the basic syntax and structure of the C# language. It describes C# data types, including variables and constants, describes the Microsoft® .NET common type system, introduces conditional and iterative statements, and explains how to create user-defined enumeration types. Understanding the syntax of the language is fundamental to writing code in C#.

Objectives

After completing this module, you will be able to:

- ■ Understand the fundamentals of a C# program.
- ■ Use C# predefined types.
- ■ Write expressions.
- ■ Create conditional statements.
- ■ Create iteration statements.

Lesson: Understanding the Fundamentals of a C# Program

- **What Is the Structure of a C# Program?**
- **How to Format Code in C#**

Introduction

This lesson describes the structure of a C# program. This information is provided as a resource for developers who have no experience with a C-style language.

Lesson objectives

After completing this lesson, you will be able to:

- Identify C# statements.
- Use braces to group statements.
- Include comments in code.

Lesson agenda

This lesson includes the following topics:

- What Is the Structure of a C# Program?
- How to Format Code in C#

What Is the Structure of a C# Program?

- **Program execution begins at Main( )**

- **The** using **keyword refers to resources in the .NET Framework class library**

- **Statements are commands that perform actions**
  - A program is made up of many separate statements
  - Statements are separated by a semicolon
  - Braces are used to group statements

```
using System;
class HelloWorld {
    static void Main() {
        Console.WriteLine ("Hello, World");
    }
}
```

Introduction

Before you write your first lines of code in C#, it is helpful to understand the structure of the language.

Definition

The structure of a programming language specifies the elements that you must include in your application and defines how to organize those elements so that the compiler understands your code.

Example of C# structure

The following code shows the basic structure of a C# application:

```
using System;

class HelloWorld {
  static void Main() {
      Console.WriteLine ("Hello, World");
  }
}
```

The elements and organizing principles that are shown in the preceding six lines of code are briefly described line by line in the following sections.

The using keyword

The **using** keyword refers to resources in the Microsoft .NET Framework class library. Typically, you insert this keyword at the beginning of the program file, usually several times, to reference various resources.

The System namespace

System is a *namespace* that provides access to all of the system functionality upon which your application is built.

Class

Programming in C#, or any object-oriented language, consists of writing classes, which are used to create objects. In the preceding code example, the class is named **HelloWorld**.

The Main method

Methods describe the behavior of a class. In the third line, **static void Main** is a global method that tells the compiler where to begin execution of the application. Every C# application must include a **Main** method in one of the classes.

Statements

Statements are instructions that are completed to perform actions in C# applications. Statements are separated by a semicolon to enable the compiler to distinguish between them.

Some languages place one statement on one line. In C#, you can include multiple statements on one line, or one statement on multiple lines. It is good practice to write one statement per line; although, for the purpose of readability, you may want to break a long statement into several lines.

Braces

Braces, { and }, are used to identify the beginning and end of blocks of code in your application. Braces are used to group statements together. Every opening brace must have one matching closing brace.

In the example, the braces following "class HelloWorld" enclose the items that are in the **HelloWorld** class. The braces following "Main" are used to enclose the statements that are in the **Main** method.

Microsoft Visual Studio® .NET provides several visual cues that help to ensure that your braces are correctly matched. When you type a closing brace, the enclosing element is briefly shown in bold. Also, the document outline indicators to the left show the extent of a group of statements.

```
using System;

class HelloWorld {
    static void Main() {
        Console.WriteLine("Hello, World");
    }
}
```

Note You do not need to add a semicolon after braces because the braces themselves indicate the end of a group of statements, implying that the statements within the braces are complete and separate blocks of code.

How to Format Code in C#

- **Use indentation to indicate enclosing statements**
- **C# is case sensitive**
- **White space is ignored**
- **Indicate single line comments by using //**
- **Indicate multiple-line comments by using /* and */**

```
using System;
class HelloWorld {
    static void Main() {
        Console.WriteLine ("Hello, World");
    }
}
```

Introduction

Formatting is another element of program design that helps you to organize your code. You are encouraged to use formatting conventions to improve the structure and readability of your code.

Example

The following code sample demonstrates how to apply the formatting principles of indentation, case sensitivity, white space, and comments:

```
using System;

class HelloWorld {
  static void Main() {
      Console.WriteLine ("Hello, World");
      //writes Hello, World
  }
}
```

Indentation

Indentation indicates that a statement is within an enclosing statement. Statements that are in the same block of statements should all be indented to the same level. This is an important convention that improves the readability of your code. Although indenting is not a requirement, or enforced by the compiler, it is a recommended best practice.

Case sensitivity

C# is case sensitive, which means that the compiler distinguishes between uppercase and lowercase characters. For example, the words "code," "Code," and "CODE" are differentiated in your application; you cannot substitute one for the other.

White space

White space is ignored by the compiler. Therefore, you can use spaces to improve the readability and formatting of your code. The only exception is that the compiler does not ignore spaces between quotation marks.

Comments

You can include single-line comments in your application by inserting a double slash (//) followed by your comment.

Alternately, if your comment is lengthy and spans multiple lines, you can use slash asterisk (/*) to indicate the beginning of a comment and asterisk slash (*/) to indicate the end of your comments. The following example of a multiple line comment includes an asterisk at the beginning of each line. These asterisks are optional and you can include them to make your comment easier to identify.

Multiple-line comment example

```
/*
 * Multiple line comment
 * This example code shows how to format
 * multiple line comments in C#
 */

/* alternative use of this comment style */
```

Layout

You can place the opening brace at the end of the line that starts a statement group, or you can place the opening brace on the line following the method or class, as shown in the following example:

```
using System;

class HelloWorld
{
  static void Main()
  {
      Console.WriteLine("Hello, World");
  }
}
```

Both layouts are acceptable and correct. It is important, however, to be consistent. In the examples in Course 2609, *Introduction to C# Programming with Microsoft .NET*, the opening brace is placed at the end of the line. Your organization should choose one layout that everyone uses.

Lesson: Using C# Predefined Types

- **What Are Predefined Types?**
- **How to Declare and Initialize Variables**
- **How to Declare and Initialize Strings**
- **How to Create and Use Constants**
- **How to Create and Use Enumeration Types**
- **How to Convert Between Types**

Introduction

This lesson introduces the basic syntax of the C# language and the .NET common type system, including how to use types, variables, constants, enumerations, and strings.

When you write any application, you must represent data in some way. This process fundamentally depends upon working with types.

Lesson objectives

After completing this lesson, you will be able to:

- Declare and initialize variables.
- Create and use strings.
- Create and use constants.
- Create and use enumerated types.
- Convert between types.

Lesson agenda

This lesson includes the following topics and activity:

- What Are Predefined Types?
- How to Declare and Initialize Variables
- How to Declare and Initialize Strings
- How to Create and Use Constants
- How to Create and Use Enumeration Types
- How to Convert Between Types
- Practice: Using C# Types

What Are Predefined Types?

- **Types are used to declare variables**
- **Variables store different kinds of data**
  - Let the data that you are representing determine your choice of variable
- **Predefined types are those provided by C# and the .NET Framework**
  - You can also define your own
- **Variables must be declared before you can use them**

Introduction

Whenever your application must store data temporarily for use during execution, you store that data in a *variable*. You can think of variables as storage boxes. These boxes come in different sizes and shapes, called *types*, which provide storage for various kinds of data. For example, the type of variable that is used to store a number is different than one that is used to store a person's name.

Definition

Predefined types are those that are supplied by the C# language and the .NET Framework. The following table lists the predefined types and describes the data that they are designed to store.

Predefined type	Definition	# Bytes
byte	Integer between 0 and 255	1
sbyte	Integer between -128 and 127	1
short	Integer between -32768 and 32767	2
ushort	Integer between 0 and 65535	2
int	Integer between -2147483648 and 2147483647	4
uint	Integer between 0 and 4294967295	4
long	Integer between -9223372036854775808 and 9223372036854775807	8
ulong	Integer between 0 and 18446744073709551615	8
bool	Boolean value: true or false	1
float	Single-precision floating point value (non-whole number)	4
double	Double-precision floating point value	8
decimal	Precise decimal value to 28 significant digits	12
object	Base type of all other types	N/A
char	Single Unicode character between 0 and 65535	2
string	An unlimited sequence of Unicode characters	N/A

Storing data

Suppose that you are writing an application that allows a user to purchase items over the Internet with a credit card. Your application must handle several pieces of information: the person's name, the amount of the purchase, the credit card number, and the expiration date on the card. To represent this information in your application, you use different types.

Choosing a type

Let the data that you are representing determine your choice of type. For example, if something can be only true or false, a **bool** type is the obvious choice. A **decimal** type is a good choice for currency. When working with integers, an **int** type is the typical choice, unless there is a specific reason to choose another type.

In addition to the predefined types that are supplied by the .NET Framework, you can define your own types to hold whatever data you choose.

How to Declare and Initialize Variables

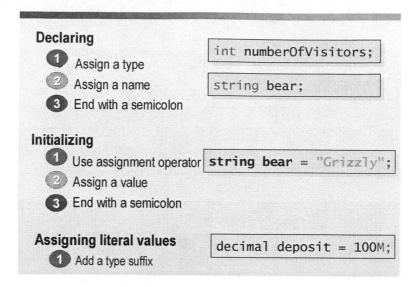

Declaring
1. Assign a type
2. Assign a name
3. End with a semicolon

```
int numberOfVisitors;
```

```
string bear;
```

Initializing
1. Use assignment operator
2. Assign a value
3. End with a semicolon

```
string bear = "Grizzly";
```

Assigning literal values
1. Add a type suffix

```
decimal deposit = 100M;
```

Introduction

A *variable* is a storage location for a particular type. For example, if your application must process a currency value, it requires a variable to hold that value.

Before you can use a variable, you must declare it. By declaring a variable, you are actually reserving some storage space for that variable in memory. After declaring a variable, you must initialize it by assigning a value to it.

Syntax

The syntax for declaring a variable is the type declaration followed by the variable name. For example:

```
int   myInteger;
bool  fileWasClosed;
```

Naming variables

The following list identifies some best practices for naming your variables:

- Assign meaningful names to your variables.

- Use camel case. In camel case, the first letter of the identifier is lowercase, and the first letter of each subsequent word in the identifier is capitalized, such as newAccountBalance.

- Do not use C# keywords.

- Although C# is case sensitive, do not create variables that differ only by case.

Initializing variables

To initialize a variable, you assign it a value. To assign a value to a variable, use the assignment operator (=), followed by a value, and then a semicolon, as shown in the following example:

```
int myVariable;
myVariable = 1;
```

You can combine these steps, as shown in the following example:

```
int myVariable = 1;
```

More examples of declaring variables are shown in the following code:

```
int x = 25;
int y = 50;
bool isOpen = false;
sbyte b = -55;
```

Assigning literal values

When you assign 25 to x in the preceding code, the compiler places the literal value 25 in the variable x. The following assignment, however, generates a compilation error:

```
decimal bankBalance = 3433.20;    // ERROR!
```

This code causes an error because the C# compiler assumes than any literal number with a decimal point is a double, unless otherwise specified. You specify the type of the literal by appending a suffix, as shown in the following example:

```
decimal bankBalance = 3433.20M;
```

The literal suffixes that you can use are shown in the following table. Lowercase is permitted.

Category	Suffix	Description
Integer	U	Unsigned
	L	Long
	UL	Unsigned long
Real number	F	Float
	D	Double
	M	Decimal
	L	Long

Characters

You specify a character (char type) by enclosing it in single quotation marks:

```
char myInitial = 'a';
```

Escape characters

Some characters cannot be specified by being placed in quotation marks—for example, a newline character, a beep, or a quotation mark character. To represent these characters, you must use **escape** characters, which are shown in the following table.

Escape sequence	Character name
\'	Single quotation mark
\"	Double quotation mark
\\	Backslash
\0	Null
\a	Alert
\b	Backspace
\f	Form feed
\n	New line
\r	Carriage return
\t	Horizontal tab
\v	Vertical tab

\u   *unicode representation*

For example, you can specify a quotation mark as follows:

```
char quoteMark = '\'';
```

Examining variables in Visual Studio .NET

The Visual Studio .NET development environment provides useful tools that enable you to examine the values of variables while your application is running.

To examine the value of a variable, set a breakpoint at the variable that you want to examine, run your application in debug mode, and then use the debug windows to examine the values.

1. Set a breakpoint by clicking in the left margin in the source window. The breakpoint is indicated by a red dot. You can also set breakpoints by clicking **New Breakpoint** on the **Debug** menu, or by pressing SHIFT+B.

2. Run your application in debug mode by clicking **Start** on the standard toolbar, or by clicking **Start** on the **Debug** menu, or by pressing F5.

3. Your application runs until it encounters a breakpoint. When the application encounters a breakpoint, it pauses, and the development environment highlights the line of code that will be executed next.

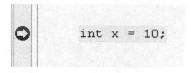

4. Use the debug windows to view the value of the variables. To open debug windows, on the **Debug** menu, point to **Windows**, and then click **Autos**, or click **Locals**, or click **This**.

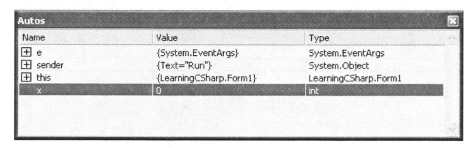

Name	Value	Type
⊞ e	{System.EventArgs}	System.EventArgs
⊞ sender	{Text="Run"}	System.Object
⊞ this	{LearningCSharp.Form1}	LearningCSharp.Form1
x	0	int

The **Autos** window displays variables used in the current and previous statements. By default, the **Autos** window is visible at the bottom of the development environment when you are in debug mode.

The Locals window displays local variables, and the **This** window shows objects that are associated with the current method.

5. To proceed to the next breakpoint when you are ready to continue executing your program, you can press F5 or click **Continue** in the **Debug** menu. Or, you can execute one program step at a time by pressing F10 or clicking **Step Over** on the **Debug** menu.

How to Declare and Initialize Strings

- **Example string**

```
string s = "Hello World"; // Hello World
```

- **Declaring literal strings**

```
string s = "\"Hello\""; // "Hello"
```

- **Using escape characters**

```
string s = "Hello\nWorld"; // a new line is added
```

- **Using verbatim strings**

```
string s = @"Hello\n"; // Hello\n
```

- **Understanding Unicode**

```
The character "A" is represented by "U+0041"
```

Introduction

Strings are one of the most commonly used types.

Definition

A *string* variable contains a sequence of alphanumeric characters that are used as input for calculations or searches.

Note   There is no limit to the number of characters that can make up a string.

Syntax

You declare a string the same way you declare any other variable, by assigning a type (string) and giving it a name.

Declaring literal strings

You can assign a literal value to the string variable by enclosing the value in quotation marks.

```
string sample = "Hello World";
```

Using escape characters

You can also include escape characters in a string.

For example, if you want to create a string that is written on two lines, you can insert a line break within your string by using the \n escape character, as shown in the following example:

```
string sample = "Hello\nWorld";
```

This code produces the following output:

```
Hello
World
```

If you want to insert a tab, use the \t escape character, as shown in the following example:

```
string sample = "Hello\tWorld"; // produces Hello    World
```

To insert a backslash, which is useful for including file path locations, use the \\ escape character, as shown in the following example:

```
string sample = "c:\\My Documents\\sample.txt";
// produces c:\My Documents\sample.txt
```

Using verbatim strings

A *verbatim* string is a string that is interpreted by the compiler exactly as it is written, which means that even if the string spans multiple lines or includes escape characters, these are not interpreted by the compiler and they are included with the output. The only exception is the quotation mark character, which must be escaped so that the compiler can recognize where the string ends.

A verbatim string is indicated with an at sign (@) character followed by the string enclosed in quotation marks. For example:

```
string sample = @"Hello";
string sample = @"Hello\tWorld"; // produces "Hello\tWorld"
```

The following code shows a more useful example:

```
string sample = @"c:\My Documents\sample.txt";
// produces c:\My Documents\sample.txt
```

If you want to use a quotation mark inside a verbatim string, you must escape it by using another set of quotation marks. For example, to produce "Hi" you use the following code:

```
string s = @"""Hi"""; // Note: three quotes on either side
```

The preceding code produces the following string:

```
"Hi"
```

Understanding Unicode

The .NET Framework uses Unicode UTF-16 (Unicode Transformation Format, 16-bit encoding form) to represent characters. C# also encodes characters by using the international Unicode Standard. The Unicode Standard is the current universal character encoding mechanism that is used to represent text in computer processing. The previous standard was ASCII.

The Unicode Standard represents a significant improvement over ASCII because Unicode assigns a unique numeric value, called a code point, and a name to each character that is used in all the written languages of the world. ASCII defined only 128 characters, which meant that some languages could not be correctly displayed in a computer application.

For example, the character "A" is represented by the code point "U+0041" and the name "LATIN CAPITAL LETTER A". Values are available for over 65,000 characters, and there is room to support up to one million more. For more information, see The Unicode Standard at www.unicode.org.

How to Create and Use Constants

- Declared using the const keyword and a type
- You must assign a value at the time of declaration

```
const int earthRadius = 6378;//km

const long meanDistanceToSun = 149600000;//km

const double meanOrbitalVelocity = 29.79D;//km sec
```

Introduction

A constant is a variable whose value remains constant. Constants are useful in situations where the value that you are using has meaning and is a fixed number, such as pi, the radius of the earth, or a tax rate.

Benefits

Constants make your code more readable, maintainable, and robust. For example, if you assign a value of **6378** to a constant named **earthRadius**, when you use this value in calculations it is immediately apparent what value you are referring to, and it is not possible for someone to assign a different value to **earthRadius**.

Syntax

You declare a constant by using the **const** keyword and a type. You must assign a value to your constants at the time that you declare them.

Examples

```
const int earthRadius = 6378; // km
const long meanDistanceToSun = 149600000; // km
const double meanOrbitalVelocity = 29.79D; // km/sec
```

How to Create and Use Enumeration Types

> ■ **Defining Enumeration Types**
>
> ```
> enum Planet {
>         Mercury,
>         Venus,
>         Earth,
>         Mars
> }
> ```
>
> ■ **Using Enumeration Types**
>
> ```
> Planet aPlanet = Planet.Mars;
> ```
>
> ■ **Displaying the Variables**
>
> ```
> Console.WriteLine("{0}", aPlanet); //Displays Mars
> ```

Introduction

An *enumeration type* specifies a group of named numeric constants. An enumeration type is a *user-defined type,* which means that you can create an enumeration type, declare variables of that type, and assign values to those variables. The purpose of an enumeration type is to represent constant values.

Benefits

In addition to providing all the advantages of constants, enumerations:

- Make your code easier to maintain by ensuring that your variables are assigned only anticipated values.

- Allow you to assign easily identifiable names to the values, thereby making your code easier to read.

- Make your code easier to type, because as you assign enumeration values, Microsoft IntelliSense® displays a list of the possible values that you can use.

- Allow you to specify a set of constant values and define a type that will accept values from only that set.

Syntax

You create an enumeration type by using the **enum** keyword, assigning a name, and then listing the values that your enumeration can take.

It is recommended that you use Pascal case for the type name and each enumeration member. In Pascal case, you capitalize the initial letter of each word in the identifier, such as **ListOfThePlanets**.

Example

An enumeration type is shown in the following example:

```
enum Planet {
    Mercury,
    Venus,
    Earth,
    Mars
}
```

The preceding code creates a new type, **Planet**. You can declare variables of this type and assign them values from the enumeration list.

Referring to a specific member

When you want to refer to a specific member in an enumeration, you use the enumeration name, a dot, and the member name.

For example, the following code declares a variable **innerPlanet** of type **Planet**, and assigns it a value:

```
Planet innerPlanet = Planet.Venus;
```

You can declare an enumeration in a class or a namespace but not in a method.

Assigning values to enumeration members

If the members of your enumeration must have a specific value, you can assign that value when you declare the enumeration. The following code assigns a value based on the equatorial radius of the inner planets:

```
enum Planets {
  Mercury = 2437,
  Venus = 6095,
  Earth = 6378
}
```

Enumeration base types

You can use any integer except char as the base type that is used for the enumeration by specifying the type after the name of the enumeration type. For example:

```
enum Planets : uint {
  Mercury = 2437,
  Venus = 6095,
  Earth = 6378
}
```

How to Convert Between Types

- **Implicit**

  - Performed by the compiler on operations that are guaranteed not to truncate information

```
int x = 123456; // int is a 4-byte integer
long y = x; // implicit conversion to a long
```

- **Explicit**

  - Where you explicitly ask the compiler to perform a conversion that otherwise could lose information

```
int x = 65537;
short z = (short) x;
// explicit conversion to a short, z == 1
```

Introduction

When designing applications, you often must convert data from one type to another. Conversion can be necessary when you perform operations on two types that are not the same.

Definitions

There are two types of conversions in the .NET Framework: *implicit* and *explicit* conversions.

- An *implicit* conversion is a conversion that is automatically performed by the common language runtime on operations that are guaranteed to succeed without truncating information.

- An *explicit* conversion is a conversion that requires you to explicitly ask the compiler to perform a conversion that otherwise could lose information or produce an error.

Why convert?

For example, when a currency value is entered on a Web page, the type of the data may actually be text. A programmer must then convert that text to a numeric value.

Another reason for conversion is to avoid number overflow. If you try to add two bytes, the compiler returns an **int**. It returns an **int** because a byte can hold only eight bits, up to a value of 255, so the result of adding two bytes could easily result in a number greater than 255. Therefore, the resulting value is converted by the compiler and returned as an **int**.

Implicit conversions

The following table shows the implicit type conversions that are supported in C#:

From	To
sbyte	short, int, long, float, double, decimal
byte	short, ushort, int, uint, long, ulong, float, double, decimal
short	int, long, float, double, decimal
ushort	int, uint, long, ulong, float, double, decimal
int	long, float, double, decimal
uint	long, ulong, float, double, decimal
long, ulong	float, double, decimal
float	double
char	ushort, int, uint, long, ulong, float, double, decimal

Notice that implicit conversions can be performed only from a smaller type to a larger type or from an unsigned integer to a signed integer.

Example

The following example shows an implicit conversion:

```
int x = 123456; // int is a 4-byte integer
long y = x; // implicit conversion to a long
```

Explicit conversions

The syntax for performing an explicit conversion is shown in the following code:

```
type variable1 = (cast-type) variable2;
```

The type in the parentheses indicates to the compiler that the value on the right side is to be converted to the type specified in the parentheses.

Example

The following example shows explicit type conversion:

```
int x = 500;
short z = (short) x;
// explicit conversion to a short, z contains the value 500
```

It is important to remember that explicit conversions can result in data loss. For example, in the following code, a decimal is explicitly converted to an int:

```
decimal d = 1234.56M;
int x = (int) d;
```

The result of this conversion is that x is assigned a value of **1234**.

Other conversions

The .NET Framework class library also provides support for type conversions in the **System.Convert** class.

Practice: Using C# Types

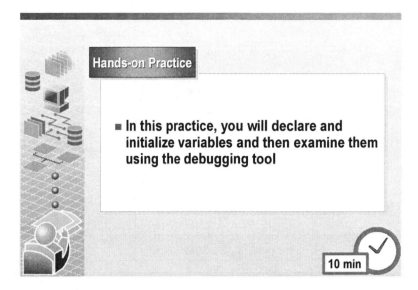

In this practice, you will declare and initialize several variables and then examine them with the debugging tool.

The starter code contains descriptions of several tasks for you to perform. Under each task is a line similar to the following:

```
Output( null );
```

When you replace the word **null** with the variable that you declared, the value of the variable appears in the form. For example, if you are asked to declare an integer and assign it the value **42**, write the following code:

```
int x = 42;
Output( x );
```

The solution code for this practice is located in *install_folder*\Practices\Mod02\Types_Solution \Types.sln. Start a new instance of Visual Studio .NET before opening the solution.

Tasks	Detailed steps
1. Start Visual Studio .NET, and then open *install_folder*\ Practices\Mod02 \Types\Types.sln.	a. Start a new instance of Visual Studio .NET. b. On the **Start** Page, click **Open Project**. c. In the **Open Project** dialog box, browse to *install_folder*\Practices \Mod02\Types, click **Types.sln**, and then click **Open**. d. In Solution Explorer, click **Form1.cs**, and then press F7 to open the Code Editor.
2. Review the tasks for this practice.	a. On the **View** menu, point to **Show Tasks**, and then click **All**. b. Review the tasks that are listed in the Task List window.

Tasks	Detailed steps
3. Declare, initialize, and display a variable with the value **Suzan Fine**.	a. In the Task List, double-click **TODO: 1 Initialize the suzanName variable with the value "Suzan Fine"**. b. Assign the value **Suzan Fine** to the variable **suzanName**. c. Change the word **null** on the following line to **suzanName**.
4. Declare, initialize, and display a variable with the value **135.20**.	a. In the Task List, double-click **TODO: 2 Declare and initialize a variable to hold a currency amount (135.20)**. b. Declare a variable, and assign it the value **135.20**. Remember that the value **135.20** is assumed to be a double, unless you append a suffix that indicates otherwise. c. Change the word **null** on the following line to the name of your variable.
5. Declare a **Planet** variable, assign the value **Planet.Earth** to it, and display its value.	a. In the Task List, double-click **TODO 3: Using the Planet enumeration**, assign **Planet.Earth** to **ourPlanet**. b. At the top of the source code file, locate the **Planet** enumeration. c. Declare a variable of the enumeration type: `Planet ourPlanet;` d. Assign the value **Planet.Earth** to the variable. e. Change the word **null** on the following line to the name of your variable.
6. Use the debugging tool to step through your code, examining the values of the variables by using the Locals window. [toolbar: Hex / Step Over]	a. Locate the line **int x = 42;** and set a breakpoint at that line. b. Press F5 to compile and run your application. c. In Visual Studio .NET, on the **Debug** menu, point to **Windows**, and then click **Locals**. d. In your application window, click **Run**. e. Step through your code, one line at a time, by clicking the **Step Over** button shown on the left, or by pressing F10. f. Examine the Locals and Autos windows to check that your program is assigning values correctly.
7. Save your application, and then quit Visual Studio .NET.	a. Save your application. b. Quit Visual Studio .NET.

Optional: The solution code declares additional variables.

- Use the debugging tool to examine the value of the variables.
- Explain why **myShort** has the value of **1** after the assignment.

Lesson: Writing Expressions

- **What Are Expressions and Operators?**
- **How to Determine Operator Precedence**

Introduction

This lesson explains how to use operators to create expressions.

Lesson objective

After completing this lesson, you will be able to use operators to create expressions.

Lesson agenda

This lesson includes the following topics and activity:

- What Are Expressions and Operators?
- How to Determine Operator Precedence
- Practice: Using Operators

What Are Expressions and Operators?

- Operators Are Symbols Used in Expressions

Common Operators	Example
· Increment / decrement	++ --
· Arithmetic	* / % + -
· Relational	< > <= >=
· Equality	== !=
· Conditional	&& || ?:
· Assignment	= *= /= %= += -= <<= >>= &= ^= |=

Introduction

The purpose of writing an expression is to perform an action and return a value. For example, you can write an expression to perform a mathematical calculation, assign a value, or compare two values.

Definitions

An *expression* is a sequence of operators and operands. An *operator* is a concise symbol that indicates the action that you want to occur in your expression. An *operand* is the value on which an operation is performed. An operator is specifically designed to produce a new value from the value that is being operated on.

Types of operators

Some of the common types of operators that you can use in your C# applications include:

- *Increment and decrement.* Used to increase or decrease a value by one.

- *Arithmetic.* Used to perform arithmetic calculations like addition.

- *Relational.* Used to define greater than, greater than or equal to, less than, and so on.

- *Equality.* Used to state equal to, or not equal.

- *Conditional.* Used to define and/or situations.

- *Assignment.* Used to assign a value to a variable.

Most operators work only with numeric data, but equality and assignment operators can also work on strings of text.

The following table lists all the operators that can be used in a C# application:

Operator type	Operator
Primary	(x), x.y, f(x), a[x], x++, x--, new, typeof, sizeof, checked, unchecked
Unary	+, -, !, ~, ++x, --x, (T)x
Mathematical	+ , - ,*, /, %
Shift	<< , >>
Relational	< , > , <= , >= , is
Equality	==
Logical	& ,	, ^
Conditional	&& , || , ?
Assignment	= , *= , /= , %= , += , -= , <<=, >>= , &= , ^= , |=

Note It is important to notice the difference between the assignment operator and the equality operator. Notice that "is equal to" is represented by two equal signs (==), because a single equal sign (=) is used to assign a value to a variable.

Example

```
int x = 10;      // assignment
int y = 20;
int z = x + y;   // mathematical plus (z == 30)
```

Operator shortcuts

C# makes it possible for you to use concise syntax to manipulate data in complex ways. The following table lists the C# operator shortcuts.

Shortcut	Identical Expression
x++ , ++x	x = x + 1 The first form increments x after the expression is evaluated; the second form increments x before the expression is evaluated.
x-- , --x	x = x - 1
x += y	x = x + y
x -= y	x = x – y
x *= y	x = x * y
x /= y	x = x / y
x %= y	x = x % y
x >>= y	x = x >> y
x <<= y	x = x << y
x &= y	x = x & y
x |= y	x = x	y
x ^= y	x = x ^ y

Example

```
int x = 11;
int z = 20;
z += x;
```

After the preceding expressions are evaluated, z has the value **31**.

Increment and decrement

The increment and decrement operators can occur either before or after an operand. For example, x++ and ++x are both equivalent to x=x+1. However, when these operators occur in expressions, x++ and ++x behave differently.

++x increments the value of x *before* the expression is evaluated. In other words, x is incremented and then the new value of x is used in the expression.

Example 1

```
int x = 5;
(++x == 6) // true or false?
```

The answer is **true**.

x++ increments the value of x after the expression is carried out; therefore, the expression is evaluated using the original value of x.

Example 2

```
x = 5
(x++ == 6) // true or false?
```

The answer is **false**.

Example 3

```
int x = 10
int y = x++; // y is equal to ten
int z = x + y; // z is equal to twenty-one
```

Tip   To improve the readability of your code, place increment and decrement operators in separate statements.

Logical negation operator

An exclamation point (!) is the logical negation operator. It is used in an assignment to reverse the value of a Boolean.

If bool b is false, !b is true.

If b is true, !b is false.

For example:

```
bool isAwake = true;
bool isAsleep = !isAwake;
```

Mathematical operators

In addition to the obvious + - * and / operators, there is a remainder operator (**%**) that returns the remainder of a division operation. For example:

```
int x = 20 % 7;     // x == 6
```

Logic operators

C# provides logic operators, as shown in the following table.

Logic operator type	Operator	Description
Conditional	&&	x && y returns true if x is true AND y is true; y is evaluated only if x is true
	||	x || y returns true if x is true OR y is true; y is evaluated only if x is false
Boolean	&	x & y returns true if x AND y are both true
	|	x | y returns true if either x OR y is true
	^	x ^ y returns true if x OR y is true, but false if they are both true or both false

Developers often use conditional logic operators. These operators follow the same rules as Boolean logic operators but have the useful characteristic that the expressions are evaluated only if they need to be evaluated.

Using operators with strings

You can also apply the plus and the equality operators to string types. The plus concatenates strings whereas the string equality operator compares strings.

```
string a = "semi";
string b = "circle";
string c = a + b;
string d = "square";
```

The string c has the value **semicircle**.

```
bool sameShape = ( "circle" == "square" );

sameShape = ( b == d );
```

The Boolean **sameShape** is **false** in both statements.

How to Determine Operator Precedence

- **Expressions are evaluated according to operator precedence**

```
10 + 20 / 5          result is 14
```

- **Parentheses can be used to control the order of evaluation**

```
(10 + 20) / 5        result is 6
10 + (20 / 5)        result is 14
```

- **Operator precedence is also determined by associativity**
  - Binary operators are left-associative
  - Assignment and conditional operators are right-associative

Introduction

Developers often create expressions that perform more than one calculation, comparison, or a combination of the two. In these situations, the *precedence* of the operators controls the order in which the expression is evaluated. If you want the operations performed in a different order; you must tell the compiler to evaluate the expression differently by using parentheses.

Evaluation order

The order in which operators are evaluated in an expression is shown in the following precedence table.

Operator type	Operator
Primary	x.y, f(x), a[x], x++, x--, new, typeof, checked, unchecked
Unary	+, -, !, ~, ++x, --x, (T)x
Multiplicative	*, /, %
Additive	+ , -
Shift	<< , >>
Relational	< , > , <= , >= , is, as
Equality	== , !=
Logical	& , ^ , |
Conditional	&& , || , ?:
Assignment	= , *= , /= , %= , += , -= , <<=, >>= , &= , ^= , |=

For example, the plus operator + has a lower precedence than the multiplication operator, so a + b * c means multiply b and c, and then add the sum to a.

Parentheses

Use parentheses to show the order of evaluation and to make the evaluation order of your expressions more readable. Extra parentheses are removed by the compiler and do not slow your application in any way, but they can make an expression much more readable.

For example, in the following expression, the compiler will multiply b by c and then add d.

```
a = b * c + d
```

Using parentheses, in the following expression, the compiler first evaluates what is in parentheses, (c + d), and then multiplies by b.

```
a = b * (c + d)
```

The following examples demonstrate operator precedence and the use of parentheses for controlling the order of evaluation in an expression:

```
10 + 20 / 5   (result is 14)
(10 + 20) / 5   (result is 6)
10 + ( 20 / 5 )   (result is 14)
((10 + 20) * 5) + 2   (result is 152)
```

Associativity

All binary operators, those that take two operands, are left-associative, meaning that the expression is evaluated from left to right, except for assignment operators. Assignment operators and conditional operators are right-associative.

For example:

x + y + z is evaluated as (x + y) + z

x = y = z is evaluated as x = (y = z)

Practice: Using Operators

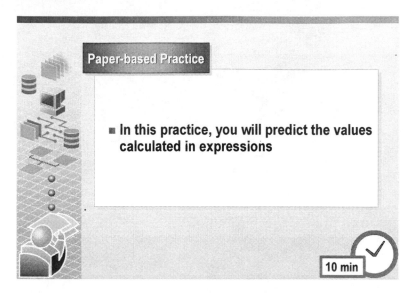

In this paper-based practice, look at each line of code, and then answer the question. Assume that the code is executed in sequence, as written.

Tasks	Detailed steps

1. Read the code in the right column, and then answer the following question.	a. Read the following code:
	
	`int x = 10;`
	`int y = x++;`
	
	b. Answer the following question.

? What is the value of **y**? Why? y=10, x = 11	
2. Read the code in the right column, and then answer the following question.	a. Read the following code, which is continued from the preceding step: `x += 10;` b. Answer the following question.
? What is the value of **x**? Why? 21	

Tasks	Detailed steps
3. Read the code in the right column, and then answer the following question.	a. Read the following code, which is continued from the preceding step: ```csharp\nint z = 30;\nint a = x + y * z;\n``` b. Answer the following question.

What is the value of **a**? Why? Write this in a more readable form.

$$x + y * z \;=\; x + (10 * 30)$$
$$=\; 21 + 300 \;=\; 321$$

| 4. Read the code in the right column, and then answer the following question. | a. Read the following code, which is continued from the preceding step:

```csharp\nint a = 10;\nint b = a++;\nbool myBool = (a == b);\n``` $b = 10,\ a = 11$

b. Answer the following question. |

What does this code do? What is the value of **myBool**?

$$(11 == 10) = False$$

| 5. Start Visual Studio .NET, and then open *install_folder*\Practices \Mod02\Operators \Operators.sln. | a. Start a new instance of Visual Studio .NET.

b. On the **Start** Page, click **Open Project**.

c. In the **Open Project** dialog box, browse to *install_folder*\Practices\Mod02\Operators, click **Operators.sln**, and then click **Open**.

d. In Solution Explorer, click **Form1.cs**, and then press F7 to open the Code Editor. |

Tasks	Detailed steps
6. Check your answers by stepping through the code.	**a.** Locate the line **int x = 10;** and set a breakpoint at that line.
	b. Press F5 to compile and run the application.
	c. If the Locals window is not visible, in Visual Studio .NET, on the **Debug** menu, point to **Windows**, and then click **Locals**.
	d. In your application window, click **Run**.
	e. Step through your code, a line at a time, by clicking the **Step Over** button, or by pressing F10.
	f. Examine the Locals and Autos windows to check that your application assigns values correctly.
7. Quit Visual Studio .NET.	▪ Quit Visual Studio .NET.

Lesson: Creating Conditional Statements

- **How and When to Use the** if **Statement**
- **How and When to Use the** switch **Statement**

Introduction

This lesson introduces you to conditional statements. You learn how and when to use **if** and **switch** statements.

Lesson objectives

After completing this lesson, you will be able to:

- Use the **if...else** conditional statement to manage the flow of control in an application.
- Use the **switch** conditional statement to manage the flow of control in an application.

Lesson agenda

This lesson includes the following topics and activity:

- How and When to Use the **if** Statement
- How and When to Use the **switch** Statement
- Practice: Using Conditional Statements

How and When to Use the *if* Statement

- **if**

```
if ( sales > 10000 ) {
    bonus += .05 * sales;
}
```

- **if else if**

```
if ( sales > 10000 ) {
    bonus += .05 * sales;
}
else if ( sales > 5000 ) {
    bonus = .01 * sales;
}
else  {
    bonus = 0;
    if ( priorBonus == 0 ) {
        //ScheduleMeeting;
    }
}
```

- **if else**

```
if ( sales > 10000 ) {
    bonus += .05 * sales;
}
else {
    bonus = 0;
}
```

Introduction

A conditional statement allows you to control the flow of your application by selecting the statement that is executed, based on the value of a Boolean expression. There are three variations to the conditional **if** statement, including: **if**, **if else**, and **if else if**.

When the expression that is being evaluated is **true**, the code following the **if** statement is executed.

Declaring an if statement

The syntax of an **if** statement is as follows:

```
if (boolean-expression) statement
```

In the following example, if the value of **sales** is greater than **10000**, the bonus calculation statement is performed:

```
if ( sales > 10000 ) {
    bonus += .05 * sales;
}
```

Declaring an if else statement

The syntax for declaring an **if else** statement is as follows:

```
if ( boolean-expression ) statement1 else statement2
```

Statement1 is executed if the Boolean expression is **true.** Otherwise, statement2 is executed.

For example:

```
if ( sales > 10000 ) {
    bonus += .05 * sales;
}
else {
    bonus = 0;
}
```

Declaring an if else if statement

You can nest **if** statements by writing them in the form of an **if else if** statement, as shown in the following example:

```
if ( sales > 10000 ) {
    bonus += .05 * sales;
}
else if ( sales > 5000 ) {
    bonus = .01 * sales;
}
else {
    bonus = 0;
    if ( priorBonus == 0 ) {
        // Schedule a Meeting;
    }
}
```

Evaluating multiple expressions

You can evaluate more than one expression in an **if** statement. For example, the following **if** statement evaluates to **true** if the value of **sales** is greater than 10,000 but less than 50,000:

```
if ( (sales > 10000) && (sales < 50000) ) {
  // sales are between 10001 and 49999 inclusive
}
```

Using the ternary operator

The ternary operator (?) is a shorthand form of the **if...else** statement. It is useful when you want to perform a comparison and return a Boolean value.

For example, the following expression assigns the value **0** to **bonus** if the value of **sales** is less than 10000:

```
bonus = ( sales > 10000 ) ? ( sales * .05) : 0 ;
```

if Sales > 1000
then
*bonus = Sales * .05*
Else
bonus = 0

How and When to Use the *switch* Statement

```
int moons;
switch (aPlanet){
   case Planet.Mercury:
        moons = 0;
        break;
   case Planet.Venus:
        moons = 0;
        break;
   case Planet.Earth:
        moons = 1;
        break;
   }
```

- **Default case**

Introduction

A **switch** statement selects the code to execute based upon the value of a test. However, a **switch** statement enables you to test for multiple values of an expression rather than just one condition.

Switch statements are useful for selecting one branch of execution from a list of mutually-exclusive choices. Using **switch** statements makes your application more efficient and your code more readable than using multiple, nested **if** statements.

Syntax

A **switch** statement takes the form of a switch expression followed by a series of switch blocks, indicated by case labels. When the expression in the argument evaluates to one of the values in a particular case, the code immediately following that case executes. When no match occurs, a default condition is executed, if one is defined.

Break

You must include a break statement at the end of each switch block, or a compile error occurs. It is not possible to fall through from one switch block to the following switch block.

Example

In the following **switch** statement, assume that "x" is an integer:

```
switch ( x ) {
  case 0:
     // x is 0
     break;
  case 1:
     // x is 1
     break;
  case 2:
     // x is 2
     break;
}
```

Execution sequence

The execution sequence is as follows:

1. x is evaluated.

2. If one of the constant values in the case label is equal to the value of the switch expression, control is passed to the statement following that case label.

3. If none of the case labels match the value of the expression, control is passed to the end point of the case statement, or to the default case, which is described in the following section.

If x has the value **1**, the statements following the case 1 label are selected and executed.

Defining a default condition

Often, you want to define a default condition so that values that are not handled specifically can still be caught. The following example shows how to define a default condition:

```
switch ( x ) {
  case 0:
      // x is 0
      break;
  case 1:
      // x is 1
      break;
  case 2:
      // x is 2
      break;
  default:
      // x is not 0, 1 or 2
      break;
}
```

The default label catches any values that are not matched by the case labels.

Using enumerations with switch statements

The type that is evaluated in the expression must be an integer type, a character type, a string, an enumeration type; or a type that can be implicitly converted to one of these types. You will often use **switch** statements with enumeration types.

In the following example, the **switch** statement selects the case based on the value of the enumeration type. This **switch** statement makes the code very readable.

```
enum Animal {
  Antelope,
  Elephant,
  Lion,
  Osprey
}
. . .

switch( favoriteAnimal ) {
  case Animal.Antelope:
      // herbivore-specific statements
      break;
  case Animal.Elephant:
      // herbivore-specific statements
      break;
  case Animal.Lion:
      // carnivore-specific statements
      break;
  case Animal.Osprey:
      // carnivore-specific statements
      break;
}
```

Combining cases

You can use multiple case labels on a single switch expression as shown in the following example:

```
switch( favoriteAnimal ) {
  case Animal.Antelope:
  case Animal.Elephant:
      // herbivore-specific statements
      break;
  case Animal.Lion:
  case Animal.Osprey:
      // carnivore-specific statements
      break;
}
```

In this case, if **favoriteAnimal** is either **Lion** or **Osprey**, the carnivore-specific statements are executed.

You cannot place a statement between the Antelope and the Elephant cases unless you also place a **break** statement between them.

Note If you are familiar with switch statements in C or C++, it is important to note that C# does not allow you to fall through a switch expression to the next switch expression. In C#, every case that has statements must also have a break statement.

Practice: Using Conditional Statements

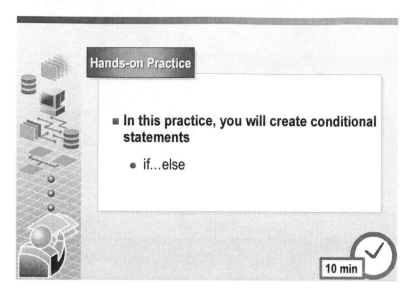

In this practice, you will complete code that lacks appropriate conditional logic.

Suppose that a zoo needs 5000 visitors per week to meet a budget projection. You will use an **if** statement to check the number of visitors and write a message indicating whether the number of visitors was above or below the goal of 5000 visitors.

The solution code for this practice is located in *install_folder*\Practices\Mod02\Conditions_Solution \conditions.sln. Start a new instance of Visual Studio .NET before opening the solution.

Tasks	Detailed steps
1. Start Visual Studio .NET, and then open *install_folder*\Practices\Mod02 \Conditions\Conditions.sln.	a. Start a new instance of Visual Studio .NET. b. On the **Start** Page, click **Open Project**. c. In the **Open Project** dialog box, browse to *install_folder*\Practices \Mod02\Conditions, click **Conditions.sln**, and then click **Open**. d. In Solution Explorer, click **Form1.cs**, and then press F7 to open the Code Editor.
2. Locate the task TODO 1: using if statements.	a. On the **View** menu, point to **Show Tasks**, and then click **All**. b. In the Task List, double-click **TODO 1: using if statements**.
3. If the value in **visitors** is 5000 or more, then use the **Output** method to display a message indicating that the target was achieved. Otherwise, display a message saying that the target was not achieved.	a. Use an **if** statement to test whether the value of visitors is 5000 or more. b. If **visitors** is 5000 or more, use the **Output** method to display a message that says that the target has been achieved. For example: `Output("Visitor target achieved");`

Tasks	Detailed steps
4. Test your code. `3000` ⇅	**a.** Press F5 to build and run your application. **b.** In your application window, click **Run**, and verify that the output matches the rules listed above. **c.** In the **NumericUpDown** control, shown at the left, delete the existing value, and then type **5000** **d.** Click **Run** and verify that the output matches the rules listed above. **e.** In the **NumericUpDown** control, change the value to **4999** **f.** Click **Run** and verify that the output matches the rules listed above.
5. Use the debugging tool to step through the code.	**a.** In Solution Explorer, click **Form1.cs**, and then press F7. **b.** Locate the following line and set a breakpoint at that line. `int visitors = (int) visitorsUpDown.Value;` **c.** Press F5 to compile and run the application. **d.** If the Locals window is not visible, in Visual Studio .NET, on the **Debug** menu, point to **Windows**, and then click **Locals**. **e.** In your application window, click **Run**. **f.** Step through your code, a line at a time, by clicking the **Step Over** button, or by pressing F10. **g.** Examine the Locals and Autos windows to check that your application assigns values correctly. **h.** Stop debugging by clicking the **Close** button in the application that you are debugging or by pressing SHIFT+F5. **i.** Repeat this task and alter the input values to the application, so that the execution follows a different path.
6. Save your application, and then quit Visual Studio .NET.	**a.** Save your application. **b.** Quit Visual Studio .NET.

Lesson: Creating Iteration Statements

- **How to Use a** for **Loop**
- **How to Use a** while **Loop**
- **How to Use a** do **Loop**

Introduction

C# provides several looping mechanisms, which enable you to execute a block of code repeatedly until a certain condition is met. In each case, a statement is executed until a Boolean expression returns **true**. By using these looping mechanisms, you can avoid typing the same line of code over and over.

Lesson objectives

After completing this lesson, you will be able to:

- Write a **for** loop.
- Write a **while** loop.
- Write a **do** loop.

Lesson agenda

This lesson includes the following topics and activity:

- How to Use a **for** Loop
- How to Use a **while** Loop
- How to Use a **do** Loop
- Practice: Using Iteration Statements

How to Use a *for* Loop

- **Use when you know how many times you want to repeat the execution of the code**

```
for (initializer; condition; iterator) {
    statements;
}
```

Example

```
for (int i = 0; i < 10; i++) {
    Console.WriteLine("i = {0}",i);
}


for ( int j = 100; j > 0; j -= 10 ) {
    Console.WriteLine("j = {0}", j);
}
```

Introduction

A **for** loop is used to execute a statement block a set number of times. A **for** loop is a commonly-used way of executing a block of statements several times. The **for** loop evaluates a given condition, and while the condition is true, it executes a block of statements.

The **for** loop is called a pretest loop because the loop condition is evaluated before the loop statements are executed. If the loop condition tests false, the statements are not executed.

You use a **for** loop when you know in advance the number of times that you want to repeat execution of your code statement.

Example

For example, suppose that you are designing an application to calculate the amount of money that you will have in your savings account after 10 years with a given starting balance, and you want to display the total that you will have at the end of each year. One way that you can write this code is to write a statement like **balance *= interestRate** in your code ten times, or you can simply write a **for** loop.

Syntax

The syntax for declaring a **for** loop is:

```
for (initializer; condition; iterator) {
  statement-block
}
```

Example

```
for ( int i = 0; i < 10; i++ ) {
  Console.WriteLine( "i = {0}",i );
}
```

```
for ( int j = 100; j > 0; j -= 10 ) {
  Console.WriteLine( "j = {0}", j );
}
```

This **for** structure is very flexible. For example, the loop counter can be incremented or decremented for each loop. In this case, you must know the number of loops before you write the loop.

Example of a decrementing loop

In the following example, **i** has decrementing values from **10** through **1**:

```
for ( int i = 10; i > 0; i-- ) {
  loop statements;
}
```

Example of an incrementing loop

In the following example, **i** has values of **0** to **100**, in incrementing steps of 10:

```
for ( int i = 0; i <= 100; i = i+10 ) {
  loop statements;
}
```

Declaring multiple variables

The **initializer** and **iterator** statements can contain more than one local variable declaration, as shown in the following example:

```
for ( int i = 0, j = 100; i < 100; i++, j-- ) {
  Console.WriteLine("{0}, {1}", i, j );
}
```

This sample would produce the following output:

```
0, 100
1, 99
2, 98
 .
 .
 .
99, 1
```

How to Use a *while* Loop

- A Boolean test runs at the start of the loop and if it tests as False, the loop is never executed

- The loop executes until the condition becomes false

```
bool readingFile;

// . . .

while ( readingFile == true ) {
   GetNextLine();
}
```

- continue, break

Introduction

Similar to the **for** loop, the **while** loop is a pretest loop, which means that if the first test evaluates **false**, the statement does not execute. This is useful when you want to make sure that something is true before executing the code in your loop. You also use a **while** loop when you do not know exactly how many times you must execute the loop statements.

Syntax

The syntax for declaring a **while** loop is:

```
while (true-condition) {
   statement-block
}
```

Example

```
while ( readingFile == true ) {
   GetNextLine();
}
```

Using the continue keyword

You can use the **continue** keyword to start the next loop iteration without executing any remaining statements. The following example reads a set of commands from a file. **GetNextLine** gets a line of text; there is one command per line.

```
while ( readingFile == true ) {
   string command = GetNextLine();
   if ( command == "Comment" ) {
      continue;
   }
   if ( command == "Set" ) {
      // do other processing
   }
}
```

When the command is a comment, there is no need to process the rest of the line, so the **continue** keyword is used to start the loop again.

The break keyword

You can also break out of a loop. When the **break** keyword is encountered, the loop is terminated, and execution continues at the statement that follows the loop statement.

```
while ( readingFile == true ) {
  string command = GetNextLine();
  if ( command == "Exit" ) {
      break;
  }
  if ( command == "Set" ) {
      // do other processing
  }
}
```

How to Use a *do* Loop

- **Executes the code in the loop and then performs a Boolean test. If the expression tests as True then the loop repeats until the expression tests as False.**

```
do {
    // something that is always going to happen
    //at least once
} while (test is true);
```

Example

```
int i = 1;
do {
    Console.WriteLine ("{0}", i++);
} while (i <= 10);
```

Introduction

In a **do** loop, the statement is executed, a condition is tested, and then the statement is executed again. This process repeats for as long as the condition tests **true**. This is known as a post-test loop. The **do** loop is useful when you want to execute a statement at least once.

Syntax

The syntax for a **do** loop is:

```
do {
    statements
} while (boolean-expression);
```

Note The semicolon after the statement is required.

Example

In the following example, a **do** loop is used to write out the numbers from 1 to 10 in a column:

```
int i = 1;
do {
    Console.WriteLine("{0}", i++);
} while ( i <= 10 );
```

In this example, the increment operator is used to increment the value of **i** after the statement is written to the screen for the first time.

Practice: Using Iteration Statements

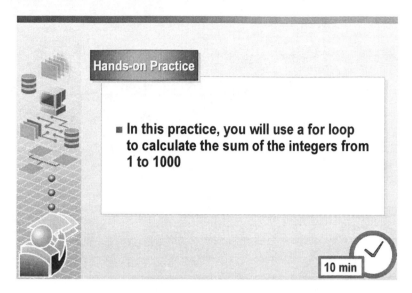

In this practice, you will use a **for** loop to calculate the sum of the integers from 1 to 1000.

If time permits, perform the same calculation using a **while** loop and a **do** loop.

The solution code for this practice is located in *install_folder*\Practices\Mod02\Loops_Solution \Loops.sln. Start a new instance of Visual Studio .NET before opening the solution.

Tasks	Detailed steps
1. Start Visual Studio .NET, and then open *install_folder* Practices\Mod02 \Loops\Loops.sln.	a. Start a new instance of Visual Studio .NET. b. On the **Start** Page, click **Open Project**. c. In the **Open Project** dialog box, browse to *install_folder*\Practices \Mod02\Loops, click **Loops.sln**, and then click **Open**. d. In Solution Explorer, click **Form1.cs**, and then press F7 to open the Code Editor.
2. Locate the task **TODO 1: writing loops**.	a. On the **View** menu, point to **Show Tasks**, and then click **All**. b. In the Task List, double-click **TODO 1: writing loops**.
3. Use a **for** loop to add all of the integers from 1 to 1000.	a. Write a **for** loop to add all of the integers from 1 to 1000. b. Place the result in an integer variable named **total**.
4. Display the result using the code shown in the right column.	▪ Display the result by using the following code: `Output("result: " + total);`
5. (Optional) Repeat steps 3 and 4, using a **while** loop instead of a **for** loop.	▪ (Optional) Repeat steps 3 and 4, using a **while** loop instead of a **for** loop.

Tasks	Detailed steps
6. (Optional) Repeat steps 3 and 4, using a **do** loop instead of a **for** loop.	▪ (Optional) Repeat steps 3 and 4, using a **do** loop instead of a **for** loop.
7. Press F5 to build and run your application.	▪ In your application window, click **Run**, and verify that the output is correct.
8. Save your application and quit Visual Studio .NET.	a. Save your application. b. Quit Visual Studio .NET.

Review

■ **Understanding the Fundamentals of a C# Program**

■ **Using C# Predefined Types**

■ **Writing Expressions**

■ **Creating Conditional Statements**

■ **Creating Iteration Statements**

1. What symbol indicates a single-line comment in your code?

   //

2. True or false: You end a statement with a closing brace and a semicolon.

   False

3. What is the largest value that can fit in a byte?

   255

4. In the following expression, what is the value of y?

   ```
   int x = 50;
   int y = ++x;
   ```

   51

conditional

5. Fill in the blank: A _____ statement allows you to control the flow of your application by selecting the statement that is executed, based on the value of a Boolean expression.

6. True or False: The **while** loop is a pre-test loop.

yes→true

Lab 2.1: Writing a Savings Account Calculator

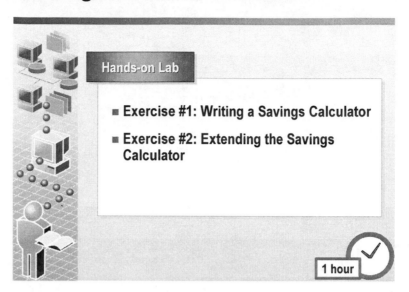

Hands-on Lab

- **Exercise #1: Writing a Savings Calculator**
- **Exercise #2: Extending the Savings Calculator**

1 hour

Objectives

After completing this lab, you will be able to:

- Declare variables and assign values to them.
- Convert between types.
- Write looping statements.
- Write conditional statements.

Note This lab focuses on the concepts in this module and as a result may not comply with Microsoft security recommendations.

Prerequisites

Before working on this lab, you must have:

- Knowledge of C# pre-defined types.
- The ability to write looping statements in C#.
- The ability to write conditional statements in C#.

Estimated time to complete this lab: 60 minutes

Exercise 0
Lab Setup

The Lab Setup section lists the tasks that you must perform before you begin the lab.

Task	Detailed steps
▪ Log on to Microsoft Windows® as **Student** with a password of **P@ssw0rd**.	▪ Log on to Windows with the following account. ● User name: **Student** ● Password: **P@ssw0rd** Note that the 0 in the password is a zero.

Note that by default the *install_folder* is C:\Program Files\Msdntrain\2609.

Exercise 1
Write a Savings Calculator

Scenario

Your bank wants to provide a simple savings calculator for account holders.

Details

In this exercise, you will write the code to complete a simple compound interest savings calculator. The user interface portion of the application is complete, but the code that performs the calculation is not written.

The application is shown in the following illustration:

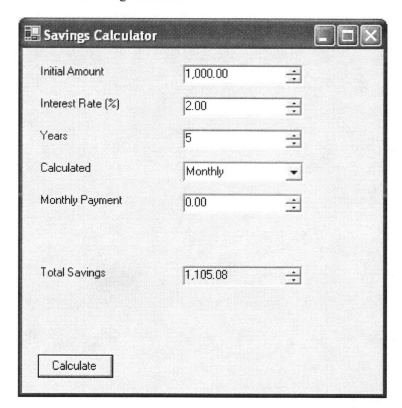

Users enter the values, and when they click the **Calculate** button, the total is displayed in the **Total Savings** line.

To illustrate the logic of the program, three usage examples are described, each followed by a description of the logic.

Example 1:

The customer makes an initial payment of 1000, the annual interest rate for the account is 2%, and the calculation is for 5 years. The interest is calculated monthly and the extra money is added to the account.

This scenario requires that the application calculates the monthly interest rate by dividing the annual rate by 12, and then increases the account balance by the monthly interest every month for the period of the calculation.

Example 2:

The customer makes an initial payment of 2000, the annual interest rate for the account is 2.5%, and the calculation is for 10 years. The interest is calculated monthly and an extra monthly payment of 10 is added to the account.

This scenario requires an extra step of adding the extra monthly payment to the new monthly balance. Add this payment *after* the interest has been added to the balance. This will result in a total of 3929.10 (rounded to two decimal places).

Example 3:

Initial Amount = 5000, interest rate = 6%, years = 15, interest calculated monthly, monthly payments made of 100. Total is 41352.34.

Tasks	Detailed steps
1. Start Microsoft Visual Studio .NET, and then open *install_folder*\ Labfiles\Lab02_1 \Exercise1\Saving.sln .	a. Start a new instance of Visual Studio .NET. b. On the **Start** Page, click **Open Project**. c. In the **Open Project** dialog box, browse to *install_folder*\ Labfiles\Lab02_1\Exercise1, click **Saving.sln**, and then click **Open**.
2. View the code of Form1.cs, and review the tasks to be performed in this exercise.	a. In Solution Explorer, click **Form1.cs**, and then press F7 to open the Code Editor. b. On the **View** menu, point to **Show Tasks**, and then click **All**. c. In the Task List, double-click **TODO: calculate the value of the account**.

3. Using the information provided in the introduction to this lab, write code that calculates the value of the savings account.	▪ Note the following:
	
	  • The variable **startAmount** contains the initial amount.
	
	  • The variable **rate** contains the selected interest rate.
	
	  • The variable **years** contains the number of years.
	
	  • The variable **calcFrequency** is a variable of enumeration type **Compound**. This is defined at the top of the code file. It has one possible value—Compound.Monthly.
	
	  • The variable **additional** contains the additional amount that the customer plans to save every month.
	
	  • Assign your calculated total to the variable **totalValue** to have it displayed on the Windows form.

Tasks	Detailed steps
4. Test your application.	▪ Use the following values to check if your solution is correct (be sure to set the value of **Calculated** to **Monthly**): • Initial Amount: 1000; Interest Rate 2%; Years: 5; Calculated: Monthly; Monthly Payment 0. Total Savings: *1105.08*. • Initial Amount: 3500; Interest Rate 3.3%; Years: 7; Calculated: Monthly; Monthly Payment 50. Total Savings: *9125.56*. • Initial Amount: 5000; Interest Rate 6.25%; Years: 10; Calculated: Monthly; Monthly Payment 250. Total Savings: *50856.56*.
5. Save your application, and then quit Visual Studio .NET.	a. Save your application. b. Quit Visual Studio .NET.

Exercise 2
Extending the Savings Calculator

In this exercise, you will add an option for quarterly interest calculations to the savings calculator. If you want to continue to use the application that you developed in Exercise 1, skip step 1.

When the quarterly interest option is selected, the interest is calculated per quarter, starting from the third month following the initial deposit. Any additional deposits are added to the balance after the interest for that ~~month~~ has been added.
quarter

The solution code for this lab is located at *install_folder*\Labfiles\Lab02_1\Exercise2 \Solution_Code\Saving.sln. Start a new instance of Visual Studio .NET before opening the solution.

Tasks	Detailed steps
1. Start Microsoft Visual Studio .NET and then open *install_folder*\ Labfiles\Lab02_1 \Exercise2\Saving.sln.	a. Start a new instance of Visual Studio .NET. b. On the **Start Page**, click **Open Project**. c. In the **Open Project** dialog box, browse to the folder *install_folder*\ Labfiles\Lab02_1\Exercise2, click **Saving.sln**, and then click **Open**.
2. Add a new value called **Quarterly** to the enumeration type **Compound**.	a. In Solution Explorer, click **Form1.cs**, and then press F7 to open the Code Editor. b. Locate the enumeration **Compound**, at the top of the Code Editor. c. Add a new value **Quarterly** to the enumeration.

3. Follow the steps on the right to add the enumeration to the **calculationFrequency** combo box on the form.	a. Locate the following line of code:
	
	 `calculationFrequency.Items.Add(Compound.Monthly);`
	
	 b. Immediately after this line, add the following code:
	
	 `calculationFrequency.Items.Add(Compound.Quarterly);`
	
	 Note that t his code assumes that you have named your new enumeration value as described in step 2.
	
	 This code adds the enumeration value to the combo box on the main form.

4. Using the information provided in the introduction to this lab, write code that calculates the value of the savings account when interest is computed quarterly.	▪ Note the following: • The variable **calcFrequency** is a variable of enumeration type **Compound**, and when the user selects **Quarterly** from the menu, **calcFrequency** will have the value **Quarterly**, as defined in step 2.

Tasks	Detailed steps
5. Test your solution.	▪ Use the following values to check if your solution is correct: • Initial Amount: 1000; Interest Rate 2%; Years: 5; Calculated: Quarterly; Monthly Payment 0. Total Savings: *1104.90*. • Initial Amount: 3500; Interest Rate 3.3%; Years: 7; Calculated: Quarterly; Monthly Payment 50. Total Savings: *9134.21*. • Initial Amount: 5000; Interest Rate 6.25%; Years: 10; Calculated: Quarterly; Monthly Payment 250. Total Savings: *50969.31*.
6. Save your application, and then quit Visual Studio .NET.	**a.** Save your application. **b.** Quit Visual Studio .NET.

msdn training

Module 3: Creating Objects in C#

Contents

Microsoft

Overview

- **Defining a Class**
- **Declaring Methods**
- **Using Constructors**
- **Using Static Class Members**

Introduction

This module introduces the fundamentals of object-oriented programming, including the concepts of objects, classes, and methods. It explains how to define classes and create objects, how to organize classes by using namespaces, and how to define, write, and call methods. Finally, it describes how to use constructors.

Objectives

After completing this module, you will be able to:

- Define a class
- Declare methods
- Use constructors
- Use static class members

Lesson: Defining a Class

- **What Are Classes and Objects?**
- **What Are Value Types and Reference Types?**
- **How to Define a Class and Create an Object**
- **How to Organize Classes Using Namespaces**
- **How to Define Accessibility and Scope**

Introduction

This lesson discusses how to define classes, instantiate objects, access class members, and use namespaces to organize classes.

Lesson objectives

After completing this lesson, you will be able to:

- Define a class.
- Create an object.
- Use access modifiers to define the scope of class members.
- Organize classes by using namespaces.

Lesson agenda

This lesson includes the following topics and activities:

- Multimedia: Introduction to Classes and Objects
- What Are Classes and Objects?
- What Are Value Types and Reference Types?
- How to Define a Class and Create an Object
- How to Organize Classes Using Namespaces
- How to Define Accessibility and Scope
- Practice: Defining Classes and Creating Objects

Multimedia: What Are Objects and Classes?

This animation introduces you to the fundamental user-defined type in C#, the class.

What Are Classes and Objects?

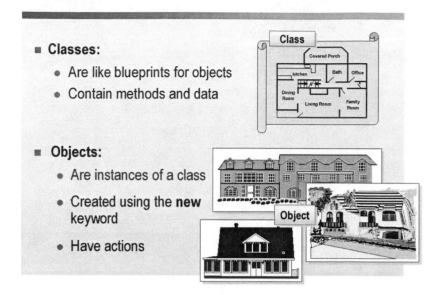

Classes:
- Are like blueprints for objects
- Contain methods and data

Objects:
- Are instances of a class
- Created using the **new** keyword
- Have actions

Introduction

A class is the fundamental user-defined type in C#. You must define a class before you can create an object.

Definition

A *class* is essentially like a blueprint, from which you can create objects. A class defines the characteristics of an object, including properties that define the types of data that the object can contain and methods that describe the behavior of the object. These characteristics determine how other objects can access and work with the data that is contained in the object.

An *object* is an instance of a class. If a class is like a blueprint, then an object is what is created from that blueprint. The class is the *definition* of an item; the object *is* the item. The blueprint for your house is like a class; the house that you live in is an object.

Example 1

For example, if you want to build objects that represent ducks, you can define a **Duck** class that has certain behaviors, such as walking, quacking, flying, and swimming—and specific properties, such as height, weight, and color. It is important to notice that the behaviors are relevant to the object. Although it is obviously illogical to create a duck object that barks like a dog, relating behavior to objects is not always so clear when you work with the type of data that a programmer typically manipulates.

The **Duck** *class* defines what a duck is and what it can do. A **Duck** *object* is a specific duck that has a specific weight, color, height, and behavioral characteristics. The duck that you feed is a duck object.

Example 2

Suppose that a programmer must write a function that changes a customer's address in a database. In a traditional approach, the programmer may write a **ChangeAddress** function that takes a database table and row as a parameter and changes the address information in that row. Or, the programmer may use the person's name as a parameter, search the table for that name, and then change the address in the record. The disadvantage of this approach is that when you want to change the information about the person, you must know something about how that information is represented, in this case, in a specific table in a database.

An object-oriented approach is to define a class that represents customers and provides the ability to change addresses. The application that uses the **Customer** class is likely to manage multiple customer objects, each representing one customer. Each customer object contains information about the location of that customer's record in the database, so when the application must change the address information, it can simply invoke the **ChangeAddress** action or method for that particular customer. The application tells the **Customer** object to change its address, in effect.

In C#, everything behaves like an object. When you create an object, you are creating a new type, called a reference type.

What Are Value Types and Reference Types?

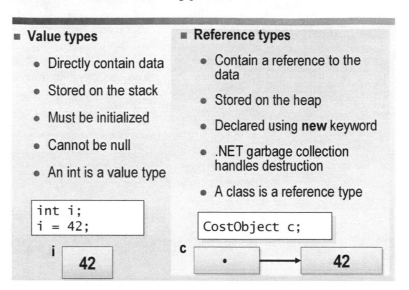

Introduction

There are two kinds of types: value types and reference types. Most of the predefined types are value types. For example, an integer is a value type.

Value types

Value types directly contain their data. Therefore, each value type variable directly contains the value that it is assigned.

Value types store themselves, and the data that they contain, in an area of memory called the *stack*. The stack is an area of memory that is used to store items in a last-in, first-out manner.

Reference types

Reference type variables contain a reference to their data. Objects are reference types.

More than one reference type variable can reference the same object. Therefore, it is possible for operations on one reference type variable to affect other variables that refer to the same object, the same data. Reference types contain a reference to data that is allocated on the *heap*. The heap is an area of memory where objects are allocated.

Initializing a value type

When you declare a value type variable, you must then initialize it before it can be used. To initialize a value type variable, you simply assign a value to that variable, as shown in the following example:

```
int anInteger;
anInteger = 42;
```

The first line declares the value type variable **int** by naming it **anInteger** and the second line initializes the variable by assigning it a value of **42**.

Initializing a reference type

When you declare a reference type variable, you then initialize it by using the **new** keyword. This keyword allocates some memory on the heap for your variable. For example, suppose that you have a class named **Customer**.

```
Customer bestCustomer = new Customer();
```

The variable **bestCustomer** refers to an object of type **Customer**.

Boxing

C# allows you to treat value types like reference types. For example, you can declare an integer, assign a value to it, and call the **ToString** method. **Console.WriteLine** method uses *boxing* in exactly this manner, to write the string format of the parameters that are passed to it.

```
int x = 25;
Console.WriteLine( x );
```

x is declared as a value type, but when the **ToString** method is invoked, it is converted to an object, which is what provides the **ToString** method. This process is called boxing. Boxing occurs implicitly when you use a value type where a reference type is expected. You can also explicitly box a value type by converting it to an object type, as shown in the following example:

```
object boxedValue = (object) x;
```

You can convert x back to a value type, although you must do so explicitly. This is called *unboxing*. To do this, simply copy the boxed variable to a value type variable, explicitly converting it to the correct value type, as shown in the following example:

```
int y = (int) boxedValue;
```

You can unbox a value only if it can be assigned to the unboxed value type.

How to Define a Class and Create an Object

- **How to define a class**

```
public class Customer {
  public string    name;
  public decimal   creditLimit;
  public uint      customerID;
}
```

- **How to instantiate a class as an object**

```
Customer nextCustomer = new Customer();
```

- **How to access class variables**

```
nextCustomer.name = "Suzan Fine";
```

Introduction

A class is like a blueprint that is used to create objects, in the same way that a blueprint for a house is used to create many individual houses.

Syntax

To define a class, you place the **class** keyword before the name of your class, and then you insert the class members between braces.

```
[attributes] [access-modifiers] class identifier {class-body}
```

Pascal case

It is recommended that you use Pascal case for your class name, for example, **MyClassName**. Pascal case means that the initial letter of each word in the identifier is capitalized.

Example

The following example defines a new class, **Customer**, with three associated pieces of relevant information—the customer's name, the credit limit of the customer, and a customer ID. Although the **Customer** class is defined in the example, there are no **Customer** objects yet. They still must be created.

```
class Customer {
  public string  name;
  public decimal creditLimit;
  public uint    customerID;
}
```

A class is a user-defined type, as opposed to a system-provided type. When you define a class, you actually create a new type in your application. To use a class that you have defined, you must first instantiate an object of that type by using the **new** keyword.

Syntax

```
<class> <object> = new <class>

Customer nextCustomer = new Customer();
```

Accessing class variables

After you instantiate an object, to access and use the data that the object contains, you type the name of the instantiated class, followed by a period and the name of the class member that you want to access.

For example, you can access the **name** member of the **Customer** class and assign it a value in your **nextCustomer** object, the name of the instantiated class, as follows:

```
nextCustomer.name = "Suzan Fine";
```

Example 2

The following code defines a new class named **Lion** with one class member, **weight,** and creates an instance of the **Lion** class, an object named **zooLion**. A value is assigned to the **weight** member of the **zooLion** class.

```
public class Lion {
  public int weight;
}


. . .


Lion zooLion = new Lion();
zooLion.weight = 200;
```

Classes are reference types

Each **Lion** object that is created is a separate object, as shown in the following code:

```
Lion largerLion = new Lion();
Lion smallerLion = new Lion();
largerLion.weight = 200;
```

The preceding code does not change the **weight** member of **smallerLion** object. That value is zero, which is the default value for an integer.

The following code does change the **weight** member of the **smallerLion** object:

```
Lion largerLion = new Lion();
largerLion.weight = 225;

Lion smallerLion = new Lion();
smallerLion.weight = 175;

Lion recentlyWeighedLion = smallerLion;

recentlyWeighedLion.weight = 185;

// smallerLion's weight is now 185.
```

In the preceding code, the value of **smallerLion.weight** is **185**.

Because **Lion** is a reference type, the assignment to **recentlyWeighedLion** causes **smallerLion** and **recentlyWeighedLion** to reference the same object.

Object destruction

When you create an object, you are actually allocating some space in memory for that object. The Microsoft® .NET Framework provides an automatic memory management feature called *garbage collection*.

Garbage collection

The garbage collector monitors the lifetime of objects and frees the memory that is allocated to them when they are no longer being referenced. By working in the .NET Framework, a programmer no longer needs to worry about de-allocation and destruction of objects in memory.

When the garbage collector locates objects that are no longer being referenced, it implicitly executes the termination code that de-allocates the memory and returns it to the pool.

The garbage collector does not operate on a predictable schedule. It can run at unpredictable intervals, usually whenever memory becomes low.

Occasionally, you may want to dispose of your objects in a deterministic manner. For example, if you must release scarce resources over which there may be contention, such as terminating a database connection or a communication port, you can do so by using the **IDisposable** interface.

Note   For more information about interfaces, see Module 5, "Programming with C#," in Course 2609, *Introduction to C# Programming with Microsoft .NET.*

How to Organize Classes Using Namespaces

- **Declaring a namespace**

```
namespace CompanyName {
  public class Customer () { }
}
```

- **Nested namespaces**

```
namespace CompanyName {
  namespace Sales {
      public class Customer () { }
  }
}
// Or
namespace CompanyName.Sales { ... }
```

- **The using statement**

```
using System;
using CompanyName.Sales;
```

Introduction

You use namespaces to organize classes into a logically related hierarchy. Namespaces function as both an internal system for organizing your application and as an external way to avoid name clashes (collisions) between your code and other applications.

Because more than one company may create classes with the same name, such as "Customer," when you create code that may be seen or used by third parties, it is highly recommended that you organize your classes by using a hierarchy of namespaces. This practice enables you to avoid interoperability issues.

Definition

A *namespace* is an organizational system that is used to identify groups of related classes.

Creating a namespace

To create a namespace, you simply type the keyword **namespace** followed by a name.

Best practices

It is recommended that you use Pascal case for namespaces.

It is also recommended that you create at least a two-tiered namespace, which is one that contains two levels of classification, separated by a period. Typically, you use your company name, followed by the name of a department or a product line.

Example

The following code shows an example of a two-tiered namespace:

```
namespace CompanyName.Sales {
  // define your classes within this namespace
  public class Customer() {

  }
}
```

The preceding two-tiered namespace declaration is identical to writing each namespace in a nested format, as shown in the following code:

```
namespace CompanyName {
  namespace Sales {
      public class Customer() {

      }
  }
}
```

In both cases, you can refer to the class by using the following code:

```
CompanyName.Sales.Customer()
```

This is the *fully qualified name* of the **Customer** class. Users of the **Customer** class can use the fully qualified name to refer to this specific customer class and avoid name collisions with other **Customer** classes.

Note   You should avoid creating a class with the same name as a namespace.

Commonly used namespaces in the .NET Framework

The Microsoft .NET Framework is made up of many namespaces, the most important of which is named **System**. The **System** namespace contains the classes that most applications use to interact with the operating system.

For example, the **System** namespace contains the **Console** class, which provides several methods, including **WriteLine,** which is a command that enables you to write code to an on-screen console. You can access the **WriteLine** method of the **Console** class as follows:

```
System.Console.WriteLine("Hello, World");
```

A few of the other namespaces that are provided by the .NET Framework through the **System** namespace are listed in the following table.

Namespace	Definition
System.Windows.Forms	Provides the classes that are useful for building applications based on Microsoft Windows®
System.IO	Provides classes for reading and writing data to files
System.Data	Provides classes that are useful for data access
System.Web	Provides classes that are useful for building Web Forms applications

The using directive

There is no limit to the number of tiers that a namespace can contain and, therefore, namespaces can grow long and cumbersome. To make code more readable, you can apply the **using** directive.

The **using** directive is a shortcut that tells your application that the types in the namespace can be referenced directly, without using the fully qualified name. Normally, at the top of your code file, you simply list the namespaces that you use in that file, prefixed with the **using** statement. You can put more than one **using** directive in the source file.

Example

```
using System;
using CompanyName.Sales;
...
Console.WriteLine("Hello, World");
Customer nextCustomer = new Customer();
```

How to Define Accessibility and Scope

- **Access modifiers are used to define the accessibility level of class members**

Declaration	Definition
public	Access not limited.
private	Access limited to the containing class.
internal	Access limited to this program.
protected	Access limited to the containing class and to types derived from the containing class
protected internal	Access limited to the containing class, derived classes, or to members of this program

Introduction

By using access modifiers, you can define the scope of class members in your applications. It is important to understand how access modifiers work because they affect your ability to use a class and its members.

Definition of scope

Scope refers to the region of code from which an element of the program can be referenced. For example, the **weight** member of the **Lion** class can be accessed only from within the **Lion** class. Therefore, the *scope* of the weight member is the **Lion** class.

Items that are nested within other items are within the scope of those items. For example, **Lion** is within the **ClassMain** class, and therefore can be referenced from anywhere within **ClassMain**.

C# access modifiers

The following table lists the access modifiers that can be added to your class members to control their scope at the time of declaration.

Declaration	Definition
public	Access is not limited: any other class can access a public member.
private	Access is limited to the containing type: only the class containing the member can access the member.
internal	Access is limited to this assembly: classes within the same assembly can access the member.
protected	Access is limited to the containing class and to types derived from the containing class.
protected internal	Access is limited to the containing class, derived classes, or to classes within the same assembly as the containing class.

An *assembly* is the collection of files that make up a program.

Rules

The following rules apply:

- Namespaces are always (implicitly) public.

- Classes are always (implicitly) public.

- Class members are private by default.

- Only one modifier can be declared on a class member. Although *protected internal* is two words, it is one access modifier.

- The scope of a member is never larger than that of its containing type.

Recommendations

The accessibility of your class members determines the set of behaviors that the user of your class sees. If you define a class member as private, the users of that class cannot see or use that member.

You should make public only those items that users of your class need to see. Limiting the set of actions that your class makes public reduces the complexity of your class from the point of view of the user, and it makes it easier for you to document and maintain your class.

Example 1

If a class named **Animal** contains a member named **weight**, the member is private by default and is accessible only from within the **Animal** class. If you try to use the **weight** member from another class, you get a compilation error, as shown in the following code:

```
using System;

namespace LearnCSharp.ClassExample {
  class ClassMain {

      public class Lion {
          public int    age;
          private int    weight;
      }

      static void Main(string[] args) {
          Lion zooLion = new Lion();
          zooLion.age = 7;
          // the following line causes a compilation error
          zooLion.weight = 200;
      }
  }
}
```

Compiling the preceding code produces the following error:

```
'LearnCSharp.ClassExample.ClassMain.Lion.weight' is
inaccessible due to its protection level
```

Practice: Defining Classes and Creating Objects

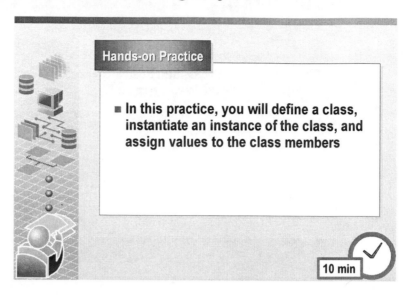

In this practice, you will create a class that represents an Antelope and create an instance of that class.

The solution code for this practice is located in *install_folder*\Practices\Mod03\Classes_Solution \ExampleClass.sln. Start a new instance of Microsoft Visual Studio® .NET before opening the solution.

Tasks	Detailed steps
1. Start Visual Studio .NET, and then open *install_folder*\ Practices\Mod03\Classes \ExampleClass.sln.	a. Start a new instance of Visual Studio .NET. b. On the **Start Page**, click **Open Project**. c. In the **Open Project** dialog box, browse to *install_folder*\Practices\Mod03\Classes, click **ExampleClass.sln**, and then click **Open**.
2. Review the tasks for this practice.	a. In Solution Explorer, click **Form1.cs**, and then press F7 to open the Code Editor. b. On the **View** menu, point to **Show Tasks**, and then click **All**. c. Review the tasks listed in the Task List.

3. Write code to define an **Antelope** class.	a. In the Task List, double-click **TODO 1: Define an Antelope class**.
	b. The **Antelope** class should have at least the following characteristics:
	  • Exhibit number
	  • Age

Tasks	Detailed steps
4. Create an instance of an **Antelope** object, and assign values to the members.	**a.** Locate the task **TODO 2: Create an instance of the Antelope class.** Any code that you place in the **runExample_Click** method will run when you click the **Run** button in the application window. **b.** Create an instance of the **Antelope** object, and assign a value to the Exhibit number member.
5. Use the supplied **Output** method to display the exhibit number for the **Antelope** object.	▪ Use the provided **Output** method to display the information, replacing the word **null** in the provided example with the value that you want to display.
6. Compile your application, and then step through it in the debugging tool to ensure that your application is working as expected. 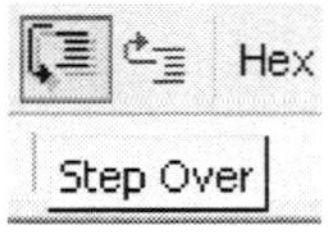 ![Step Over button] Hex Step Over	**a.** Set a breakpoint at the line where you instantiate your first object. **b.** Press F5 to compile and run your application in debug mode. **c.** Click **Run** in your application. **d.** Step through your code by using the **Step Over** button, shown on the left, or by pressing F10.
7. Save your application, and then quit Visual Studio .NET.	**a.** Save your application. **b.** Quit Visual Studio .NET.

Lesson: Declaring Methods

- **How to Write a Method**
- **How to Pass Parameters to a Method**
- **How to Pass Parameters by Reference**
- **How to Pass a Reference Type**
- **How to Overload a Method**
- **How to Use XML Code Comment Features**

Introduction

This lesson explains how to implement actions in C# by using methods.

Lesson objectives

After completing this lesson, you will be able to:

- Write a method.
- Pass parameters to a method.
- Use the **ref** keyword to modify a parameter in a method.
- Use the **out** keyword to initialize a value in a method.
- Overload a method.
- Use the XML comment feature in Visual Studio .NET.

Lesson agenda

This lesson includes the following topics and activity:

- How to Write a Method
- How to Pass Parameters to a Method
- How to Pass Parameters by Reference
- How to Pass a Reference Type
- How to Overload a Method
- How to Use XML Code Comment Features
- Practice: Writing and Calling a Method

How to Write a Method

> ■ **A method is a command for action**

```
class Lion {
  private int weight;
  public bool IsNormalWeight () {
      if ((weight < 100)||(weight > 250)) {
            return false;
      }
      return true;
  }
  public void Eat() { /* some action */ }
  public int GetWeight() {return this.weight;}
}
. . .
Lion bigLion = new Lion();
bool weightNormal = bigLion.IsNormalWeight();
bigLion.Eat();
int weight = bigLion.GetWeight();
```

Introduction

A method is a class member that is used to define the actions that can be performed by that object or class.

Syntax

The syntax for declaring a method is as follows:

```
[attributes] [modifiers] return-type method-name ( [parameter-
list] ) statement-block
```

Rules

The following rules apply to methods:

- In the method declaration, you must always specify a return type. If the method is not designed to return a value to the caller, you specify a return type of **void**.

- Even if the method takes no arguments, you must include a set of empty parentheses after the method name.

- When calling a method, you must match the input parameters of the method exactly, including the return type, the number of parameters, their order, and their type. The method name and parameter list is known as the method *signature*.

Recommendation

The following are recommendations for naming methods:

- The name of a method should represent the action that you want to carry out. For this reason, methods usually have action-oriented names, such as **WriteLine** and **ChangeAddress**.

- Methods should be named using Pascal case.

Returning a value from a method

When you call a method, the execution jumps to that method and it executes until either a **return** statement or the end of the method is reached. At that point, the execution returns to the calling method.

When you want a method to return a value to the caller, use the **return** keyword followed by the value, where the type of the value is the same as the return-type of the method. If the return type of the method is **void**, you do not need to use the **return** keyword, or you can use return with no value specified.

Example

In the following code, the **IsNormalWeight** method checks the value of weight and returns **false** if the weight is outside the normal range. In the following example, **IsNormalWeight** must return **true** or **false,** because the **return-type** is **bool**:

```
class Lion {
  private int  weight;

  public bool IsNormalWeight() {
      if ( ( weight < 100 ) || ( weight > 250 ) ) {
          return false;
      }
      return true;
  }
  public void Eat() { }
  public int GetWeight() {
      return weight;
  }
}
```

You create the object as follows:

```
Lion bigLion = new Lion();
```

The **IsNormalWeight** method returns a Boolean value, so it can be used in an **if** statement as follows:

```
if ( bigLion.IsNormalWeight() == false ) {
  Console.WriteLine("Lion weight is abnormal");
}
```

The **Eat** method does not return a value, having a return type of **void**, so the following line of code simply instructs the **bigLion** object to perform the **Eat** action:

```
bigLion.Eat();
```

The **GetWeight** method returns an **int**, and it can be used to assign the resulting value to an int in the calling method as follows:

```
int bigLionWeight = bigLion.GetWeight();
```

The this keyword

The **this** keyword is used to refer to the current instance of an object. When **this** is used within a method, it allows you to refer to the members of the object.

For example, the **GetWeight** method can be modified to use **this** as follows:

```
public int GetWeight() {
  return this.weight;
}
```

In this case, the statement **this.weight** refers to the weight member of this object. This is functionally identical to the **GetWeight** method shown in the **Lion** class in the above example.

Using **this** can help to make your code more readable because it is immediately apparent to the person reading the code that you are referring to a member of this object. In addition, Microsoft IntelliSense® provides a list of class members when you type **this**.

Note   The code used in this topic is available on the Student Materials compact disc in Samples\Mod03\Methods\Methods.sln.

How to Pass Parameters to a Method

■ **Passing by value**

```
class Lion {
  private int weight;
  public void SetWeight(int newWeight) {
      weight = newWeight;
  }
}
. . .

Lion bigLion = new Lion();

int bigLionWeight = 250;
bigLion.SetWeight( bigLionWeight );
```

Introduction

When a value type variable is passed to a method, the method receives a copy of the value that was assigned to the variable. The method uses this value to perform an action.

Example 1

For example, given the following class:

```
class Lion {
  private int weight;
  public void SetWeight( int newWeight ) {
      weight = newWeight;
  }
}
```

If you pass the value of **200** to the **SetWeight** method:

```
Lion bigLion = new Lion();

int bigLionWeight = 200;
bigLion.SetWeight( bigLionWeight );
```

When the method is called, the value of **bigLionWeight** is copied to the *newWeight* parameter, and this changes the private member **weight** to **200**.

Example 2

In this example, two parameters are passed to an **Add** method that adds the numbers and returns the result. The result, 50, is assigned to the integer variable **total**, as shown in the following code:

```
class SimpleMath {
  public int Add( int x, int y ) {
      return x + y;
  }
}

SimpleMath sums = new SimpleMath();
int total = sums.Add ( 20, 30 );
```

Passing by value

When you pass a variable as a parameter, the method works on a copy of that variable. This is called *passing by value*, because the value is provided to the method, yet the object that contains the value is not changed.

In the following example, the attempt to double the variable fails:

```
public void Double( int doubleTarget ) {
  doubleTarget = doubleTarget * 2;
}

int numbertoDouble = 10;
sums.Double ( numbertoDouble);
// numbertoDouble is still 10
```

When the **Double** method is called, the **numberToDouble** variable is copied into the *doubleTarget* parameter. This copy, in the **doubleTarget** variable, is a local variable within the scope of the **Double** method and is discarded when the method returns. The value in **numberToDouble** is unchanged.

The this keyword

An alternative implementation of the **SetWeight** method follows:

```
class Lion {
  private int weight;
  public void SetWeight( int weight ) {
      this.weight = weight;
  }
}
```

In this example, the parameter weight has the same name as the class member. When weight is referenced within the scope of the method, the compiler will use the parameter value, so **this** is used to reference the class member.

This example illustrates the scope of parameters, and the use of the **this** keyword. You should make every attempt to avoid name collisions in your code.

Note   The code used in this topic is available on the Student Materials compact disc in Samples\Mod03\ValueParameters\Value.sln.

How to Pass Parameters by Reference

- **Using the** ref **keyword**

```
public void GetAddress(ref int number,
            ref string street) {
            number = this.number;
            street = this.street;
}
. . .
int sNumber = 0; string streetName = null;
zoo.GetAddress( ref sNumber, ref streetName );
// sNumber and streetName have new values
```

- **Definite assignment**
- **Using the** out **parameter keyword**
  - Allows you to initialize a variable in a method

Introduction

Methods return only a single value, but sometimes you want a method to modify or return multiple values. You can achieve this by passing the method a *reference* to the variable that you want to modify. The method can use the reference to access the actual value and change the value.

When a value is passed by reference, the method receives a reference to the actual value—so any changes that the method makes to the variable are actually made to the object that was passed to the method.

The ref keyword

You declare that a parameter is a reference parameter by using the **ref** keyword. Use the **ref** keyword in the parameter list to indicate to the compiler that the value is being passed by reference. You also must use the **ref** keyword when you call the method.

Non-example

Suppose that you have a class representing a Zoo that attempts to implement a **GetAddress** method, as shown in the following code:

```
class Zoo {
     private int    streetNumber = 123;
     private string streetName = "High Street";
     private string cityName = "Sammamish";
     public void GetAddress(int number, string street,
                                            string city) {
         number = streetNumber;
         street = streetName;
         city = cityName;
     }
}
```

The attempt to retrieve the address fails, as shown in the following code:

```
Zoo localZoo = new Zoo();
int zooStreetNumber = 0;
string zooStreetName = null;
string zooCity = null;
localZoo.GetAddress(zooStreetNumber, zooStreetName, zooCity);
// zooStreetNumber, zooStreetName, and zooCity still 0 or null
```

The **GetAddress** method in the preceding example operates on copies of the parameters, so **zooStreetNumber** is still **0** and **zooStreetName** and **zooCity** are still null after the method is called.

Example

Using the **ref** keyword allows this code to work as planned:

```
public void GetAddress( ref int number,
                        ref string street,
                        ref string city) {
  number = streetNumber;
  street = streetName;
  city = cityName;
}
```

You must also use the **ref** keyword when you call the function:

```
localZoo.GetAddress(ref zooStreetNumber, ref zooStreetName,
ref zooCity);

if ( zooCity == "Sammamish" ) {
  Console.WriteLine("City name was changed");
}
```

The variables **zooStreetNumber**, **zooStreetName**, and **zooCity** are assigned the values that are stored in the object.

Definite assignment

C# imposes definite assignment, which requires that all variables are initialized before they are passed to a method. This eliminates a common bug caused by the use of unassigned variables.

Even if you have a variable that you know will be initialized within a method, definite assignment requires that you initialize the variable before it can be passed to a method. For example, in the preceding code, the lines that initialize **zooStreetNumber**, **zooStreetName**, and **zooCity** are required to make the code compile, even though the intent is to initialize them in the method.

The out keyword

By using the **out** keyword, you can eliminate the redundant initialization. Use the **out** keyword in situations where you want to inform the compiler that variable initialization is occurring within a method. When you use the **out** keyword with a variable that is being passed to a method, you can pass an uninitialized variable to that method.

Example

The following code modifies the zoo **GetAddress** method to demonstrate use of the **out** keyword:

```
using System;

namespace LearnCSharp.MethodExample1 {
  class Zoo {
      private int    streetNumber = 123;
      private string streetName = "High Street";
      private string cityName = "Sammamish";

      public void GetAddress(  out int number,
                               out string street,
                               out string city) {
          number = streetNumber;
          street = streetName;
          city = cityName;
      }
  }

  class ClassMain {
      static void Main(string[] args) {
          Zoo localZoo = new Zoo();
          // note these variables are not initialized
          int    zooStreetNumber;
          string zooStreetName;
          string zooCity;
          localZoo.GetAddress(  out zooStreetNumber,
                                out zooStreetName,
                                out zooCity);

          Console.WriteLine(zooCity);
          // Writes "Sammamish" to a console
      }
  }
}
```

How to Pass a Reference Type

- **When you pass a reference type to a method, the method can alter the actual object**

```
class Zoo {
  public void AddLion( Lion newLion ) {
      newLion.location = "Exhibit 3";
      . . .
  }
}

. . .

Zoo myZoo = new Zoo();
Lion babyLion = new Lion();
myZoo.AddLion( babyLion );
// babyLion.location is "Exhibit 3"
```

Introduction

When you pass a reference type variable to a method, the method can alter the actual value because it is operating on a reference to the *same object*.

Example 1

In the following example, a **babyLion** object is passed to an **AddLion** method, where the **location** member of **babyLion** is assigned the value **Exhibit 3**. Because the reference to the actual object is passed to the method, the method can change the value of **location** in the **babyLion** object.

```
using System;

namespace LearningCSharp {
  class MainClass {
        static void Main(string[] args) {
        Zoo myZoo = new Zoo();
        Lion babyLion = new Lion();

        myZoo.AddLion( babyLion );
        // babyLion.location is Exhibit 3
    }
  }

  class Lion {
     public string location;
  }

  class Zoo {
     public void AddLion( Lion newLion ) {
        newLion.location = "Exhibit 3";
     }
  }
}
```

Example 2

The following code defines an **Address** class. It creates an **Address** object, **zooLocation**, in the **Main** method and passes the object to the **GetAddress** method. Because **Address** is a reference type, **GetAddress** receives a reference to the same object that was created in **Main**. **GetAddress** assigns the values to the members, and when control returns to **Main**, the **zooLocation** object has the address information.

```csharp
using System;

namespace LearningCSharp {
  class Address {
      public int number;
      public string street;
      public string city;
  }

  class Zoo {
      private int    streetNumber = 123;
      private string streetName = "High Street";
      private string cityName = "Sammamish";

      public void GetAddress(   Address zooAddress ) {
          zooAddress.number = streetNumber;
          zooAddress.street = streetName;
          zooAddress.city = cityName;
      }
  }

  class ClassMain {
      static void Main(string[] args) {
          Zoo localZoo = new Zoo();
          Address zooLocation = new Address();

          localZoo.GetAddress( zooLocation );

          Console.WriteLine( zooLocation.city );
          // Writes "Sammamish" to a console
      }
  }
}
```

Example 3

You can use different types of parameters in a single method. For example, you may want to request a specific exhibit for the new lion.

```csharp
public void AddLion(Lion newLion, int preferedExhibit) { }
```

How to Overload a Method

- **Overloading enables you to create multiple methods within a class that have the same name but different signatures**

```
class Zoo {
  public void AddLion(Lion newLion) {
  ...
  }
  public void AddLion(Lion newLion,
                        int exhibitNumber) {
  ...
  }
}
```

Introduction

When calling a method, you must match the input parameters exactly; including the return type, the number of parameters, and their order.

Definition

Method overloading is a language feature that enables you to create multiple methods in one class that have the same name but that take different signatures.

By overloading a method, you provide the users of your class with a consistent name for an action while also providing them with several ways to apply that action.

Example 1

Your **Zoo** class includes an **AddLion** method that allows you to add new **Lion** objects, but sometimes you want to place them in a specific exhibit and other times you do not want to specify this information. You can write two **AddLion** methods, one that accepts a *Lion* parameter, and one that accepts Lion and exhibit number parameters.

```
class Zoo {
  public void AddLion( Lion newLion ) {
      // Place lion in an appropriate exhibit
  }
  public void AddLion( Lion newLion, int exhibitNumber ) {
      // Place the lion in exhibitNumber exhibit
  }
}
```

When you subsequently call the **AddLion** method, you call the correct method by matching the parameters, as shown in the following code:

```
Zoo myZoo = new Zoo();
Lion babyLion = new Lion();

myZoo.AddLion( babyLion );
myZoo.AddLion( babyLion, 2 );
```

Example 2

Suppose you have a Web site that allows people to sign up for a newsletter about a zoo. Some information is necessary, such as name and e-mail address, but some is optional, such as favorite animal. You can use one method name to handle this situation, as shown in the following code:

```
class ZooCustomer {
  private string name;
  private string email;
  private string favoriteAnimal;

  public void SetInfo(  string webName,
                        string webEmail,
                        string animal ) {
    name = webName;
    email = webEmail;
    favoriteAnimal = animal;
  }

  public void SetInfo(string webName, string webEmail) {
    name = webName;
    email = webEmail;
  }
}
```

Why overload?

Consider the following guidelines as you decide whether to use method overloading:

- Use overloading when you have similar methods that require different parameters.

- Overloaded methods are a good way for you to add new functionality to existing code.

- Use overloaded methods only to implement methods that provide similar functionality.

How to Use XML Code Comment Features

- **Three forward slashes (///) inserts XML comments**

- **Hovering over a section of code produces a pop-up menu for accessing class member information**

```
static void Main(string[] args) {
    Lion zooLion = new Lion();
    zooLion.age = 7;
}
              age              int Lion.age
              Equals
              GetHashCode
              GetType
              ToString
```

Introduction

Visual Studio .NET provides several useful features for working with classes and accessing class members. These features include pop-up menus for accessing class member information, and an XML code comment feature.

Pop-up menus

For example, in the Code Editor, when you type the dot operator after an object name, Visual Studio .NET displays all the members of that class in a list from which you can select the member you want to access, as shown in the following illustration:

```
static void Main(string[] args) {
    Lion zooLion = new Lion();
    zooLion.age = 7;
}
              age              int Lion.age
              Equals
              GetHashCode
              GetType
              ToString
```

You can also access this list from the **Edit** menu by pointing to **IntelliSense** and then clicking **List Members**, or by pressing CTRL+J.

XML comments

Visual Studio .NET also provides an XML code comment feature that makes it easy for you to include useful comments in your code.

When you type three forward slashes (///), Visual Studio.NET inserts several lines of XML code for you, and all you have to do is enter the actual description of the type and type members. Even the correct values for the parameter names are included for you in the <param> tags.

The following table shows the <param> tags that you can use:

Declaration	Definition
<summary>	One line summary of a class, method, or property
<remarks>	May contain <para> and <list> formatting tags, as well as <cref> for creating hyperlinks
<value>	Description of a property
<exception>	Exceptions arising from methods and properties
<param>	Method parameters

IntelliSense enables you to hover your mouse pointer over a section of code to reveal the comments and type information.

Adding comments to a method

Use the following procedures to include XML comments in your code:

1. Type /// on the line above the method.

```
///
public void SetInfo(string webName, string webEmail) {
    name = webName;
    email = webEmail;
}
```

2. Examine the XML template that is provided by Visual Studio .NET.

3. Document your method.

```
/// <summary>
/// Sets customer information from the Web page
/// </summary>
/// <param name="webName">Name supplied by customer</param>
/// <param name="webEmail">Email supplied by customer</param>
public void SetInfo(string webName, string webEmail) {
    name = webName;
    email = webEmail;
}
```

4. Use the method to see how your code comments are integrated with IntelliSense.

```
SetInfo(
```
```
void Form1.SetInfo (string webName, string webEmail)
webName:
    Name supplied by customer
```

The C# compiler can extract the XML elements from your comments and generate an XML file for you.

Practice: Writing and Calling a Method

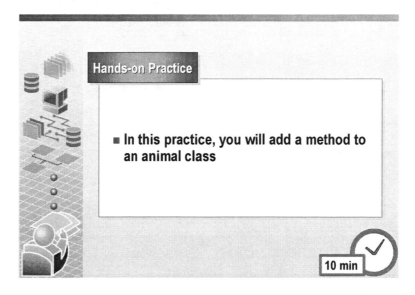

In this practice, you will add a method to an animal class.

The solution code for this practice is provided in *install_folder*\Practices\Mod03\Methods \MethodExample.sln. Start a new instance of Visual Studio .NET before opening the solution.

Tasks	Detailed steps
1. Start Visual Studio .NET, and then open *install_folder*\ Practices\Mod03\Methods \MethodExample.sln.	a. Start a new instance of Visual Studio .NET. b. On the **Start Page**, click **Open Project**. c. In the **Open Project** dialog box, browse to *install_folder*\Practices \Mod03\Methods, click **MethodExample.sln**, and then click **Open**.
2. Review the tasks for this practice.	a. In Solution Explorer, click **Form1.cs**, and then press F7 to open the Code Editor. b. On the **View** menu, point to **Show Tasks**, and then click **Comment**.
3. Write a method in the **Antelope** class that sets the private member **weight** to a value that is specified in a parameter.	a. In the Task List, double-click **TODO 1: Write a SetWeight method, that sets the weight member**. b. In the **Antelope** class, write a **SetWeight** method that takes one parameter, representing the weight of the animal. c. Use the parameter that is passed to the method to set the private member **weight** in the **Antelope** class.

Tasks	Detailed steps
4. Call the **SetWeight** method with a weight of **100**.	a. Locate the task **TODO 2: Call the method to set the Antelope's weight**. b. In the **runExample_Click** method, write code that calls the **SetWeight** method of the **babyAntelope** object, with the value **100** as a parameter.
5. Compile your program and run it. The value **500** should be displayed in the text window.	a. Press F5 to compile and run your application. b. In your application window, click **Run**. c. Ensure that the value **100** appears in the text window.
6. Save your application, and then quit Visual Studio .NET.	a. Save your application. b. Quit Visual Studio .NET.

Optional:

Add a **GetWeight** method to the **Antelope** class. **GetWeight** should take no parameters and return the weight of the **babyAntelope** object. If you do this, make the **weight** member private.

Modify the **Output** method so that it uses the **GetWeight** method.

Lesson: Using Constructors

- ■ **How to Initialize an Object**
- ■ **How to Overload a Constructor**

Introduction	This lesson defines class constructors and explains how to use them to initialize objects.
Lesson objectives	After completing this lesson, you will be able to:
	■ Write constructors.
	■ Overload constructors.
Lesson agenda	This lesson includes the following topics and activity:
	■ How to Initialize an Object
	■ How to Overload a Constructor
	■ Practice: Using Constructors

How to Initialize an Object

- **Instance constructors are special methods that implement the actions required to initialize an object**
  - Have the same name as the name of the class
  - Default constructor takes no parameters

```
public class Lion {
  public Lion() {
      Console.WriteLine("Constructing Lion");
  }
}
```

- **Readonly**
  - Used to assign a value to a variable in the constructor

Introduction

Every class implicitly or explicitly includes an *instance constructor*, which is a method that is automatically called by the runtime whenever an instance of the class is created.

Definition

Constructors are special methods that implement the actions that are required to initialize an object.

Creating a class constructor

The constructor method is defined by using the same name as the class in which it is declared.

Syntax

```
[attributes] [modifiers] constructor-name ( [parameters] )
[initializer] statement-block
```

For example, the following code contains a constructor:

```
public class Lion {
  public Lion() {
      Console.WriteLine("Constructing Lion");
  }
}
```

When the following code is executed, the Lion constructor is called when the object is instantiated:

```
Lion babyLion = new Lion();
Console.WriteLine("Made a new Lion object");
```

The following output is produced:

```
Constructing Lion
Made a new Lion object
```

If you do not write an instance constructor, C# automatically provides a default instance constructor. For example, you can write a class as follows:

```
public class Lion {
  private string name;
}
```

This is exactly equivalent to:

```
public class Lion {
  private string name;
  public Lion() {
  }
}
```

Constructor parameters

Constructors can take parameters, like any other method. When you specify a constructor with a parameter, the default constructor for that object is not provided. For example, if you want users of your class to always specify the name of the lion when they create it, you can write a constructor as shown in the following code:

```
public class Lion {
  private string name;
  public Lion( string newLionName ) {
      this.name = newLionName;
  }
}
```

When users create this object, they must specify a name:

```
Lion babyLion = new Lion("Leo");
```

Failure to provide a name will result in a compilation error.

Class initialization

When an object is created, the instance members in the class are implicitly initialized. For example, in the following code, **zooName** is initialized to **null**:

```
class Zoo {
  public string zooName;
}
```

Usually, the purpose of writing your own constructor is to perform some initialization of the members of the object. For example:

```
class Zoo {
  public string zooName;
  public Zoo() {
      zooName = "Sammamish Zoo";
  }
}
```

The **zooName** member of every instance of the **Zoo** class is now set to "Sammamish Zoo". When a new **Zoo** class is instantiated:

```
Zoo localZoo = new Zoo();
Console.WriteLine(localZoo.zooName);
```

The following output is produced:

```
Sammamish Zoo
```

A better way to write this class is as follows:

```
class Zoo {
  public string zooName = "Sammamish Zoo";
}
```

When an instance of **Zoo** is created, the instance member variables are initialized. Because any values are assigned before the constructor is executed, the constructor can use the values.

```
class Zoo {
  public string zooName = "Sammamish Zoo";
  public Zoo() {
      if ( zooName == "Duwamish Zoo" ) {
          // This can never happen
      }
  }
}
```

readonly

When you use the **readonly** modifier on a member variable, you can only assign it a value when the class or object initializes, either by directly assigning the member variable a value, or by assigning it in the constructor.

Use the **readonly** modifier when a **const** keyword is not appropriate because you are not using a literal value—meaning that the actual value of the variable is not known at the time of compilation.

In the following example, the value of **admissionPrice** is set in the constructor, and subsequent attempts to set the value will fail, resulting in a compilation error.

```
class Zoo {
  private int           numberAnimals;
  public readonly decimal    admissionPrice;

  public Zoo() {
      // Get the numberAnimals from some source...
      if ( numberAnimals > 50 ) {
          admissionPrice = 25;
      }
      else {
          admissionPrice = 20;
      }
  }
}
```

How to Overload a Constructor

- **Create multiple constructors that have the same name but different signatures**

  - Specify an initializer with **this**

```
public class Lion {
  private string    name;
  private int       age;

  public Lion() : this( "unknown", 0 ) {
      Console.WriteLine("Default: {0}", name);
  }
  public Lion( string theName, int theAge ) {
      name = theName;
      age = theAge;
      Console.WriteLine("Specified: {0}", name);
  }
}
```

Introduction

It is often useful to overload a constructor to allow instances to be created in more than one way.

Syntax

You overload a constructor in the same way that you overload a method: create a base class that contains two or more constructors with the same name but different input parameters.

Example 1

For example, if you create a new record for an adopted lion, you can create different constructors depending upon the information that is available at the time that you create the record, as shown in the following code:

```
class Lion {
    private string name;
    private int    age;

    public Lion( string theName, int theAge ) {
        name = theName;
        age = theAge;
    }

    public Lion( string theName ) {
        name = theName;
    }

    public Lion( int theAge ) {
        age = theAge;
    }
}

Lion adoptedLion = new Lion( "Leo", 3 );
Lion otherAdoptedLion = new Lion( "Fang" );
Lion newbornLion = new Lion( 0 );
```

Now, when you create a lion record, you can add the information that you have available. You can assume that other methods exist to allow you to update the object information.

Specifying an initializer

Often when you have multiple constructors, you initialize each one in a similar manner. Rather than repeating the same code in each constructor, attempt to centralize common code in one constructor and call that from the other constructors.

To call a specific constructor that is defined in the class itself, use the **this** keyword. When you add **this** to the constructor declaration, the constructor that matches the specified parameter list (has the same signature) is invoked. An empty parameter list invokes the default constructor.

Example 2

```
public class Lion {
  private string name;
  private int    age;

  public Lion() : this ( "unknown", 0 ) {
      Console.WriteLine("Default {0}", name);
  }

  public Lion( string theName, int theAge ) {
      name = theName;
      age = theAge;
      Console.WriteLine("Specified: {0}", name);
  }
}

. . .

Lion adoptedLion = new Lion();
```

In this example, when the user of the class creates the **adoptedLion** object, the class invokes the matching constructor, which is **Lion()**. Before **Lion()** executes the code in the body of the constructor, it invokes an alternative instance constructor that has parameters matching those specified in the **this** initializer (a **string** and an **int**). Before any of the code in the constructors is executed, however, the member variables are initialized and assigned.

The output from this sample is:

```
Specified unknown
Default unknown
```

Practice: Using Constructors

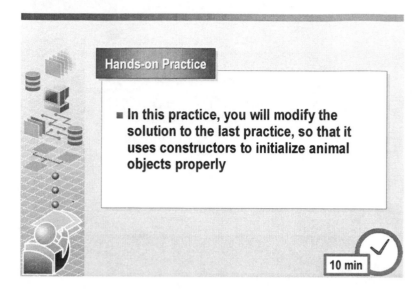

In this practice, you will modify the solution to the last practice, so that it uses constructors to initialize animal objects properly.

The solution code for this practice is provided in *install_folder*\Practices\Mod03\ Ctor_Solutions\CtorExample.sln. Start a new instance of Visual Studio .NET before opening the solution.

Tasks	Detailed steps
1. Start Visual Studio .NET, and then open *install_folder*\ Practices\Mod03\Ctor \CtorExample.sln.	a. Start a new instance of Visual Studio .NET. b. On the **Start Page**, click **Open Project**. c. In the **Open Project** dialog box, browse to *install_folder*\Practices \Mod03\Ctor, click **CtorExample.sln**, and then click **Open**.
2. Review the tasks for this practice.	a. In Solution Explorer, click **Form1.cs**, and then press F7 to open the Code Editor. b. On the **View** menu, point to **Show Tasks**, and then click **Comment**.
3. Specify the antelope's gender in the constructor call.	■ In the Task List, double-click TODO 1: Change the constructor call to specify the gender. • Specify the gender as a string, for example **"male"**.

Tasks	Detailed steps
4. Test your code and observe the error.	a. Press F5 to compile and run your application. b. You will receive an error. This is because the **Antelope** class does not contain a constructor that takes a parameter.
5. Write an Antelope constructor that accepts a string.	a. In the Task List, double-click **TODO 2: Add a constructor.** b. Add a constructor that accepts the string that you added in step 3, and uses it to set the Antelope member **gender**.
6. Test your code and verify that a male antelope is created.	a. Press F5 to compile and run your application. b. In the application window, click **Run**, and verify that you receive a message stating that a male antelope object was created.
7. Save your application, and then quit Visual Studio .NET.	a. Save your application. b. Quit Visual Studio .NET.

Lesson: Using Static Class Members

- **How to Use Static Class Members**
- **How to Initialize a Class**

Introduction

This lesson introduces you to static class members. Static members belong to the class, rather than an instance. Static constructors are used to initialize a class.

Lesson objective(s)

After completing this lesson, you will be able to:

- Use static class members.
- Initialize a class using a static constructor.

Lesson Agenda

This lesson includes the following topics and activity:

- How to Use Static Class Members
- How to Initialize a Class
- Practice: Using Static Class Members

How to Use Static Class Members

- **Static Members**
  - Belong to the class
  - Initialize before an instance of the class is created
  - Shared by all instances of the class

```
class Lion {
  public static string family = "felidae";
}
...
// A Lion object is not created in this code
Console.WriteLine( "Family: {0}", Lion.family );
```

Introduction

Classes can have static members, such as properties, methods and variables.

Static members are associated with the class, not with a specific instance of the class. Static members are useful when you want to initialize or provide a value that is shared by all instances of a class.

Static members

Because static members belong to the class, rather than an instance, they are accessed through the class, not through an instance of the class. The following complete code example shows how to use the static member **family**.

```
using System;

namespace StaticExample {
  class ZooDemo {
    static void Main(string[] args) {
      Console.WriteLine( "Family: {0}", Lion.family );
      Console.ReadLine();
    }
  }

  class Lion {
    public static string family = "felidae";
  }
}
```

This code samples produces the following output:

```
fedilae
```

Static methods

Methods can also be static. When the static access modifier is applied to a method, the method is accessible only through the class, not an object instance.

Because static methods are part of the class, you can invoke them without creating an instance of the object. In C#, you cannot access a static method from an instance.

The static modifier provides global methods. When you add a static declaration to a method, you declare that there will be only one copy of the method, no matter how many times that class is created.

Use static members when they refer to or operate on information that is about the class, rather than about an instance of a class. For example, you can use a static method to maintain a count of the number of objects that are created from a class, or to log information about objects of a specific class.

The following example counts the number of male or female lions that are added to the Zoo:

```csharp
using System;

namespace StaticExample {
  enum Gender {
      Male,
      Female
  }

  class ZooDemo {
      static void Main(string[] args) {
          Lion male1 = new Lion( Gender.Male );
          Lion male2 = new Lion( Gender.Male );
          Lion male3 = new Lion( Gender.Male );

          Console.WriteLine("Males {0}", Lion.NumberMales() );
      }
  }

  class Lion {
      private static int males;
      private static int females;

      public Lion(Gender lionGender) {
          if ( lionGender == Gender.Male ) {
              males++;
          }
          else {
              females++;
          }
      }
      public static int NumberMales() {
          return males;
      }
  }
}
```

The preceding code is provided on the Student Materials compact disc in the Samples\Mod03\Static folder.

How to Initialize a Class

- ■ **Static Constructors**
  - Will only ever be executed once
  - Run before the first object of that type is created
  - Have no parameters
  - Do not take an access modifier
  - May co-exist with a class constructor
  - Used to initialize a class

Introduction

Instance constructors are used to initialize an object. You can, however, write a constructor that initializes a class. This type of constructor is called a *static constructor*. You create a static constructor by using a **static** modifier.

Static constructor

A static constructor is sometimes referred to as a *shared* or *global* constructor because it does not operate on a specific instance of a class.

You cannot call a static constructor directly. It is executed at most *once* before the first instance of the class is created or before any static methods are used. Therefore, a static constructor is useful for initializing values that will be used by all instances of the class.

Syntax

Like instance constructors, static constructors have the same name as the class, and an empty parameter list. You declare a static constructor by using the **static** modifier. It does not take an access modifier and it can coexist with an instance constructor.

```
class Lion {
  static Lion() {
     // class-specific initialization
  }
}
```

Example 1

For example, suppose that there are several zoo animal classes, each of which has a class member **family**. All Lions belong to the family *felidae*, so it is useful to set this information for the class.

```
class Lion {
  static private string family;
  static Lion() {
      family = "felidae";
  }
}
```

Example 2

For example, if your code must initialize a series of values that are required for a calculation, or load a set of data that will be used by all instances of the class, such as a look-up table, then it can be useful to perform this task only once for the class, rather than every time an instance is created.

The following example uses **System.Random**, the pseudo-random number generator that is provided in the .NET Framework, to generate random numbers. It creates a single instance of **Random**, and every instance of the **RandomNumberGenerator** class uses this object.

```
using System;

namespace StaticConstructor {

  class RandomNumberGenerator {
      private static Random randomNumber;

      static RandomNumberGenerator() {
          randomNumber = new Random();
      }

      public int Next() {
          return randomNumber.Next();
      }
  }

  class Class1 {
      static void Main(string[] args) {
          RandomNumberGenerator r
                  = new RandomNumberGenerator();

          for ( int i = 0; i < 10; i++ ) {
              Console.WriteLine( r.Next() );
          }
      }
  }
}
```

In this example, the **randomNumber** member of the class is declared as **static**. This member variable must be static for the static constructor to be able to assign a value to it. Instance members are not initialized until an instance of the class is created, so an attempt to assign to an instance variable from a static constructor results in a compilation error.

For example, the following code will not compile, because **firstNumber** does not exist when the constructor is called.

```
class RandomNumberGenerator {
 private static Random randomNumber;
  private int          firstNumber;  // ERROR!

  static RandomNumberGenerator() {
      randomNumber = new Random();
      firstNumber = randomNumber.Next();
  }
}
```

Practice: Using Static Class Members

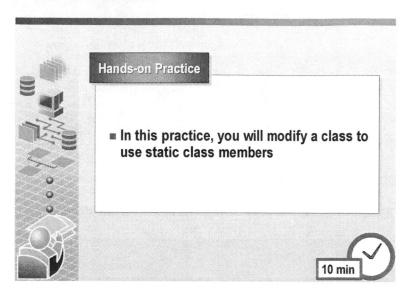

In this practice, you will maintain a count of the number of **Antelope** objects that are created, by adding a static member to the **Antelope** class and incrementing it in the antelope constructor.

The solution code for this practice is located in *install_folder*\Practices\Mod03\Static_Solution\StaticExample.sln. Start a new instance of Visual Studio .NET before opening the solution.

Tasks	Detailed steps
1. Start Visual Studio .NET, and then open *install_folder*\Practices\Mod03\Static\StaticExample.sln.	a. Start a new instance of Visual Studio .NET. b. On the **Start Page**, click **Open Project**. c. In the **Open Project** dialog box, browse to *install_folder*\Practices\Mod03\Static, click **StaticExample.sln**, and then click **Open**.
2. Review the tasks for this practice.	a. In Solution Explorer, click **Form1.cs**, and then press F7 to open the Code Editor. b. On the **View** menu, point to **Show Tasks**, and then click **Comment**.
3. Add an public static **int** variable to the **Antelope** class, and name it **numberOfAntelopes**.	a. In the Task List, double-click **TODO 1: Add a public static int called numberOfAntelopes**. b. Add the following line of code to the class: `public static int numberOfAntelopes;`

Tasks	Detailed steps
4. In the Antelope constructor, increment the **numberOfAntelopes** member variable.	**a.** Locate the task **TODO 2: Increment the numberOfAntelopes variable**. **b.** Every time an **Antelope** object is created, increment the **numberOfAntelopes** variable by adding the following code to the constructor: `numberOfAntelopes++;`

5. Display the number of antelopes that are created.	**a.** Locate the task **TODO 3: Display the number of antelopes created**.
	
	 b. Replace the null parameter in the **Output** method with a reference to the static **numberOfAntelopes** method. For example:
	
	 `Output( "Number of Antelopes: " +`
	 `        Antelope.numberOfAntelopes );`

6. Test your code.	**a.** Set a breakpoint at the first statement in the **runExample_Click** method. **b.** Press F5 to compile and run your application. **c.** In your application window, click **Run**. **d.** Step through the code and ensure that your program is functioning as expected. Note that the **numberOfAntelopes** variable is shared by both of the Antelope objects. **e.** When you are finished, stop debugging by closing your application or pressing SHIFT+F5.
7. Save your application, and quit Visual Studio .NET.	**a.** Save your application. **b.** Quit Visual Studio .NET.

Review

- ■ **Defining a Class**
- ■ **Declaring Methods**
- ■ **Using Constructors**
- ■ **Using Static Class Members**

1. What is the default accessibility level of a class member?

   a. Public

   b. Private

   c. Internal

2. What is the keyword that is used to inform the compiler that a variable is initialized within a method?

   out

3. What is the purpose of overloading a constructor?

4. When and how often does a static constructor execute?

once before the very first instance

5. Can you invoke a static method without instantiating an object? Why or why not?

Yes

Lab 3.1: Creating Classes in C#

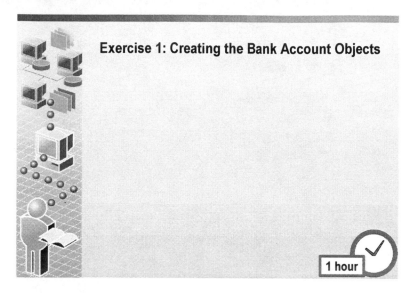

Exercise 1: Creating the Bank Account Objects

1 hour

Objectives

After completing this lab, you will be able to:

- Create classes and objects.
- Write methods.
- Pass parameters to methods.

Note   This lab focuses on the concepts in this module and as a result may not comply with Microsoft security recommendations.

Scenario

You are a programmer at a bank and have been asked to define objects for the types of bank accounts that customers can open. These accounts are:

- Checking account
- Savings account

Checking account

Each checking account has the following characteristics:

- The account holder's name can be assigned only when the account is created.
- The opening balance must be specified when the account is created.
- The account number must be assigned when the account is created.

  Checking account numbers range from 100000 to 499999, and every checking account must have a unique account number. You do not need to check the upper limit of the account number in this lab.

A checking account holder can:

- Order a checkbook.
- Check the account balance.
- Add money to the checking account.
- Withdraw money if the account has sufficient funds.

Savings account

A savings account has the following characteristics:

- The account holder's name can be assigned only when the account is created.
- Saving account numbers range from 500000 to 999999. You do not need to check the upper limit of the account number in this lab.
- The account earns interest.

  The interest rate depends on the account balance. If the balance is above 1000, the rate is 6%; otherwise, it is 3%.

A savings account holder can:

- Check the account balance.
- Add money to the account.
- Withdraw money if the account has sufficient balance.

Estimated time to complete this lab: 60 minutes

Exercise 0
Lab Setup

The Lab Setup section lists the tasks that you must perform before you begin the lab.

Task	Detailed steps
▪ Log on to Windows as **Student** with a password of **P@ssw0rd**.	▪ Log on to Windows with the following account: • User name: **Student** • Password: **P@ssw0rd** Note that the 0 in the password is a zero.

Note that by default the *install_folder* is C:\Program Files\Msdntrain\2609.

Exercise 1
Creating the Bank Account Objects

In this exercise, you will write the objects that represent the bank account classes that are outlined in the scenario.

A sample solution is shown in the following illustration:

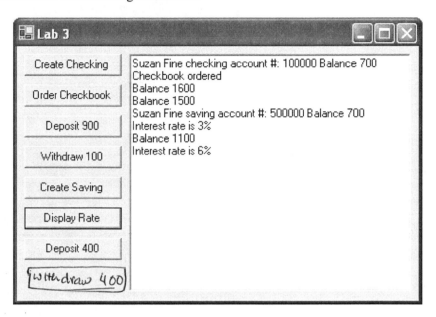

The solution code for this lab is located at *install_folder*\Labfiles\Lab03_1\
Exercise1\Solution_Code. Start a new instance of Visual Studio .NET before opening the solution.

Tasks	Detailed steps
1. Start Microsoft Visual Studio .NET, and then open *install_folder*\Labfiles \Lab03_1\Exercise1 \Bank.sln.	a. Start a new instance of Visual Studio .NET. b. On the **Start** Page, click **Open Project**. c. In the **Open Project** dialog box, browse to *install_folder*\Labfiles \Lab03_1\Exercise1, click **Bank.sln**, and then click **Open**. **Form1.cs** provides the user interface.
2. In Solution Explorer, locate the **BankAccount.cs** file.	▪ In Solution Explorer, click the C# file **BankAccount.cs**, and then press F7 to open the Code Editor. This file is provided as a place for you to implement the bank account class or classes.

Tasks	Detailed steps
3. Write the checking account class.	**a.** Define a class named **CheckingAccount**. **b.** Write a constructor that implements the following rules: • An account holder's name can be assigned only when the account is created. • The opening balance must be specified when the account is created. • An account number must be assigned when the account is created. Checking account numbers range from 100000 to 499999, and every checking account must have a unique account number. You do not need to check the upper limit of the account number in this lab. Use a static member to implement this rule.
4. Test your code by performing the actions listed on the right. Place your test code in the methods that are provided in the **Form1** class in the sample code.	**a.** In the **checking_Click** method in the **Form1** class, create a new checking account for the customer Suzan Fine, with a balance of 700. The object should be declared in **Form1**, but not in the **checking_Click** method. Look for the comment **//TODO: place bank account objects here**. **b.** Display the information about the account in the text box window by using the provided **Output** method. **c.** Run your application by pressing F5, and then in the application window, click **Create Checking**.
5. In the **CheckingAccount** class, write a method to order a checkbook.	**a.** In the **CheckingAccount** class, write a method named **OrderCheckBook** that always returns **true**. **b.** Call the **OrderCheckBook** method from the **Form1** class, in the **checkbook_Click** method. **c.** Compile and test your application.
6. Write **Deposit** and **Withdraw** methods in the **CheckingAccount** class.	**a.** In the **CheckingAccount** class, write a method named **Deposit** that adds money to the account. **b.** In the **CheckingAccount** class, write a method named **Withdraw** that removes money from the account. Do not permit the balance to fall below zero, and return **false** if the withdrawal amount is greater than the balance.
7. Call the **Withdraw** and **Deposit** methods from the **Form1** class.	**a.** In the **deposit_Click** method in the **Form1** class, write code to deposit 700 into the checking account, and display the new balance. **b.** In the **withdraw_Click** method in the **Form1** class, write code to withdraw 100 from the checking account, and display the new balance.

Tasks	Detailed steps
8. Write a **SavingAccount** class.	▪ In the **BankAccount.cs** file, define a **SavingAccount** class that implements the following rules: • An account holder's name can be assigned only when the account is created. Savings account numbers range from 500000 to 999999. You do not need to check the upper limit of the account number in this lab. Hint: use a static member to manage the account numbers. • The interest rate depends on the account balance. If the balance is above 1000, the rate is 6%; otherwise it is 3%.
9. Create a **SavingAccount** object.	a. In the **saving_Click** method in the **Form1** class, create a new ~~checking~~ account for the customer Suzan Fine, with a balance of 700. The object should be declared in **Form1**, but not in the **saving_Click** method. Look for the comment **//TODO: place bank account objects here**. b. Display the information about the account in the text box window by using the provided **Output** method. c. Run your application by pressing F5, and then in the application window click **Create Saving**.
10. Write a **GetRate** method for the **SavingAccount** class, that returns the current interest rate, and call it from the **interest_Click** method in **Form1**.	a. In the **SavingAccount** class, write a method that returns the current interest rate. b. In the **interest_Click** method in **Form1**, call the **SavingAccount** method, and display the current interest rate by using the **Output** method. c. Compile, run, and test your application.
11. Write **Deposit** and **Withdraw** methods in the **SavingAccount** class.	a. In the **SavingAccount** class, write a method named **Deposit** that adds money to the account. Adjust the interest rate accordingly. b. In the **SavingAccount** class write a method named **Withdraw** that removes money from the account. Do not permit the balance to fall below zero, and return **false** if the withdrawal amount is greater than the balance. Adjust the interest rate accordingly.
12. Call the **Deposit** method from the Form1 class.	a. In the **deposit_Click** method in the **Form1** class, write code to deposit 400 into the ~~checking~~ account, and display the new balance. b. Compile, run and test your application.
13. Save your application, and then quit Visual Studio .NET.	a. Save your application. b. Quit Visual Studio .NET.

msdn® training

Module 4: Implementing Object-Oriented Programming Techniques in C#

Contents

Microsoft®

Overview

- ■ **Designing Objects**
- ■ **Using Inheritance**
- ■ **Using Polymorphism**

Introduction

This module describes the most important principles of object-oriented design: encapsulation, inheritance, and polymorphism. It discusses the benefits of object-oriented programming, and it explains how to design classes so that they encapsulate functionality but limit accessibility to information that the users of your objects do not need.

This module also explains how to create classes that other classes can use through the process of inheritance, so that you can reuse previous work and increase productivity. Finally, this module explains how to override methods that are provided by a base class and how to define abstract classes that specify a set of functionality that a derived class must follow.

Objectives

After completing this module, you will be able to:

- ■ Encapsulate information in an object.
- ■ Create an object that inherits functionality from another object.
- ■ Implement polymorphism to use abstract classes.

Lesson: Designing Objects

- **What Are the Benefits of Object-Oriented Programming?**
- **What Is Encapsulation?**
- **What Are Properties?**

Introduction

This lesson explains how to use the design principals of abstraction and encapsulation to create classes that present a useful programming model to the object user.

Lesson objectives

After completing this lesson, you will be able to:

- List the benefits of object oriented programming.
- Encapsulate data in an object.
- Use properties to manage access to encapsulated data.

Lesson agenda

This lesson includes the following topics and activity:

- What Are the Benefits of Object-Oriented Programming?
- What Is Encapsulation?
- What Are Properties?
- Practice: Writing and Using Properties

What Are the Benefits of Object-Oriented Programming?

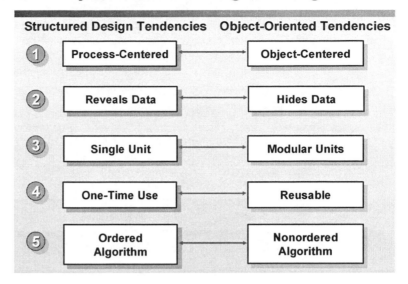

Structured Design Tendencies	Object-Oriented Tendencies
① Process-Centered	→ Object-Centered
② Reveals Data	← Hides Data
③ Single Unit	Modular Units
④ One-Time Use	→ Reusable
⑤ Ordered Algorithm	→ Nonordered Algorithm

Introduction

An object-oriented approach to programming provides many benefits over the structured approach.

Process-centered vs. object-centered

The structured approach to programming is process-centered, meaning that it takes a problem and focuses on a hierarchy of processes that must be performed sequentially to arrive at a solution.

Object-oriented analysis and design focuses on objects. The objects have certain behaviors and attributes that determine how they interact and function. No attempt is made to provide an order for those actions at design time because objects function based on the way other objects function.

Object-oriented programming allows developers to create objects that reflect real-world scenarios. Most people find the object-oriented approach a much more natural design model than other methodologies. This is because it meshes well with the way people naturally interpret the world. Human understanding largely rests on identification and generalization (objects and classes), finding relationships between groups, and interacting through the normal interface of an entity (behaviors).

Reveals data vs. hides data

The structured approach packages data and procedures, which are revealed or accessible to the rest of the program. There is little effort to actually hide information from other processes. The structured approach leaves this decision up to the implementer.

The object-oriented implementations hide data, which shows only behaviors to users and hides the underlying code of an object. The behaviors that the programmer exposes are the only items that the user of the object can affect.

Single unit vs. modular unit

The structured approach is based on a single unit of code, where processes call other processes and are dependent on each other.

The object-oriented approach allows objects to be self-contained. Objects stand on their own, with the functionality to call behaviors of other objects. Using the object-oriented approach, developers can create applications that reflect real-world objects such as rectangles, ellipses, and triangles, in addition to money, part numbers, and items in inventory.

One-time use vs. reusable

Structured processes may not be reusable, depending on the implementation.

In the object-oriented approach, objects are by definition modular in their construction. That is, they are complete entities and therefore tend to be highly reusable.

Consider the example of buying a new car. The manufacturer builds a base model car. If you prefer additional features such as air conditioning, power windows, and a sunroof, these items can be added to the car. By adding features, you extend the characteristics of the base model instead of building an entirely new car.

Ordered algorithm vs. nonordered algorithm

Structured approaches with processes tend to result in linear, or top down, algorithm-based implementations.

Object-oriented applications are constructed on a message-based or event-driven paradigm, where objects send messages to other objects, such as the Microsoft® Windows® operating system.

Summary of benefits

In summary, object-oriented programming benefits developers because:

- Programs are easier to design because objects reflect real-world items.

- Applications are easier for users because data they do not need is hidden.

- Objects are self-contained units.

- Productivity increases because you can reuse code.

- Systems are easier to maintain and adapt to changing business needs.

What Is Encapsulation?

■ **Grouping related pieces of information and processes into self-contained unit**

    • Makes it easy to change the way things work under the cover without changing the way users interact

■ **Hiding internal details**

    • Makes your object easy to use

Introduction

Non-object-oriented programming languages consist of data, either in a database or in computer memory, and separate instructions for manipulating that data. These languages do not usually enforce any sort of relationship between the data and the code that manipulates the data. If any aspect of the data changes—for example, if a year field is changed from 2 digits to 4 digits then all of the code that uses that data must also be changed. Because the code is not closely related to the data, changing the code can be difficult and time-consuming.

Definition

In object-oriented programming, *encapsulation* is the enclosing of both properties and methods (the data and the code that manipulates that data) together in a common structure. Encapsulating both data and the actions that manipulate that data together in this way, and specifying the actions and properties of the object, creates a new data type called a *class*.

Benefit of encapsulation

When data and methods are encapsulated, you can specify methods and properties that define how the external user sees your information and how they can request actions from the object. By hiding information that users do not need, such as implementation information, the user can concentrate on only the useful characteristics of the object.

For example, the internal mechanism of a telephone is hidden from the user. The wires, switches, and other internal parts of a telephone are encapsulated by its cover to allow the user to focus on using the phone and not on the internal operations of the telephone.

This abstraction also enables you to easily change the implementation details of your application without the users of your object experiencing any change in the way they interact with the object.

Design considerations

When you design a class, there are several questions to consider. What will the class represent? What actions should the class provide? What elements does a user of the class need to see?

When you design a class, you should attempt to hide as much of the implementation detail as possible and expose only those actions and values that the users of your class need to know about. This enables you to improve and change the implementation details of your class later, without changing the way users interact with the class. Therefore, do not expose elements just because you think that they might be useful. As you refine your design, you can always add elements to the public definition when you clearly see a need.

Example

At a zoo, visitors can look at a monitor outside an exhibit to learn about the animals. The monitor at the elephant exhibit shows visitors educational information about the elephant, including its size, dietary requirements, reproductive rate, and life span. The application that runs the display uses an **Elephant** object to access information about the elephant. The **Elephant** object hides internal information that the display application does not need to see, such as where the animal-specific data is stored, and how the data is structured in the database.

When you design your application in this way, it is easy for you to change the implementation details without changing the interface. For example, you can move the files to a different database location or even database type without the visitors seeing anything different on the display and without the application that uses your objects changing its implementation.

By preventing access to internal data structures, you also prevent users of your object from accessing information that could corrupt your object.

What Are Properties?

- **Properties are methods that protect access to class members**

```
private int animalWeight;
public int Weight {
      get {
              return animalWeight;
      }
      set {
              animalWeight = value;
      }
}
```

Introduction

To separate the implementation details of your objects from what the user sees, you can define the scope of the class members and thereby control access to the data in your objects.

Although you can control access to class members by using access modifiers, an even more powerful way to manage access is through the use of properties. By using properties, you can manage the access that other objects have to data in your class.

Definition

Properties are class members that provide access to elements of an object or class.

Syntax

The syntax for defining a property consists of an access modifier, such as **public** or **protected**, followed by a type, the property name, the keywords **get** and **set**, and the property code for each in curly braces, as shown in the following code:

```
public int myIntegerProperty {
  get {
      // Property get code
  }
  set {
      // Property set code
  }
}
```

The **get** and **set** statements are called *accessors*.

The **get** accessor must return a type that is the same as the property type, or one that can be implicitly converted to the property type. The **set** accessor is equivalent to a method that has one implicit parameter, named **value**.

Non-Example 1

You are writing an application to track the amount of food that zoo animals consume so that you can use this value to predict the size of future food purchases. You decide to represent this consumption value as **DailyFoodIntake**, as shown in the following code:

```
class Elephant {
    // Not a good idea!
    public decimal DailyFoodIntake;
}

class Zoo {
    static void Main(string[] args) {
        Elephant zooElephant = new Elephant();
        zooElephant.DailyFoodIntake = 300M;
    }
}
```

This code allows the user of the object to directly access the **DailyFoodIntake** value of **zooElephant** and alter it. This is a design flaw because the programmer has no ability to ensure that the change is allowable or that the value is correct.

Non-Example 2

You gain more control over the variable by making it private and using a method to access it, as shown in the following example:

```
class Elephant {
    private decimal dailyFoodIntake;

    public decimal GetDailyFoodIntake() {
        return dailyFoodIntake;
    }

    public void SetDailyFoodIntake(decimal newRate) {
        if ( newRate < dailyFoodIntake - 25 ) {
            // call the vet
        }
        else {
            dailyFoodIntake = newRate;
        }
    }
}

class Zoo {
    static void Main(string[] args) {
        Elephant e = new Elephant();
        e.SetDailyFoodIntake( 300M );
    }
}
```

However, this approach also has some disadvantages. This code contains two methods: one to set the amount of food that is eaten daily, and one to get the amount. The **dailyFoodIntake** member is private so you control the values that can be set, but this implementation requires the user of the object to remember and use two method names rather than only one element.

**Example using
properties**

Using properties is the best way to declare **DailyFoodIntake**, as shown in the
following code:

```
using System;

namespace LearningCSharp {
  class Elephant {
      private decimal dailyConsumptionRate;

      public decimal DailyFoodIntake {
          get {
              return dailyConsumptionRate;
          }
          set {
              if ( value < dailyConsumptionRate - 25 ) {
                  // notify medical center
              }
              else {
                  dailyConsumptionRate = value;
              }
          }
      }
  }

class Zoo {
      static void Main(string[] args) {
          Elephant e = new Elephant();
          e.DailyFoodIntake = 300M;
      }
    }

}
```

In this example, users of the **Elephant** object can access the **DailyFoodIntake**
method in the same way that they would access a public member variable in the
class. The implementer of the class can separate the interface that it provides,
DailyFoodIntake, from the member variable that is used internally by the
class, **dailyConsumptionRate**, to predict animal food purchases. In future
implementations, the programmer can change **dailyConsumptionRate** to
another type, but users of the **Elephant** class will not have to modify their code.

Note that the **set** accessor uses the **value** keyword to retrieve the new value.

This code sample is available on the Student Materials compact disc as
Properties.sln in the folder Samples\Mod04\Properties.

Practice: Writing and Using Properties

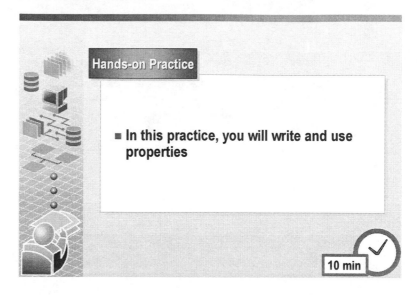

In this practice, you will write and use properties.

Scenario: the Zoo Medical Center requires a way to represent information about the animals in its care. You have been asked to develop an object that represents information about lions, such as name, age, weight, gender. You are given an example of how the user of this object wants it to behave.

In this practice, you will change the **Gender** member of the **Lion** class from a member variable to a property.

The solution code for this practice located in *install_folder*\Practices\Mod04\Properties_Solution\Properties_Solution.sln. Start a new instance of Microsoft Visual Studio® .NET before opening the solution.

Tasks	Detailed steps
1. Start Visual Studio .NET, and then open *install_folder*\ Practices\Mod04 \Properties\Properties.sln. Examine the **Lion** class, which is located near the top of the code window.	a. Start a new instance of Visual Studio .NET. b. On the **Start Page**, click **Open Project**. c. In the **Open Project** dialog box, browse to *install_folder*\Practices\Mod04\Properties, click **Properties.sln**, and then click **Open**. d. In Solution Explorer, click **Form1.cs**, and then press F7 to open the Code Editor. Review the **Lion** class, which is located near the top of the code window.
2. Examine the Task List.	▪ On the **View** menu, point to **Show Tasks**, and then click **All**.

Tasks	Detailed steps
3. Implement the rule that the **Gender** can be **Male** or **Female**.	a. To view the Task List, on the **View** menu, point to **Show Tasks**, and then click **All**. b. In the Task List, double-click **TODO: Change Gender member of Lion class to be a property**. c. Modify **Gender** so that it is a property. d. Compile and run your program. e. In your application, click **Run**, and then check that the output is as follows: `Leo: Male age 8; weighs 280kg`
4. Save your application, and then quit Visual Studio .NET.	a. Save your application. b. Quit Visual Studio .NET.

Optional:

- Change the other members of the **Lion** class to be properties.
- Represent the gender as an enumeration.

Lesson: Using Inheritance

- **What Is Inheritance?**
- **How to Create a Derived Class**
- **How to Call a Base Constructor from a Derived Class**
- **How to Use a Sealed Class**

Introduction

This lesson explains how to implement inheritance by creating base classes from which other classes can be derived.

Lesson objectives

After completing this lesson, you will be able to:

- Design a base class.
- Create a derived class.
- Create a sealed class.

Lesson agenda

This lesson includes the following topics and activity:

- What Is Inheritance?
- How to Create a Derived Class
- How to Call a Base Class Constructor from a Derived Class
- How to Use a Sealed Class
- Practice: Creating a Derived Class

What Is Inheritance?

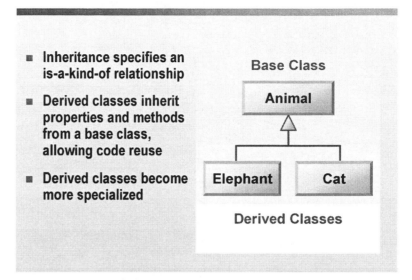

- Inheritance specifies an is-a-kind-of relationship
- Derived classes inherit properties and methods from a base class, allowing code reuse
- Derived classes become more specialized

Introduction

When you design an application, you often must manage similar but not identical items. The object-oriented principle of inheritance enables you to create a generalized class and then derive more specialized classes from it. The general class is referred to as the *base* class. A more specific class is referred to as the *derived* class. Derived classes inherit properties and methods from the base class.

Definition

Inheritance is the ability of a derived class to take on the characteristics of the class or derived class on which it is based. Inheritance allows a common set of behaviors, defined as properties and methods, to be included in a base class and reused in derived classes. It is a means for creating new, more specific types from an existing, more general type. Inheritance also defines one type as a subcategory of another type.

Benefits

The primary benefit of inheritance is code reuse. In a base class, you can write code once that all derived classes will automatically inherit. Inheritance facilitates reusability.

Example of an inheritance hierarchy

In a hierarchy that uses inheritance, you can design several classes, each one deriving from the class above it. When you design classes using inheritance, look for the common features of the objects, and then factor these into a hierarchy of classes with increasingly more specific attributes, as shown in the following example:

Animal

    Mammal

	Monotremes	Duck-billed platypus
	Multitubercules	Extinct
	Marsupials	Kangaroo
	Utherians	Mouse, Bat, Human

The most general features and functions that are common to all animals are defined at the highest level of the hierarchy. In lower levels, previously-defined features and functionality are inherited and new features are added so that each level becomes more specific and more specialized.

Note When you create a derived class in C#, you specify only one base class.

Non-example

In an application that manages animals, you may need to implement objects for a cat, a mouse, and an elephant. You can set up your application by creating three separate classes, one for each type of animal, as shown in the following code.

Note *{ }indicates where the implementation of the methods would exist.*

```
public class Antelope {
    public bool IsSleeping;
    public void Sleep() { }
    public void Eat() { }
}

public class Lion {
    public bool IsSleeping;
    public void Sleep() { }
    public void EatAntelope( ) { }
    public void StalkPrey() { }
}

public class Elephant {
    public bool IsSleeping;
    public void Sleep() { }
    public int CarryCapacity;
    public void Eat() { }
}

Elephant e = new Elephant();
e.Sleep();
```

Why the non-example is poor design

The design in the previous example has two obvious disadvantages:

- *Duplication of code.* For example, the **Sleep** method must be implemented multiple times.

- *User confusion.* The eating methods have different names in different objects.

A better way of designing this application is by using inheritance. You can place the common features of the animals in a base class, derive new classes that inherit these features from the base class, and then refine the derived class to implement any object-specific changes.

How to Create a Derived Class

```
public class Animal {
   protected bool IsSleeping;
   public void Sleep() { }
   public void Eat() { }
}

public class Lion : Animal {
   public void StalkPrey() { }
}
...
Lion adoptedLion = new Lion();
adoptedLion.StalkPrey();
adoptedLion.Eat();
```

Introduction

You can use many of the classes that are available in the Microsoft .NET class library as base classes from which you can derive new classes. For example, when you create a new Windows application in Visual Studio .NET, the main form that is created by the integrated development environment is a new class that is derived from the **System.Windows.Forms** class.

Syntax

To create a derived class, use the following syntax:

[attributes] [access-modifiers] class identifiers [:base-class] {class-body}

Example

The previous example requires you to create objects that represent types of animals. To use inheritance, first create a base class named **Animal**, and then include any methods that are common to all your derived classes, as shown in the following example:

```
public class Animal {
    public bool IsSleeping;
    public void Sleep() { }
    public void Eat() { }
}
```

Then, you can create your derived classes. The following code creates the **Antelope**, **Lion**, and **Elephant** classes with animal-specific behavior:

```
public class Animal {
    public bool IsSleeping;
    public void Sleep() {
        Console.WriteLine("Sleeping");
    }
    public void Eat() { }
}

public class Antelope : Animal {
}

public class Lion : Animal {
    public void StalkPrey() { }
}

public class Elephant : Animal {
    public int CarryCapacity;
}
```

Note that the **Sleep** and **Eat** methods are defined only once in the **Animal** base class. The derived **Antelope**, **Lion**, and **Elephant** classes each inherit these methods, and they can be invoked as follows:

```
Elephant e = new Elephant();
e.Sleep();
```

The preceding code produces the following output:

```
Sleeping
```

Design considerations

Remember that when you define a new class, you create a new reference type.

Avoid overusing inheritance in your applications. For example, although it is possible to create new versions of Windows user interface components, such as buttons, there is rarely a good reason to do so.

You can inherit from any class that is not sealed, so you can inherit derived classes. The following code declares a **Mammal** class that inherits from the **Animal** class. The code then defines classes for specific animals that inherit the **Mammal** class.

```
public class Animal {
    public bool IsSleeping;
    public void Sleep() {
        Console.WriteLine("Sleeping");
    }
    public void Eat() { }
}

public class Mammal : Animal {
    public MammalGroup    PhylogenicGroup;
}

public class Antelope : Mammal {
}

public class Lion : Mammal {
    public void StalkPrey() { }
}

public class Elephant : Mammal {
    public int CarryCapacity;
}
```

The **MammalGroup** enumeration is defined as follows:

```
public enum MammalGroup {
    Monotremes,
    Multitubercules,
    Marsupials,
    Utherians
}
```

You can also write code that uses the public members of any object in the inherited hierarchy, as shown in the following example:

```
Elephant e = new Elephant();
e.Sleep();
e.PhylogenicGroup = MammalGroup.Utherians;
```

**Protected access
modifier**

The purpose of the protected access modifier is to limit the scope of the
members of the protected class to only that class and those classes that inherit
it.

For example, in the following code, the Boolean value **IsSleeping** is declared as
protected, so it can be used only by the base **Animal** class and derived classes.

```
public class Animal {
    protected bool IsSleeping = false;
    public void Sleep() { }
    public void Eat() { }
}
```

How to Call a Base Constructor from a Derived Class

- **The base keyword is used in derived classes to specify a non-default base class constructor**

```
public class Animal {
    public Animal(GenderType gender) {
        // . . .
        Console.WriteLine("Constructing Animal");
    }
}

public class Elephant : Animal {
    public Elephant(GenderType gender): base(gender) {
        //Elephant code
        Console.WriteLine("Constructing Elephant");
    }
}
```

Introduction

When you create an object, the instance constructor is executed. When you create an object from a derived class, the instance constructor for the base class is executed first, and then the instance constructor for the derived class is executed.

Order of execution

Because the derived class uses the base class, the base class must be instantiated before the derived class.

```
public class Animal {
    public Animal() {
        Console.WriteLine("Constructing Animal");
    }
}

public class Elephant : Animal {
    public Elephant() {
        Console.WriteLine("Constructing Elephant");
    }
}
```

When an **Elephant** object is created, as shown in the following code:

```
Elephant e = new Elephant();
```

The following output is produced:

```
Constructing Animal
Constructing Elephant
```

Notice that the constructor for the base class is executed before the constructor for the derived class. The base class of the hierarchy is constructed first, so in a hierarchy that consists of an **Elephant** class that is derived from a **Mammal** class, which in turn is derived from an **Animal** class, the order of constructor execution is **Animal**, followed by **Mammal**, followed by **Elephant**.

Calling a specific constructor

If the base class has a non-default constructor that you want to use, you must use the **base** keyword.

For example, the **Animal** class may allow you to specify the gender of the animal when it is created, as shown in the following code:

```
public enum GenderType {
    Male,
    Female
}

public class Animal {
    public Animal() {
        Console.WriteLine("Constructing Animal");
    }

    public Animal( GenderType gender ) {
        if ( gender == GenderType.Female ) {
            Console.WriteLine("Female ");
        }
        else {
            Console.WriteLine("Male ");
        }
    }
}
```

You use the **base** keyword in the derived class constructor to call the base class constructor with a matching signature.

If your base class does not have a default constructor, you *must* use the **base** keyword to specify which constructor to call when your derived class is instantiated, as shown in the following code:

```
public class Elephant : Animal {
    public Elephant( GenderType gender ) : base( gender ) {
        Console.WriteLine("Elephant");
    }
}
```

You can then create an **Elephant** object as follows:

```
Elephant e = new Elephant(GenderType.Female);
```

The preceding code produces the following output:

```
Female
Elephant
```

This code sample is available on the Student Materials compact disc as BaseConstructor.sln in the folder Samples\Mod04\BaseConstructor.

How to Use a Sealed Class

- **You cannot derive from a sealed class**
- **Prevents the class from being overridden or extended by third parties**

```
public sealed class MyClass {
  // class members
}
```

Introduction

You cannot inherit from a sealed class. Any attempt to derive a class from a sealed class causes a compile-time error. You can add the **sealed** keyword to any class or method to create a class that cannot be inherited from to prevent the class from being overridden or extended by third parties.

Designing a sealed class

Creating a sealed class is useful when you want to prevent a class or a method from being overridden. For example, you may apply the **sealed** keyword when the class you are writing is crucial to the functionality of your program and any attempts to override it will cause problems. Or, you may also use it to mark certain classes in your program as proprietary to prevent third-party users from extending them.

Example

The .NET Framework class **System.String** is a sealed class because it has a very strict set of conditions under which its internal data structures must operate, and derived classes may break these rules.

Many of the classes in the **System.Security** and **System.Security.Cryptography** namespaces are sealed to prevent users from overriding their functionality.

Syntax

The syntax for using the **sealed** keyword is as follows:

[*attributes*] [*access-modifiers*] **sealed** *class identifiers* {*class-body*}

```
public sealed class Elephant {
  ...
}
```

Practice: Creating a Derived Class

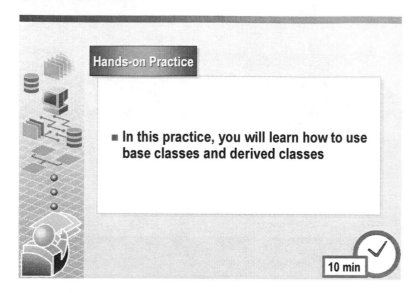

In this practice, you will learn how to use base classes and derived classes.

The solution code for this practice is provided in *install_folder*\Practices\Mod04
\Inheritance_Solution\Inheritance_Solution.sln. Start a new instance of Visual Studio .NET before
opening the solution.

Tasks	Detailed steps
1. Start Visual Studio .NET and open *install_folder*\Practices\Mod04 \Inheritance\Inheritance.sln.	a. Start a new instance of Visual Studio .NET. b. On the **Start Page**, click **Open Project**. c. In the **Open Project** dialog box, browse to *install_folder*\Practices\Mod04\Inheritance, click **Inheritance.sln**, and then click **Open**. d. In Solution Explorer, click **Form1.cs**, and then press F7 to open the Code Editor, and then review the provided code.
2. Examine the Task List.	▪ On the **View** menu, point to **Show Tasks**, and then click **All**.
3. Write a **Dolphin** class that derives from the **Animal** class.	a. In the Task List, double-click **TODO 1: Create a Dolphin class, derived from Animal**. b. Write a class named **Dolphin** that is derived from the **Animal** class. You do not need to write any methods or properties in your **Dolphin** class.

Tasks	Detailed steps
4. Create a **Dolphin** object.	**a.** In the Task List, double-click **TODO 2: Create a Dolphin object**. **b.** Create an instance of the **Dolphin** class.
5. Test your code.	**a.** Build and run your application by pressing F5. **b.** In your application window, click **Run**. A message appears informing you that an animal object has been created. Note that this method is defined in the **Animal** class.
6. Call the **Sleep** method on the **Dolphin** object, and then test your code.	**a.** In the Task List, double-click **TODO 3: Call the Sleep method on the dolphin object**. **b.** Add code that calls the **Sleep** method of the **Dolphin** object that you created in step 4. **c.** Test your code by pressing F5.
7. Save your application, and then quit Visual Studio .NET.	**a.** Save your application. **b.** Quit Visual Studio .NET.

Lesson: Using Polymorphism

- What Is Polymorphism?
- How to Write Virtual Methods
- How to Use Base Class Members from a Derived Class
- What Are Abstract Methods and Classes?

Introduction

This lesson explains how to use polymorphism in a C# application.

Lesson objectives

After completing this lesson, you will be able to:

- Implement polymorphism by using virtual methods in base classes.
- Create and use abstract classes.

Lesson agenda

This lesson includes the following topics and activity:

- What Is Polymorphism?
- How to Write Virtual Methods
- How to Use Base Class Members from a Derived Class
- What Are Abstract Methods and Classes
- Practice: Using Polymorphism

What Is Polymorphism?

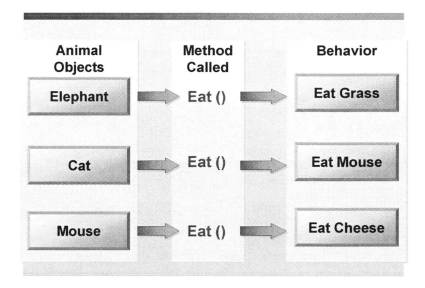

Introduction

Classes can inherit functionality from a base class, and a derived class can provide new functionality when you change the details of an inherited behavior. In fact, the purpose of creating a derived class is to extend the functionality of the base class and provide multiple ways to accomplish a task.

Definition

Polymorphism is an object-oriented concept that enables you to treat your derived classes in a similar manner, even though they are different. When you create derived classes, you provide more specialized functionality; polymorphism enables you to treat these new objects in a general way.

Example

You are writing an application for a zookeeper to use to manage feeding of the animals. First, you design a base class named **Animal**. In that base class, you include a method named **Eat** that determines how much food the animal will receive. Then, you create the derived classes, such as one for an elephant and one for a cat. Because the dietary requirements of these two types of animals are different, you change the method in each derived class to apply a different set of rules. For example, the **Eat** method for the elephant may calculate a quantity of grass, whereas the **Eat** method for the cat may calculate a quantity of protein.

Although the **Eat** method performs differently in each derived class, polymorphism enables you to simply call **Eat()** on an instance of either derived class without knowing anything about the differences in dietary requirements of these animals.

How to Write Virtual Methods

```
public class Animal {
    public virtual void Eat() {
        Console.WriteLine("Eat something");
    }
}
public class Cat : Animal {
    public override void Eat() {
        Console.WriteLine("Eat small animals");
    }

}
```

Introduction

When you create a method in a base class that you expect to be altered in the derived classes, define the method in your base class as a **virtual** method.

Definition

A **virtual** method is one whose implementation can be replaced by a method in a derived class.

Using the virtual keyword

To define a method in your base class as a **virtual** method, use the keyword **virtual** as shown in the following code:

```
public class Animal {
    public virtual void Eat() {
        Console.WriteLine("Eat something");
    }
}
```

In the preceding code, any class that is derived from **Animal** can implement a new **Eat** method.

Using the override keyword

To indicate that a method in a derived class is overriding the base class method, you use the **override** keyword, as shown in the following code:

```
public class Cat : Animal {
    public override void Eat() {
        Console.WriteLine("Eat small animals");
    }
}
```

When you override a virtual method, the overriding method must have the same signature as the virtual method.

Calling virtual methods

You can use polymorphism to treat derived classes in a generalized manner. To achieve this, you can treat derived objects as though they are of their base class type. In the following example, when you use an **Animal** object, you can call the **Eat** method, and the appropriate method for the object will be called.

For example, in the following code, the **FeedingTime** method takes a parameter of **Animal** and calls the **Eat** method to produce the action that is appropriate for that particular animal. The **FeedingTime** method uses polymorphism to invoke the desired action. The **FeedingTime** method can accept as a parameter any object that is derived from **Animal**.

```
public void FeedingTime( Animal someCreature ) {
    if ( someCreature.IsHungry ) {
        someCreature.Eat();
    }
}
```

The **FeedingTime** method can be passed a **Cat** object, for example:

```
Cat myCat = new Cat();
FeedingTime(myCat);
```

When you invoke a virtual method in your application, a run-time decision determines which method is actually invoked. The most derived implementation of the method is invoked. The most derived method is the original virtual method if no overriding method is provided (**Animal.Eat** in this example); otherwise, the most derived method is the overriding method in the object for which the method has been invoked (**Cat.Eat** in this example).

```csharp
using System;
namespace LearningCSharp {
    public class Animal {  // base class
        public Animal() { }
        public void Sleep() { }
        public bool IsHungry = true;
        public virtual void Eat() {
            Console.WriteLine("Eat something");
        }
    }

    public class Elephant : Animal {
        public int CarryCapacity;
        public override void Eat() {
            Console.WriteLine("Eat grass");
        }
    }

    public class Mouse : Animal {
        public override void Eat() {
            Console.WriteLine("Eat cheese");
        }
    }

    public class Cat : Animal {
        public void StalkPrey() { }
        public override void Eat() {
            Console.WriteLine("Eat mouse");
        }
    }

    public class WildLife {
        public WildLife() {
            Elephant myElephant = new Elephant();
            Mouse myMouse = new Mouse();
            Cat myCat = new Cat();

            FeedingTime(myElephant);
            FeedingTime(myMouse);
            FeedingTime(myCat);
        }

        public void FeedingTime( Animal someCreature ) {
            //Notice use of polymorphism here
            if ( someCreature.IsHungry ) {
                someCreature.Eat();
            }
        }

        static void Main(string[] args) {
            WildLife w = new WildLife();
        }
    }
}
```

When run, the preceding code produces the following result:

```
Eat grass
Eat cheese
Eat mouse
```

This code sample is provided on the Student Materials compact disc in Samples\Mod04\Polymorphism\Polymorphism.sln.

How to Use Base Class Members from a Derived Class

- The **base** keyword is used to call a method in the base class from a derived class

```
public class Cat : Animal {
  public override void Eat() {
        base.Eat();
        Console.WriteLine("Eat small animals");
    }
}
```

Introduction

The **base** keyword is used in derived classes to access members of the base class.

Example

To call the **Animal.Eat** method from the **Cat.Eat** method, you specify **base.Eat()** in the **Cat** object, as shown in the following code:

```
public class Animal {
  public virtual void Eat() {
        Console.WriteLine("Eat something");
  }
}

public class Cat : Animal {
    public void StalkPrey() { }
    public override void Eat() {
        base.Eat();
        Console.WriteLine("Eat small animals");
    }
}
```

The following code creates a **Cat** object and calls the **Eat** method:

```
Cat c = new Cat();
c.Eat();
```

The following output is produced:

```
Eat something
Eat small animals
```

You will find it useful to call base methods from your derived class when you want to extend the functionality of a method in a base class. You can call the base method from your overriding method, reuse the base method code, and then provide your own extra functionality.

What Are Abstract Methods and Classes?

- **An abstract class is a generic base class**
  - Contains an abstract method that must be implemented by a derived class
- **An abstract method has no implementation in the base class**

```
public abstract class Animal {
  public abstract void Eat();
  public abstract Group PhylogenicGroup { get; }
}
```

- **Can contain non-abstract members**

Cannot be sealed.

Introduction

Often, it is useful to create a class that contains methods that must be implemented by all derived classes but not by the base class itself.

Definitions

An *abstract method* is an empty method—one that has no implementation. Instead, derived classes are required to provide an implementation.

An *abstract class* is a class that can contain abstract members, although it is not required to do so. Any class that contains abstract members must be abstract. An abstract class can also contain non-abstract members.

Because the purpose of an abstract class is to act as a base class, it is not possible to instantiate an abstract class directly, nor can an abstract class be sealed.

Syntax

The syntax for creating an abstract method is to use the **abstract** modifier with the name of the method and the parameters, followed by a semicolon instead of a statement block.

[*access-modifiers*] **abstract** *return-type method-name* ([*parameters*]) ;

Example

The following example shows how to create an abstract class **Animal** class with an abstract **Eat** method:

```
public abstract class Animal {
  public abstract void Eat();
}
```

Benefits

The benefit of creating abstract methods is that it enables you to add methods to your base class that subsequently must be implemented by all derived classes, but the implementation details for these methods do not have to be defined in the base class.

The **Eat** method in the preceding examples is a good use of an abstract method because although all animals eat, the implementation details of **Eat** vary enough between animals that it is not useful to provide a default implementation.

Override

When a derived class inherits an abstract method from an abstract class, it must override the abstract methods. This requirement is enforced at compile time.

The following example shows how a **Mouse** class, which is derived from **Animal,** uses the *override* keyword to implement the **Eat** method:

```
public class Mouse : Animal {
  public override void Eat() {
      Console.WriteLine("Eat cheese");
  }
}
```

When you call the **Eat** method on the **Mouse** object, the following output is produced:

```
Eat cheese
```

Abstract class with virtual method

You can also create an abstract class that contains virtual methods, as shown in the following example:

```
public abstract class Animal {
  public virtual void Sleep() {
      Console.WriteLine("Sleeping");
  }
  public abstract void Eat();
}
```

In this case, a derived class does not have to provide an implementation of the **Sleep** method because **Sleep** is defined as virtual. Therefore, if you have a generic method that is common to all derived classes, and you want to force each derived class to implement the method, you must define the method as abstract in the base class.

Example

Because some animals sleep in different ways—some sleep while standing, others sleep for long periods, and so on—you decide that sleep is a good candidate for an abstract method.

To do this, you change the definition of **Sleep** to abstract and remove the implementation, as shown in the following code:

```
public abstract class Animal {
    public abstract void Sleep();
    public abstract void Eat();
}
```

When the application is compiled, because the mouse object does not implement the **Sleep** method, you receive the following error:

```
LearningCSharp.Mouse' does not implement inherited abstract
member 'LearningCSharp.Animal.Sleep()'
```

Note   **LearningCSharp** is the namespace that contains the **Animal** classes.

By changing **Sleep** to an abstract method, you force the derived classes to implement their own version of the method.

The following code shows an implementation of both the **Eat** and the **Sleep** methods in the **Mouse** class:

```
public class Mouse : Animal {
    public override void Eat() {
        Console.WriteLine("Eat cheese");
    }
    public override void Sleep() {
        Console.WriteLine("Mouse sleeping");
    }
}
```

Abstract properties

Properties may also be declared as abstract.

To declare an abstract property, specify the property name and the accessors that the derived property should implement.

Example 1

The following example shows how to create an animal class and declare an abstract property named **PhylogenicGroup** (**Group** is an enumeration that contains phylogenic group names):

```
public abstract class Animal {
    public abstract Group PhylogenicGroup{get; set;}
}
```

To make the property read-only or write-only, you can remove the corresponding accessor.

Example 2

The following code produces a compilation error because the code attempts to set a value while the property is declared as read-only:

```
public abstract class Animal {
    public abstract Group PhylogenicGroup{get;}
}

public class Cat : Animal {
  public override Group PhylogenicGroup{
      get{
          return Group.Utherians;
      }
  }
}

. . .

Cat c = new Cat();
//The following line causes a compilation error
c.PhylogenicGroup = Group.Utherians;
```

Practice: Using Polymorphism

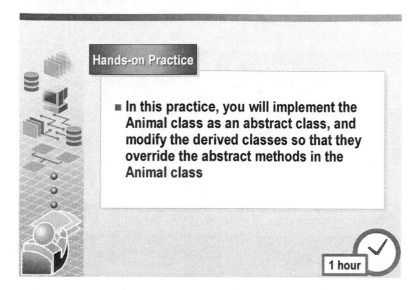

In this practice, you will implement the **Animal** class as an abstract class, and modify the derived classes so that they override the virtual functions in the **Animal** class.

The solution code for this practice is provided in *install_folder*\Practices\Mod04\ Abstract_Solution\Abstract.sln. Start a new instance of Visual Studio .NET before opening the solution.

Tasks	Detailed steps
1. Start Visual Studio .NET, and then open *install_folder* \Practices\Mod04\Abstract \Abstract.sln.	a. Start a new instance of Visual Studio .NET. b. On the **Start Page**, click **Open Project**. c. In the **Open Project** dialog box, browse to *install_folder*\Practices \Mod04\Abstract, click **Abstract.sln**, and then click **Open**.
2. Examine the tasks, and double-click **Next button code**.	a. In Solution Explorer, click **Form1.cs**, press F7 to open the Code Editor, and then review the provided code. b. On the **View** menu, point to **Show Tasks**, and then click **All**.

Tasks	Detailed steps
3. Change the methods in the **Animal** class so that they are abstract methods.	a. In the Task List, double-click **TODO 1: Make the methods in the class abstract**. b. Change the methods **Sleep** and **Eat** to abstract methods. c. Test your code by pressing **F5**. *The compiler should list errors indicating that the Lion and Antelope classes do not implement the abstract members of Animal.*
4. Change the derived classes to correctly inherit from the **Animal** class.	a. Double-click **TODO 2: Change Lion and Antelope to work with the abstract Animal class**. b. Change the **Lion** and **Antelope** classes so that they correctly inherit from the **Animal** class. c. Test your code by pressing **F5**.
5. Save your application, and then quit Visual Studio .NET.	a. Save your application. b. Quit Visual Studio .NET.

Review

- ■ **Designing Objects**
- ■ **Using Inheritance**
- ■ **Using Polymorphism**

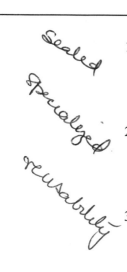

1. What keyword do you add to your class definition if you do not want other classes to inherit from it?

2. Should a derived class be more specialized or more generalized than its base class?

3. What are some of the benefits of object-oriented programming?

Lab 4.1: Creating Classes in C#

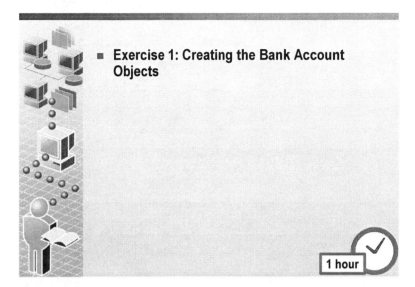

- Exercise 1: Creating the Bank Account Objects

1 hour

Objectives

After completing this lab, you will be able to:

- Use properties to provide access to data in a class.
- Create base classes and derive classes from them.
- Create abstract classes and derive classes from them.

Note This lab focuses on the concepts in this module and as a result may not comply with Microsoft security recommendations.

Prerequisites

Before working on this lab, you must have:

- Knowledge of how to create derived classes.
- Knowledge of how to write properties.

Scenario

You are a programmer at a bank and have been asked to define an object hierarchy for the types of bank accounts that customers can open. These accounts are:

- Checking account
- Savings account

Note If you have a working solution from module 3, then you can use it in this lab, rather than the starter code.

Checking account

A checking account has the following characteristics:

- The account holder's name can be assigned only when the account is created.
- The opening balance must be specified when the account is created.
- The account number must be assigned when the account is created.
  - Checking account numbers range from 100000 to 499999, and every checking account must have a unique account number. You do not need to check the upper limit of the account number in this lab.

A checking account holder can:

- Order a checkbook.
- Check the account balance.
- Add money to the checking account.
- Withdraw money if the account has sufficient funds.

Savings account

A savings account has the following characteristics:

- The account holder's name that can be assigned only when the account is created.

  Saving account numbers range from 500000 to 999999. You do not need to check the upper limit of the account number in this lab.
- The account earns interest.

  The interest rate depends on the account balance. If the balance is above 1000, the rate is 6%; otherwise, it is 3%.

A savings account holder can:

- Check the account balance.
- Add money to the account.
- Withdraw money if the account has sufficient balance.

Your bank is likely to add more account types in the future, so it is important to reuse as much code as possible, while ensuring that the different account objects implement a standard set of features.

Estimated time to complete this lab: 60 minutes

Exercise 0
Lab Setup

The Lab Setup section lists the tasks that you must perform before you begin the lab.

Task	Detailed steps
▪ Log on to Windows as **Student** with a password of **P@ssw0rd**.	▪ Log on to Windows with the following account. • User name: **Student** • Password: **P@ssw0rd** Note that the 0 in the password is a zero.

Note that by default the *install_folder* is C:\Program Files\Msdntrain\2609.

Exercise 1
Creating the Bank Account Objects

In this exercise, you will write the objects that represent the bank account classes that are outlined in the scenario.

A sample application is shown in the following illustration:

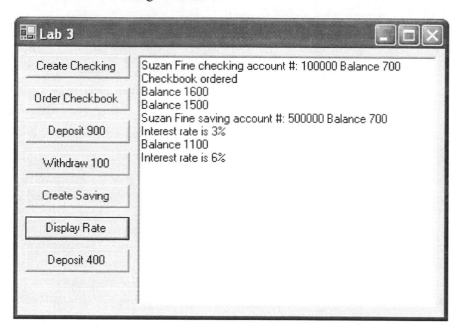

The solution code for this lab is provided in *install_folder*\Labfiles\Lab04_1\Exercise1
\Solution_Code\Bank.sln. Start a new instance of Visual Studio .NET before opening the solution.

Tasks	Detailed steps
1. Start Visual Studio .NET, and then open *install_folder*\Labfiles \Lab04_1\Exercise1 \Bank.sln.	a. Start a new instance of Visual Studio .NET. b. On the **Start Page**, click **Open Project**. c. In the **Open Project** dialog box, browse to *install_folder*\ Labfiles\ Lab04_1\Exercise1, click **Bank.sln**, and then click **Open**. **Form1.cs** provides the user interface. **BankAccount.cs** is provided as a place for you to implement the bank account class or classes.
2. In Solution Explorer, locate the BankAccount.cs file.	▪ In Solution Explorer, click the C# file **BankAccount.cs**, and then press F7 to open the Code Editor. This file provides a sample implementation of the checking account and saving account classes.

Tasks	Detailed steps
3. Write a base class called **BankAccount** and modify the **CheckingAccount** and **SavingsAccount** classes so that they inherit **BankAccount**.	The sample solution provides two classes, **CheckingAccount** and **SavingsAccount**. These classes duplicate some code, and allow uncontrolled access to information. In this step you will create a base class, and in the next step you will implement the methods and properties of the base class. a. At the top of the BankAccount.cs file, locate **TODO: Implement BankAccount class here**, and declare a base class for **CheckingAccount** and **SavingsAccount**. b. Modify **CheckingAccount** and **SavingsAccount** so that they inherit **BankAccount**.
4. Decide which properties should be provided by the base class, add them to the base class, and modify the **CheckingAccount** and **SavingsAccount** classes to remove public variables.	a. Examine the public variables in the **CheckingAccount** and **SavingsAccount** classes, and change them to properties, moving them to the base class where appropriate. b. Use Pascal case for your properties, and change the calling code in **Form1.cs** appropriately. ■ Note that you can use the protected keyword to limit access to a variable to derived classes only. ■ Some properties should be read only: you can make a property read only by omitting the **set** accessor.
5. Decide which methods should be provided by the base class, add them to the base class, and modify the **CheckingAccount** and **SavingsAccount** classes to reuse code.	a. Examine the methods in **CheckingAccount** and **SavingsAccount** to determine which should be provided by the **BankAccount** class, and then change the code so that they are provided by **BankAccount**. b. Use Pascal case for your properties, and change the calling code in **Form1.cs** appropriately. ■ Note that you can use the protected keyword to limit access to a variable to derived classes only.
6. Provide a **BankAccount** constructor that forces the derived classes to specify the account holder name and initial balance.	a. Examine the constructors in **CheckingAccount** and **SavingsAccount** to determine what features should be provided by a **BankAccount** constructor. b. Add a **BankAccount** constructor that requires the account holder's name and an initial balance. c. Change the **CheckingAccount** and **SavingsAccount** constructors so that they pass the correct values to the **BankAccount** constructor.

Tasks	Detailed steps
7. If any existing methods would be more appropriately implemented as properties, then change them to properties.	▪ Examine the methods in **CheckingAccount** and **SavingsAccount** to determine if any should be properties, and change any that you identify.
8. Test your code by running the application, and then clicking the buttons in sequence from top to bottom.	a. Press F5 to compile and run your application. b. Click each button in sequence and ensure that your application produces the expected output: • **Create Checking**: a message stating that Suzan Fine has created a checking account with a balance of 700. • **Order Checkbook**: a message stating that a checkbook has been ordered. • **Deposit 900**: a balance of 1600. • **Withdraw 100**: a balance of 1500. • **Create Saving**: a message stating that Suzan Fine has created a saving account with a balance of 700. • **Display Rate**: an interest rate of 3%. • **Deposit 400**: a balance of 1100. c. Click **Display Rate** once more to check that the interest rate has increased to 6%.
9. Save your application and quit Visual Studio .NET.	a. Save your application. b. Quit Visual Studio .NET.

training

Module 5: Programming with C#

Contents

Microsoft®

Overview

- ■ **Using Arrays**
- ■ **Using Collections**
- ■ **Using Interfaces**
- ■ **Using Exception Handling**
- ■ **Using Delegates and Events**

Introduction

This module introduces various data structures including arrays (the **System.Array** class) and collections (classes in the **System.Collections** namespace), and explains when to use each of these data structures in an application. The module also introduces interfaces, describes the concepts and syntax of exception handling, and explains delegates and their use in event handling.

Objectives

After completing this module, you will be able to:

- ■ Create and use arrays.
- ■ Use classes in the **System.Collections** namespace.
- ■ Use the **ArrayList** class.
- ■ Use interfaces.
- ■ Handle exceptions.
- ■ Create and call a delegate.
- ■ Use delegates to handle events.

Lesson: Using Arrays

- **What Is an Array?**
- **How to Create an Array**
- **How to Initialize and Access Array Members**
- **How to Iterate Through an Array Using the foreach Statement**
- **How to Use Arrays as Method Parameters**
- **How to Index an Object**

Introduction

This lesson introduces arrays and the **Array** class in the **System** namespace. It explains how to use arrays to hold a series of objects, and how to index the array.

Lesson objectives

After completing this lesson, students will be able to:

- Create an array.
- Index an array.
- Use the **foreach** statement to iterate through the items in the array.

Lesson agenda

This lesson includes the following topics and activity:

- What Is an Array?
- How to Create an Array
- How to Initialize and Access Array Members
- How to Iterate Through an Array Using the **foreach** Statement
- How to Use Arrays as Method Parameters
- How to Index an Object
- Practice: Using **foreach** with an Array
- Practice (optional): Using an Indexer

What Is an Array?

- **A data structure that contains a number of variables called elements of the array**
- **All of the array elements must be of the same type**
- **Arrays are zero indexed**
- **Arrays are objects**
- **Arrays can be:**
  - Single-dimensional, an array with the rank of one
  - Multidimensional, an array with a rank greater than one
  - Jagged, an array whose elements are arrays
- **Array methods**

Introduction

An array can be thought of as a list. By using arrays, you can store a group of elements that have the same data type under one variable name. You can also easily access, use, and store values of the same type. An array is a good choice when you want to maintain a list of items.

Definition

An *array* is a data structure that contains a number of variables called the *elements* of the array. To refer to a specific element in the series, you use a number, or *index*. C# arrays are *zero indexed*; that is, the array indexes start at zero. Arrays are objects.

[0]	[1]	[2]	[3]	[4]	[5]	[6]

Index 0   Index 6

Single dimensional array

An array that consists of a single list or sequence is called a *single-dimensional array*. An array has one or more dimensions.

Multidimensional array

A *multidimensional array* is indexed by more than one value. Multidimensional arrays of specific sizes are often referred to by size, such as two-dimensional arrays and three-dimensional arrays. You can think of a two-dimensional array as a grid. For example, you can store a set of graph coordinates, such as x and y, in a 2-dimensional array.

Analogy

Consider a shelf full of books as a single-dimensional array. The shelf is the array dimension and a book is an element in the array. A bookcase is more like a multidimensional array, with the shelves being one dimension on the array, and the books being another dimension. For example, you would refer to the third book on the second shelf.

Jagged array

The elements of an array can be any type, including an array type. An array of arrays is called a *jagged array*.

Array methods

C# natively supports arrays, based on the Microsoft® .NET Framework class **System.Array**. The **System.Array** class is an abstract class that provides many methods that you can use when working with arrays.

The following table includes some of the most commonly used methods.

Method	Description
Sort	Sorts the elements in an array
Clear	Sets a range of elements to zero or **null**
Clone	Creates a copy of the array
GetLength	Returns the length of a given dimension
IndexOf	Returns the index of the first occurrence of a value
Length	Gets the number of elements in the specified dimension of the array

How to Create an Array

- **Declare the array by adding a set of square brackets to end of the variable type of the individual elements**

```
int[] MyIntegerArray;
```

- **Instantiate to create**
  - int[ ] numbers = new int[5];
- **To create an array of type Object**
  - object [ ] animals = new object [100];

Introduction

Before you can use an array, you must create it by declaring it and then instantiating it.

Syntax

You create or declare arrays in code just as you declare other variables. You follow the same guidelines for naming, scoping, and choosing data types. When you declare an array, you place the brackets ([ ]) after the type. These square brackets are called the *index operators*.

```
int[] MyIntegerArray;

int[] table;
```

Declaring an array

To declare an array, use the following syntax:

```
type[] array-name;
```

For example:

```
int[] numbers;
```

Instantiating an array

Arrays in C# are objects and must be instantiated. When you instantiate the array, you set aside memory, on the heap, to hold the elements of the array.

The following code allocates space for 5 integers:

```
int[] numbers;
numbers = new int[5];
```

As with other variable declarations, you can combine these statements as follows:

```
int[] numbers = new int[5];
```

Initial values

When you create an array of value types, the contents of the array are initialized to the default value for that type. For an integer array, the default value is zero.

Examples

The array can be of any type. For example, you can maintain a list of names or bank account balances in an array.

```
string[] names = new names[7];
decimal[] balances = new balances[10];
```

You can also create an array of type **Object** as shown in the following example. Creating this type of array can be useful if you must manage a list of many different types of objects.

```
object[] animals = new object[100];
```

How to Initialize and Access Array Members

- **Initializing an array**

```
int[] numbers = {10, 9, 8, 7, 6, 5, 4, 3, 2,
   1, 0};

numbers[4] = 5;
```

- **Accessing array members**

```
string[] animal = {"Mouse", "Cat", "Lion"};
animal[1]= "Elephant";
string someAnimal = animal[2];
```

Introduction

C# provides simple ways to initialize arrays and access array members.

Initializing a single-dimensional array

To initialize a single-dimensional array when it is declared, enclose the initial values in curly braces { }.

Note If an array is not initialized when it is declared, array members are automatically initialized to the default initial value for the array type.

The following examples show various ways to initialize single-dimensional arrays:

```
int[] numbers = new int[5] {1, 2, 3, 4, 5};
```

```
string[] animals = new string[3] {"Elephant", "Cat", "Mouse"};
```

If an initializer is provided, you can omit the **new** statement, as shown in the following examples:

```
int[] numbers = {1, 2, 3, 4, 5};
```

```
string[] animals = {"Elephant", "Cat", "Mouse"};
```

Note that the size of the array is inferred from the number of elements that are specified.

Accessing array members

Accessing array members in C# is straightforward. For example, the following code creates an array called **numbers** and then assigns **5** to the fifth element of the array:

```
int[ ] numbers = {10, 9, 8, 7, 6, 5, 4, 3, 2, 1, 0};
numbers[4] = 5;
```

Example

The following code creates an array of 100 integers and fills them with the values **100** down to **1**:

```
int[] countdown = new int[100];

for ( int i = 0, j = 100; i < 100; i++, j-- ) {
  countdown[i] = j;
}
```

When you declare an array to include a number of elements, you must access only valid array elements. If you attempt to access an element that is out of range, you generate an **IndexOutOfRange** exception, a type of run-time error.

For example, the following code generates a run-time error because the array allocates 5 integers but attempts to access the sixth element in the array. Remember that arrays are zero-indexed.

```
int[] errorArray = new int[5];
errorArray[5] = 42;  // runtime error
```

Examining arrays using the debugging tool

It is very useful to check the contents of an array while your application is running. The debugging tool provides excellent access to array element values through the various debugging windows such as the **Autos** window and the **Watch** window:

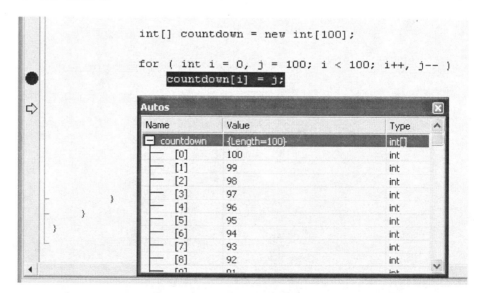

To examine the contents of an array, set a breakpoint at the array, and then, in the Debug window, click the expand button next to the array name.

How to Iterate Through an Array Using the *foreach* Statement

> ■ Using *foreach* statement repeats the embedded
> statement(s) for each element in the array

```
int[] numbers = {4, 5, 6, 1, 2, 3, -2, -1, 0};
foreach (int i in numbers) {
    Console.WriteLine(i);
}
```

Introduction

Code that iterates through an array and executes the same statements on each element is very common. Although you can use any looping statement to iterate through an array, the **foreach** statement simplifies this common process by eliminating the need for you to check the size of the array.

Syntax

The syntax of the **foreach** statement is:

```
foreach ( type identifier in expression )
    statement-block
```

Using the foreach statement

The following code creates an array named **numbers**, iterates through the array with the **foreach** statement, and then writes the values out to the console, one per line:

```
int[] numbers = {4, 5, 6, 1, 2, 3, -2, -1, 0};
foreach (int i in numbers) {
    Console.WriteLine(i);
}
```

Important   You must not modify the iteration variable in a **foreach** loop. In the preceding example, **i** is the iteration variable.

Example

This example shows how the **foreach** statement can be useful when you work with an array of objects. Two classes, **Lion** and **Elephant**, are derived from **Animal**. Both of the derived classes implement the **Eat** method. The classes are instantiated, and then a **Lion** and an **Elephant** object are placed in an array. The **foreach** statement is used to iterate through the array so that the polymorphic **Eat** method is called. Note that the base object type is used to specify the type of the identifier.

```csharp
using System;

namespace ArraySample {
  public abstract class Animal {
      abstract public void Eat();
  }

  public class Lion : Animal {
      public override void Eat() {
          // eats meat
      }
  }

  public class Elephant : Animal {
      public override void Eat() {
          // eats vegetation
      }
  }

  class ClassZoo {
      static void Main(string[] args) {
          Lion aLion = new Lion();
          Elephant anElephant = new Elephant();

          Animal[] zoo = new Animal[2];
          zoo[0] = aLion;
          zoo[1] = anElephant;

          foreach ( Animal a in zoo ) {
             a.Eat();
          }
      }
  }
}
```

How to Use Arrays as Method Parameters

- **Pass an array to a method**

- **Use the *params* keyword to pass a variable number of arguments to a method**

```
public int Sum(params int[] list) {
        int total = 0;
        foreach ( int i in list ) {
                total += i;
        }
        return total;
}

...
// pe is the object providing Sum()
...
int value = pe.Sum( 1, 3, 5, 7, 9, 11 );
```

Introduction

You may want to write a method that can accept an unpredictable number of parameters, for example, a method that would return the sum of any set of integers.

Passing an array to a method

To write this type of method, you can place the integers in an array, pass the array to the method, and then use the **foreach** statement to iterate through the array.

Example

The following example shows how to do this with the **Sum** method. Note the declaration of the **Sum** method and note the declaration and initialization of the **tester** array.

```
using System;

namespace ParameterExample {
  public class ParamExample {
      public int Sum(int[] list) {
          int total = 0;
          foreach ( int i in list ) {
              total += i;
          }
          return total;
      }
  }

  class Tester {
      static void Main(string[] args) {
          ParamExample pe = new ParamExample();
          int[] tester = {1, 2, 3, 4, 5, 6, 7 };

          int total = pe.Sum( tester );

          Console.WriteLine( total );  // 28
      }
  }
}
```

Using params keyword

Although this approach works, C# provides a better solution by allowing you to use the **params** keyword rather than creating the array yourself. When you place the **params** keyword before the array declaration in the parameter list, you can use the method as shown in the following example:

```
using System;

namespace ParameterExample {
  public class ParamExample {
      public int Sum(params int[] list) {
          int total = 0;
          foreach ( int i in list ) {
              total += i;
          }
          return total;
      }
  }

  class Tester {
      static void Main(string[] args) {
          ParamExample pe = new ParamExample();

          int total = pe.Sum( 1, 2, 3, 4, 5, 6, 7 );

          Console.WriteLine( total );  // 28
      }
  }
}
```

The **params** keyword can modify any type of parameter. A **params** parameter need not be the only parameter. For example, you can add the following method to the **ParamExample** class:

```
class ParamExample {
    public string Combine(string s1, string s2,
                                    params object[] others) {
        string combination = s1 + " " + s2;
        foreach ( object o in others ) {
            combination += " " + o.ToString();
        }
        return combination;
    }
}
```

You can use this method as follows:

```
string combo = pe.Combine("One", "two", "three", "four" );
// combo has the value "One two three four"

combo = pe.Combine("alpha", "beta");
// combo has the value "alpha beta"
```

Notice how this method is implemented in the preceding example. The first call to **pe.Combine** matches the method that has the **params** parameter, and the compiler creates an array and then passes that array to your method. The second call to **pe.Combine** matches the method that takes two string parameters, and the compiler does not create an array. When using the **params** keyword, you must consider the overhead that is involved.

Tip   If you expect that the users of your method are normally going to pass one, two, or three parameters, it is a good idea to create several overloads of the method that can handle those specific cases.

How to Index an Object

■ Use *this* keyword, and *get* and *set* accessors

```
public class Zoo {
      private Animal[] theAnimals;
      public Animal this[int i] {
            get {
                  return theAnimals[i];
            }
            set {
                  theAnimals[i] = value;
            }
      }
}
```

Introduction

When a class contains an array, or a collection, it is useful to access the information as though the class itself were an array. An *indexer* is a property that allows you to index an object in the same way as an array.

Declaring an indexer

To declare an indexer in C#, you use the **this** keyword. Like properties, indexers can contain **get** and **set** clauses, as shown in the following example:

```
type this [ type index-argument ] { get-accessor; set-
accessor; }
```

The get accessor

The **get** accessor uses the same index-argument as the indexer, as shown in the following example:

```
public numbers this[int i] {
  get {
      return myIntegerArray[i];
  }
}
```

The set accessor

The **set** accessor uses the same index-argument as the indexer, in addition to the **value** implicit parameter, as shown in the following example:

```
set {
    myArray[i] = value;
}
```

Example

In the following complete example, the **Zoo** class maintains a private array of **Animal** objects named **theAnimals**. An indexer is provided so that users of the **Zoo** class can access the animals in **Zoo** just like an array, as shown in **Main** method.

```
using System;

namespace IndexExample {

    public class Zoo {
        private Animal[] theAnimals;
        public Animal this[int i] {
            get {
                return theAnimals[i];
            }
            set {
                theAnimals[i] = value;
            }
        }

        public Zoo() {
            // Our Zoo can hold 100 animals
            theAnimals = new Animal[100];
        }
    }

    class ZooKeeper {
        static void Main(string[] args) {
            Zoo myZoo = new Zoo();
            myZoo[0] = new Elephant();
            myZoo[1] = new Lion();
            myZoo[2] = new Lion();
            myZoo[3] = new Antelope();

            Animal oneAnimal = myZoo[3];
            // oneAnimal gets an antelope
        }
    }

    public abstract class Animal {
        abstract public void Eat();
    }
    public class Lion : Animal {
        public override void Eat() { }
    }
    public class Elephant : Animal {
        public override void Eat() { }
    }
    public class Antelope : Animal {
        public override void Eat() { }
    }
}
```

Instead of using the indexer, you can either make the array public, which violates the design principals of encapsulation, or write methods to add and remove animals from the array.

The preceding code is available on the Student Materials compact disc in the IndexObject.sln file in the Samples\Mod05\Indexers folder.

Practice: Using a *foreach* Statement with an Array

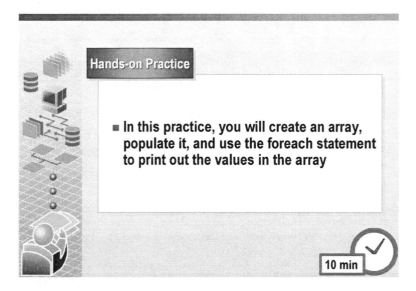

In this practice, you will use a **foreach** loop to list the contents of an array. Each **Animal** object in the array has a property named **Species** that returns the animal species as a string. You can display this property by using the **Output** method that is provided in the starter code as shown in the following code, assuming **anAnimal** is an **Animal** object:

```
Output ( anAnimal.Species );
```

The array **animalArray** is defined as follows:

```
Animal animalArray[] = new Animal[5];
```

Animals are assigned to the array as follows:

```
animalArray[0] = new Lion();
```

The output is shown in the following illustration:

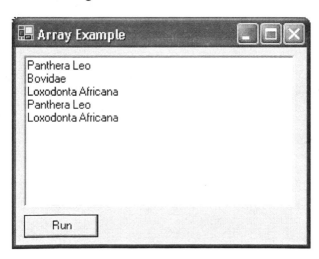

The solution for this practice is located in *install_folder*\Practices\Mod05\Arrays_Solution \ArrayExample.sln. Start a new instance of Microsoft Visual Studio® .NET before opening the solution.

Tasks	Detailed steps
1. Start Visual Studio .NET, and then open *install_folder* \Practices\Mod05\Arrays \ArrayExample.sln.	a. Start a new instance of Visual Studio .NET. b. On the **Start Page**, click **Open Project**. c. In the **Open Project** dialog box, browse to *install_folder*\Practices \Mod05\Arrays, click **ArrayExample.sln**, and then click **Open**. d. In Solution Explorer, click **Form1.cs**, and then press F7 to open the Code Editor.
2. Review the Task List.	a. On the **View** menu, point to **Show Tasks**, and then click **All**. b. Review the tasks in the Task List.
3. Write a **foreach** loop that lists the contents of the **animalArray** array.	a. Double-click the task **TODO: Write a foreach loop that lists the animals**. Note that the **animalArray** has been declared and initialized with some animals. b. Write a **foreach** loop that displays the **Species** of every animal in the **animalArray**. c. Press F5 to compile and run your application. In your application window, click **Run**. Your application output should be the same as that shown in the introduction to this practice.
4. Save your solution, and the quit Visual Studio .NET.	a. On the **File** menu, click **Save All**. b. On the **File** menu, click **Exit**.

Practice (optional): Using an Indexer

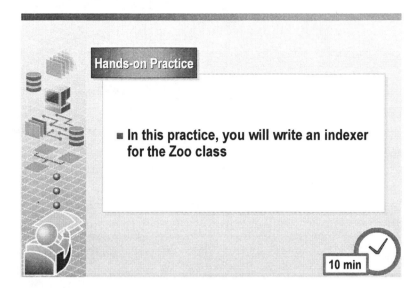

In this practice, you will write an indexer for the **Zoo** class. Currently, the **Zoo** class maintains **Animal** objects in a public array named **animalsArray**. When you click the **Run** button, a **Zoo** object named **myZoo** is created, and three **Animal** objects are created and placed in the **animalsArray** array in **myZoo**.

Next, a **for** loop is used to display the species of the animals in the **animalsArray** in the **Zoo** object.

Your tasks are to:

- Write an indexer to modify the array.

- Use the indexer to add the animals to the array (code is provided).

- Display the animals in the array, using the indexer (code is provided).

The solution will look like this:

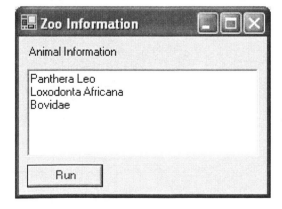

The solution for this practice is located in *install_folder*\Practices\Mod05\
Indexers_Solution\Indexers.sln. Start a new instance of Visual Studio .NET before opening the solution.

Tasks	Detailed steps
1. Start Visual Studio .NET, and then open *install_folder* \Practices\Mod05\Indexers \Indexers.sln.	a. Start a new instance of Visual Studio .NET. b. On the **Start Page**, click **Open Project**. c. In the **Open Project** dialog box, browse to *install_folder*\Practices\Mod05\Indexers, click **Indexers.sln**, and then click **Open**. d. In Solution Explorer, click **Form1.cs**, and then press F7 to open the Code Editor.
2. Review the Task List.	a. On the **View** menu, point to **Show Tasks**, and then click **All**. b. Review the tasks in the Task List.
3. Locate and complete the task **Write an Indexer for this class, based on animalArray**.	a. Double-click the task **TODO: Write an Indexer for this class, based on animalArray**. b. Write an indexer for the **Zoo** class. In the **get** accessor, return an **Animal** object from the **animalArray**. In the **set** accessor, add an **Animal** object to the **animalArray**.
4. Comment out the lines in the **Zoo** class **runExample_Click** method that directly use **animalArray**.	To test your indexer, you will comment out the code in the **runExample_click** method that uses **animalArray** directly, and uncomment the code that uses the indexer. a. Double-click the task **TODO 2 : Comment out the following:** b. Comment out the lines that assign animals to the **animalArray**, and comment out the for loop immediately following these assignments. Note that you can use the **Comment Selection** function to comment out selected lines of code. This function is available on the **Edit** menu under **Advanced**, and also as a toolbar button, as shown on the left.
5. Uncomment the code that uses the Zoo indexer to read assign the animals and display them.	a. Locate the task **TODO 3: Uncomment the following lines**. b. Remove the comments from the lines following this task description.
6. Compile and run your application, and test that the animal names display correctly when you click **Run**.	■ Press F5 to compile and run your application, and then click **Run** on your application window. The output should list the three animal species.
7. Quit Visual Studio .NET, saving your solution.	a. On the **File** menu, click **Save All**. b. On the **File** menu, click **Exit**.

Lesson: Using Collections

- **What Are Lists, Queues, Stacks, and Hash Tables?**
- **How to Use the ArrayList Class**
- **How to Use Queues and Stacks**
- **How to Use Hash Tables**

Introduction

This lesson introduces the various data structures in the **Collections** namespace, with special attention given to the **ArrayList** class. The lesson explains how to create an **ArrayList** class, add items to a collection, iterate through the items in a collection, and use hash tables to access collection elements.

Lesson objectives

After completing this lesson, you will be able to:

- Create and use collections.
- Use a hash table to access collection elements.

Lesson agenda

This lesson includes the following topics and activity:

- What Are Lists, Queues, Stacks, and Hash tables?
- How to Use the **ArrayList** Class
- How to Use Queues and Stacks
- How to Use Hash Tables
- Practice: Creating and Using Collections

What Are Lists, Queues, Stacks, and Hash Tables?

Lists, queues, stacks, and hash tables are common ways to manage data in an application

- **List:** A collection that allows you access by index

    Example: An array is a list; an ArrayList is a list

- **Queue:** First-in, first-out collection of objects

    Example: Waiting in line at a ticket office

- **Stack:** Last-in-first-out collection of objects

    Example: A pile of plates

- **Hash table:** Represents a collection of associated keys and values organized around the hash code of the key

    Example: A dictionary

Introduction

An array is a useful data structure, but it has some limitations. For example, when you create an array, you must know how many elements you will need, and accessing the element by a sequential index may not be the most convenient method for your application. Lists, queues, stacks, and hash tables are other common ways to manage data in an application.

Definition

The **System.Collections** namespace contains interfaces and classes that define various collections of objects, such as lists, queues, stacks, and hash tables, that provide a useful variety of data structures.

Many of the objects in the .NET Framework classes use collections to manage their data, so understanding these data structures is critical to your ability to successfully create C# applications.

Description

The following table shows some of the classes in the **System.Collections** namespace and illustrates their best uses through examples.

Class	Description	Use	Example
ArrayList	Represents an ordered collection of objects that can be individually indexed.	Use an ArrayList when you want to access elements by using an index. In almost every situation, an ArrayList is a good alternative to an array.	Mailboxes: items can be inserted or removed at any position.
Queue	Represents a first-in, first-out collection of objects.	Use a queue when you need first-in, first-out access. A queue is often used to hold elements in that are discarded immediately thereafter, such as information in a buffer.	Waiting in line at a ticket office, where you join at the back and leave from the front. Requests coming over a network are queued and then discarded after they are processed.
Stack	Represents a simple last-in, first-out collection of objects.	Use a stack when you need last-in, first-out access. A stack is often used to hold items during calculations.	A pile of plates, in a cupboard, where you place them on top, and remove them from the top.
Hashtable	Uses a key to access the elements in the collection.	Use a hash table when you must access elements by using an index and you can identify a useful index value.	You can access book titles by their ISBN numbers.

How to Use the ArrayList Class

- ArrayList does not have a fixed size; it grows as needed
- Use Add(object) to add an object to the end of the ArrayList
- Use [] to access elements in the ArrayList
- Use TrimToSize() to reduce the size to fit the number of elements in the ArrayList
- Use Clear to remove all the elements
- Can set the capacity explicitly

Introduction

The **ArrayList** class solves the main disadvantage of an array, which is that you must know the capacity of the data structure when you instantiate the array, by providing a data structure that behaves like an array but can grow as required. As elements are added to an **ArrayList** object, the capacity is automatically increased. An **ArrayList** object initially allocates 16 elements. When you add a seventeenth element, the **ArrayList** expands to 32 elements.

Accessing elements in an ArrayList

You can access elements in an **ArrayList** object in the same way that you access arrays. You can also use **ArrayList** methods to add elements to or remove elements from an **ArrayList**. To decrease the capacity of an **ArrayList**, you can call the **TrimToSize** method or explicitly set the **Capacity** property.

Use the **Add** method to add items to an **ArrayList**.

You can also use **foreach** to iterate over items in an **ArrayList**.

Note that **ArrayList** elements are objects, such as **System.Object**, so when you retrieve the elements from the list, you most likely must perform type conversion.

Methods

Method	Use
Add	Adds an object to the end of the ArrayList.
Remove	Removes the first occurrence of a specific object from the ArrayList.
Clear	Removes all elements from the ArrayList.
Insert	Inserts an element into the ArrayList at the specified index.
TrimToSize	Sets the capacity to the actual number of elements in the ArrayList.
Sort	Sorts the elements in the ArrayList.
Reverse	Reverses the elements in the ArrayList.

Example

The following code shows how to use an **ArrayList**. Note the following points:

- You must include the **System.Collections** namespace.

- The ArrayList (**theAnimals**) is initialized without specifying its size, because it will grow as needed.

- The **Add** and **Insert** methods are used to add elements to the array. This is the difference between arrays and ArrayLists.

- In both of the places where elements are retrieved from the ArrayList, they must be converted to the type of the variable to which they are being assigned.

- You can access the elements of the ArrayList by using the index operator [].

```csharp
using System;
using System.Collections;

namespace ArrayListExample {
  public class Zoo {
      private ArrayList theAnimals;
      public ArrayList ZooAnimals {
          get {
              return theAnimals;
          }
      }
      public Animal this[int i] {
          get {
              return (Animal) theAnimals[i];
          }
          set {
              theAnimals[i] = value;
          }
      }
      public Zoo() {
          theAnimals = new ArrayList();
      }
  }

  public class ZooKeeper {
      static void Main(string[] args) {
          Zoo myZoo = new Zoo();
          myZoo.ZooAnimals.Add( new Lion() );
          myZoo.ZooAnimals.Add( new Elephant() );
          myZoo.ZooAnimals.Insert( 1, new Lion() );

          Animal a = myZoo[0];
          myZoo[1] = new Antelope();
      }
  }

  public abstract class Animal {
      abstract public void Eat();
  }

  public class Lion : Animal {
      public override void Eat() { }
  }

  public class Elephant : Animal {
      public override void Eat() { }
  }

  public class Antelope : Animal {
      public override void Eat() { }
  }
}
```

The preceding code is available on the Student Materials compact disc in the
ArrayListExample.sln file in the Samples\Mod05\ArrayList folder.

How to Use Queues and Stacks

- ■ **Queues: first-in, first-out**
  - ● Enqueue places objects in the queue
  - ● Dequeue removes objects from the queue
- ■ **Stacks: last-in, first-out**
  - ● Push places objects on the stack
  - ● Pop removes objects from the stack
  - ● Count gets the number of objects contained in a stack or queue

Introduction

Queue objects and **Stack** objects are collection objects in the **System.Collections** namespace. The **Queue** class tracks objects on a first-in, first-out basis. The **Stack** class tracks objects on a first-in, last-out basis. By using the public methods of both **Queue** and **Stack** classes, you can move objects to different locations.

Using queues

The table below shows some of the public methods of the **Queue** class and a description of how they move objects:

Public methods	Description
Enqueue-Queue	Adds an object to the end of the **Queue**.
Dequeue-Queue	Removes and returns the object at the beginning of the **Queue**.

Example

The following example shows how to use a **Queue** object to handle messages. The **Messenger** class in this code calls the **SendMessage** method to send messages in the sequence "One", "Two", "Three", and "Four". The **Queue** object places the messages in the buffer by using the **Enqueue** method. When it is ready to receive the messages, it writes them to the console; in this case, by calling the **Dequeue** method.

```
using System;
using System.Collections;

namespace QueueExample {
  class Message {
      private string messageText;
      public Message (string s) {
          messageText = s;
      }
      public override string ToString() {
          return messageText;
      }
  }

  class Buffer {
      private Queue  messageBuffer;
      public void SendMessage( Message m ) {
          messageBuffer.Enqueue( m );
      }
      public void ReceiveMessage( ) {
          Message m = (Message) messageBuffer.Dequeue();
          Console.WriteLine( m.ToString() );
      }
      public Buffer() {
          messageBuffer = new Queue();
      }
  }

  class Messenger {
      static void Main(string[] args) {
          Buffer buf = new Buffer();
          buf.SendMessage( new Message("One") );
          buf.SendMessage( new Message("Two") );
          buf.ReceiveMessage ();
          buf.SendMessage( new Message("Three") );
          buf.ReceiveMessage ();
          buf.SendMessage( new Message("Four") );
          buf.ReceiveMessage ();
          buf.ReceiveMessage ();
      }
  }
}
```

The preceding code produces the following output:

```
One
Two
Three
Four
```

The preceding code is available on the Student Materials compact disc in the
Queues.sln file in the Samples\Mod05\Queue folder.

Using stacks

The following table shows some of the public methods of the **Stack** class and a description of how they move objects to different locations.

Public methods	Description
Count	Gets the number of objects contained in a stack.
Push	Inserts an object at the top of the stack.
Pop	Removes and returns the object at the top of the stack.

Example

The following code uses a **Stack** object instead of a **Queue** object. Note that the messages are added by using the **Push** method and removed by using the **Pop** method.

```csharp
using System;
using System.Collections;

namespace StacksExample {
  class Message {
      private string messageText;
      public Message (string s) {
          messageText = s;
      }
      public override string ToString() {
          return messageText;
      }
  }

  class Buffer {
      private Stack  messageBuffer;
      public void SendMessage( Message m ) {
          messageBuffer.Push( m );
      }
      public void ReceiveMessage( ) {
          Message m = (Message) messageBuffer.Pop();
          Console.WriteLine( m.ToString() );
      }
      public Buffer() {
          messageBuffer = new Stack();
      }
  }

  class Messenger {
      static void Main(string[] args) {
          Buffer buf = new Buffer();
          buf.SendMessage( new Message("One") );
          buf.SendMessage( new Message("Two") );
          buf.ReceiveMessage ();
          buf.SendMessage( new Message("Three") );
          buf.ReceiveMessage ();
          buf.SendMessage( new Message("Four") );
          buf.ReceiveMessage ();
          buf.ReceiveMessage ();
      }
  }
}
```

The preceding code produces the following output:

```
Two
Three
Four
One
```

This code is available on the Student Materials compact disc in the Stacks.sln file in the Samples\Mod05\Stack folder.

How to Use Hash Tables

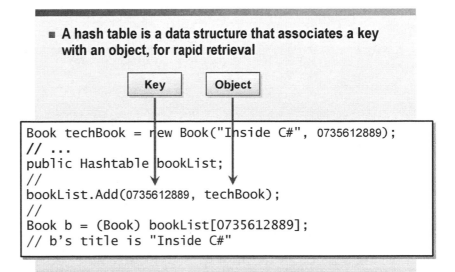

- A hash table is a data structure that associates a key with an object, for rapid retrieval

```
Book techBook = new Book("Inside C#", 0735612889);
// ...
public Hashtable bookList;
//
bookList.Add(0735612889, techBook);
//
Book b = (Book) bookList[0735612889];
// b's title is "Inside C#"
```

Introduction

A hash table is a data structure that is designed for fast retrieval. It does this by associating a key with each object that you store in the table. When you use this key to retrieve a value, the hash table can quickly locate the value.

Methods

Use a hash table when the data that you want to manage has some attribute that can act as the key. For example, if you are representing customers at a bank, you can use their taxpayer ID or their name. Or, a car rental company can use the rental agreement number as the key to the customer record.

In the .NET Framework, you can create hash tables by using the **Hashtable** class. After you have created a **Hashtable** object, you can use the **Add** method to add entries to it. The method takes two parameters, the key and the value, as shown in the following example:

```
myHashTable.Add( rentalAgreementNumber, someCustomerRecord );
```

You can retrieve objects from a **Hashtable** object by using the index operator and the key value, as shown in the following code.

```
Customer cr = (Customer) myHashTable[rentalAgreementNumber];
```

When you select the key value, choose one that is as short as possible and that will not change over the life of the object.

Example

The following example maintains a list of books by using the ISBN number as the key. Remember that the **Hashtable** class stores the data as type **Object**, so it is necessary to convert the retrieved object to the correct type before use.

```csharp
using System;
using System.Collections;

namespace HashExample {

    // A library contains a list of books.
    class Library {
        public Hashtable bookList;
        public Library() {
            bookList = new Hashtable();
        }
    }

    // Books are placed in the library
    class Book {
        public Book( string t, int n) {
            Title = t; ISBN = n;
        }
        public string Title;
        public int ISBN;
    }

    class ClassMain {
        static void Main(string[] args) {
            Book b1 = new Book("Programming Microsoft Windows with C#", 0735613702 );
            Book b2 = new Book("Inside C#", 0735612889 );
            Book b3 = new Book("Microsoft C# Language Specifications", 0735614482 );
            Book b4 = new Book("Microsoft Visual C# .NET Lang. Ref.", 0735615543 );

            Library myReferences = new Library();
            myReferences.bookList.Add(b1.ISBN, b1);
            myReferences.bookList.Add(b2.ISBN, b2);
            myReferences.bookList.Add(b3.ISBN, b3);
            myReferences.bookList.Add(b4.ISBN, b4);

            Book b = (Book) myReferences.bookList[0735612889];
            Console.WriteLine( b.Title );
        }
    }
}
```

The preceding code is available on the Student Materials compact disc in the HashExample.sln file in the Samples\Mod05\Hashtable folder.

Practice: Creating and Using Collections

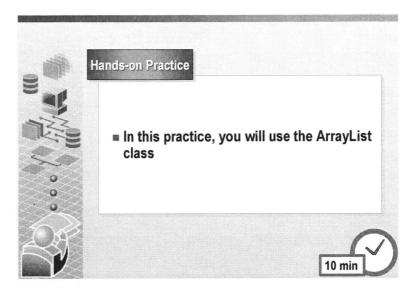

The **Zoo** class uses an object of type ArrayList to maintain a list of **Animal** objects. You will add missing code to initialize the list and to add animals to the list.

The solution for this practice is located in *install_folder*\Practices\Mod05\Collections_Solution \Collections.sln. Start a new instance of Visual Studio .NET before opening the solution.

Tasks	Detailed steps
1. Start Visual Studio. NET, and then open *install_folder* \Practices\Mod05\Collections \Collections.sln.	a. Start a new instance of Visual Studio .NET. b. On the **Start Page**, click **Open Project**. c. In the **Open Project** dialog box, browse to *install_folder*\Practices \Mod05\Collections, click **Collections.sln**, and then click **Open**. d. In Solution Explorer, click **Form1.cs**, and then press F7 to open the Code Editor.
2. Review the Task List.	a. On the **View** menu, point to **Show Tasks**, and then click **All**. b. Review the tasks in the Task List.
3. Create the ArrayList.	a. Double-click the task **TODO: Instantiate the ArrayList**. b. Use the **new** keyword to create the ArrayList.

Tasks	Detailed steps
4. Ensure that the indexer returns an **Animal** type.	▪ Double-click the task **TODO: Fix the return type**, and return an **Animal** object from the **get** block in the indexer.
5. Implement the **Add** method in the **Zoo** class.	a. Double-click the task **TODO: Implement the Add method**. b. Write an **Add** method that adds an animal to the ArrayList.
6. Test your application.	▪ Press F5 to test your application. Fix any problems.
7. Quit Visual Studio .NET, saving your solution.	a. On the **File** menu, click **Save All**. b. On the **File** menu, click **Exit**.

Lesson: Using Interfaces

- ■ **What Is an Interface?**
- ■ **How to Use an Interface**
- ■ **How to Work with Objects That Implement Interfaces**
- ■ **How to Inherit Multiple Interfaces**
- ■ **Interfaces and the .NET Framework**

Introduction

This lesson describes why interfaces are an important part of C# programming and explains how to implement interfaces in a C# application. This lesson explains how to work with objects that implement interfaces and how to implement multiple inheritances. How interfaces work in the .NET Framework is also covered in this lesson.

Lesson objectives

After completing this lesson, you will be able to:

- ■ Describe an interface.
- ■ Work with objects that implement interfaces.
- ■ Use interfaces to implement multiple inheritance.

Lesson agenda

This lesson includes the following topics and activity:

- ■ What Is an Interface?
- ■ How to Use an Interface
- ■ How to Work with Objects That Implement Interfaces
- ■ How to Inherit Multiple Interfaces
- ■ Interfaces and the .NET Framework
- ■ Practice: Using Interfaces

What Is an Interface?

An interface:

- **Is a reference type that defines a contract**

- **Specifies the members that must be supplied by classes or interfaces that implement the interface**

- **Can contain methods, properties, indexers, events**

- **Does not provide implementations for the members**

- **Can inherit from zero or more interfaces**

Introduction

An interface is in some ways like an abstract class. It defines a set of methods, properties, indexers, and events, just like any other class. However, it provides no implementation. The class that inherits the interface must provide the implementation.

Definition

Interface is a reference type that defines a contract in that a class that implements an interface must implement every aspect of that interface exactly as it is defined. Like classes, interfaces can contain methods, properties, indexers, and events as members. Other types implement an interface to guarantee that they support certain operations. The interface specifies the members that must be supplied by classes or other interfaces that implement it. Providing an implementation of the methods, properties, indexers, and events that are declared by the interface is called *implementing* the interface.

Although C# imposes a single inheritance rule for classes, the language is designed so that a class can inherit multiple interfaces.

Design considerations

A well-designed interface combines a set of closely related features that define a specific behavior. When an object uses this interface, it implements that behavior.

You can develop enhanced implementations for your interfaces without jeopardizing existing code, thus minimizing compatibility problems. You can also add new features at any time by developing additional interfaces and implementations.

Interface invariance

Although interface implementations can evolve, interfaces themselves cannot be changed after they are published. This is called *interface invariance*. Changes to a published interface may break existing code. When an interface needs enhancement, you must create a new interface.

You are less likely to make errors when you design an interface than when you create a large inheritance tree. If you start with a small number of interfaces, you can have parts of a system running relatively quickly. The ability to evolve the system by adding interfaces allows you to gain the advantages that object-oriented programming is intended to provide.

Purpose

There are several reasons that you may want to use interfaces instead of class inheritance:

- Interfaces are better suited to situations in which your applications require many possibly unrelated object types to provide certain functionality.

- Interfaces permit polymorphism between classes with different base classes.

- Interfaces are more flexible than base classes because you can define a single implementation that can implement multiple interfaces.

- Interfaces are better in situations in which you do not need to inherit implementation from a base class.

- Interfaces are useful in cases where you cannot use class inheritance.

How to Use an Interface

- An interface defines the same functionality and behavior to unrelated classes

- Declare an interface

- Implement an interface

```
interface ICarnivore {
      bool IsHungry { get; }
      Animal Hunt();
      void Eat(Animal victim);
}
```

Introduction

Interfaces define a standard set of properties, methods, indexers, and events that are found in any class that implements the interface. As such, interfaces are useful when you want to maintain the same functionality and behavior in unrelated classes.

Declaring an interface

You use the **interface** keyword to declare an interface. The syntax is:

```
[attributes] [access-modifier] interface interface-name
[:base-list] { interface-body }
```

Example

The following example defines an interface named **ICarnivore** with one method and one property. The class that implements this interface must implement the **EatMeat** method and the **IsHungry** property. The compiler enforces this implementation.

```
interface ICarnivore {
  bool    IsHungry { get; }
  Animal  Hunt();
  void    Eat(Animal victim);
}
```

If you want the user of the interface to be able to set the **IsHungry** property, define it as follows:

```
bool IsHungry { get; set; }
```

Note   Interface names normally start with an upper case **I**. The language does not enforce this, but it is a good practice.

Implementing an interface

To implement a specific interface, a class must inherit that interface. In the following example, the **Lion** class implements the **ICarnivore** interface.

```
public class Lion: ICarnivore {
  private bool hungry;
  public bool IsHungry {
      get {
          return hungry;
      }
  }

  public Animal Hunt() {
      // hunt and capture implementation
      // return animal object
  }

  public void Eat( Animal victim ) {
      // implementation
  }
}
```

The preceding code defines the **Lion** class as having the behaviors of the **ICarnivore** interface. The primary benefit of this approach is that any other object that can work with objects that implement the **ICarnivore** interface can now work with your object.

The class that implements an interface can be a derived class that includes some unique class members. The following example shows a **Lion** class that inherits the **Animal** class and implements the **ICarnivore** interface.

The following example is also provided on the Student Materials compact disc in the Carnivore.sln file in the Samples\Mod05\Interfaces folder.

```csharp
Using System;

namespace LearningCSharp {

    interface ICarnivore {
        bool IsHungry { get; }
        Animal Hunt();
        void Eat(Animal victim);
    }

    public abstract class Animal {
        public abstract void Sleep();
    }

    public class Antelope: Animal {
        public override void Sleep() { }
    }

    public class Lion: Animal, ICarnivore {

        public Lion() {
            hungry = true;
        }

        // ICarnivore implementation
        private bool hungry;
        public bool IsHungry {
            get {
                return hungry;
            }
        }

        public Animal Hunt( ) {
            // hunt and capture implementation
            return new Antelope();
        }

        public void Eat( Animal prey ) {
            // implementation
            Console.WriteLine("Lion is no longer hungry");
        }

        // Inherited from base class
        public override void Sleep() {
            // sleeping
        }

        public void JoinPride() {
            // Join with a Pride of other Lions
        }
    }
```

Code continued on the following page.

```csharp
class Tester {
    static void Main(string[] args) {
        Lion aLion = new Lion();
        Antelope a = new Antelope();

        // carnivore-like behavior
        if ( aLion.IsHungry ) {
            Animal victim = aLion.Hunt();
            if ( victim != null ) {
                aLion.Eat( victim );
            }
        }

        // Lion specific
        aLion.JoinPride();

        // Animal behavior
        aLion.Sleep();
    }
}
```

How to Work with Objects That Implement Interfaces

- **is**

```
if ( anAnimal is ICarnivore ) {
    ICarnivore meatEater = (ICarnivore) anAnimal;
    Animal prey = meatEater.Hunt();
    meatEater.Eat( prey );
}
```

- **as**

```
ICarnivore meatEater = anAnimal as ICarnivore;
if ( meatEater != null ) {
    Animal prey = meatEater.Hunt();
    meatEater.Eat( prey );
}
```

```
// is and as with an object
if ( prey is Antelope ) { ... }
```

Introduction

At run time, your application may not know if an object implements a certain interface. You can use the **is** and **as** keywords to determine whether an object implements a specific interface.

Example

For example, you may want to know whether the objects in the preceding examples implement the **ICarnivore** or **IHerbivore** interface, so that you can call only the **GatherFood** method for the animals that are herbivores:

```
interface ICarnivore {
    bool IsHungry { get; }
    Animal Hunt();
    void Eat(Animal victim);
}
interface IHerbivore {
    bool Hungry { get; }
    void GatherFood();
}

public class Chimpanzee: Animal, IHerbivore, ICarnivore {
    // implement members of IHerbivore and ICarnivore
}
public class Lion: Animal, ICarnivore {
    // implement members of ICarnivore
}
public class Antelope: Animal, IHerbivore {
    // implement members of IHerbivore
}
public class elephant: Animal, IHerbivore {
    // implement members of IHerbivore
}
```

Suppose that you have an ArrayList **zoo** that contains objects that are derived from the **Animal** class, some of which are **Lion**, which implements **ICarnivore**, **Antelope**, which implements **IHerbivore** and others such as **Elephant**. To discover if the animal implements **IHerbivore**, use the **is** keyword.

After you determine that the object implements the interface, you must obtain a reference to the interface. To obtain a reference to the interface, you can cast to the interface, as shown in the following example, where **someAnimal** is cast to type **IHerbivore** as it is assigned to **veggie**.

```
foreach ( Animal someAnimal in zoo ) {
  if ( someAnimal is IHerbivore ) {
      IHerbivore veggie = (IHerbivore) someAnimal;
      veggie.GatherFood();
  }
}
```

Note that when the application tries to perform a type cast, it checks to make sure that it will succeed. In the preceding example, checking is performed twice, because the **is** operator also checks the type of **someAnimal**. Because this is a fairly common situation, C# provides a way to avoid the double check, by using the **as** operator.

The **as** operator combines the check with the type cast, allowing you to rewrite the preceding code as follows:

```
foreach ( Animal someAnimal in zoo ) {
  IHerbivore veggie = someAnimal as IHerbivore;
  if ( veggie != null ) {
      veggie.EatPlant();
  }
}
```

Using is and as with other types

Note that the **is** and **as** operators work with other types. You can use them to determine the type of a class at run time. For example, the **Eat** method can be rewritten as follows:

```
public void Eat( Animal prey ) {
  // implementation
  if ( prey is Antelope ) {
      Console.WriteLine("Favorite meal");
  }
  Console.WriteLine("Lion is no longer hungry");
}
```

How to Inherit Multiple Interfaces

```
class Chimpanzee: Animal, ICarnivore, IHerbivore { ... }
```

- **Interfaces should describe a type of behavior**
- **Examples:**
  - Lion is-a-kind-of Animal; Lion has Carnivore behavior
  - Shark is-a-kind-of Animal; has Carnivore behavior
  - Derive Lion and Shark from abstract class Animal
  - Implement Carnivore behavior in an Interface

Introduction

A class can inherit multiple interfaces. Interfaces can also inherit from one or more interfaces.

Inheriting multiple interfaces

To implement multiple interface inheritance, you list the interfaces in a comma-separated list, as shown in the following example:

```
class Chimpanzee: Animal, ICarnivore, IHerbivore { ... }
```

The **Chimpanzee** class must provide the implementation of all of the members of **ICarnivore** and of **IHerbivore**, as shown in the following code:

```
interface ICarnivore {
  bool IsHungry { get; }
  Animal Hunt();
  void Eat(Animal victim);
}

interface IHerbivore {
    bool IsHungry { get; }
    void GatherFood();
}
```

Interfaces inheriting interfaces

An interface can inherit from other interfaces. Unlike classes, interfaces can inherit more than one other interface. To inherit more than one interface, the interface identifier is followed by a colon and a comma-separated list of base interface identifiers. An interface inherits all members of its base interfaces and the user of the interface must implement all the members of all the inherited interfaces.

For example, if an **IOmnivore** interface inherits both **ICarnivore** and **IHerbivore**, any class that implements **IOmnivore** must write an implementation of **IsHungry**, **Hunt()**, **Eat(Animal)**, and **GatherFood()**, as shown in the following code:

```
interface ICarnivore {
  bool IsHungry { get; }
  Animal Hunt();
  void Eat(Animal victim);
}
interface IHerbivore {
  bool IsHungry { get; }
  void GatherFood();
}

interface IOmnivore: IHerbivore, ICarnivore {
}
```

You can extend the **IOmnivore** interface by adding another member, as shown in the following code:

```
interface IOmnivore: IHerbivore, ICarnivore {
  void DecideWhereToGoForDinner();
}
```

Explicit interface implementation

In the preceding example, it is not possible to determine whether the **IsHungry** property in the **Chimpanzee** class implements **IHerbivore.IsHungry** or **ICarnivore.IsHungry**. To make this implementation explicit, you must declare the interface in the declaration, as shown in the following example:

```
public class Chimpanzee: Animal, IHerbivore, ICarnivore {
...// implement other interface members
  bool ICarnivore.IsHungry {
      get {
          return false;
      }
  }

  bool IHerbivore.IsHungry {
      get {
          return false;
      }
  }
}
```

Access modifiers are not permitted on explicit interface implementations, so to access these members you must convert the object to the interface type, as shown in the following code:

```
Chimpanzee chimp = new Chimpanzee();
IHerbivore vchimp = (IHerbivore) chimp;
bool hungry = vchimp.IsHungry;
```

Interfaces vs. abstract classes

Deciding whether to design your functionality as an interface or an abstract class is sometimes difficult. An abstract class is a class that cannot be instantiated, but must be inherited from. An abstract class may be fully implemented, but is more usually partially implemented or not implemented at all, thereby encapsulating common functionality for inherited classes.

An interface, by contrast, is a totally abstract set of members that can be thought of as defining a contract for conduct. The implementation of an interface is left completely to the developer.

Abstract classes provide a simple and easy way to manage versions of your components. By updating the base class, all inheriting classes are automatically updated with the change. Interfaces, on the other hand, cannot be changed after they are created. If an interface needs revisions, you must create a new interface.

Recommendations

The following recommendations suggest when to use an interface or an abstract class to provide polymorphism for your components:

When you:	Use:
Create multiple versions of your component	Abstract class
Create a function that is useful across a wide range of disparate objects	Interface
Design small, concise bits of functionality	Interface
Design large functional units	Abstract class

Note   Abstract classes should be used primarily for objects that are closely related, whereas interfaces are best suited for providing common functionality to unrelated classes.

Interfaces and the .NET Framework

- **Allows you to make your objects behave like .NET Framework objects**

- **Example: Interfaces used by Collection classes**

  - ICollection, IComparer, IDictionary, IDictionary Enumerator, IEnumerable, IEnumerator, IHashCodeProvider, IList

```
public class Zoo : IEnumerable {
. . .
public IEnumerator GetEnumerator() {
      return (IEnumerator)new ZooEnumerator(
this );
}
```

Introduction

Interfaces are used in many places in the .NET Framework. You can enhance the usefulness of classes that you develop by implementing appropriate interfaces.

One area of the .NET Framework that makes extensive use of interfaces is the set of classes in the **System.Collections** namespace.

Definitions

Collection classes use the following interfaces:

ICollection	Defines size, enumerators, and synchronization methods for all collections.
IComparer	Exposes a method that compares two objects.
IDictionary	Represents key-value pairs, as used by hash tables.
IDictionaryEnumerator	Enumerates the elements in a dictionary (a hashtable is a dictionary).
IEnumerable	Exposes the enumerator, for iteration over a collection.
IEnumerator	Supports iteration over a collection. **IEnumerator** is the base interface for all enumerators. Enumerators only allow reading the data in the collection. Enumerators cannot be used to modify the underlying collection.
IHashCodeProvider	Defines a method for getting a hash code.
IList	Supports array-like indexing.
ICloneable	Supports cloning, which creates a new instance of a class with the same value as an existing instance.

Collection requirements   By implementing specific interfaces, you can make your objects behave like collection objects, as shown in the following two examples.

Example 1   Suppose that you have a class that maintains a set of objects as follows:

```
public class Zoo {
  private int insertPosition = 0;
  private Animal[] animals;

  public Zoo() {
      animals = new Animal[100];
  }

  public void Add(Animal a) {
      if ( insertPosition >= 100 ) {
          return;
      }
      animals[insertPosition++] = a;
  }
}
```

The user of the class may find it useful to use the **foreach** statement to iterate through the elements of your class.

To iterate through a collection, a class (or struct or interface) must implement the **IEnumerable** interface. The **IEnumerator** interface contains one instance method named **GetEnumerator** that returns an object that implements **IEnumerator**.

A class that implements **IEnumerator** must contain:

- A property named **Current** that returns the current element of the collection.

- A **bool** method named **MoveNext** that increments an item counter and returns **true** if there are more items in the collection.

- A void method named **Reset** that resets the item counter.

Example 2

In this example, animals are added to a **Zoo** object. The **Zoo** object implements the **IEnumerable** interface:

```
public class Zoo : IEnumerable {
. . .
public IEnumerator GetEnumerator() {
  return (IEnumerator) new ZooEnumerator( this );
}
```

The **GetEnumerator** method returns an instance of **ZooEnumerator**. The **ZooEnumerator** class provides the specific **IEnumerator** implementation for moving through the data structure that contains the animals in the zoo. Although this data structure is an array, the programmer can use any data structure to maintain the **Animal** objects.

Because the **ZooEnumerator** class is so closely linked to the **Zoo** class, it is declared in the **Zoo** class. The full code sample is included at the end of this topic.

```
private class ZooEnumerator : IEnumerator {
  private Zoo z;
  private int currentPosition = -1;

  public ZooEnumerator(Zoo aZoo) {
      z = aZoo;
  }
. . .
}
```

The constructor simply saves the reference to the **Zoo** object **aZoo** that is passed in as a parameter. Note that **currentPosition** is set to **-1**. This is because the **MoveNext** method will increment this to zero and then check to see if this is a valid position in the data.

```
public bool MoveNext() {
  ++currentPosition;
  if ( currentPosition < z.insertPosition ) {
      return true;
  }
  return false;
}
```

z.insertPosition is the first unassigned position. The code returns **false** if the current position moves beyond this point, and this will cause the **foreach** loop that is using your **Zoo** class collection to exit.

The **Current** property is used to retrieve the current element:

```
public object Current {
  get {
      return z.animals[currentPosition];
  }
}
```

And the **Reset** method simply resets **currentPosition**:

```
public void Reset() {
  currentPosition = -1;
}
```

The preceding code implements the **IEnumerable** and **IEnumerator** interfaces, and it is now possible to iterate through **Zoo** with the **foreach** statement:

```
Zoo z = new Zoo();
z.Add( new Antelope() );
z.Add( new Elephant() );
z.Add( new Antelope() );

foreach ( Animal a in z ) {
  a.Sleep();
  Console.WriteLine( a.ToString() );
}
```

The complete code follows:

```csharp
using System;
using System.Collections;

namespace LearningCSharp {
  public abstract class Animal {
      public abstract void Sleep();
  }

  public class Elephant : Animal {
      public override void Sleep() { }
  }

  public class Antelope : Animal {
      public override void Sleep() { }
  }

  public class Zoo : IEnumerable {
      private int insertPosition = 0;
      private Animal[] animals;

      // Constructor
      public Zoo() {
          animals = new Animal[100];
      }

      // public methods
      public void Add(Animal a) {
          if ( insertPosition >= 100 ) {
              return;
          }
          animals[insertPosition++] = a;
      }

      // IEnumerable
      public IEnumerator GetEnumerator() {
          return (IEnumerator)new ZooEnumerator( this );
      }

      // ZooEnumerator as private class
      private class ZooEnumerator : IEnumerator {
          private Zoo z;
          private int currentPosition = -1;
```

Code continued on the following page.

```
                    public ZooEnumerator(Zoo aZoo) {
                        z = aZoo;
                    }

                    // IEnumerator
                    public object Current {
                        get {
                            return z.animals[currentPosition];
                        }
                    }
                    public bool MoveNext() {
                        ++currentPosition;
                        if ( currentPosition < z.insertPosition ) {
                            return true;
                        }
                        return false;
                    }
                    public void Reset() {
                        currentPosition = -1;
                    }
                }
            }

            class Tester {
                static void Main(string[] args) {
                    Zoo z = new Zoo();
                    z.Add( new Antelope() );
                    z.Add( new Elephant() );
                    z.Add( new Antelope() );

                    foreach ( Animal a in z ) {
                        a.Sleep();
                        Console.WriteLine(a.ToString());
                    }
                }
            }
        }
```

This preceding code produces the following output:

```
LearningCSharp.Antelope
LearningCSharp.Elephant
LearningCSharp.Antelope
```

This code is available on the Student Materials compact disc in the Interfaces2.sln file in the Samples\Mod05\Interfaces2 folder.

Practice: Using Interfaces

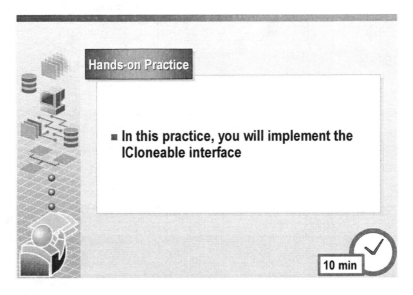

In this practice, you will add the **ICloneable** interface to the **Zoo** class. The **ICloneable** interface consists of one method: **object Clone()**. The Clone method creates and returns a copy of an object.

The solution for this practice is located in *install_folder*\Practices\Mod05\Interfaces_Solution \Interfaces.sln. Start a new instance of Visual Studio .NET before opening the solution.

Tasks	Detailed steps
1. Start Visual Studio .NET, and then open *install_folder*\Practices \Mod05\Interfaces\Interfaces.sln.	a. Start a new instance of Visual Studio .NET. b. On the **Start Page**, click **Open Project**. c. In the **Open Project** dialog box, browse to *install_folder* \Practices\Mod05\Interfaces, click **Interfaces.sln**, and then click **Open**. d. In Solution Explorer, click **Form1.cs**, and then press F7 to open the Code Editor.
2. Review the Task List.	a. On the **View** menu, point to **Show Tasks**, and then click **All**. b. Review the tasks in the Task List.
3. Add the **ICloneable** interface reference to the class. Compile your application and read the error message.	a. Double-click **TODO: State that this class implements the ICloneable Interface**. b. Add the **ICloneable** interface to the class definition. c. Press F5 to test your application. Read the error message. d. On the **View** menu, point to **Show Tasks**, and then click **All**.

Tasks	Detailed steps
4. Add the **Clone** method to the **Zoo** class.	a. Double-click **TODO: Implement ICloneable**. b. Remove the comments from the **Clone** method. c. Note that the **Clone** method creates and returns a new **Zoo** object.
5. Test your implementation of **ICloneable** by declaring a new **Zoo** object **zooTwo**, and cloning **myZoo**.	a. Double-click **TODO: Test ICloneable**. b. Uncomment the call to **Clone**, and to **DisplayZooInformation**. c. Press F5 to test your application. Fix any problems.
6. Quit Visual Studio .NET, saving your solution.	a. On the **File** menu, click **Save All**. b. On the **File** menu, click **Exit**.

Lesson: Using Exception Handling

- ■ **How to Use Exception Handling**
- ■ **How to Throw Exceptions**

Introduction

This lesson describes error handling using exception handlers, including user exceptions and basic exception handling syntax, such as **try**, **catch**, and **finally**. It also explains how to use exception types. The lesson also covers throwing exceptions by using the **throw** keyword.

Lesson objectives

After completing this lesson, you will be able to:

- ■ Explain exception handling.
- ■ Use the **throw** keyword.
- ■ Use the **try**, **catch**, and **finally** keywords.
- ■ Catch specific exception types.

Lesson agenda

This lesson includes the following topics and activity:

- ■ How to Use Exception Handling
- ■ How to Throw Exceptions
- ■ Practice: Using Exception Handling

How to Use Exception Handling

- **Exception handling syntax**

```
try {
        // suspect code
}
catch {
        // handle exceptions
}
finally {
        // always do this
}
```

Introduction

An *exception* is any error condition or unexpected behavior that is encountered by an executing program. Exceptions can be raised because of a fault in your code or in code that you call, resources not being available, such as running out of memory or not being able to locate a particular file, or other unexpected conditions.

You should, of course, attempt to eliminate all bugs in your code. Exceptions are not designed to handle programming errors; they are designed to provide control in situations where there is a true exception to the expected behavior of the application. When possible, make every effort to avoid a condition that could throw an exception. Under normal circumstances, your application should not encounter any exceptions.

Note The code samples in this topic are intended to illustrate exception handling. As such, these samples do not try to anticipate and avoid error conditions.

Using try/catch to catch exceptions

The following examples represent situations that might cause exceptions:

Scenario	Solution
Opening a file	Before opening a file, check that the file exists and that you can open it.
Reading an XML document	You will normally read well-formed XML documents, but you should deal with the exceptional case where the document is not valid XML. This is a good example of where to rely on exception handling.
Accessing an invalid member of an array	If you are the user of the array, this is an application bug that you should eliminate. Therefore, you should not use exception handling to catch this exception.
Dividing a number by zero	This can normally be checked and avoided.
Converting between types using the **System.Convert** classes	With some checking, these can be avoided.

You can handle these error conditions by using **try**, **catch**, and **finally** keywords.

To write an exception handler, place the sections of code that may throw exceptions in a **try** block, and then place code that handles exceptions in a **catch** block. The **catch** block is a series of statements that begin with the **catch** keyword, followed by an exception type and an action to be taken.

Example

The following code shows a Microsoft Windows® text box named **numberOfTickets** into which the user types the number of tickets that they want to purchase. Text boxes provide access to their contents through the **Text** property, which is a **string** type, so the user input must be converted to an integer. The following code uses a byte to hold the number of tickets:

```
numberOfTickets = new TextBox();
...
byte tickets = Convert.ToByte(numberOfTickets.Text);
```

The **Convert.ToByte** method throws an exception, **System.FormatException** if the user enters a character string. The following code demonstrates how to handle this situation:

```
try {
  byte tickets = Convert.ToByte(numberOfTickets.Text);
}
catch {
  MessageBox.Show("Please enter a number");
}
```

The **try** block encloses the code that may throw an exception. The **catch** block catches all exceptions that are thrown in the **try** block, because **catch** does not specify the exception that it will handle.

Handling specific exceptions

You can also specify the type of the exception that you want to catch, as shown in the following code:

```
try {
  byte tickets = Convert.ToByte(numberOfTickets.Text);
}
catch (FormatException) {
  MessageBox.Show("Format Exception: please enter a number");
}
```

When the user enters text instead of numbers, a message box appears containing an appropriate message.

Multiple catch blocks

Suppose that the user wants to buy 400 tickets. This quantity exceeds the capacity of the byte, so a **System.OverflowException** is thrown. To handle the **OverflowException** and the **FormatException**, you must specify more than one **catch** block, as shown in the following example:

```
try {
  byte tickets = Convert.ToByte(numberOfTickets.Text);
}
catch (FormatException e) {
  MessageBox.Show("Format Exception: please enter a number");
}
catch (OverflowException e) {
  MessageBox.Show("Overflow: too many tickets");
}
```

When the user tries to purchase 400 tickets, the overflow message is displayed. When the user enters text, the format exception message is displayed.

Planning the catch sequence

The order in which the exceptions are listed is significant. For example, **System.DivideByZeroException** is derived from **System.ArithmeticException**. If you try to catch an ArithmeticException before a DivideByZeroException, the DivideByZeroException is not caught because the DivideByZeroException is a type of ArithmeticException—that is, it derived from ArithmeticException. Fortunately, the C# compiler checks for this situation and provides a warning message if you try to catch exceptions in an order that does not work.

Although these examples simply inform the user that the exception has occurred, in a real application you should make some attempt to correct the situation that caused the error. However, you should also keep the code in the **catch** block as small as possible to avoid the possibility of throwing another exception while handling the first.

Using the finally keyword

When an exception occurs, execution stops and control is given to the closest exception handler. This often means that lines of code that you expect to always be called are not executed. However, some resource cleanup, such as closing a file, must always be executed even if an exception is thrown. To accomplish this, you can use a **finally** block. A **finally** block is always executed, regardless of whether an exception is thrown.

```
FileStream xmlFile = null;
try {
  xmlFile = new FileStream("XmlFile.xml", FileMode.Open);
}
catch( System.IO.IOException e ) {
  return;
}
finally {
  if ( xmlFile != null ) {
      xmlFile.Close();
  }
}
```

In this example, the **finally** block is used to close the file, if it was open.

Scope of exception handlers

When an exception occurs, as shown in the following code, where **ReadSetupFile** does not have a **try/catch** block in the method, the application looks up through the stack for the first exception handler that can handle the current exception type. If you do not provide any exception handler, the runtime provides a handler as in the following code:

```
try {
      zoo.ReadSetupFile();
}
catch {
      // error handling
}
```

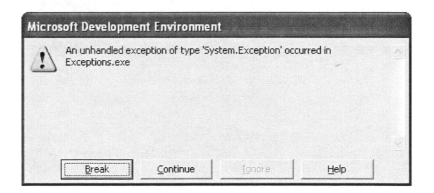

You may have seen this handler if any of your programs have ever thrown an exception.

How to Throw Exceptions

- **Throw keyword**
- **Exception handling strategies**
- **Exception types**
  - The predefined common language runtime exception classes

    Example: ArithmeticException, FileNotFoundException
  - User-defined exceptions

Introduction

Sometimes you may want to catch an exception, do some work to handle the exception, and then pass an exception on to the calling code. This is called *throwing an exception*. It is good coding practice to add information to an exception that is rethrown to provide more information when debugging.

You use the **throw** keyword to throw an exception, as shown in the following code:

```
Exception e = new Exception();
throw e;
```

The preceding code is equivalent to:

```
throw new Exception();
```

Exception handling strategies

There are several strategies for handling exceptions:

- You can decide to ignore an exception, relying instead on the caller to handle the exception. This strategy can leave your object in an incorrect state, but it is sometimes necessary.

- You can catch the exception, try to fix the error, ensuring that at least your object is in a known state, and then rethrow the exception. This strategy has the advantage of leaving your object in a usable state, but it does not give the caller much useful information.

- You can catch the exception and add information to it by throwing a new exception that wraps around the old exception. This strategy is preferable because your object can then provide additional information about the error.

System.Exception

Exceptions inherit from the **System.Exception** base class. There are two important classes that are derived from **System.Exception**:

- **System.SystemException** is the base class for exceptions that are defined by the system.

- **System.ApplicationException** is the base class for exceptions that are defined by applications.

Example 1

This example throws an exception if the contents of a text box cannot be converted to a number, and catches **FormatException**. If the problem occurred because the user did not type a value, it creates a new exception that wraps up the **FormatException**, and adds information.

```
private int ReadData() {
  byte tickets = 0;
  try {
      tickets = Convert.ToByte(textBox1.Text);
  }
  catch ( FormatException e ) {
      if ( textBox1.Text.Length == 0 ) {
          throw (new FormatException("No user input ", e));
      }
      else {
          throw e;
      }
  }
  return tickets;
}
```

In a real application, you check the user input rather than throwing an exception.

The user of the **ReadData** method can catch the new **FormatException** and retrieve the additional information provided by the object that threw the exception, as shown in the following code:

```
private void run_Click(object sender, System.EventArgs ea) {
  int tickets = 0;
  try {
      tickets = ReadData();
  }
  catch ( FormatException e ) {
      MessageBox.Show( e.Message + "\n" );
      MessageBox.Show( e.InnerException.Message );
  }
}
```

When the exception is caught by the **run_Click** method, **e** references the new **FormatException** object thrown in **ReadData**, so the value of **e.Message** is **No user input**. The property **e.InnerException** refers to the original exception, so the value of **e.InnerException.Message** is **Input string was not in a correct format**, which is the default message for **FormatException**.

This code sample is provided on the Student Materials compact disc in the Exception.sln file in the Samples\Mod05\Exception folder.

Throwing user-defined exceptions

You can create your own exception classes by deriving from the **Application.Exception** class. When creating your own exceptions, it is good coding practice to end the class name of the user-defined exception with the word "Exception".

Example 2

This example defines a new class named **TicketException** that is thrown when there is an error in the ticket ordering process. **TicketException** is derived from **ApplicationException**.

```
class TicketException: ApplicationException {
  private bool purchasedCompleted = false;
  public bool PurchaseWasCompleted {
      get {
          return purchasedCompleted;
      }
  }
  public TicketException( bool completed, Exception e )
                        : base ("Ticket Purchase Error", e ){
      purchasedCompleted = completed;
  }
}
```

The **ReadData** and run_**Click** methods can use **TicketException**:

```
private int ReadData() {
  byte tickets = 0;
  try {
      tickets = Convert.ToByte(textBox1.Text);
  }
  catch ( Exception e ) {
      // check if purchase was complete
      throw ( new TicketException( true, e ) );
  }
  return tickets;
}
```

```
private void run_Click(object sender, System.EventArgs ea) {
  int tickets = 0;
  try {
      tickets = ReadData();
  }
  catch ( TicketException e ) {
      MessageBox.Show( e.Message );
      MessageBox.Show( e.InnerException.Message );
  }
}
```

Typically, you should overload the constructor so that the user can provide more detailed information about the error.

When an error occurs, this sample produces the **Ticket Purchase Error** message, and also provides access to the original exception through the **InnerException** property.

This code sample is provided on the Student Materials compact disc in the UserException.sln file in the Samples\Mod05\UserException folder.

Practice: Using Exception Handling

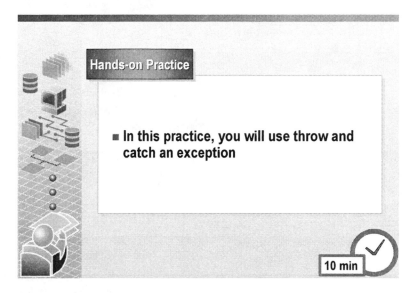

In this practice, you will use exception handling to prevent a run-time error from occurring when you attempt to access an invalid index of the **Zoo** class.

The solution for this practice is located in *install_folder*\Practices\Mod05\Exceptions_Solution \Exceptions.sln. Start a new instance of Visual Studio .NET before opening the solution.

Tasks	Detailed steps
1. Start Visual Studio .NET, and then open *install_folder* \Practices\Mod05\Exceptions \Exceptions.sln.	a. Start a new instance of Visual Studio .NET. b. On the **Start Page**, click **Open Project**. c. In the **Open Project** dialog box, browse to *install_folder*\Practices \Mod05\Exceptions, click **Exceptions.sln**, and then click **Open**. d. In Solution Explorer, click **Form1.cs**, and then press F7 to open the Code Editor.
2. Cause a run-time error by attempting to access an animal in the zoo that does not exist.	a. Double-click the task **TODO: catch the error thrown in this assignment.** The assignment **from myZoo[10]** throws an exception because the **myZoo** only has 3 elements. b. Press F5 to compile and run your application, and note the error message that results. c. You will receive a **System.ArgumentOutOfRangeException** exception, along with some explanatory text. *In the **Microsoft Development Environment** dialog box, you can click **Break** to debug your application. When you click **Break**, the line that threw the exception is displayed in the code window (the Zoo Indexer). To see the code that called the Indexer, in the **Call Stack** window, double-click the line immediately below the line that is highlighted with the green arrow. To access the **Call Stack** window, on the **Debug** menu, point to **Windows** and then click **Call Stack**, or press CTRL+ALT+C.*
3. Use a **try...catch** block to catch the ArgumentOutOfRangeException and use the following code to display your own message: `MessageBox.Show("Zoo access error");`	a. Enclose the **myZoo[10]** statement in a **try** block. b. Write a **catch** block that catches an ArgumentOutOfRangeException exception. c. In the **catch** block, use the following code to display a message box: `MessageBox.Show("Zoo access error");`
4. Test the application.	▪ Press F5 to test your application. Fix any problems.
5. Quit Visual Studio .NET, saving your solution.	a. On the **File** menu, click **Save All**. b. On the **File** menu, click **Exit**.

Lesson: Using Delegates and Events

- How to Create a Delegate
- What Is an Event?
- How to Write an Event Handler

Introduction

This lesson introduces delegates, describes the purpose and syntax of delegates, and explains how to create and use a delegate function. This lesson also introduces event handling and explains how events are handled in C#.

Lesson objectives

After completing this lesson, you will be able to:

- Describe a delegate.
- Create a delegate.
- Use a delegate.
- Describe an event.
- Write an event handler.

Lesson agenda

This lesson includes the following topics and activity:

- How to Create a Delegate
- What Is an Event?
- How to Write an Event Handler
- Practice: Declaring and Calling a Delegate

How to Create a Delegate

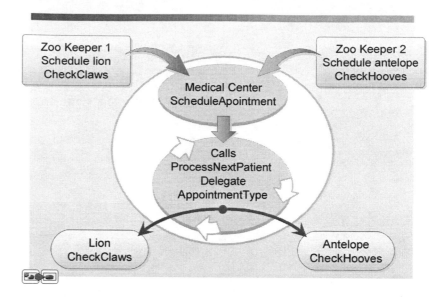

Introduction

A delegate is an object that contains a reference to a method.

Definition

A *delegate* is a variable, a reference type that can contain a reference to a method. Using delegates is useful when you know that your application must perform an action by calling a method; but, at compile time, you do not know what that action will be.

Delegates allow you to specify at runtime the method to be invoked. Delegates are object-oriented, type-safe, and secure.

Declaring a delegate

A delegate specifies the return type and parameters that each method must provide.

Example

The following example shows how to declare a delegate type for a method that takes a single argument of type **Image** and has a **void** return type:

```
delegate void ImageFunctionsDelegateType(Image i);
```

Instantiating a delegate

After you declare a delegate type, you can create a delegate object and associate it with a particular method. A new delegate object is created with the **new** operator.

For example, the **Invert** method is in the **ImageUtility** class, as shown in the following code:

```
class ImageUtility {
  void Invert( Image i ) {
      // inverts an image
  }
}
```

The class is instantiated, as shown in the following code:

```
ImageUtility utilities = new ImageUtility();
```

You create an instance of the delegate as shown in the following code:

```
ImageFunctionsDelegateType someUtility;
someUtility = new ImageFunctionsDelegateType(
utilities.Invert );
```

The preceding code initialized **someUtility**, which is an instance of the delegate type **ImageFunctionsDelegateType**. The **someUtility** variable is then initialized, like any other reference type. The parameter that is passed to the delegate constructor is the name of a method that can be called through the delegate. Note that this must have the same signature as the delegate.

Calling a delegate

When the **someUtility** method delegate instance is subsequently called, the actual method that is invoked is **utilities.Invert**.

```
this.someUtility( imageToBeProcessed );
```

A delegate does not need to know the class of the object that it references. A delegate can reference any object as long as the signature of the method matches the signature of the delegate.

Example

For example, The Zoo Medical Center creates a class that zookeepers use when they check the health of the animals. The medical checkup to be performed, such as a tooth check or a claw check, is specific to the animal and therefore is listed as part of the animal definition. The following example shows how the **MedicalCenter** class uses a delegate instance called **animalCheckup** to reference and call the method instance passed as a parameter to **ScheduleAppointment**.

1. Define the animals and include the information about the types of checkup they need:

```
public abstract class Animal { }

public class Antelope : Animal {
   public void CheckHooves() {
       Console.WriteLine("Schedule Hoof Checkup");
   }
}
public class Lion: Animal {
   public void CheckClaws() {
       Console.WriteLine("Schedule Claw Checkup");
   }
}
```

2. Define the delegate:

```
public delegate void AppointmentType();
```

The signature of the delegate matches the **CheckHooves** and **CheckClaws** methods.

3. Define the medical center:

```
public class MedicalCenter {
    private AppointmentType animalCheckup;

    public void ScheduleAppointment(AppointmentType a) {
        animalCheckup = a;
    }
    public void ProcessNextPatient() {
        animalCheckup();
    }
}
```

The **MedicalCenter** class has a private member **animalCheckup**, which is the delegate instance. The **ScheduleAppointment** method is called by the user of the **MedicalCenter** class to schedule an animal for a check-up or a medical procedure. It assigns the instance method passed in the **AppointmentType** parameter to **animalCheckup**.

To use this system, create or obtain a **MedicalCenter** object and some animals:

```
MedicalCenter animalHospital = new MedicalCenter();
Antelope bigMaleAntelope = new Antelope();
Lion notVeryBraveLion = new Lion();
```

4. Schedule a medical check-up.

```
animalHospital.ScheduleAppointment( new AppointmentType(
bigMaleAntelope.CheckHooves ) );
```

This code creates a new **AppointmentType** delegate instance that will call the **CheckHooves** method and passes it to the **MedicalCenter** object.

In this implementation, only one appointment is stored, and it can be processed by invoking:

```
animalHospital.ProcessNextPatient();
```

This code in turn calls **animalCheckup()**, which invokes the **CheckHooves** method.

In a more realistic implementation, the medical center may maintain a queue of animals that are expecting procedures, and the **ProcessNextPatient** method would dequeue animals when facilities became available, always calling the **animalCheckup** method to invoke the specific medical procedure for that animal.

The complete code sample follows:

```csharp
using System;

namespace DelegateExample {
  class Zoo {
      public abstract class Animal { }

      public class Antelope : Animal {
          public void CheckHooves() {
              Console.WriteLine("Schedule Hoof Checkup");
          }
      }
      public class Lion: Animal {
          public void CheckClaws() {
              Console.WriteLine("Schedule Claw Checkup");
          }
      }

      public class MedicalCenter {
          public delegate void AppointmentType();
          public AppointmentType animalCheckup;

          public void ScheduleAppointment(AppointmentType a) {
              animalCheckup = a;
          }
          public void ProcessNextPatient() {
              if ( animalCheckup != null ) {
                  animalCheckup();
              }
          }
      }

      static void Main(string[] args) {
          MedicalCenter animalHospital = new MedicalCenter();
          Lion notVeryBraveLion = new Lion();
          Antelope bigMaleAntelope = new Antelope();

          animalHospital.ScheduleAppointment( new
MedicalCenter.AppointmentType( bigMaleAntelope.CheckHooves )
);
          animalHospital.ProcessNextPatient();

          animalHospital.ScheduleAppointment ( new
MedicalCenter.AppointmentType( notVeryBraveLion.CheckClaws )
);

          animalHospital.ProcessNextPatient();
      }
  }
}
```

This code sample is provided on the Student Materials compact disc in the DelegateSample.sln file in the Samples\Mod05\DelegateSample folder.

Multicasting

In the preceding example, it is only possible to schedule one appointment at a time. To schedule two or more procedures for one animal, you could maintain a queue, or array, of the methods and call them in sequence. However, a delegate can call more that one method. This is called multicasting. The delegate maintains a list of methods that it calls in order. This list is called the delegate's *invocation list*.

Multicasting is used frequently in the .NET Framework to allow a user interface object to have multiple event handlers.

Syntax

To combine delegates, use the following syntax:

```
DelegateType d1 = d2 + d3;
```

When d2 and d3 are combined, the methods that they encapsulate are added to the d1's invocation list. Invoking d1 invokes both methods that are referenced in d2 and d3.

A more common way to add delegates is to use the += operator to add delegates. This syntax is used to add event handlers to Windows controls, as shown in the following example:

```
Button myButton.Click += new System.EventHandler(myAction);
```

You can also use – and -= to remove delegates as follows:

```
d1 -= d3;
```

This removes the last delegate from d1 that contains a method that matches the method *named* in d3. This means that you can also remove a delegate as follows:

```
myClass.d1 += new DelegateType ( myMethod );
. . .
d1 -= new DelegateType ( myMethod );
```

The removal statement removes a **myMethod** method from the invocation list.

Example

For example, the code in the Zoo Medical Center application can be modified so that one animal can be scheduled for multiple procedures, as shown in the following example. The following code invokes both **CheckHooves** and **TakeBloodSample** from one delegate. The methods simply write a string to the console.

```
public class Antelope : Animal {
  public void CheckHooves() {
      Console.WriteLine("Schedule Hoof Checkup");
  }
  public void TakeBloodSample() {
      Console.WriteLine("Schedule Blood Check");
  }
}
```

Then instantiate the **Antelope** object, just as before, but this time the **ScheduleAppointment** method is called twice.

```
Antelope bigMaleAntelope = new Antelope();

animalHospital.ScheduleAppointment( new
MedicalCenter.AppointmentType( bigMaleAntelope.CheckHooves )
);
animalHospital.ScheduleAppointment( new
MedicalCenter.AppointmentType( bigMaleAntelope.TakeBloodSample
) );
```

In the original **ScheduleAppointment** method, the **TakeBloodSample** method replaces the **CheckHooves** method in the delegate, so the **ScheduleAppointment** method must be modified slightly, as shown in the following code:

```
public void ScheduleAppointment(AppointmentType a) {
  animalCheckup += a
}
```

The **animalCheckup** delegate now adds the second delegate to itself. The **ProcessNextPatient** code is unchanged:

```
public void ProcessNextPatient() {
  if ( animalCheckup != null ) {
      animalCheckup();
  }
}
```

A single call to **ProcessNextPatient** produces the following output:

```
Schedule Hoof Checkup
Schedule Blood Check
```

What Is an Event?

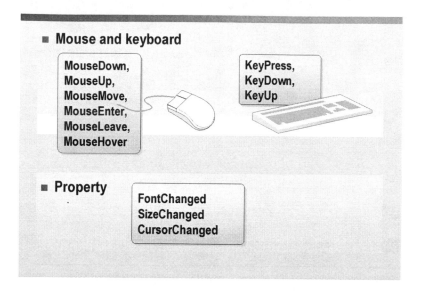

- **Mouse and keyboard**

  MouseDown,
  MouseUp,
  MouseMove,
  MouseEnter,
  MouseLeave,
  MouseHover

  KeyPress,
  KeyDown,
  KeyUp

- **Property**

  FontChanged
  SizeChanged
  CursorChanged

Introduction

When you create a Windows-based application or a Web application, you create an event-driven application. Event-driven applications execute code in response to an event. Each form that you create and control that you use exposes a predefined set of events that you can program against. When one of these events occurs and there is code in the associated event handler, that code is invoked.

Definition

An *event* is an action that you can respond to, or handle, in code. Events can be generated by a user action, such as clicking a button with the mouse or pressing a key. Events can also be programmatically generated. The primary use of multicasting is to handle events by using program code or the operating system.

Types of events

The types of events that are raised by an object vary, but many types of events are common to most controls. For example, most objects handle a **Click** event—when a user clicks a form, code in the **Click** event handler of the form is executed. The most commonly used events are keyboard, mouse, and property events. If your application supports drag-and-drop operations, it will handle drag-and-drop events.

Mouse and keyboard events

Several events are related to the user's use of the mouse and keyboard. Each of these events has an event handler for which you can write code in your Windows-based applications. These events include **MouseDown**, **MouseUp**, **MouseMove**, **MouseEnter**, **MouseLeave**, **MouseHover**, **KeyPress**, **KeyDown**, and **KeyUp**. The mouse-related event handlers receive an argument of type **EventArgs**, which contain data related to their events. The key-related event handlers receive an argument of type **KeyEventArgs**, which contains data related to their events.

Property events

Property events occur when a property changes. For example, a control can register to receive a **SizeChanged** event when its **Size** property changes.

How to Write an Event Handler

- **Declare events using delegates**

  - **System.EventHandler** is declared as a delegate

```
button1.Click += new
   System.EventHandler(button1_Click);
```

- **Event handler is called when the event occurs**

  - EventArgs parameter contains the event data

```
private void button1_Click(object sender,
   System.EventArgs e) {

      MessageBox.Show( e.ToString() );

}
```

Introduction

The most familiar use for events is in graphical user interfaces. Typically, the classes that represent controls in the graphical user interface include events that are notified when a user manipulates the control, such as when a user clicks a button.

Events also allow an object to signal state changes that may be useful to clients of that object. Delegates are particularly suited for event handling and are used to implement event handling in C#.

Delegates as event handlers

The .NET framework event model uses delegates to bind events to the methods that are used to handle them. The delegate allows other classes to register for event notification by specifying a handler method. When the event occurs, the delegate calls the bound method or methods. The method that is called when the event occurs is referred as the *event handler*.

Tip   Remember that multicasting allows a delegate to call several methods.

Receiving an event

The most common use of events in the .NET Framework is to handle activity in the user interface.

The easiest way to register to receive events is to use the Visual Studio .NET development environment.

The Properties window in the development environment contains an **Events** icon, as shown below:

Clicking this icon displays a list of events that can be sent from the selected object.

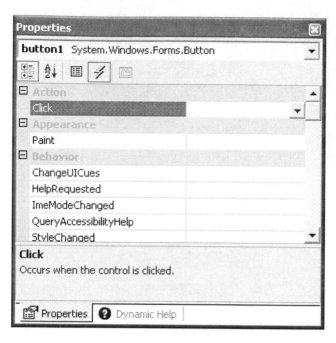

When you double-click the name of an event, the development environment creates an event handler for that event. The following code, which is generated in the initialization method, adds the **button1_Click** method to the delegate:

```
this.button1.Click += new
System.EventHandler(this.button1_Click);
```

Visual Studio .NET inserts the **button1_Click** method into the code, and you place your event-handling code in this method:

```
private void button1_Click(object sender, System.EventArgs e)
{

}
```

The **sender** parameter passes a reference to the object that caused the event. In the preceding example, this is a reference to the **button1** object.

The **System.EventArgs** class contains useful information about the event. Certain events pass a specific **EventArgs** class. For example, the **MouseUp**, **MouseDown**, and **MouseMove** events pass a **MouseEventArgs** object to the subscribed event handler. The **MouseEventArgs** class defines the X and Y position of the mouse, in addition to button click and mouse wheel information.

Example

The following example shows how to handle mouse events.

This Windows form displays the current coordinates of the mouse when the left mouse button is held down. As the mouse moves, the coordinates are updated. When the button is released, the display is cleared.

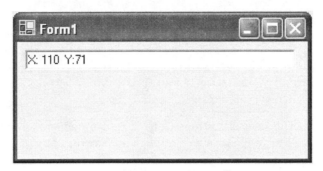

The text box is named **MouseCoordinateDisplay**. Three event handlers are registered for the form (**Form1**), one each for **MouseDown**, **MouseUp**, and **MouseMove** event.

When the mouse button is pressed, a **MouseDown** event is sent to the handler, which sets a Boolean variable **tracking** to **true**.

When the mouse is moved, the **MouseMove** event handler is called. If tracking is set to **true**, this handler updates the display with the current mouse position.

When the button is released, the **MouseUp** event handler is called, which sets **tracking** to **false** and clears the display.

The event-handling code follows:

```csharp
private bool tracking = false;
string coordinateDisplay = null;

private void Form1_MouseDown(object sender,
System.Windows.Forms.MouseEventArgs e) {
  tracking = true;
}

private void Form1_MouseUp(object sender,
System.Windows.Forms.MouseEventArgs e) {
  tracking = false;
  MouseCoordinateDisplay.Clear();
}

private void Form1_MouseMove(object sender,
System.Windows.Forms.MouseEventArgs e) {
  if ( tracking ) {
      coordinateDisplay = "X: " + e.X + "  Y:" + e.Y;
      MouseCoordinateDisplay.Text = coordinateDisplay;
  }
}
```

The following code registers the event handlers (**this** is Form1):

```
this.MouseDown += new
System.Windows.Forms.MouseEventHandler(this.Form1_MouseDown);
this.MouseUp += new
System.Windows.Forms.MouseEventHandler(this.Form1_MouseUp);
this.MouseMove += new
System.Windows.Forms.MouseEventHandler(this.Form1_MouseMove);
```

MouseEventHandler is the delegate type that is declared in the **Forms** class, and **MouseDown**, **MouseUp**, and **MouseMove** are the **Forms** class delegates that provide the event notification.

This code sample is available on the Student Materials compact disc, in the WinEventExample.sln file in the Samples\Mod05\WinEventSample folder.

Sending (declaring) events

When you declare an event in a class, you state that your class will notify other objects that have registered an event handler with your object.

To declare an event inside a class, you must first declare a delegate type for the event. The delegate type defines the set of arguments that are passed to the method that handles the event.

Example

Suppose that the Zoo Medical Center wants to allow users to receive an event when an animal is released. This example uses two classes: the **MedicalCenter** class, which implements an event, and the **ZooKeeper** class, which must be notified when animals are released. The example uses **Lion** and **Antelope** objects, the implementation of which can be seen in the full code example at the end of this topic.

The delegate type for the event is declared in the **MedicalCenter** class:

```
public delegate void AnimalCollectionHandler(Animal a);
```

The event itself is also declared in the **MedicalCenter** class. You declare an event as you would declare a field of **delegate** type, except that the **event** keyword follows the modifiers and precedes the **delegate** type. Events usually are declared public, but any accessibility modifier is allowed.

```
public event AnimalCollectionHandler
OnAnimalReadyForCollection;
```

It is normal to prefix your event with **On**.

The **ZooKeeper** class must have a method that will be invoked by the event. This method is as follows:

```
public void ReleasedNotification (Animal a) { . . . }
```

The purpose of this method is to notify the keeper when an animal is released from the medical center. Because it is invoked by the event delegate, it must have a matching signature.

The **Keeper** class registers this method as an event handler for **OnAnimalReadyForCollection** events:

```
public void GetReleaseNotifications(MedicalCenter hospital) {
  hospital.OnAnimalReadyForCollection += new
MedicalCenter.AnimalCollectionHandler(this.ReleasedNotificatio
n);
}
```

The **MedicalCenter** object will continue to process animals until none are left, sending an event as each animal is released. Pending work is stored on the **queuedProcedures** queue, and the event handlers are invoked by the **OnAnimalReadyForCollection** call. The **if** statement that checks against **null** is to test if any event handlers are registered.

```
public void ProcessPatients() {
  Animal a;
  for(;;) {
      if ( queuedProcedures.Count == 0 )
         break;
      a = (Animal) queuedProcedures.Dequeue();
      a.Checkup();
      if ( OnAnimalReadyForCollection != null ) {
         OnAnimalReadyForCollection( a );
      }
   }
}
```

Note the use of **for (; ;)** to loop forever.

The complete code example follows:

```csharp
using System;
using System.Collections;

namespace EventExample {
    class Zoo {
        // represents a Zoo medical center
        public class MedicalCenter {
            private Queue queuedProcedures;

            // User of this class can register for the following event
            public delegate void AnimalCollectionHandler(Animal a);

            public event AnimalCollectionHandler OnAnimalReadyForCollection;

            public MedicalCenter() {
                // procedures are stored in a queue
                queuedProcedures = new Queue();
            }

            public void Add(Animal sickAnimal) {
                // Add animals to the work queue
                queuedProcedures.Enqueue(sickAnimal);
            }

            public void ProcessPatients() {
                Animal a;
                for(;;) {
                    if ( queuedProcedures.Count == 0 )
                        break;
                    a = (Animal) queuedProcedures.Dequeue();
                    a.Checkup(); // Do the medical procedure
                    if ( OnAnimalReadyForCollection != null ) {
                        // Call the event handler
                        OnAnimalReadyForCollection( a );
                    }
                }
            }
        }


        // User of the MedicalCenter
        public class ZooKeeper {
            // This is called when an animal is released
            public void ReleasedNotification (Animal a) {
                Console.WriteLine("Keeper: " + a + " was just released from the
medical center");
            }

            // This method registers the event handler
            public void GetReleaseNotifications(MedicalCenter hospital) {
                hospital.OnAnimalReadyForCollection += new
MedicalCenter.AnimalCollectionHandler(this.ReleasedNotification);
            }
        }
```

Code continued on the following page.

```
        static void Main(string[] args) {
            MedicalCenter animalHospital = new MedicalCenter();

            Lion notVeryBraveLion = new Lion();
            Antelope bigMaleAntelope = new Antelope();

            ZooKeeper manager = new ZooKeeper();
            manager.GetReleaseNotifications(animalHospital);

            animalHospital.Add( notVeryBraveLion );
            animalHospital.Add( bigMaleAntelope );

            animalHospital.ProcessPatients();

            Console.ReadLine();
        }
    }

    public abstract class Animal {
        public abstract void Checkup();
    }
    public class Antelope : Animal {
        public override void Checkup() {
            Console.WriteLine("Antelope: Checkup ");
        }
        public override string ToString() {
            return "Antelope";
        }
    }
    public class Lion: Animal {
        public override void Checkup() {
            Console.WriteLine("Lion: Checkup");
        }
        public override string ToString() {
            return "Lion";
        }
    }
}
```

The preceding code produces the following output:

```
Lion: Checkup
Keeper: Lion was just released from the medical center
Antelope: Checkup
Keeper: Antelope was just released from the medical center.
```

This code sample is available on the Student Materials compact disc, in the EventExample.sln file in the Samples\Mod05\EventSample folder.

Practice: Declaring and Calling a Delegate

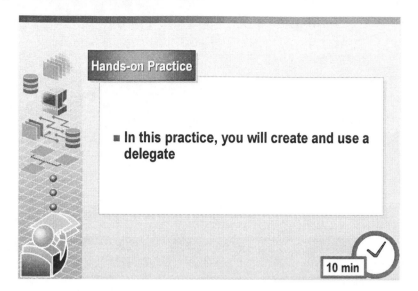

In this practice, you will create and use a delegate.

The zoo has some interactive displays, where visitors can locate information about the animals in the zoo. One of the displays is oriented to children and displays information about dolphin behaviors and tricks that they can perform.

Because these tricks may change from time to time as old dolphins are taught new tricks; the trick implementation is referenced in the **Dolphin** class by a delegate.

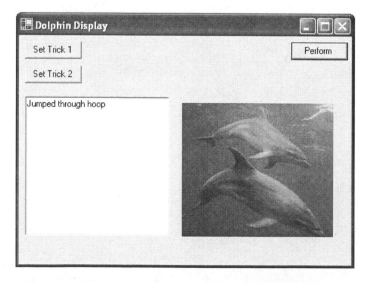

In this application, clicking a **Set Trick** button attaches a method to the dolphin's **Trick** delegate. Clicking **Perform** calls the method referenced in the delegate.

The solution for this practice is located in *install_folder*\Practices\Mod05\Delegates_Solution \Dolphin.sln. Start a new instance of Visual Studio .NET before opening the solution.

Tasks	Detailed steps
1. Start Visual Studio .NET, and then open *install_folder* \Practices\Mod05\Delegates \Dolphin.sln.	**a.** Start a new instance of Visual Studio .NET. **b.** On the **Start Page**, click **Open Project**. **c.** In the **Open Project** dialog box, browse to *install_folder*\Practices \Mod05\Delegates, click **Dolphin.sln**, and then click **Open**. **d.** In Solution Explorer, click **Dolphin.cs**, and then press F7 to open the Code Editor. The **Dolphin** class is located in the file **Dolphin.cs**.
2. Examine the Delegate declaration.	**a.** On the **View** menu, point to **Show Tasks**, and then click **All.** **b.** Double-click the task **TODO 1: Examine the delegate: void TrickType().** Note that the delegate declaration is for a method that takes no parameters and has a void return type.
3. In the **Dolphin** class, add a property called **Trick** that allows the user of the class to assign a method to the private delegate instance member **dolphinTrick**.	**a.** Locate the task **TODO 2: Write a public property called Trick.** **b.** Add a property called **Trick** that allows the user of the class to assign a method to **dolphinTrick** by removing the comments from the lines that follow the TODO comment.
4. In **Form1.cs**, locate the method **setTrick2_Click** and write code to assign a trick to **zooDolphin.Trick**.	**a.** In Solution Explorer, click **Form1.cs**, and then press F7 to open the Code Editor. **b.** Locate the task **TODO 3: Assign a trick to the dolphin**. **c.** In the **setTrick2_Click** method, remove the **Select a trick** comment, and replace it with one of the methods that implements a trick. Trick methods are located at the bottom of this file. The **JumpThroughHoop** method is already assigned to the **Set Trick 1** button. Note that this statement creates a new Delegate and assigns it to the **Trick** property of the **zooDolphin** object.
5. Test the application.	**a.** Press F5 to test your application. **b.** In the **Dolphin Display** window, click **Perform**. Nothing should happen because no methods have been assigned to the dolphin's delegate. **c.** Click **Set Trick 1**, and then click **Perform**. **d.** Click **Set Trick 2**, and then click **Perform**.
6. Quit Visual Studio .NET, saving your solution.	**a.** On the **File** menu, click **Save All**. **b.** On the **File** menu, click **Exit**.

Review

> - Using Arrays
> - Using Collections
> - Using Interfaces
> - Using Exception Handling
> - Using Delegates and Events

1. In the array int[] number = {1, 2, 3, 4 } how do you access the value 3?

2. Create an array that contains the integers 1, 2, and 3. Then use the **foreach** statement to iterate over the array and output the numbers to the console.

```
int[] iarr = {1,2,3}

{foreach(i in iarry)
{
console.write( i.Tostring())
}
```

3. Name two collection objects in **System.Collections** namespace, and describe how these classes track objects.

queue, stack

4. What is a delegate, what is the benefit of using a delegate, and when should you use it?

runtime

async - delegate

Lab 5:1: Using Arrays

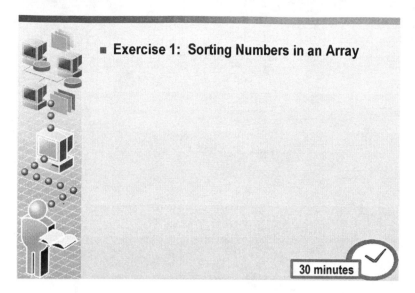

- Exercise 1: Sorting Numbers in an Array

30 minutes

Objectives

After completing this lab, you will be able to use an array to sort numbers.

Prerequisites

Before working on this lab, you must have the ability to:

- Declare and initialize arrays.
- Assign to and from arrays.

Note This lab focuses on the concepts in this module and as a result may not comply with Microsoft security recommendations.

Estimated time to complete this lab: 30 minutes

Exercise 0
Lab Setup

The Lab Setup section lists the tasks that you must perform before you begin the lab.

Task	Detailed steps
▪ Log on to Windows as **Student** with a password of **P@ssw0rd**.	▪ Log on to Windows with the following account: • User name: **Student** • Password: **P@ssw0rd** Note that the 0 in the password is a zero.

Note that by default the *install_folder* is C:\Program Files\Msdntrain\2609.

Exercise 1
Sorting Numbers in an Array

In this exercise, you will sort numbers in an array.

Scenario

Although C# and the .NET Framework provide sorting algorithms, as a programmer you will find it useful to understand how data is held in an array and what happens when that data is sorted.

In this lab, you will implement the **BubbleSort** method as shown in the following code:

```
private void BubbleSort( int[] anArray)
```

The **anArray** integer array contains randomly generated numbers. Your **BubbleSort** method will sort the numbers in the array, with the lower numbers at the beginning of the array.

You will use the following simple algorithm to sort the numbers in the array:

```
For every element in array a
    For every unsorted element in array a
        If a[n] > a[n + 1]
            swap them
```

To move the lowest numbers to the beginning of the array, pass through the array multiple times in the **BubbleSort** method, each time moving the highest unsorted number to the end of the list.

Within the loop, you examine each element n in array a and compare the element to the one that follows it, $n + 1$. If $a[n]$ is greater than $a[n + 1]$, the elements must be swapped. Continue to move down the list comparing adjacent elements. In this way, higher values are moved down the list until they are in place.

On each pass, you must compare only the unsorted elements of the array.

The solution code for this lab is provided in *install_folder*\Labfiles\Lab05_1\Exercise1 \Solution_Code\Bubble Sort.sln. Start a new instance of Visual Studio .NET before opening the solution.

Tasks	Detailed steps
1. Start Visual Studio .NET, and then open *install_folder* \Labfiles\Lab05_1\Exercise1 \Bubble Sort.sln.	**a.** Start a new instance of Visual Studio .NET. **b.** On the **Start Page**, click **Open Project**. **c.** In the **Open Project** dialog box, browse to i*nstall_folder*\Labfiles \Lab05_1\Exercise1, click **Bubble Sort.sln**, and then click **Open**.
2. Examine the code and run the sample application.	**a.** In Solution Explorer, click **Bubble.cs**, and then press F7. **b.** Locate the **sort_Click** method, located at the bottom of the file, and examine the code. The **sort_Click** method is called when you click the **Sort** button in the application. It generates 1000 random integers and places in them in array **a**. It then calls the **BubbleSort** method, passing the array. Finally it lists the contents of the array in the application window. **c.** Build and run the application by pressing F5. **d.** In the application window, click **Sort**. **e.** Close the application window.
3. Write the **BubbleSort** method.	■ Locate the **BubbleSort** method and write code to sort the elements in the array, using the algorithm outlined in the scenario.
4. Test your method by running the program and clicking the **Sort** button.	**a.** In Visual Studio .NET, press F5 to compile and run your program. **b.** In the **Sorting an Array** window, click **Sort**.
5. Quit Visual Studio .NET, saving your solution.	**a.** On the **File** menu, click **Save All**. **b.** On the **File** menu, click **Exit**.

Lab 5.2 (optional): Using Indexers and Interfaces

- Exercise 1: Writing the Check Pick-up Application
- Exercise 2: Using Interfaces

1 hour

Objectives

After completing this lab, you will be able to:

- Use collection classes to manage objects.
- Write indexers to provide indexed access to the data in your objects.
- Implement interfaces for an object.
- Use exception handling to handle unexpected errors.

Note This lab focuses on the concepts in this module and as a result may not comply with Microsoft security recommendations.

Prerequisites

Before working on this lab, you must have the ability to:

- Declare, initialize, and use indexers.
- Implement interfaces.

Scenario

When bank customers who order traveler's checks ask to pick them up in person, the check numbers and amounts are placed in a list for the bank teller who subsequently retrieves the checks and places them in an envelope for the customers.

You have been asked to create a prototype for a system that reads the list of checks and displays them to the teller. This system consists of three parts:

- The user interface where the data operator will retrieve, view, and clear the check information, which is provided to you.

- The component that generates the list of checks, which is simulated and provided to you.

- A data structure that holds the collection of the checks that the teller retrieved but has not yet processed.

Estimated time to complete this lab: 60 minutes

Exercise 0
Lab Setup

The Lab Setup section lists the tasks that you must perform before you begin the lab.

Task	Detailed steps
▪ Log on to Windows as **Student** with a password of **P@ssw0rd**.	▪ Log on to Windows with the following account: • User name: **Student** • Password: **P@ssw0rd** Note that the 0 in the password is a zero.

Note that by default the *install_folder* is C:\Program Files\Msdntrain\2609.

Exercise 1
Writing the Check Pick-up Application

In this exercise, you will write the traveler's check customer pick-up application.

Scenario

A bank provides a service that allows users to order traveler's checks by using the Web site, and then pick them up in person.

The **Get Checks** button retrieves the checks that are waiting for collection and then displays the number of retrieved checks. The code that generates the checks is provided to you. The application is shown in the following illustration:

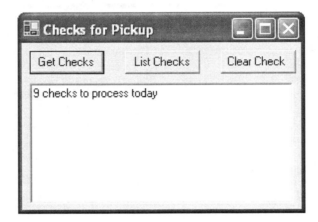

The **List Checks** button lists the checks that were retrieved, as shown in the following illustration:

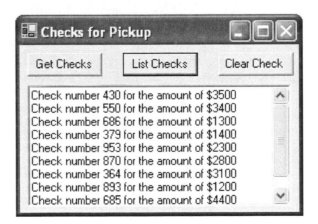

The **Clear Check** button removes a check from the top of the list:

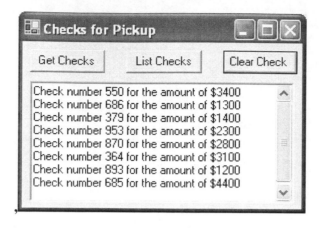

You have been provided with a sample user interface to the traveler's check customer pick-up application. It currently consists of the following C# source files:

- *Checks.cs.* Implement your check collection class in this file. The file contains two classes, **Checks** and **TravelerCheck**. **TravelerCheck** is a simple implementation of the information that is required to locate a traveler's check, and **Checks** is the class that you will implement. You do not need to modify the **TravelerCheck** class. **Checks** will maintain a collection of **TravelerCheck** objects, and provide methods and properties that allow users of the class to do the following:

  - Add **TravelerCheck** objects to the **Checks** collection

  - Reference **TravelerCheck** objects in **Checks** by index, for example:

    ```
    myTravelerCheck = todaysChecks[0];
    ```

  - Remove **TravelerCheck** objects from **Checks**

- *Form1.cs.* The main window. The code that calls your check collection class is in this file.

- *CheckSource.cs.* Contains the code that generates the list of checks that will be collected today. It contains one class, **CheckSource**, with one method, **Next**, that you use to retrieve checks, as shown in the following code:

  ```
  // source is the CheckSource object
  TravelerCheck someCheck = source.Next();
          while (someCheck != null ) {
              someCheck = source.Next();
              // add to todaysChecks
          }
  ```

You will not need to modify the **CheckSource** class.

The solution for this lab is provided in *install_folder*\Labfiles\Lab05_2\Exercise1\Solution_Code \Checkprocess.sln. Start a new instance of Visual Studio .NET before opening the solution.

Tasks	Detailed steps
1. Start Visual Studio .NET, and then open *install_folder*\Labfiles \Lab05_2\Exercise1 \Checkprocess.sln.	**a.** Start a new instance of Visual Studio .NET. **b.** On the **Start** Page, click **Open Project**. **c.** In the **Open Project** dialog box, browse to *install_folder*\Labfiles \Lab05_2\Exercise1, click **Checkprocess.sln**, and then click **Open**.
2. Review the code in Form1.cs and in Checks.cs.	**a.** In Solution Explorer, click **Form1.cs**, and then press F7 to open the Code Editor. **b.** Find the constructor for Form1 and note that the objects **source** and **todaysChecks** are created. • The **source** object is used to produce a list of checks, by using the algorithm described above. • The **todaysChecks** object is an instance of the **Checks** class which you will implement. **c.** Locate the **getChecks_Click**, **listChecks_Click**, and **clearCheck_click** methods, and then review the comments and code in them. **d.** In Solution Explorer, click **Checks.cs**, and then press F7 to open the Code Editor. Review the code. This file contains two classes, **TravelerCheck** and **Checks**. The **TravelerCheck** class represents a single traveler's check, and the **Checks** class represents the collection of checks.
3. Write code that allows the user of the **Checks** class to add **TravelerCheck** objects to a data structure maintained within the class.	**a.** Choose an appropriate data structure for the **Checks** class, and use it to maintain a collection of **TravelerCheck** objects: • Declare the data structure below the declaration of **Count**. • Add a constructor and initialize the data structure in the constructor. **b.** Write a method that adds items to the data structure.
4. Complete the code in the **getChecks_Click** method, and then test your code.	**a.** On the **View** menu, point to **Show Tasks**, and then click **All**. **b.** In the Task List, double-click **TODO 1: Get the list of checks from the check source**. **c.** Complete the **getChecks_Click** method. **d.** Build your application. **e.** Run your application, and then click **Get Checks**. You should see a message indicating that you have some checks to process.

Tasks	Detailed steps
5. Complete the code in the **listChecks_Click** method, and then test your code.	a. On the **View** menu, point to **Show Tasks**, and then click **All**. b. In the **Task List**, double-click **TODO 2: Write an indexer and use it to list the contents**. After you write the indexer, you can use the code that is commented out in the method to display the list of checks. c. Complete the **listChecks_Click** method. d. Build your application. e. Run your application, click **Get Checks**, and then click **List Checks**. You should see a list of the checks to process.
6. Write a method that removes the top item from the list of checks.	a. In Solution Explorer, click **Checks.cs**, and then press F7. b. In the **Checks** class, write a method that removes the top item from the list of checks.
7. Complete the code in the **clearCheck_Click** method, and then test your code.	a. On the **View** menu, point to **Show Tasks**, and then click **All**. b. In the Task List, double-click **TODO 3: Remove the top check**. c. Complete the method **clearCheck_Click**. d. Include code to refresh the display. An easy way to do this is to simulate a click of the **List Checks** button: `listChecks.PerformClick();` e. Build your application. f. Run your application, and then click **Clear Check**. You should see that the top check is removed from the list.
8. Save your solution.	▪ On the **File** menu, click **Save All**.

Exercise 2
Using Interfaces

In this exercise, you will implement the **IEnumerable** interface for the **Checks** class, and test this interface by replacing the **for** statement in **listChecks_Click** with a **foreach** statement.

You can either continue to use your application from Exercise 1, or you can use the starter code that is provided.

The solution for this lab is provided in *install_folder*\Labfiles\Lab05_2\Exercise2\Solution_Code\ Checkprocess.sln. Start a new instance of Visual Studio .NET before opening the solution.

Tasks	Detailed steps
1. In Visual Studio .NET, either use the application that you wrote in Exercise 1, or open *install_folder*\Labfiles \Lab05_2\Exercise2 \Checkprocess.sln.	a. If you want to use the starter code, then in Visual Studio .NET, on the **File** menu, point to **Open**, and then click **Project**. b. In the **Open Project** dialog box, browse to *install_folder*\Labfiles \Lab05_2\Exercise2. c. Click **Checkprocess.sln**, and then click **Open**.
2. Modify the **Checks** class so that it implements the **IEnumerable** interface.	a. Change the **Checks** class so that it inherits **IEnumerable**. b. Implement **GetEnumerator**. c. In the **Checks** class, create a **CheckEnumerator** class that implements **IEnumerator**.
3. Test your code by modifying the **listChecks_Click** method in the **Form1** class so that it uses a **foreach** loop.	a. Delete the **for** statement in your code and substitute a **foreach** statement. b. Build your application, and then run it. c. Check **Get Checks,** and then click **List Checks**. You should see a list of the checks to process.
4. Save your solution, and then quit Visual Studio .NET.	a. On the **File** menu, click **Save All**. b. On the **File** menu, click **Exit**.

Lab 5.3 (optional): Using Delegates and Events

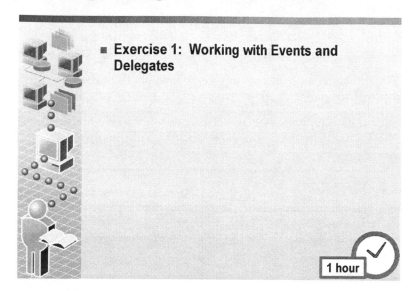

Objectives

After completing this lab, you will be able to:

- Create and use delegates.
- Write event procedures and send events to registered event handlers.

Note This lab focuses on the concepts in this module and as a result may not comply with Microsoft security recommendations.

Prerequisites

Before working on this lab, you must have the ability to use delegates, events, and event handlers.

Scenario

In this lab, you will write an application that allows the user to buy and sell stock by setting a buy value and a sell value.

Estimated time to complete this lab: 60 minutes

Exercise 0
Lab Setup

The Lab Setup section lists the tasks that you must perform before you begin the lab.

Task	Detailed steps
▪ Log on to Windows as **Student** with a password of **P@ssw0rd**.	▪ Log on to Windows with the following account: • User name: **Student** • Password: **P@ssw0rd** Note that the 0 in the password is a zero.

Note that by default the *install_folder* is C:\Program Files\Msdntrain\2609.

Exercise 1
Working with Events and Delegates

In this exercise, you will complete an application that simulates a detail page on a stock trader's application.

You will write code that represents a stock. The stock will raise three events: **OnStockChange**, **OnStockFall**, and **OnStockRise**. The trader's application allows the trader to use the **OnStockFall** event to buy the stock at a given price. The **OnStockRise** price is used to specify the sale price of the stock.

The application is shown in the following illustrations:

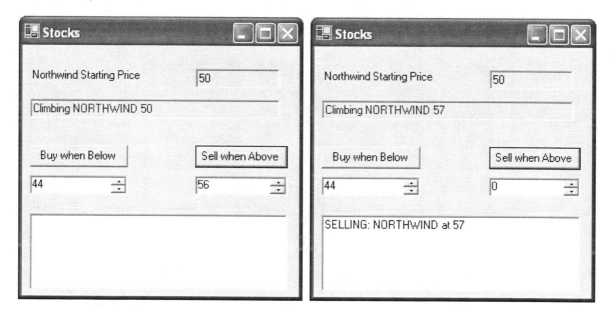

When the application runs, it monitors the current price of the stock for a fictitious company, Northwind Traders, displaying the current price in the center area. The trader can set a Buy or Sell price, by using the **NumericUpDown** boxes, and then click **Buy when Below** or **Sell when Above** to place the order. If the price drops below the buy price, stock is purchased and the order is removed. Similarly, if the price rises above the sell price, the stock is sold and the order is removed.

Because this lab is about using delegates and events to place and act on the orders, the quantities of stock being bought and sold are not considered.

The code for the user interface and the stock price changes is provided to you. Your task is to implement the **OnStockRise** and **OnStockFall** events, and to register handlers for them.

How the Code Works

The **StockTicks** class contains a **StockTicker** method that regularly updates the price of a stock. When the application initializes, the Northwind Traders stock is passed to the **StockTicker**, and thereafter the **Price** property is automatically updated.

When the **Price** property changes, you should raise the **Stock** class appropriate event. For example, when the stock price goes up, raise the **OnStockRise** and **OnStockChange** events.

The **Form1** class, the code for the main window, uses the **Stock** class in the following ways:

▪ To update the stock price display, the **Form1** class registers for **OnStockRise** and **OnStockFall** events.

When a button is clicked, the **Form1** class also registers either a **Buy** event handler or **Sell** event handler for the events, depending on the button that is clicked. For example, the **Buy** event handler is registered for the **OnStockFall** event, and when the price drops below the value in the **NumericUpDown** box, it buys the stock.

When a **Buy** or **Sell** decision is made, you clear the order by removing the event handler.

Note: Some of the starter code in this lab uses events and properties of the **Stock** class that you will write. For that reason, the starter code will not compile until you provide those elements in the **Stock** class.

The solution for this lab is provided in *install_folder*\Labfiles\Lab05_3\Exercise1\Solution_Code \StockPrice.sln. Start a new instance of Visual Studio .NET before opening the solution.

Tasks	Detailed steps
1. Start Visual Studio .NET, and then open *install_folder* \Labfiles\Lab05_3\Exercise1 \StockPrice.sln.	a. Start a new instance of Visual Studio .NET. b. On the **Start** Page, click **Open Project**. c. In the **Open Project** dialog box, browse to *install_folder*\Labfiles \Lab05_3\Exercise1, click **StockPrice.sln**, and then click **Open**. d. In Solution Explorer, click **Stock.cs**, and then press F7 to open the Code Editor.
2. In the **Stock** class, declare a delegate named **StockChange**.	a. On the **View** menu, point to **Show Tasks**, and then click **Comment**. b. In the Task List, double-click **TODO 1: Declare a delegate named StockChange**. c. In the **Stock** class, under the comment, declare a delegate named **StockChange**.
3. Declare two event handlers named **OnStockRise**, and **OnStockFall**.	a. In the Task List, double-click TODO 2: Declare two more event handlers. b. Under the comment, declare two event handlers named **OnStockRise**, and **OnStockFall**.

Tasks	Detailed steps
4. Write a property named **Price** that raises the following events: • **OnStockRise**: raise this event when the new stock price is higher than the previous stock price. • **OnStockFall**: raise this event when the new stock price is lower than the previous stock price.	a. In the Task List, double-click TODO 3: Complete the property named Price. b. The **Price** property encapsulates the **stockPrice** private member. c. Raise an **OnStockRise** event every time the **Price** property is assigned a value that is higher than its previous value. d. Raise an **OnStockFall** event every time the **Price** property is assigned a value that is lower than its previous value.
5. In the **Form1** class, in the **buying_Click** method, write code to add the method **Buy** as an event handler for the **OnStockFall** method.	a. In Solution Explorer, click **Form1.cs**, and then press F7. b. In the Code Editor, locate the **buying_Click** method. This method is called when the user clicks the **Buy when Below** button in the user interface. c. Add the **Buy** method as an event handler for the **OnStockFall** method.
6. In the **Buy** method, add code to remove **Buy** from the **OnStockFall** delegate after a successful stock purchase.	a. Locate the **Buy** method, directly below the **buying_Click** method. b. Add code to remove the **Buy** method from the invocation list of **OnStockFall**.
7. Write the code to sell stock at a price specified in **sell.Value**.	■ Locate the task TODO 4: Write code to sell at a price specified in sell.Value, and write the code.
8. Test your application.	■ Compile and run your application.
9. Save your solution, and then quit Visual Studio .NET.	a. On the **File** menu, click **Save All**. b. On the **File** menu, click **Exit**.

msdn training

Module 6: Building .NET-based Applications with C#

Contents

Overview

- **Examining the .NET Framework Class Library**
- **Overriding Methods from System.Object**
- **Formatting Strings and Numbers**
- **Using Streams and Files**

Introduction

This module presents the Microsoft® .NET Framework class library, focusing on the **System.Object** class and several of its most useful derived classes.

Every programming language requires access to computer features so that it can accomplish tasks such as read a file, accept input from a user, convert data types, and so on. In languages such as C and C++, an application often includes files that contain common functions so that the developer does not have to re-invent common functions. The .NET Framework class library provides common functions for all of the languages that .NET supports. This module examines some of the namespaces that convert data types, read a file, and so on, for .NET-based applications.

Objectives

After completing this module, you will be able to:

- Identify a namespace in the .NET Framework class library by its function.
- Override and implement the **ToString** method.
- Format strings, currency, and date values.
- Read and write both binary and text files.

Lesson: Examining the .NET Framework Class Library

- .NET Framework Class Library
- The Object Browser

This lesson describes the hierarchy of namespaces in the .NET Framework class library and also describes the Object Browser, the Microsoft Visual Studio® .NET feature that is used to browse the object hierarchy.

Lesson objectives

After completing this lesson, you will be able to:

- Identify a namespace in the .NET Framework class library by its function.
- Use the Object Browser.

Lesson agenda

This lesson includes the following topics and activity:

- .NET Framework Class Library
- The Object Browser
- Practice: Using the Object Browser

.NET Framework Class Library

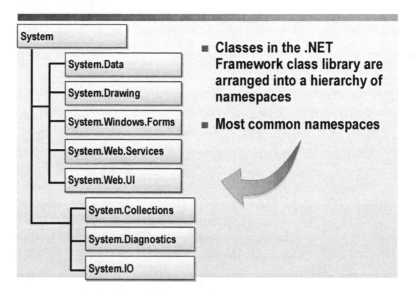

Introduction

Classes in the .NET Framework class library are arranged into a hierarchy of namespaces. For example, all of the classes for data collection management are in the **System.Collections** namespace.

Tip For more information about the namespaces and classes in the .NET Framework class library, see the Visual Studio .NET documentation. Use the Help index and look for **Class Library**.

Common .NET Framework class library namespaces

Some of the most common namespaces in the .NET Framework class library are described in the following table.

Namespace	Description
System	Contains fundamental classes and base classes that define commonly-used value and reference data types, events and event handlers, interfaces, attributes, and processing exceptions.
System.Data	Contains most of the classes that constitute the Microsoft ADO.NET architecture. The ADO.NET architecture enables you to build components that manage data from multiple data sources.
System.Drawing	Provides access to the Graphical Device Interface (GDI+) functions. More advanced functions are provided in the **System.Drawing.Drawing2D**, **System.Drawing.Text**, and **System.Drawing.Imaging** namespaces. GDI+ is the set of classes that you use to produce any sort of drawing, graph, or image.
System.Windows.Forms	Contains classes for creating applications based on Microsoft Windows®.
System.Web.Services	Contains the classes that you use to build and use XML Web Services.
System.Web.UI	Contains classes and interfaces that allow you to create controls and pages that will appear in your Web applications as user interface on a Web page.
System.Collections	Contains interfaces and classes that define various collections of objects, such as **lists**, **queues**, **bitarrays**, **hash tables**, and **dictionaries**.
System.Diagnostics	Contains classes that allow you to interact with system processes, event logs, and performance counters. This namespace also provides classes that allow you to debug your application and to trace the execution of your code.
System.IO	Contains types that allow you to read and write files.

The Object Browser

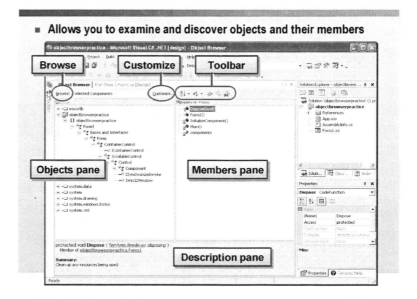

■ **Allows you to examine and discover objects and their members**

Introduction

Use the Visual Studio .NET Object Browser to examine objects such as namespaces, classes, structures, interfaces, types, and object members such as properties, methods, events, and constants from projects in your solution, referenced components within those projects, and external components.

Tip To open the Object Browser by using shortcut keys, press CTRL+ALT+J.

Object Browser elements

Elements of the Object Browser are described in the following table.

Element	Description
Objects pane	Namespaces and their members are displayed in the Objects (left) pane. As you browse objects in this pane, you can display the inheritance hierarchy that makes up a particular member.
Members pane	If an object in the Objects pane includes members such as properties, methods, events, variables, constants, and enumerated items, those members are displayed in the Members (right) pane.
Description pane	This pane displays detailed information about the currently selected object or member, such as:
	• Name and parent object.
	• Syntax, based on the current programming language.
	• Links to related objects and members.
	• Description, comments, or Help text.
	• Attributes.
	Not every object or member has all of this information.
	You can copy text from the Description pane to the editor window.

(continued)

Element	Description
Browse	This element allows you to locate an object within the namespace hierarchy, or to select either the **Active Project** browsing scope or the **Selected Components** browsing scope. You can determine what components are shown by choosing and customizing the browsing scope.
	The Active Project browsing scope is the contents of the active project and its referenced components. The Object Browser updates as the active project changes.
	The Selected Components browsing scope allows you to choose specific components to browse. These components can include projects in your solution and their referenced components, and any other external components, such as .NET Framework components.
Customize button	This button is available when you select **Selected Components** as your browsing scope. This displays the **Selected Components** dialog box where you specify the components that you want to browse—projects and their referenced components, and external components.
Toolbar	This element allows you to specify and customize the browsing scope, sort and group the contents of the Object Browser, move around within it, and search for symbols by using the **Find Symbol** dialog box.

Note   You can also use Class View to view projects in your solution. Class View gives you a hierarchical view of symbols restricted to only the projects in your solution. You can use Class View to discover and edit the structure of your code and the relationships between objects in it.

To use Class View, in Visual Studio .NET, on the **View** menu, click **Class View**, or press CTRL+ALT+C.

Practice: Using the Object Browser

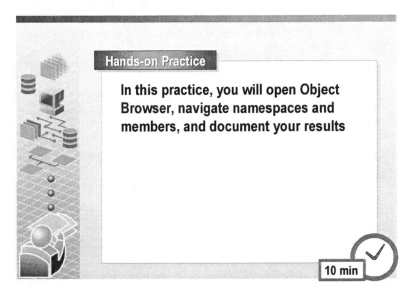

Hands-on Practice

In this practice, you will open Object Browser, navigate namespaces and members, and document your results

10 min

In this practice, you will open Object Browser, browse namespaces and members, and document your results.

Tasks	Detailed steps
1. Start Visual Studio .NET, and then create a new project. Project Type: **Visual C#** Template: **Windows Application** Name: **ObjectBrowserPractice**	**a.** Start a new instance of Visual Studio .NET. **b.** On the **Start Page**, click **New Project**. **c.** In the **New Project** dialog box, under **Project Types**, click **Visual C# Projects**. **d.** Under **Templates**, click **Windows Application**. **e.** In the **Name** box, type **ObjectBrowserPractice** **f.** In the Location box, browse to *install_folder***Practices\Mod06** and then click **OK**.
2. Display the Object Browser.	▪ On the **View** menu, point to **Other Windows**, and then click **Object Browser**.
❓ Using the Object Browser, document the **Equals** method of the **Object** object. Include the access modifiers in your documentation. _____ _____	

Tasks	Detailed steps
❓	Using the Object Browser, document how many implementations of the method **Compare** are supported by the **String** object.
❓	Using the Object Browser, find the **Convert** class and document the class modifiers that are listed for the class. In your document, include what effect the modifier has on the class.
❓	Using the Object Browser, find the **ReadUInt16** method. What does this method do?
❓	Using the Object Browser, find the **ArrayList** class. Can you set the **IsReadOnly** property to **true** or **false**?
❓	Using the Object Browser, find the **FileStream** class. What namespace contains this class?
❓	Using the Object Browser, find the **ReadUInt32** method. What does this method do?

Lesson: Overriding Methods from System.Object

- **Methods Inherited from System.Object**
- **How to Override and Implement ToString**

Introduction

Every object in the .NET Framework inherits **ToString**, **GetHashCode**, **Equals**, and **GetType** methods from **System.Object**. When you create a new object, you can override these built-in functions to improve how these functions fit your object.

Lesson objectives

After completing this lesson, you will be able to:

- Name the methods that are inherited from the **Object** class.
- Override and implement the **ToString** method.

Lesson agenda

This lesson includes the following topics and activity:

- Methods Inherited from **System.Object**
- How to Override and Implement **ToString**
- Practice: Overriding the **ToString** Method

Methods Inherited from System.Object

- **ToString**

  Creates and returns a human-readable text string that describes an instance of the class

- **GetHashCode**

  Returns an integer number as a hashcode for the object

- **Equals**

  Determines whether two objects are equal

- **GetType**

  Returns the type of the current instance

Introduction

Every object in the .NET Framework inherits from the **System.Object** base class. This class implements a small number of methods that are available on all objects. These methods are **ToString**, **GetHashCode**, **Equals**, and **GetType**. When you create a new class, the new class inherits these methods.

Overriding methods

The default implementation of **Object** class methods may not provide the function that you need for your new class, requiring you to override the method. Generally, only the **ToString**, **GetHashCode**, and **Equals** are overridden.

ToString method

The **ToString** method creates and returns a human-readable text string that describes an instance of the class.

The following code demonstrates how to call the **ToString** method:

```
object o = new object();
MessageBox.Show(o.ToString());
```

GetHashCode method

The **GetHashCode** method returns an integer number as a hash code for the object. Other .NET Framework class library classes and .NET-compatible languages such as C# use this method to quickly locate instances of an object when the object is contained in a hash table. For example, the C# statement **switch**, uses a hash table that is populated with hash entries from the **GetHashCode** method to improve the efficiency of the statement.

Equals method

The **Equals** method determines whether two objects are equal.

The following code demonstrates how to call the **Equals** method:

```
object o1 = new object();
object o2 = o1;
MessageBox.Show(o1.Equals(o2).ToString());
```

GetType method

The **GetType** method obtains the type of the current instance.

The following code demonstrates how to call the **GetType** method:

```
object o = new object();
```

```
MessageBox.Show(o.GetType().FullName);
```

It is unlikely that you would ever override the **GetType** method. It is included here because it is inherited from the **System.Object** class.

How to Override and Implement ToString

- **Inherited ToString() returns the name of the class**

```
public enum CarSize {
    Large,
    Medium,
    Small,
}
public class Car {
    public CarType  Size;
    public int TopSpeed;
}
Car myCar = new Car();
myCar.Size = CarSize.Small;
MessageBox.Show(myCar.ToString());
```

    `WindowsApplication1.Form1.Car`

- **Override ToString to provide a more useful string**

```
public override string ToString() {
    return ( this.Size.ToString() + " Car");
}
```

    `Small Car`

Introduction

When you create a class, the class inherits the **ToString** method.

The following code contains a **Car** class with two public fields. The code under the class writes to the console the output from the default **ToString** method that was inherited from the **System.Object** object.

Example

```
public enum CarSize {
  Large,
  Medium,
  Small,
}
public class Car {
    public CarType  Size;
    public int TopSpeed;
}
Car myCar = new Car();
myCar.Size = CarSize.Small;
MessageBox.Show(myCar.ToString());
```

The preceding line of code writes the name of the executing object to the console as follows:

```
WindowsApplication1.Form1.Car
```

Overriding the ToString method

However, if you need the **ToString** method to produce the size of the car instead of the **Car** class name, you must override the default **ToString** method, as shown in the following code:

```
public override string ToString() {
    return ( this.Size.ToString() + " Car");
}
```

Using **ToString** on the **Car** class now produces the following output:

```
Small Car
```

This output is written to the console for the instance that was created in the preceding example.

Note For further information about overriding methods from the **System.Object** class, see Appendix B, "Advanced Topics," in Course 2609, *Introduction to C# Programming with Microsoft .NET*.

Practice: Overriding the ToString Method

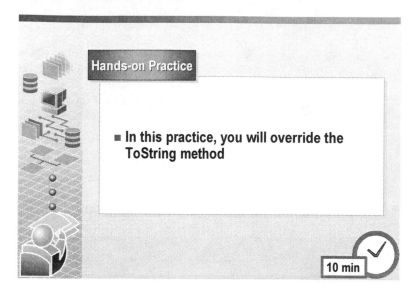

In this practice, you will override the **ToString** method.

The solution code for this practice is located in *install_folder*\Practices\Mod06\ OverrideToString_Solution\OverrideToString.sln. Start a new instance of Visual Studio .NET before opening the solution.

Tasks	Detailed steps
1. Start Visual Studio .NET, and then open the solution *install_folder*\Practices\Mod06\ OverrideToString\ OverrideToString.sln	a. Start a new instance of Visual Studio .NET. b. On the **Start Page**, click **Open Project**. c. In the **Open Project** dialog box, browse to *install_folder*\Practices\Mod06\OverrideToString. d. Click **OverrideToString.sln**, and then click **Open**.
2. Run the application, and then click **Create Car Object**.	a. On the standard toolbar, click **Start**. b. In the Module 6 Practice 2 window, click **Create Car Object**.
ⓘ Note: A message displays the output of the **myCar.ToString()** method. The message box contains **Mod06_Pratice2.Car**, which is the class name of the object.	
3. Override the **ToString** method to return the manufacturer and model name of the car.	▪ Refer to the content and code examples earlier in this module for detailed information about overriding the **ToString** method.
4. Run the application and then click **Create Car Object**.	a. On the standard toolbar, click **Start**. b. In the Module 6 Practice 2 window, click **Create Car Object**.
ⓘ Note: Your application message box should now contain the message **BIGCARS NICECAR**.	

Lesson: Formatting Strings and Numbers

- How to Format Numbers
- How to Format Date and Time
- How to Create Dynamic Strings

Introduction

This lesson introduces students to the classes in the .NET Framework class library that provide numeric and string formatting functions.

Lesson objectives

After completing this lesson, students will be able to:

- Use the **Format** method to format numbers and currencies.
- Format currency and date values.

Lesson agenda

This lesson includes the following topics and activity:

- How to Format Numbers
- How to Format Date and Time
- How to Create Dynamic Strings
- Practice: Formatting Strings

How to Format Numbers

- ■ **Some .NET Framework classes use format strings to return common numeric string types, including these methods:**
  - • String.Format, ToString, Console.WriteLine
- ■ **String.Format class example**

```
string s = String.Format( "{0:c}",
    12345.67 );
```

  - • The {0:c} is the formatting information, where
    - "0" is the index of the following objects
    - ":c" dictates that the output use the currency format
  - • Output is $12,345.67 (on a US English computer)
- ■ **Custom numeric format strings apply to any format string that does not fit the definition of a standard numeric format string**
  - • # character in the number example

Introduction

Formatting refers to the various ways that you can display a particular numeric value. You use formatting to display values in a way that is appropriate for the type of application or locale.

Example of value display formats

For example, consider the value **12345.67**. You can represent this value in several ways.

You can represent the value with or without a comma:

> 12345.67

> 12,345.67

You can also display it as a negative number in various ways:

> -12,345.67

> (12345.67)

Finally, you can display the value by using exponential notation:

> 1.2E+004

> 1.234567E+004

The .NET Framework uses formatting strings and custom formatting strings to specify the output format of numeric values such as currency amount, fixed point digits, date, time, and so on.

A number of classes within the .NET Framework use formatting strings to specify the output format. Three examples of these methods are **String.Format**, **ToString**, and **Console.WriteLine**.

'Standard numeric format strings

A string that consists of a single alphabetic character, optionally followed by a sequence of digits that form a value between 0 and 99, is considered a *standard* format string. All other strings are considered *custom* format strings.

You use standard numeric format strings to return common numeric string types. A standard format string takes the form *Axx* where *A* is an alphabetic character that is called the *format specifier*, and *xx* is a sequence of digits that are called the *precision specifier*.

The following table describes the standard numeric format strings.

Format specifier	Name	Description
C	Currency	The number is converted to a string that represents a currency amount. The conversion is controlled by the currency format information of the **NumberFormatInfo** object that is used to format the number.
D	Decimal	This format is supported for integral types only. The number is converted to a string of decimal digits (0-9), prefixed by a minus sign if the number is negative.
E	Exponential	The number is converted to a string of the form "-*d.ddd*...E+*ddd*" or "-*d.ddd*...e+*ddd*", where each *d* indicates a digit (0-9). The string starts with a minus sign if the number is negative. One digit always precedes the decimal point. The system picks fixed point or exponential.
F	Fixed Point	The number is converted to a string of the form "-*ddd.ddd*..." where *d* is a digit (0-9). The string starts with a minus sign if the number is negative.
G	General	The number is converted to the most compact decimal form, using fixed or scientific notation.
N	Number	The number is converted to a string of the form "-*d,ddd,ddd.ddd*...", where *d* is a digit (0-9). The string starts with a minus sign if the number is negative. Thousand separators are inserted between each group of three digits to the left of the decimal point.
R	Roundtrip	The roundtrip specifier guarantees that a numeric value that is converted to a string will be parsed back into the same numeric value.
X	Hexadecimal	The number is converted to a string of hexadecimal digits. The case of the format specifier indicates whether to use uppercase or lowercase characters for the hexadecimal digits greater than 9.

Tip Use numbers after D, E, and F to control the displayed decimal places. For complete information about standard numeric format strings, see the Visual Studio .NET documentation. Use the Help index and look for **Standard Numeric Format Strings**.

Tip To maintain consistency between numeric formats and system settings, use the format codes in the preceding table rather than by creating custom formatting codes.

String.Format class example

The following code shows the **String.Format method** being used to format the numbers. "{0:c}" is the formatting information, where "0" is the index of the following objects and ":c" causes the number to be formatted as currency.

```
string s = String.Format( "{0:c}", 12345.67 );
```

If a string is interpreted as a standard numeric format string and contains one of the standard numeric format specifiers, the numeric value is formatted accordingly. However, if a string is interpreted as a standard format string but does not contain one of the standard format specifiers, a **FormatException** error occurs.

Custom numeric format strings

Any numeric format string that does not fit the definition of a standard numeric format string is interpreted as a *custom* numeric format string. Also, if the standard numeric format specifiers do not provide the type of formatting that you require, you can use custom format strings to further enhance string output.

The following table shows the characters that you can use to create custom numeric format strings and their definitions.

Character	Description	Example	Example output
0	Zero placeholder	{0:00#####.##}	0012345.67
#	Digit or space placeholder.	{0:#####}	12346
,	Display a comma.	{0:##,### }	12,346
.	Display the decimal point.	{0:#####.##}	12345.67
%	Display percent	{0:#%}	2%
;	Statement separator for positive, negative, and zero.	{0:##;(#);#}	The output is dependent on the input being either +, -, or 0 (zero).

Note Some of the patterns that are produced by these characters are influenced by the values in the **Regional and Language Options** settings in Control Panel.

Custom format string example

In some circumstances, you may require a number to be formatted with a number sign character (#) in the number. In the following example, the # character is a formatting character that appears at the end of the digit sequence. Typically, the # character does not appear; instead, it is interpreted as part of the formatting.

The following code demonstrates how you can use \# to cause what is called *escaping* the character. Using \# causes # character to be treated as a normal character and not part of the formatting information.

If you want to use the # character to create 123456#, use \# as follows:

```
String.Format("{0:#\\#}",123456)
```

escape it (escape the \ to escape the #) – or better:

```
String.Format(@"{0:#\#}",123456)
```

use the verbatim string character.

How to Format Date and Time

- **DateTimeFormatInfo class**
  - Used for formatting **DateTime** objects

    ```
    System.DateTime dt = new
        System.DateTime(2002,3,20,10,30,0);

    MessageBox.Show(dt.ToString("f"));
    ```

  - String output is: Wednesday, March 20, 2002 10:30 AM

- **Custom formatting string**
  - String output is: 20 Mar 2002 - 10:30:00

    ```
    System.DateTime dt = new
        System.DateTime(2002,3,20,10,30,0);

    MessageBox.Show(dt.ToString("dd MMM
        yyyy - hh:mm:ss"));
    ```

Introduction

Like the numeric data types, the **DateTime** class implements the **IFormattable** interface, which allows you to format the value of an object as a string by using one of the overloads of the **DateTime.ToString** method. The standard format provider class that is used for formatting **DateTime** objects in the .NET Framework is **DateTimeFormatInfo**.

DateTime format string parameters are either standard format strings or custom format strings.

Tip For complete information about **DateTime** standard format strings, see the Visual Studio .NET documentation. Use the Help index and look for **Date and Time Format Strings**.

DateTime standard format strings

Format strings are interpreted as standard format specifiers if they contain only one of the single format specifiers that are listed in the following table.

Note The following table lists only a few of the most common format specifiers. For complete information about the format specifiers, see the Visual Studio .NET documentation.

Format specifier	Name	Description
d	Short date pattern	Displays a pattern defined by the **DateTimeFormatInfo.ShortDatePattern** property associated with the current thread or by a specified format provider.
D	Long date pattern	Displays a pattern defined by the **DateTimeFormatInfo.LongDatePattern** property associated with the current thread or by a specified format provider.
t	Short time pattern	Displays a pattern defined by the **DateTimeFormatInfo.ShortTimePattern** property associated with the current thread or by a specified format provider.
T	Long time pattern	Displays a pattern defined by the **DateTimeFormatInfo.LongTimePattern** property associated with the current thread or by a specified format provider.
f	Full date/time pattern (short time)	Displays a combination of the long date and short time patterns, separated by a space.
F	Full date/time pattern (long time)	Displays a pattern defined by the **DateTimeFormatInfo.FullDateTimePattern** property associated with the current thread or by a specified format provider.

Example

The following example uses the **DateTimeFormat** property.

```
System.DateTime dt = new System.DateTime(2002,3,20,10,30,0);
MessageBox.Show(dt.ToString("f"));
```

String output is:

```
Wednesday, March 20, 2002 10:30 AM
```

DateTime custom format strings

The custom format strings allow **DateTime** objects to be formatted for situations where the standard formatting strings are not useful. You can create your own custom format strings.

Tip   For complete information about **DateTime** custom format strings, see the Visual Studio .NET documentation. Use the Help index and look for **Date and Time Format Strings**.

Example

The following code example uses a custom formatting string:

```
System.DateTime dt = new System.DateTime(2002,3,20,10,30,0);
MessageBox.Show(dt.ToString("dd MMM yyyy - hh:mm:ss"));
```

String output is:

```
20 Mar 2002 - 10:30:00
```

DateTime.ToString

The **DateTime.ToString** method converts the value of an instance to its equivalent string representation.

DateTime.Now

The **DateTime.Now** method returns a **DateTime** data type that is the current local date and time of the user's computer.

How to Create Dynamic Strings

- **Question: After executing the following code, how can you preserve computer memory?**

```
for (int i=0; i < 1000; i++) {
    s = s.Concat(s, i.ToString());
}
```

- **Solution: Use the StringBuilder Class**

```
StringBuilder s = new StringBuilder();
for (int i=0; i < 1000; i++) {
    s.Append(i);
}
```

Introduction

In what circumstances do you use **StringBuilder** class with a string type? Because strings are immutable, after a string is stored in memory, the memory that is allocated for the string cannot change. If the string is changed, a new memory location is needed to store the changed string. For example, consider the following:

```
int amount = 42;
string s1 = "Your balance is ";
s1 = string.Concat( s1, amount.ToString() );
```

In the preceding code, **s1** is created and then changed, causing the old and new version of **s1** to be stored temporarily in memory. The old **s1** will be cleared from memory by the garbage collection process. If your application frequently manipulates strings, you may be holding a large amount of memory in use, while waiting for the next periodic garbage collection.

Concatenating strings

The **string.Concat** method creates a new string, and concatenates **s** with the result of the **ToString** method and then stores the result in a new memory location, which is then linked to **s**. This means that you have two strings when you only need one. When dealing with multiple strings, for example if you concatenate strings in a loop, this situation can be both a performance and memory problem.

The solution is to use the **StringBuilder** class in the **System.Text** namespace.

Using the StringBuilder class

If your code must manipulate strings, especially looped operations where large numbers of strings are left in memory, it is recommended that you use the **StringBuilder** class.

StringBuilder acts just like the **Collection** classes. It allocates an initial value of sixteen characters and if your string becomes larger than this, it automatically grows to accommodate the string size. You would rewrite your code as follows:

```
int amount = 42;
StringBuilder sb = new StringBuilder( "Your balance is " );
sb.Append( amount );
```

The preceding code contains only one string, which is referenced by "sb". Also note that the **Append** method takes an object.

Methods of the StringBuilder class

The important methods of the **StringBuilder** class are listed in the following table.

Method	Function
Append	Places an item (object) at the end of the current **StringBuilder** object.
AppendFormat	Specifies a format for the object (for example, number of decimal places).
Insert	Places the object at a specific index.
Remove	Removes characters.
Replace	Replaces characters (specific or indexed).

Example

The following code shows the creation of the object **s**. The table that follows the code shows the contents of the object **s** after the code statement is executed. Each row in the table builds on the state of the object **s** from the previous row.

```
StringBuilder s = new StringBuilder("ABCD");
```

Code	Output
`s.Append("EF");`	ABCDEF
`s.AppendFormat("{0:n}",1100);`	ABCDEF1,100.00
`s.Insert(2,"Z");`	ABZCDEF1,100.00
`s.Remove(7,6);`	ABZCDEF00
`s.Replace("0","X");`	ABZCDEFXX

Note For your reference, the sample **StringOrStringBuilder** application is located at *install_folder\Samples\StringOrStringBuilder* folder on the Student Materials compact disc. This basic application demonstrates the performance implications of using a string variable instead of an instance of the **StringBuilder** class.

Practice: Formatting Strings

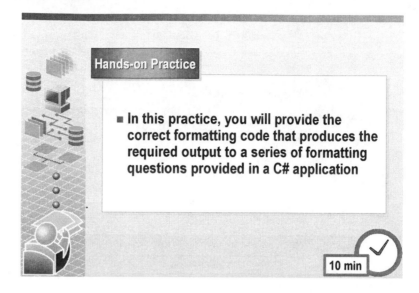

In this practice, you will provide the correct formatting code that produces the required output to a series of formatting questions that are provided in a C# application.

Tasks	Detailed steps
ℹ **Note:** In this practice, you are provided with an application. You do not use Visual Studio .NET for this practice.	
1. Start the application StringFormat.exe in *install_folder*\Practices\Mod06 \StringFormat.	a. Click **Start**, and then click **Run**. b. Type *install_folder***Practices\Mod06\StringFormat StringFormat.exe** and then click **OK**.
2. Examine the code samples and then enter the format code that completes the code samples.	▪ Study the code samples. Enter the format code that completes the code examples.
ℹ **Note:** You will progress to the next question when the correct format code is entered. You can skip a question at any time by clicking **Skip**.	

Lesson: Using Streams and Files

- **What Is File I/O?**
- **How to Read and Write Text Files**
- **How to Read and Write Binary Files**
- **How to Traverse the Windows File System**

Introduction

This lesson introduces the **System.IO** namespace and explains how to read and write binary and text files, how to browse through the file system, how to read the contents of a file, and how to write a file.

Lesson objectives

After completing this lesson, you will be able to:

- Read and write binary files.
- Read and write text files.
- Traverse the Windows file system.

Lesson agenda

This lesson includes the following topics and activity:

- What Is File I/O?
- How to Read and Write Text Files
- How to Read and Write Binary Files
- How to Traverse the Windows File System
- Practice: Using File System Information

What Is File I/O?

- *A file* is a collection of data stored on a disk with a name and often a directory path
- A *stream* is something on which you can perform read and write operations
- **FileAccess Enumerations**
  - Read, ReadWrite, Write
- **FileShare Enumerations**
  - Inheritable, None, Read, ReadWrite, Write
- **FileMode Enumerations**
  - Append, Create, CreateNew, Open, OpenOrCreate, Truncate

Introduction

The .NET Framework distinguishes between files and streams.

A *file* is a collection of data stored on a disk with a name and often a directory path. When you open a file for reading or writing, it becomes a *stream*. You can perform read and write operations on a stream.

Streams encompass more than just open disk files, however. Data coming over a network is a stream, and you can also create a stream in memory. In a console application, keyboard input and text output are also streams.

Stream operations

Streams involve these fundamental operations:

- Streams can be read from. *Reading* is the transfer of data from a stream into a data structure, such as an array of bytes.

- Streams can be written to. *Writing* is the transfer of data from a data structure into a stream.

- Streams can support seeking. *Seeking* is the querying and modifying of the current position within a stream.

FileStream class

Most file I/O support in the .NET Framework is implemented in the **System.IO** namespace. You use the **FileStream** class in the **System.IO** namespace to read from, write to, and close files. **FileStream** inherits from the abstract class **Stream**, and many of its properties and methods are derived from **Stream**.

To open an existing file or create a new file, you create an object of type **File Stream**.

File access, sharing and type

The **FileAccess**, **FileMode**, and **FileShare** enumerations define constants that are used by some of the **FileStream** and **IsolatedStorageFileStream** constructors and some of the **File.Open** overloaded methods. These constants affect the way in which the underlying file is created, opened, and shared.

FileAccess enumeration

Unless you specify a **FileAccess** enumerator, the file is opened for both reading and writing. The **FileAccess** enumerator indicates whether you want to read from the file, write to it, or both.

FileAccess members

Members of the **FileAccess** enumeration are **Read**, **ReadWrite**, and **Write**.

The following **FileStream** constructor grants read-only access to an existing file (**FileAccess.Read**).

```
FileStream s2 = new FileStream(name, FileMode.Open,
FileAccess.Read, FileShare.Read);
```

FileShare enumerations

The **FileShare** enumerator contains constants for controlling the kind of access that other **FileStream** constructors can have to the same file. A typical use of this enumeration is to define whether two processes can simultaneously read from the same file. For example, if a file is opened and **FileShare.Read** is specified, other users can open the file for reading but not for writing.

FileShare members

Members of the **FileShare** enumerator are:

- **Inheritable**, which make the file handle inheritable by child processes.
- **None**, which declines sharing of the current file.
- **Read**, which allows subsequent opening of the file for reading.
- **ReadWrite**, which allows subsequent opening of the file for reading and writing.
- **Write**, which allows subsequent opening of the file for writing.

Example

The following **FileStream** constructor opens an existing file and grants read-only access to other users (**FileShare.Read**):

```
FileStream s2 = new FileStream(name, FileMode.Open,
  FileAccess.Read, FileShare.Read);
```

FileMode enumerations

This enumerator specifies how the operating system should open a file. A **FileMode** parameter is specified in many of the constructors for **FileStream**, **IsolatedStorageFileStream**, and in the **Open** methods of **File** and **FileInfo** to control how a file is opened.

FileMode parameters control whether a file is overwritten, created, or opened, or some combination thereof. Use **Open** to open an existing file. To append to a file, use **Append**. To truncate a file or to create it if it does not exist, use **Create**.

FileMode members

Members of **FileMode** enumerations are:

- **Append**, which opens the file if it exists and seeks to the end of the file, or creates a new file.
- **Create**, which specifies that the operating system should create a new file.
- **CreateNew**, which specifies that the operating system should create a new file.
- **Open**, which specifies that the operating system should open an existing file.
- **OpenOrCreate**, which specifies that the operating system should open a file if it exists; otherwise, a new file should be created.
- **Truncate**, which specifies that the operating system should open an existing file.

Example

The following **FileStream** constructor opens an existing file (**FileMode.Open**):

```
FileStream s2 = new FileStream(name, FileMode.Open,
    FileAccess.Read, FileShare.Read);
```

How to Read and Write Text Files

Class	Example

StreamReader	```StreamReader sr = new StreamReader(@"C:\SETUP.LOG");```
	```textBox1.Text = sr.ReadToEnd();```
	```sr.Close();```

StreamWriter	```StreamWriter sw = new StreamWriter(@"C:\TEST.LOG",false);```
	```sw.WriteLine("Log Line 1");```
	```sw.WriteLine("Log Line 2");```
	```sr.Close();```

XmlTextReader	```public class XmlTextReader : XmlReader, IXmlLineInfo```

XmlTextWriter	```w.WriteStartElement("root");```
	```w.WriteAttributeString("xmlns", "x", null, "urn:1");```
	```w.WriteStartElement("item","urn:1"); w.WriteEndElement();```
	```w.WriteStartElement("item","urn:1"); w.WriteEndElement();```
	```w.WriteEndElement();```

Introduction

Use the **Stream** class to read and write data. The **Stream** class is the abstract class that supports reading and writing bytes. If you know that your file contains only text, you may use the **StreamReader** or **StreamWriter** classes. If you know that your file contains data from different inputs, such as a stream object, a **TextReader** class object, and a URL identifying a local file location, or Web site, you may use the **XMLTextReader** and **XMLTextWriter** classes.

StreamReader class

The **StreamReader** class implements a **TextReader** that reads lines of information from a standard text file such as a log file. A **TextReader** represents a reader that can read a sequential series of characters.

The following code uses the **StreamReader** class:

```
StreamReader sr = new StreamReader(@"C:\SETUP.LOG");
textBox1.Text = sr.ReadToEnd();
```

The following line places entire file into the textbox:

```
sr.Close();
```

StreamWriter class

The **StreamWriter** class inherits from the abstract class **TextWriter** for writing characters to a stream in a particular encoding. The **TextWriter** class represents a writer that can write a sequential series of characters.

The following code uses the **StreamWriter** class:

```
StreamWriter sw = new StreamWriter(@"C:\TEST.LOG",false);
sw.WriteLine("Log Line 1");
sw.WriteLine("Log Line 2");
sr.Close();
```

XmlTextReader class

The **XmlTextReader** class inherits from the class **XmlReader**, and provides a fast, performant parser. It enforces the rules that XML must be well-formed. It is neither a validating nor a non-validating parser because it does not have a document type definition (DTD) or schema information. It can read text in blocks or read characters from a stream.

The **XmlTextReader** provides the following functionality:

- Enforces the rules that XML must be well-formed.

- Checks that the DTD is well-formed. However, **XmlTextReader** does not use the DTD for validation, expanding entity references, or adding default attributes.

- Validating is not performed against DTDs or schemas.

- Checks that any DOCTYPE nodes are well-formed.

- Checks that the entities are well-formed. For node types of **EntityReference**, a single, empty **EntityReference** node is returned. An empty **EntityReference** node is one in which its **Value** property is **string.Empty**. This is because you have no DTD or schema with which to expand the entity reference. The **XmlTextReader** does ensure that the whole DTD is well-formed, including the EntityReference nodes.

- Provides a performant XML parser, because the **XmlTextReader** does not have the overhead involved with validation checking.

The **XmlTextReader** can read data from different inputs, such as a stream object, a **TextReader Class** object, and a URL identifying a local file location or Web site.

The following code defines the **XmlTextReader** class:

```
public class XmlTextReader : XmlReader, IXmlLineInfo
```

XmlTextWriter class

The **XmlTextWriter** class represents a writer that provides a fast, non-cached, forward-only way of generating streams or files containing XML data that conforms to the World Wide Web Consortium (W3C) XML 1.0 and the namespaces in XML recommendations.

XmlTextWriter maintains a namespace stack corresponding to all of the namespaces defined in the current element stack. Using **XmlTextWriter** you can declare namespaces manually.

XmlTextWriter promotes the namespace declaration to the root element to avoid having it duplicated on the two child elements. The following code generates the XML output:

```
w.WriteStartElement("root");
w.WriteAttributeString("xmlns", "x", null, "urn:1");
w.WriteStartElement("item","urn:1"); w.WriteEndElement();
w.WriteStartElement("item","urn:1"); w.WriteEndElement();
w.WriteEndElement();
```

The child elements pick up the prefix from the namespace declaration. Given the preceding code, the code output is:

```
<root xmlns:x="urn:1">
 <x:item/>
 <x:item/>
</x:root>
```

Tip **XmlTextWriter** also allows you to override the current namespace declaration.

How to Read and Write Binary Files

- **BinaryReader**
  - Reads primitive data types as binary values in a specific encoding
- **BinaryWriter**
  - Writes primitive types in binary to a stream and supports writing strings in a specific encoding

```
FileStream fs = new
  FileStream(@"C:\TEST2.DAT",FileMode.CreateNew);
BinaryWriter w = new BinaryWriter(fs);
w.Write((byte)65);
w.Write((byte)66);
w.Close();
fs.Close();
```

Introduction

You use the **BinaryReader** and **BinaryWriter** classes for writing and reading binary data. Therefore, you use a binary rather than a text file stream when you must handle binary streams of information rather than textual information.

BinaryReader class

The **BinaryReader** class reads primitive data types as binary values in a specific encoding.

BinaryWriter class

The **BinaryWriter** class writes primitive types in binary to a stream and supports writing strings in a specific encoding.

Example

The following code example demonstrates writing two bytes of data to a file:

```
FileStream fs = new
  FileStream(@"C:\TEST2.DAT",FileMode.CreateNew);
BinaryWriter w = new BinaryWriter(fs);
w.Write((byte)65);
w.Write((byte)66);
w.Close();
fs.Close();
```

How to Traverse the Windows File System

- **Using the DirectoryInfo and FileInfo classes**

```
DirectoryInfo d = new DirectoryInfo("C:\\");
DirectoryInfo[] subd = d.GetDirectories();
foreach (DirectoryInfo dd in subd) {
  if (dd.Attributes==FileAttributes.Directory) {
      FileInfo[] f = dd.GetFiles();
      foreach (FileInfo fi in f) {
            listBox1.Items.Add(fi.ToString());
      }
  }
}
```

- **Using recursion**
  - Technique where a function calls itself, repeatedly, passing in a different parameter

Introduction

The ability to look over files and subdirectories for a specific directory is essential for many programming tasks. You can work with files and directories by using the **DirectoryInfo** and **FileInfo** classes in combination, which is a very efficient way to obtain all of the information that you need about files and subdirectories in a specific directory.

DirectoryInfo class

The **DirectoryInfo** class exposes instance methods for creating, moving, and enumerating through directories and subdirectories. This class includes the **GetFiles** method which returns a file list from the current directory.

FileInfo class

The objects inside the directory can be files or directories. You can iterate through the directory twice, looking for files first, and directories next. An alternate solution is to use the **FileSystemInfo** object, which can represent a **FileInfo** or a **DirectoryInfo** object. Using the **FileSystemInfo** object allows you to iterate through the collection only once.

Example

```
DirectoryInfo d = new DirectoryInfo("C:\\");
DirectoryInfo[] subd = d.GetDirectories();
foreach (DirectoryInfo dd in subd) {
  if (dd.Attributes==FileAttributes.Directory) {
      FileInfo[] f = dd.GetFiles();
      foreach (FileInfo fi in f) {
          listBox1.Items.Add(fi.ToString());
      }
  }
}
```

Using recursion

Recursion is a programming technique where a function calls itself, repeatedly, passing in a different parameter. For example, to traverse the Windows file system, you can pass the root of a particular drive, such as C:\, into a function. The function then obtains the subdirectories of this directory and calls itself for each subdirectory, and so on.

Caution   Recursion can generate a **StackOverflowException** error.

Practice: Using File System Information

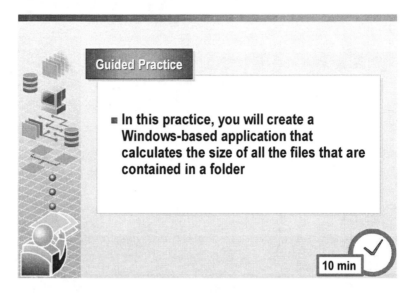

In this practice, you will create a Windows-based application that calculates the size of all the files that are contained in a folder.

The solution for this practice is located in *install_folder*\Practices\Mod06\Streams_Solution. Start a new instance of Visual Studio .NET before opening the solution.

Tasks	Detailed steps
1. Start Visual Studio .NET.	▪ Start a new instance of Visual Studio .NET.
2. Open *install_folder*\Practices \Mod06\Streams\Streams.sln.	a. On the **Start Page**, click **Open Project**. b. In the **Open Project** dialog box, browse to *install_folder*\Practices \Mod06\Streams, click **Streams.sln**, and then click **Open**.
3. Open the Code Editor for Form1.	▪ In Solution Explorer, under **Solution 'Strings'**, under project **Strings**, right-click **Form1.cs**, and then click **View Code**.

Tasks	Detailed steps
4. To the **button1_Click** procedure, add code that calculates the size of the files in the directory specified in textBox1.	a. Scroll down through the code displayed in the window and locate the **button1_Click** procedure. b. Add code into this procedure that calculates the total size of the files contained in the directory specified by textBox1. Use the **MessageBox** class to display your result to the user.
5. Run the application and test it with the C:\Program Files\Msdntrain directory.	a. On the standard toolbar, click **Start**. b. In the Streams Practice window, in the **Directory** text box type **C:\Program Files\Msdntrain** and then click **Calculate Size**. The total size of the files contained in the directory should be displayed in a message box.
	OPTIONAL: If you have time, try using recursion in your application to calculate the size of all the files contained in the folder specified and all subfolders of that folder. You might want to examine the solution *install_folder*\Practices\Mod06\Streams_Recursive\Streams.sln. Notice the use of the **ref** keyword in the **calculate_size** procedure and the calls to this procedure.

Review

- **Examining the .NET Framework Class Library**
- **Overriding Methods from System.Object**
- **Formatting Strings and Numbers**
- **Using Streams and Files**

1. The following table lists namespace contents and namespaces. Draw a line to match the namespace to its contents.

Namespace	Namespace contents
System	**A.** Types that allow you to read and write files.
System.Collections	**B.** Most of the classes that constitute the ADO.NET architecture.
System.Data	**C.** Fundamental classes and base classes that define commonly-used value and reference data types, events and event handlers, interfaces, attributes, and processing exceptions.
System.Diagnostics	**D.** Interfaces and classes that define various collections of objects.
System.IO	**E.** Classes that allow you to interact with system processes, event logs, and performance counters.

2. What methods are inherited from the **System.Object** base class when you create a new class?

1 Get type
2 ToString
3 hash value.
4

String builder

Filestream

BinaryReader Writer

3. The **Append**, **AppendFormat**, **Insert**, and **Replace** methods belong to which class?

4. What type of object do you create to open an existing file or to create a new file?

5. Which two classes are used for writing and reading binary data?

Lab 6.1: Using Streams

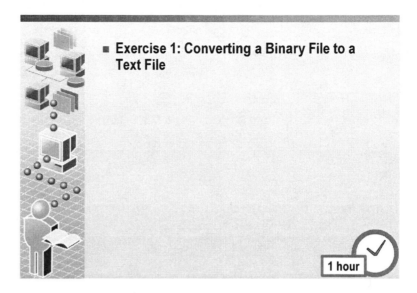

- **Exercise 1: Converting a Binary File to a Text File**

1 hour

Objectives

After completing this lab, you will be able to:

- Read data from a binary file.
- Write text to a file.
- Format strings.

Prerequisites

Before working on this lab, you must have:

- Format strings, currency, and date values.
- Read and write both binary and text files.

Scenario

In this, lab you will build a C# application that will take the data contained in a binary file and write it as a human-readable text file. The data contained in the file represents transactions from a transaction clearing company. The data consists of the account number that the money was debited from, the amount of money, and the date the transaction occurred. The data is encoded in the file as shown in the following table:

B1	B2	B3	B4	B5	B6	B7	B8	B9	B10
Account (1-999)		DayOfYear (1-365)		Year (1900-3000)		Amount Implied 2 decimal places (for example, 100.25 held as 10025)			

Your application will take the data contained in *install_folder*\Labs\ Lab06_1\data.bin and convert it into a file named *install_folder*\Labs \Lab06_1\output.txt.

Your output text file should contain the columns shown in the following table:

Column	Size
Date in Long date format	44 characters
Account	3 characters
Amount shown as a currency	8 characters

Write your conversion code to calculate the total of the Amount column. Your total should equal $223,652.00.

Estimated time to complete this lab: 60 minutes

Exercise 1
Converting a Binary File to a Text File

In this exercise, you will write an application that converts a binary file to a text file.

Tasks	Detailed steps
1. Start Visual Studio .NET, and then create a new project. Project Type: **Visual C#** Template: **Windows Application** Location: *install_folder*\Labfiles\Lab06_1 Name: **FileConversion**	a. Start a new instance of Visual Studio .NET. b. On the **Start Page**, click **New Project**. c. In the **New Project** dialog box, under **Project Types**, click **Visual C# Projects**. d. Under **Templates**, click **Windows Application**. e. In the **Location** box, type *install_folder***Labfiles\Lab06_1** f. In the **Name** box, type **FileConversion** and then click **OK**.
2. Write the code to convert the file.	▪ Write the necessary code to convert the file as described in the lab scenario.

 Application Hints. You may wish to work through the following step guidelines to create this application.

a. Add a button to the form.

b. Add the code to for this application into the button_Click event.

c. Create a **FileStream** object to open the binary file.

d. Use the opened **FileStream** object to create a **BinaryReader** object. The **BinaryReader** object provides you with binary methods to manipulate the binary file.

e. Create a **StreamWriter** object to output the text file.

f. Add definitions for variables that your code will use.

g. Create a while loop structure to loop through the binary file. The loop condition should be:

```
(binaryReaderObj.Length > binaryReader.Position)
```

h. Within the loop, use the **ReadUInt16** method to read the 2 byte data and the **ReadUInt32** method to read the 4 byte data.

i. Calculate the running total.

j. The binary file holds the date as a year and the number of days from the beginning of the year. To use this data to set a variable of type DateTime:

```
System.DateTime dt = new System.DateTime(yearfrombinaryfile,1,1);
```

k. Use the **AddDays** method of the **DateTime** class to correct for the days in the year.

```
dt = dt.AddDays(dayofyearfrombinaryfile);
```

l. Notice above that the **AddDays** method returns a new **DateTime** object.

m. Format the data to be written into the text file. Use the **WriteLine** method to output the line of text to the text file.

n. When the loop is complete, close all stream-based objects.

| 3. Run the application and create the output file. | ▪ Run your application. |

msdn training

Module 7: Using ADO.NET to Access Data

Contents

always Connected

SQL connection
Transaction
SQL Transaction

SQL Exception
Errors
SQL Error

SQL Command
Parameters
SQL parameters

SQL DataReader
SQL Data Adapter

Table mapping
· Select command
· update "
· insert "
· Delete "

always never connected
Disconnected ↔ XML

Data Table
Columns
Data Column
Rows
Data Row
constraint
Data Constraint

Relation
Data Relation
Parent columns
Data Column
child columns
Data Column

Data View
Table
· Sort / · Row filter

Overview

- ADO.NET Architecture
- Creating an Application That Uses ADO.NET to Access Data
- Changing Database Records

Introduction

This module explains how to use Microsoft® ADO.NET and the objects in the **System.Data** namespace to access data in a database. It describes how to create an application based on Microsoft Windows® that uses ADO.NET. This module also describes how to use that application to connect to a database, create a query, and use a **DataSet** object to manage the data, bind data to controls, and insert, update, and delete records in a database.

Objectives

After completing this module, you will be able to:

- Describe ADO.NET.
- Create a Windows-based application that uses ADO.NET.
- Connect to a database.
- Create a query.
- Use a **DataSet** object to manage data.
- Bind a **DataGrid** object to a data source.
- Insert, update, and delete a database record.

Lesson: ADO.NET Architecture

- ■ **What Is ADO.NET?**

- ■ **What Is a Connected Environment?**

- ■ **What Is a Disconnected Environment?**

- ■ **What Is the ADO.NET Object Model?**

- ■ **What Is the DataSet Class?**

- ■ **What Is the .NET Data Provider?**

Introduction

This lesson describes ADO.NET, the basic structure of a database, ADO.NET **DataSet** classes, and .NET data providers.

Lesson objectives

After completing this lesson, you will be able to:

- ■ Explain ADO.NET.
- ■ Explain the ADO.NET object model.

Lesson agenda

This lesson includes the following topics and activities:

- ■ What Is ADO.NET?
- ■ What Is a Connected Environment?
- ■ What Is a Disconnected Environment?
- ■ What Is the ADO.NET Object Model?
- ■ Multimedia: Using ADO.NET to Access Data
- ■ What Is the **DataSet** Class?
- ■ What Is the .NET Data Provider?
- ■ Practice: ADO.NET Architecture

What Is ADO.NET?

ADO.NET is a data access technology. It provides:

- A set of classes, interfaces, structures, and enumerations that manage data access from within the .NET Framework

- An evolutionary, more flexible successor to ADO

- A system designed for disconnected environments

- A programming model with advanced XML support

Introduction

With the evolution of computers, data access and processing models evolved from highly localized to highly distributed. As the number of users and the amount of data increased, data access models evolved from a single user on a single application to multiple users on the Internet.

An increasing number of applications use XML to encode data to be passed over network connections. ADO.NET provides a programming model that incorporates features of both XML and ActiveX® Data Objects (ADO) within the Microsoft .NET Framework to accommodate distributed data access and processing that uses Windows-based, Web, or console (command-line) applications.

Definition

ADO.NET is a data acccss technology. It provides:

- A set of classes, interfaces, structures, and enumerations that manage data access from within the .NET Framework.

- A system designed for disconnected environments.

- A programming model with advanced XML support.

Benefits

ADO.NET provides the following advantages over previous data access models:

- *Scalability*. The ADO.NET programming model encourages programmers to conserve system resources for applications that run on the Web. Because data is held locally in in-memory caches, there is no need to maintain active database connections for extended periods.

- *Programmability*. The ADO.NET programming model uses strongly typed data. Strongly typed data makes code more concise and easier to write because Microsoft Visual Studio® .NET provides statement completion.

- *Interoperability*. ADO.NET makes extensive use of XML. XML is a portable, text-based technology to represent data in an open and platform-independent way, which makes it easier to pass data between applications even if they are running on different platforms.

ADO.NET components

The ADO.NET components are designed to separate data access from data manipulation. The two components of ADO.NET that accomplish this are the **DataSet** object and the .NET data provider. The components of the .NET data provider are explicitly designed for disconnected data manipulations.

ADO.NET and Windows Forms provide data consumer components that you can use to display your data. These components include controls, such as the **DataGrid** control, that can be bound to data, and data-binding properties on most standard Windows controls, such as the **TextBox**, **Label**, **ComboBox**, and **ListBox** controls.

What Is a Connected Environment?

- ■ **A connected environment is one in which users are constantly connected to a data source**
- ■ **Advantages:**
  - ● Environment is easier to secure
  - ● Concurrency is more easily controlled
  - ● Data is more likely to be current than in other scenarios
- ■ **Disadvantages:**
  - ● Must have a constant network connection
  - ● Scalability

Introduction

A connected environment is one in which a user or an application is continuously connected to a data source. For much of the history of computers, the only available environment was the connected environment.

Advantages A connected scenario offers the following advantages:

- ■ A secure environment is easier to maintain.
- ■ Concurrency is easier to control.
- ■ Data is more likely to be current than in other scenarios.

Disadvantages

A connected scenario has the following disadvantages:

- ■ It must have a constant database connection.
- ■ It is not scalable.

Examples

The following are examples of connected environments:

- ■ A factory that requires a real-time connection to monitor production output and storage.
- ■ A brokerage house that requires a constant connection to stock quotes.

What Is a Disconnected Environment?

- In a disconnected environment, a subset of data from a central data store can be copied and modified independently, and the changes merged back into the central data store

- Advantages
  - You can work at any time that is convenient for you, and can connect to a data source at any time to process requests
  - Other users can use the connection
  - A disconnected environment improves the scalability and performance of applications

- Disadvantages
  - Data is not always up to date
  - Change conflicts can occur and must be resolved

Introduction

With the advent of the Internet and with the increasing use of mobile devices, disconnected scenarios have become commonplace. Laptop, notebook, and other portable computers allow you to use applications when you are disconnected from servers or databases.

In many situations, people do not work entirely in a connected or disconnected environment, but rather in an environment that combines the two approaches.

Definition

A disconnected environment is one in which a user or an application is not constantly connected to a source of data. Mobile users who work with laptop computers are the primary users in a disconnected environment. Users can take a subset of data with them on a disconnected computer and then merge changes back into the central data store.

Advantages

A disconnected environment provides the following advantages:

- You can work at any time that is convenient for you, and you can connect to a data source at any time to process requests.
- Others can share connection resources.
- The scalability and performance of applications is improved.

Example

When you return your rental car, the person who accepts the car uses a handheld computer to read the return information. Because the handheld device may have limited processing capacity, it is important to scale the data to the task that the user performs at any given time.

Disadvantages

A disconnected environment has the following disadvantages:

- Data is not always up to date.
- Change conflicts can occur and must be resolved.

What Is the ADO.NET Object Model?

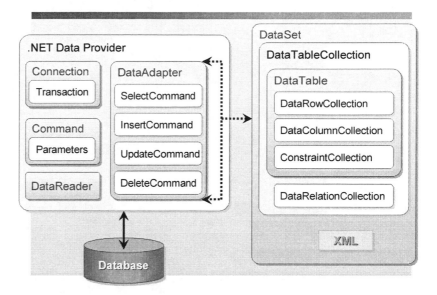

Introduction

The ADO.NET object model consists of two major parts:

- .NET data provider classes
- **DataSet** class

.NET data provider classes

The .NET data provider classes are specific to a data source. Therefore, the .NET data providers must be written specifically for a data source and will work only with that data source. The .NET data provider classes enable you to connect to a data source, retrieve data from the data source, and perform updates on the data source.

The ADO.NET object model includes the following .NET data provider classes:

- SQL Server .NET Data Provider
- OLE DB .NET Data Provider

DataSet class

The **DataSet** class allows you to store and manage data in a disconnected cache. The **DataSet** is independent of any underlying data source, so its features are available to all applications, regardless of the origin of the data in the application.

Multimedia: Using ADO.NET to Access Data

This animation demonstrates how to access data by using ADO.NET.

▶ **To view the animation**

Action	Description
Start animation.	There are two ways to access data from a database by using ADO.NET: by using a **DataSet** object or by using a **DataReader** object. This animation demonstrates how these two methods work and highlights their differences.
Click **Start**.	
Click **DataSet**.	Using the **DataSet** object is a disconnected way to access data from a database.
	In this method, when a user requests data from a database, the **DataAdapter** object is used to create a **DataSet**, which is a collection of data tables from the database that also retains the relationships between these tables. Notice that, after a **DataSet** is populated, it is disconnected from the database.
	To display the data from the **DataSet**, you bind the **DataSet** directly to a list-bound control. You can use any of the three list-bound controls, **DataGrid**, **Repeater**, or **DataList**, to display data.
	The data in the list-bound control is then displayed on the client.
Click **DataReader**.	Using the **DataReader** object is similar to the Microsoft ActiveX® Data Objects (ADO) way of accessing data by using recordsets.
	In this method, when a user requests data from a database, the **Command** object retrieves the data into a **DataReader**. A **DataReader** is a read-only/forward-only view of the data. A **DataReader** works similarly to a Recordset in ADO, allowing you to simply loop through the records. Like the ADO Recordset, the **DataReader** is connected to the database. You must explicitly close the connection when you are finished reading data.

What Is the DataSet Class?

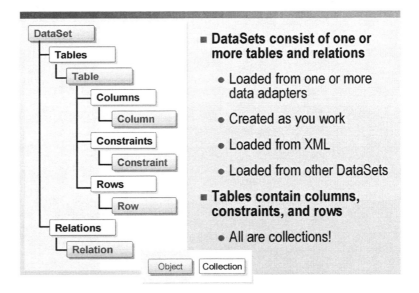

Introduction

The ADO.NET **DataSet** class is the core component of the disconnected architecture of ADO.NET.

DataSet objects

The **DataSet** objects in the **System.Data** namespace serve as a virtual cache of a database, including not only data, but also schemas, relationships, and constraints, which may be loaded from one or more data adapters, created as you work, loaded from XML, or loaded from other datasets. **DataSet** objects are disconnected from the parent data source, so you effectively have full access to the data without needing a persistent connection to the data source.

Example

When you work with a database, you most likely use only a small portion of the database. The **DataSet** class allows you to retrieve only the data that you need at a given time.

DataSet collections

The **DataSet** class contains collections of:

- *Tables*. Tables are stored as a collection of **DataTable** objects, which in turn each hold collections of **DataColumn** and **DataRow** objects.

- *Relations*. Relations are stored as a collection of **DataRelation** objects that describe the relationships between tables.

- *Constraints*. Constraints track the information that ensures data integrity.

In ADO.NET, **DataSet**, **DataTable**, and **DataColumn** objects enable you to represent data in a local cache and provide a relational programming model for the data, regardless of its source.

What Is the .NET Data Provider?

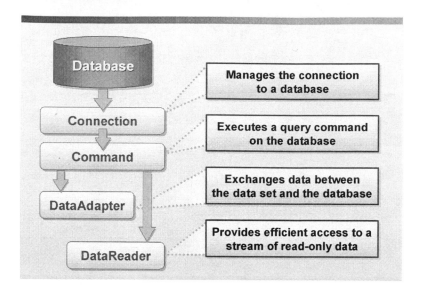

Introduction

A .NET data provider enables you to connect to a database, execute commands, and retrieve results.

Those results are either processed directly or placed in an ADO.NET **DataSet** object to be exposed to the user in an ad-hoc manner, combined with data from multiple sources, or used remotely.

.NET data providers

A .NET data provider can handle basic data manipulation, such as updates, inserts, and basic data processing. Its primary focus is to retrieve data from a data source and pass it on to a **DataSet** object, where your application can use it in a disconnected environment.

ADO.NET provides two kinds of .NET data providers:

- SQL Server .NET Data Provider

  The SQL Server .NET Data Provider accesses databases in Microsoft SQL Server™ version 7.0 or later. It provides excellent performance because it accesses SQL Server directly instead of going through an intermediate OLE DB provider.

- OLE DB. NET Data Provider

  The OLE DB .NET Data Provider accesses databases in SQL Server 6.5 or earlier, Oracle, and Microsoft Access.

.NET data provider classes

ADO.NET exposes a common object model for .NET data providers. The following table describes the core classes that make up a .NET data provider, which you can use in a disconnected scenario.

Class	Description
Connection	Establishes and manages a connection to a specific data source. For example, the **SqlConnection** class connects to OLE DB data sources.
Command	Executes a query command from a data source. For example, the **SqlCommand** class can execute SQL statements in an OLE DB data source.
DataAdapter	Uses the **Connection**, **Command**, and **DataReader** classes implicitly to populate a **DataSet** object and to update the central data source with any changes made to the **DataSet**. For example, the **SqlDataAdapter** object can manage the interaction between a **DataSet** and an Access database.
DataReader	Provides an efficient, forward-only, read-only stream of data from a data source.

Practice: ADO.NET Architecture

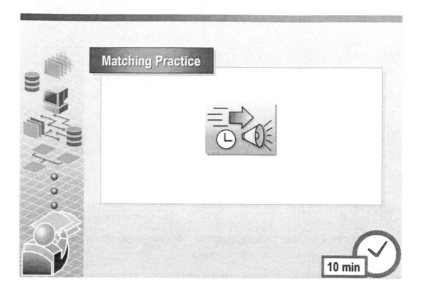

In this practice, you will use an interactive animation to manipulate various components of ADO.NET. Place the components in order, so that they show how information is read from a database and displayed on a Windows Form.

Tasks	Detailed steps
1. Start the animation located at *install_folder* Mod07\AdoArchitecture\ 2609A_ADO.Arch.htm.	▪ Using Windows Explorer, navigate to *install_folder* Mod07\AdoArchitecture and then double-click 2609A_ADO.Arch.htm.
2. Drag and drop each component to the correct location.	a. Drag and drop the **SQL Server 2000**, **SQL Data Adapter**, **DataSet**, **DataGrid**, and **Windows Form** to their appropriate squares. b. Drag and drop **Select and Connect Commands**, **Data Source**, and **Fill** to their appropriate callouts.
3. Check your answer by clicking **Reveal**.	▪ Click **Reveal** to see the correct order that these components should have been placed.
4. Close the animation window.	▪ Close the animation window.

Lesson: Creating an Application That Uses ADO.NET to Access Data

- **How to Specify the Database Connection**
- **How to Specify the Database Command**
- **How to Create the DataAdapter Object**
- **How to Create a DataSet Object**
- **How to Bind a DataSet to a DataGrid**
- **How to Use the Data Wizards in Visual Studio .NET**

Introduction

This lesson explains how to create an application that uses ADO.NET to access a database. This lesson also describes how to display database contents by binding a **DataSet** object to a **DataGrid**.

Lesson objectives

After completing this lesson, you will be able to:

- Create an application that uses ADO.NET.
- Retrieve information from a database by using ADO.NET.
- Bind a **DataSet** object to a **DataGrid** control.

Lesson agenda

This lesson includes the following topics and activities:

- How to Specify the Database Connection
- How to Specify the Database Command
- How to Create the **DataAdapter** Object
- How to Create a **DataSet** Object
- How to Bind a DataSet to a DataGrid
- Demonstration: Using the Data Wizards in Visual Studio .NET
- How to Use the Data Wizards in Visual Studio .NET
- Practice: Using the Data Adapter Configuration Wizard

How to Specify the Database Connection

- **Use the Connection object to:**
  - Choose the connection type
  - Specify the data source
  - Open the connection to the data source

- **Use the connection string to specify all of the options for your connection to the database, including the account name, database server, and database name**

```
string connectionStr = @"Data Source=localhost;
  Integrated Security=SSPI; Initial
  Catalog=northwind";
```

Introduction

Before you can work with data, you must first establish a connection to a data source. To connect to a data source, you choose the connection type, specify the data source, and then open the connection to the data source. As you connect to the data source, you should also consider certain database security issues.

Choosing the connection type

You can use the **Connection** object to connect to a specific data source. You can use either the **SqlConnection** object to connect to a SQL Server database or the **OleDbConnection** object to connect to other types of data sources.

Specifying the data source

After you choose the connection type, you use a **ConnectionString** property to specify the data provider, the data source, and other information that is used to establish the connection.

Syntax

The following table describes common parameters of connection strings. The table contains a partial list of the values.

Parameter	Description
Initial Catalog	The name of the database.
Data Source	The name of the SQL Server to be used when a connection is open, or the filename of a Microsoft Access database.
Integrated Security or Trusted Connection	The parameter that determines whether the connection is to be a secure connection. **True**, **False**, and **SSPI** are the possible values. **SSPI** is the equivalent of **True**.
User ID	The SQL Server login account.
Password	The login password for the SQL Server account.
Provider	The property used to set or return the name of the provider for the connection, used only for **OleDbConnection** objects.
Connection Timeout or Connect Timeout	The length of time in seconds to wait for a connection to the server before terminating the attempt and generating an exception. **15** is the default.
Persist Security Info	When set to **False**, security-sensitive information, such as the password, is not returned as part of the connection if the connection is open or has ever been in an open state. Setting this property to **True** can be a security risk. **False** is the default.

Example 1

The following code shows how to specify the connection to a SQL Server database by using the SQL .NET Data Provider (note the use of a verbatim string):

```
string connectionString = @"data source=localhost;integrated
security=SSPI;initial catalog=Northwind";
```

In this example, the database is located on the local computer (localhost), Windows authentication is used, and the database name is **Northwind**.

Example 2

The following code establishes a connection to an Access database by using the OLE DB .NET Data Provider:

```
string connectionString =
@"provider=Microsoft.JET.OLEDB.4.0;data
source=C:\samples\northwind.mdb";
```

In this example, the provider connects to the database that is located at C:\samples\northwind.mdb.

Database security

When you build an application that accesses data, you normally must connect to a secure database. To do so, you must pass security information, such as user name and password, to the database before a connection can be made. The database security that is available depends on the database that you access.

SQL Server can operate in one of two authentication modes:

- Microsoft Windows Authentication (recommended)
- Mixed Authentication Mode (Windows Authentication and SQL Server authentication)

Windows Authentication allows a user to connect through a Windows user account. Network security attributes for the user are established at network login time and are validated by a Windows domain controller.

When a network user tries to connect, SQL Server verifies that the user has a valid SQL Server account, and then permits or denies login access based on that network user name alone, without requiring a separate login name and password.

Although it is possible to specify the user name and password in the connection string, you should avoid using these parameters, and use the stronger security offered by Windows Authentication.

Warning If you decide to build the connection string from user input, make sure that you carefully check the input so that the user does not include extra commands in their text.

How to Specify the Database Command

```
string commandStr=@"SELECT CustomerName,
  CompanyName FROM Customers";
```

- **Create a string containing SQL statements**
  - Remember that Verbatim strings can make this much easier!
- **Examples of SQL statements:**
  - SELECT * FROM Customers
  - SELECT CustomerName FROM Customers
  - SELECT * FROM Customers WHERE Country = 'Mexico'

Introduction

After you connect to a database, you must specify the set of information that you want to retrieve from it. There are several ways to do this. This topic describes how to create a string that contains a database query and then how to send that string to a database.

The following four examples use the **Northwind Traders** database.

Example 1

The following simple query selects all of the data in the **Customers** table:

```
string queryString = "SELECT * FROM Customers";
```

Example 2

The following query selects the data rows in the **Customer** table where the value of the **CompanyName** column is equal to **Island Trading** (note the use of a verbatim string):

```
string commandString = @"SELECT * FROM Customers WHERE
CompanyName='Island Trading'";
```

Example 3

The following code selects the *CompanyName* and *ContactName* fields from only those rows in which **CompanyName** is **Island Trading**:

```
string commandString = @"SELECT CompanyName, ContactName FROM
Customers WHERE CompanyName='Island Trading'";
```

Example 4

The following more complex SQL command shows how to define a command string that selects a number of fields from the **Products** table, such as **Products.ProductID**, and a number of items from the **Suppliers** table, such as **Suppliers.CompanyName**. Note the use of the **INNER JOIN** command specifying the relationship between **Suppliers.SupplierID** and **Products.SupplierID**.

```
string commandString = @"SELECT Products.ProductID,
Products.ProductName, Products.SupplierID,
Products.CategoryID, Products.QuantityPerUnit,
Products.UnitPrice, Suppliers.CompanyName,
Suppliers.SupplierID AS Expr1 FROM Products INNER JOIN
Suppliers ON Products.SupplierID = Suppliers.SupplierID";
```

Note   For more information about the SQL Query, see the following resources.

- Online resource: MSDN® at msdn.microsoft.com
- Printed resource: Microsoft Press® SQL Book, *Microsoft SQL Server 2000 Resource Kit*, ISBN 0-7356-1266-8.
- Training resource: Course 2389, *Programming with ADO.NET*.

How to Create the DataAdapter Object

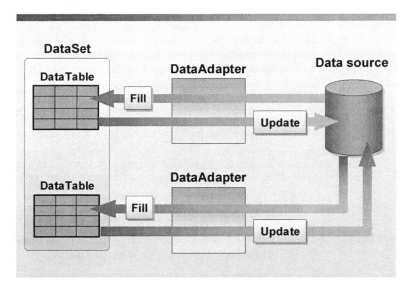

Introduction

To establish the connection to the data source and manage the movement of data to and from the data source, you use a **DataAdapter** object.

Definition

A **DataAdapter** object serves as a bridge between a **DataSet** object and a data source, such as a database, for retrieving and saving data. The **DataAdapter** object represents a set of database commands and a database connection that you use to fill a **DataSet** object and update the data source. **DataAdapter** objects are part of the .NET data providers, which also include connection objects, data-reader objects, and command objects.

Each **DataAdapter** object exchanges data between a single **DataTable** object in a dataset and a single result set from a SQL statement. Use one **DataAdapter** object for each query when you send more than one query to a database from your application.

Example

You use a **DataAdapter** object to exchange data between the data source and a **DataSet** object. In many applications, this means reading data from a database into a dataset through the data adapter, and then writing changed data from the dataset to the data adapter and back to the database. A data adapter can move data between any source and a dataset. For example, an adapter can move data between a server running Microsoft Exchange and a dataset.

Primary DataAdapters for databases

Visual Studio .NET makes two primary data adapters available for use with databases. Other data adapters can also be integrated with Visual Studio .NET.

The primary data adapters are:

- **OleDbDataAdapter**, which is suitable for use with certain OLE DB providers.

- **SqlDataAdapter**, which is specific to a Microsoft SQL Server 7.0 or later database. The **SqlDataAdapter** is faster than the **OleDbDataAdapter** because it works directly with SQL Server and does not go through an OLE DB layer.

DataAdapter properties

You use **DataAdapter** objects to act on records from a data source. You can specify which actions you want to perform by using one of the following four **DataAdapter** properties, which execute a SQL statement. The properties are actually command objects that are instances of the **SqlCommand** or **OleDbCommand** class.

Select Command	Retrieves rows from the data source.
InsertCommand	Writes inserted rows from the DataSet into the data source.
UpdateCommand	Writes modified rows from the DataSet into the data source.
DeleteCommand	Deletes rows in the data source.

Depending on how you specify your **DataAdapter**, these command objects can be generated automatically. For example, if you pass a command string and a connection string to the constructor when you create the **DataAdapter**, the **SelectComman**d property is constructed for you.

Methods used by a DataAdapter

You use **DataAdapter** methods to fill a dataset or to transmit changes in a **DataSet** table to a corresponding data store. These methods include:

- **Fill**

  Use this method of a **SqlDataAdapter** or **OleDbDataAdapter** to add or refresh rows from a data source and place them in a **DataSet** table. The **Fill** method uses the **SELECT** statement that is specified in the **SelectCommand** property.

- **Update**

  Use this method of a **DataAdapter** object to transmit changes to a **DataSet** table to the corresponding data source. This method calls the corresponding **INSERT**, **UPDATE**, or **DELETE** command for each specified row in a **DataTable** in a **DataSet**.

- **Close**

  Use this method to close the connection to the database.

Example of creating a DataAdapter programmatically

The following example uses a **SqlDataAdapter** object to define a query in the **Northwind** database:

```
using System;
using System.Data;
using System.Data.SqlClient;

namespace Samples {
  class SampleAdo {
      static void Main(string[] args) {
              string connectionString = @"data source=localhost;
Initial catalog=Northwind; integrated security=SSPI";
              string commandString = @"SELECT * FROM Customers";
              SqlDataAdapter dataAdapter = new SqlDataAdapter(
commandString, connectionString );

              DataSet myDataSet = new DataSet();
              dataAdapter.Fill( myDataSet );

              DataTable table = myDataSet.Tables[0];
              int numberRows = table.Rows.Count;
      }
    }
}
```

Example

The following example uses a **OleDbDataAdapter** object to define a query in the **Northwind** database.

```
using System;
using System.Data;
using System.Data.OleDb;

namespace Samples {
  class SampleAdo {
      static void Main(string[] args) {
              string connectionString =
@"provider=Microsoft.JET.OLEDB.4.0;data
source=c:\samples\Northwind.mdb";
              string commandString = @"SELECT * FROM Customers";
              OleDbDataAdapter dataAdapter = new
OleDbDataAdapter( commandString, connectionString );

              DataSet myDataSet = new DataSet();
              dataAdapter.Fill( myDataSet );

              DataTable table = myDataSet.Tables[0];
              int numberRows = table.Rows.Count;
      }
    }
}
```

How to Create a DataSet Object

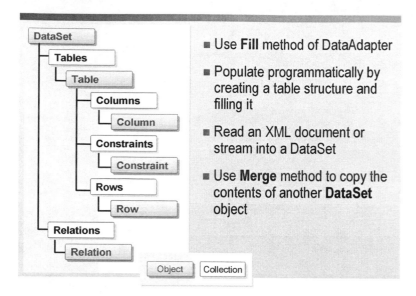

- Use **Fill** method of DataAdapter

- Populate programmatically by creating a table structure and filling it

- Read an XML document or stream into a DataSet

- Use **Merge** method to copy the contents of another **DataSet** object

Introduction

After you specify the data that you want to retrieve, the next step is to populate a **DataSet** object with data from the database. **DataSet** objects store data in a disconnected cache. The structure of a **DataSet** is similar to that of a relational database; it exposes an object model of tables, rows, and columns. It also contains constraints and relationships that are defined for the **DataSet**.

Populating DataSets

A **DataSet** is a container; therefore, you must populate it with data. You can populate a **DataSet** in a variety of ways:

- Call the **Fill** method of a data adapter

  This method causes the adapter to execute an SQL statement and fill the results into a table in the **DataSet**. If the **DataSet** contains multiple tables, you probably have separate data adapters for each table and therefore must call the **Fill** method of each adapter separately.

- Manually populate tables in the **DataSet**

  You use this method by creating **DataRow** objects and adding them to the **Rows** collection of the table. You can set the **Rows** collection only at run time, not at design time.

- Read an XML document or stream into the **DataSet**

- Copy or merge the contents of another **DataSet**

  This scenario can be useful if your application obtains DataSets from various sources, such as various XML Web services, but must consolidate them into a single DataSet.

Example 1

You use a **DataAdapter** to access data stored in a database, and store the data in **DataTable** objects in a **DataSet** in your application. The following example shows how to create a **DataSet** that contains all the data in the **Customers** table in the **Northwind Traders** database.

```
using System;
using System.Data;
using System.Data.SqlClient;

namespace Samples {
  class SampleSqlADO {
      static void Main(string[] args) {
              string connectionString = @"data source=localhost;
Initial catalog=Northwind; integrated security=SSPI";
              string commandString = @"SELECT * FROM Customers";
              SqlDataAdapter dataAdapter = new SqlDataAdapter(
commandString, connectionString );

              DataSet myDataSet = new DataSet();
              dataAdapter.Fill( myDataSet );
      }
    }
}
```

Example 2

One of the overloads of the **Fill** method allows you to specify a name that you can subsequently use to reference the table, as shown in the following example:

```
using System;
using System.Data;
using System.Data.SqlClient;

namespace Samples {
  class SampleSqlADO {
      static void Main(string[] args) {
              string connectionString = @"data source=localhost;
Initial catalog=Northwind; integrated security=SSPI";
              string commandString = @"SELECT * FROM Customers";
              SqlDataAdapter dataAdapter = new SqlDataAdapter(
commandString, connectionString );

              DataSet myDataSet = new DataSet();
              dataAdapter.Fill( myDataSet, "Customers" );

              DataTable table = myDataSet.Tables["Customers"];
      }
    }
}
```

You can use this feature to make your code more readable and therefore more maintainable.

How to Bind a DataSet to a DataGrid

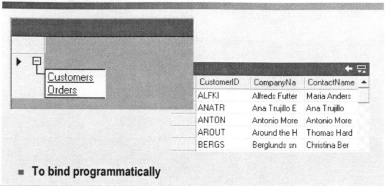

- **To bind programmatically**

```
DataGrid dataGrid1 = new DataGrid();
sqlDataAdapter1.Fill(dataSet1, "Customers");
sqlDataAdapter2.Fill(dataSet1, "Orders");
dataGrid1.DataSource = dataSet1;
```

Introduction

After you populate a **DataSet** object, you can view and modify data by using the Windows Forms **DataGrid** control. The **DataGrid** displays data in a series of rows and columns. In a simple example, the grid is bound to a data source with a single table that contains no relationships and the data appears in simple rows and columns, as in a spreadsheet.

How the DataGrid control works

If the **DataGrid** control is bound to data with multiple related tables, and if navigation is enabled on the grid, the grid displays expanders in each row. An expander allows navigation from a parent table to a child table. Clicking a node displays the child table, and clicking the **Back** button displays the original parent table. In this fashion, the grid displays the hierarchical relationships between tables.

The **DataGrid** can provide a user interface for a **DataSet**, navigation between related tables, and rich formatting and editing capabilities.

The display and manipulation of data are separate functions:

- The control handles the user interface.
- The data-binding architecture of Windows Forms and ADO.NET data providers handle data updates.

Therefore, multiple controls that are bound to the same data source stay in sync.

Binding data to the control

For the **DataGrid** control to work, you must bind it to a data source by using the **DataSource** property or by using the **SetDataBinding** method. You can set the **DataSource** property by using the Properties window in the development environment, or programmatically.

This binding points the **DataGrid** to an instantiated data-source object, such as a **DataSet** or **DataTable**, and the **DataGrid** control shows the results of actions that are performed on the data.

Scenario 1

You can bind to a **DataSet**, which may contain multiple tables, as shown in the following example:

```
        .
        .
        .
    public class Form1 : System.Windows.Forms.Form {
        private System.Windows.Forms.DataGrid dataGrid1;
        .
        .
        public Form1() {

            string connectionString = @"data source=localhost;
Initial catalog=Northwind; integrated security=SSPI";
            string commandString = @"SELECT * FROM Customers";
            dataAdapter = new SqlDataAdapter( commandString,
connectionString );

            myDataSet = new DataSet();
            dataAdapter.Fill( myDataSet, "Customers" );

            dataGrid1.DataSource = myDataSet;
        }
        .
        .
        .
    }
```

Scenario 2

Or, you can bind to a single table in a **DataSet** object, as shown in the following example:

```
dataGrid1.DataSource = myDataSet.Tables["Customers"];
```

Demonstration: Using the Data Wizards in Visual Studio .NET

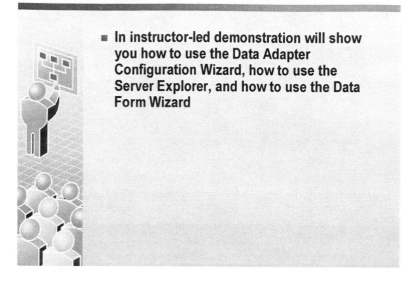

- **In instructor-led demonstration will show you how to use the Data Adapter Configuration Wizard, how to use the Server Explorer, and how to use the Data Form Wizard**

This instructor-led demonstration will show you how to use the Data Adapter Configuration Wizard, how to use Server Explorer, and how to use the Data Form Wizard.

▶ **How to Use the Data Adapter Configuration Wizard**

1. Connect to **Northwind** Database by using **SqlDataAdapter** object.

2. Specify connection and SQL command information by using the **Query Builder**.

3. Select a table and generate the dataset.

▶ **How to Use the Server Explorer**

1. Access Server Explorer.

2. Add and remove connections by using Server Explorer.

3. Drag items from Server Explorer and drop them into Windows Forms Designer.

4. View database elements by using Server Explorer.

▶ **How to Use the Data Form Wizard**

1. Start the Data Form Wizard.

2. Add a form to a project by using the Data Form Wizard.

3. Select a database connection, select tables, and then display them on the form.

Tip   The Data Form Wizard creates a new Form. You can easily display this form by changing the parameter to **Application.Run** in the **Main** method, so that it references the form created by the Wizard.

How to Use the Data Wizards in Visual Studio .NET

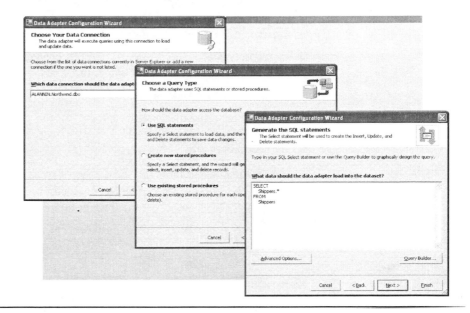

Introduction

You can use the visual tools in Visual Studio .NET to automatically generate much of the code that is required to access a database. This feature can be useful for rapidly prototyping database applications.

Visual Studio .NET provides the Data Adapter Configuration Wizard to build Data Provider objects. This wizard is complemented by Server Explorer, which lets you view and manipulate database information, such as connections, tables and records, on any server to which you have network and database access, and the Data Form Wizard, which helps you create Web-based pages and Windows-based forms containing data-bound controls.

Using the Data Adapter Configuration Wizard

The Data Adapter Configuration Wizard helps you set the properties of a new or existing data adapter. A data adapter contains SQL commands that your application can use to read data into a **DataSet** from a database and write it back again. The wizard can optionally create a data connection that allows the adapter to communicate with a database.

To use the Data Adapter Configuration Wizard:

1. Drag an **OleDbDataAdapter** or **SqlDataAdapter** object from the Toolbox onto a form or component.

2. Specify connection and SQL command information.

   The wizard displays several dialog boxes:

   a. If you ask to create a connection, the wizard displays the **Connection** tab of the **Data Link Properties** dialog box, which allows you to specify a provider, server name, database name, user name, and password for the connection.

   b. To help you create SQL statements, the wizard provides the Query Builder, a utility that allows you to create and test a **SELECT** statement by using visual tools. To launch it, click the **Query Builder** button when asked for a SQL statement.

3. In the Component Designer, select the adapter or adapters that will be used to transfer data between the data source and the **DataSet**.

   Typically, each data adapter accesses data in a single table. Therefore, to create a **DataSet** that contains multiple data tables, select all the adapters for the tables that you want to work with.

4. On the **Data** menu, click **Generate DataSet**.

   The **Generate DataSet** dialog box appears.

5. Click **New**, and then specify a name for the new DataSet. To add the DataSet to your form or component, select **Add this dataset to the designer** and then click **OK.**

6. You must add code to fill the dataset. Typically, the designer creates a data adapter named **sqlDataAdapter1**, and an instance of a dataset named **dataSet11**, so you should add the following line:

```
sqlDataAdapter1.Fill( dataSet11 );
```

Adding a DataGrid control

To bind the **DataGrid** control to a single table in the Component Designer:

1. In the Toolbox, on the **Data** tab, click the **DataGrid** control and drag it over the form.

2. Press F4 to display the Properties window.

3. Expand the **(DataBindings)** property.

4. Set the **DataSource** property of the control to the object containing the data items that you want to bind to.

5. If the data source is a **DataSet** or a data view based on a **DataSet** table, add code to the form to fill the **DataSet**.

Accessing Server Explorer

You can access Server Explorer at any time during the development process, while working with any type of project or item.

To access Server Explorer:

- On the **View** menu, click **Server Explorer**.

– or –

- If the **Server Explorer** tab is displayed on the left edge of the screen, click that tab.

Adding and removing data connections

Server Explorer displays database connections under the Data Connections node. After you establish a connection, you can design programs to open connections and retrieve and manipulate the data that is provided. By default, Server Explorer displays data connections and links to servers that you have previously used.

To add a data connection in Server Explorer:

1. On the **Tools** menu, click **Connect to Database**.

   The **Data Link Properties** dialog box opens.

2. On the **Provider** tab of the **Data Link Properties** dialog box, select a provider.

3. On the **Connection** tab of the **Data Link Properties** dialog box, provide the information requested. The input fields displayed vary, depending upon the provider that you selected on the **Provider** tab.

   For example, if you select the OLE DB Provider for SQL Server, the **Connection** tab displays fields for server name, type of authentication, and database.

4. Click **OK** to establish the data connection.

   The **Data Link Properties** dialog box closes, and the new data connection appears under the Data Connections node, named for the server and database accessed. For example, if you create a data connection to a database called **NWind** on a server named **Server1**, a new connection named **Server1.NWind.dbo** appears under the Data Connections node.

To remove a data connection from Server Explorer:

1. In Server Explorer, expand the **Data Connections** node.

2. Select the desired database connection.

3. Press DELETE.

   There is no effect on the actual database. You are removing the reference from your view.

Dragging and dropping data resources

You can drag items from Server Explorer and drop them onto the Windows Forms Designer. Putting items onto the Windows Forms Designer creates new data resources that are preconfigured to retrieve information from the selected data source.

To create a new data component by using Server Explorer, you can create a data component preconfigured to reference a particular resource.

1. In Design view, open the form to which you want to add a data component.

2. In Server Explorer, select the data item that you want to use. An example of a data item is a field or table.

3. Drag the item from Server Explorer to the designer surface.

Viewing database elements

You can use Server Explorer to view and retrieve information from all of the databases that are installed on a server. You can list database tables, views, stored procedures, and functions in Server Explorer; expand individual tables to list their columns and triggers; and right-click a table to select the Table Designer from its shortcut menu.

Using the Data Form Wizard

You use the Data Form Wizard to help create pages and forms that contain data-bound controls. The Data Form Wizard creates a new page or form in your project that contains a DataGrid, along with **Load**, **Update**, and **Cancel All** buttons.

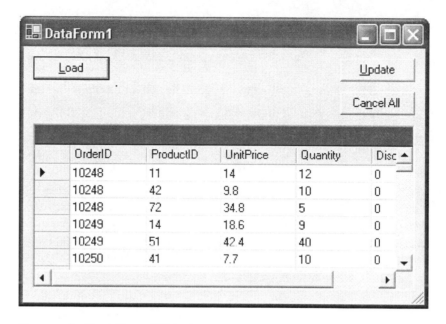

To start the Data Form Wizard:

1. Create a new Windows project.

2. In the Solution Explorer, right-click the project and on the shortcut menu, point to **Add**, and then click **Add New Item**.

3. In the **Add New Item** dialog box, select the **Data** category, select the **Data Form Wizard**, and then click **Open**.

To add a form to a project by using the Data Form Wizard, perform the following steps.

Note The following procedure assumes that you start with a blank Windows project. If your project contains existing ADO.NET components, the screen sequence and contents will differ from those in the following procedure.

---

1. On the **Welcome to the DataForm Wizard** page, click **Next**.

2. On the **Choose the DataSet you want to use** page, type the name of a new DataSet, and then click **Next**.

3. On the **Choose a data connection** page, select a database connection or create a new one, and then click **Next**.

4. On the **Choose tables or view** page, select the table or tables that you want listed on your page, and then click **Next**.

5. On the **Choose tables and columns to display on the form** page, select the items that you want to display on the form, and then click **Next**.

6. On the **Choose a display style** page, select your display options, and then click **Finish**.

To display the form, invoke the **ShowDialog** method on the form. If this form is the only one that you want to display, you can pass it as a parameter to **Application.Run** in the **Main** method. For example:

```
Application.Run( new DataForm1() );
```

Practice: Using the Data Adapter Configuration Wizard

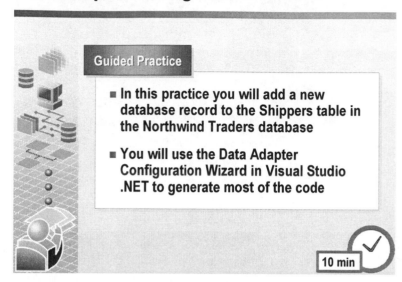

In this practice, you will add a new database record to the **Shippers** table in the **Northwind Traders** database. You will use the Database Wizard in Visual Studio .NET to generate most of the code.

The solution for this practice is located in *install_folder*\Practices\Mod07\AdoDemo1\AdoDemo\ AdoDemo.sln. Start a new instance of Visual Studio .NET before opening the solution.

Tasks	Detailed steps
1. Start Visual Studio .NET, and then create a Database Project named **AdoDemo**.	a. Start Visual Studio .NET.
	b. On the **Start Page**, click **New Project**.
	Make a note of the location of your project, in case you need to refer back to it later.
	c. In the **New Project** dialog box, in the Project Types window, expand **Other Projects**, and then click **Database Projects**.
	d. In the Templates window, click **Database Project**.
	e. In the **Name** box, delete the existing name, type **AdoDemo** and then click **OK**.
2. Set the **Data Link Properties** by using the information that is provided in the following table, and then click **OK**.	a. If you have already established a link to the database, an **Add Database Reference** dialog box is displayed. If you see this box, click **Add New Reference**.
	b. Insert the values from the following table into the **Data Link Properties** dialog box, and then click **OK**.
	For machinename, substitute the name of your computer, or type **localhost**
	c. If you see the **Add Database Reference** dialog box, click **OK**.

Tasks	Detailed steps
Item Select or enter a server name Enter information to log on to the server Select the database on the server	**Value** *machinename* or **localhost** **Use Windows NT Integrated Security** **Northwind**
3. Use Server Explorer to examine the **Shippers** table in the **Northwind** database.	**a.** In Server Explorer, expand *machinename*.**Northwind.dbo**, and then expand **Tables**. **b.** Double-click the **Shippers** table to see the contents of the database table.
4. Use Solution Explorer to add a C# Project named **AdoPractice** to the solution.	**a.** In Solution Explorer, right-click **Solution 'AdoDemo'**, point to **Add**, and then click **New Project**. **b.** Add a new C# Windows Application project to the solution, naming it **AdoPractice**.
5. Use Server Explorer to add a connection to the **Shippers** table to the application.	▪ Using a drag operation, drag the **Shippers** table from Server Explorer and drop it on the form in the Designer. Note that Visual Studio .NET creates a **SqlConnection (sqlConnection1)** object and a **SqlDataAdapter (sqlDataAdapter1)** object at the bottom of the form.
6. Use the Designer to add a **DataSet** to the application.	**a.** Right-click the Data Adapter icon **sqlDataAdapter1**, and then on the shortcut menu, click **Generate Dataset**. Note that Visual Studio usually selects both **sqlDataAdapter1** and **sqlConnection1** after adding them, so you may need to ensure that only **sqlDataAdapter1** is selected. You can easily do this by clicking anywhere else in the Designer and then clicking **sqlDataAdapter1**. **b.** In the **Generate Dataset** dialog box, click **OK**. This generates a new **DataSet** type named **DataSet1**, and creates an instance of this type, named **dataSet11**.
7. Add a **DataGrid** to the application, and then bind it to the **Shippers** table in the DataSet.	**a.** Click the **Toolbox** tab, and then drag a **DataGrid** onto the form. **b.** Resize the **DataGrid** so that it fills the top ¾ of the form. **c.** Use the Properties window to set the **DataSource** property of the DataGrid to **dataSet11.Shippers**.

Tasks	Detailed steps
8. Write code to use the **Fill** method of the Data Adapter to fill the DataSet.	a. In Visual Studio .NET, press F7 to open the Code Editor. b. Locate the TODO line (**TODO: Add any constructor code after InitializeComponent call**) in the form constructor. c. Delete the TODO comment lines and add code that calls the **Fill** method on **sqlDAtaAdapter1**, passing in **dataSet11** as the DataSet parameter: `sqlDataAdapter1.Fill( dataSet11, "Shippers" );`
9. Test your application.	▪ Press F5 to build and run your application.
10. Save your work and keep Visual Studio .NET open.	▪ Save your work and keep Visual Studio .NET open. You will use this project in the following lesson.

Lesson: Changing Database Records

- ■ **How to Access Data in a DataSet Object**
- ■ **How to Update a Database in ADO.NET**
- ■ **How to Create a Database Record**
- ■ **How to Update a Database Record**
- ■ **How to Delete a Database Record**

Introduction	This lesson describes how create, update, and delete records in a database by using ADO.NET.
Lesson objectives	After completing this lesson, you will be able to:

- ■ Examine methods for updating a database.
- ■ Create a database record.
- ■ Update a database record.
- ■ Delete a database record.

Lesson agenda

This lesson includes the following topics and activity:

- ■ How to Access Data in a DataSet Object
- ■ How to Update a Database in ADO.NET
- ■ How to Create a Database Record
- ■ How to Update a Database Record
- ■ How to Delete a Database Record
- ■ Practice: Updating a Database Record

How to Access Data in a DataSet Object

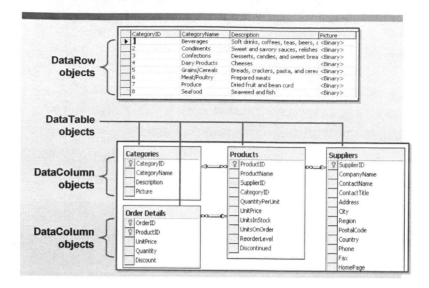

DataRow objects					
DataTable objects					
DataColumn objects					
DataColumn objects					

Introduction

The **DataSet** object contains a collection of tables and knowledge of relationships between these tables. Each table contains a collection of columns. These objects together represent the schema of the **DataSet**. Each table can have multiple rows, representing the data held by the **DataSet**. These rows track their original state along with their current state, which enables the **DataSet** to track all the changes that occur during data manipulation.

Using tables in a DataSet

A **DataSet** can contain multiple tables. You can retrieve multiple sets of data from a database and store them in separate tables in a **DataSet**. For example, you can query the supplier table and the products table, and hold both results in the same **DataSet**. The tables are stored in the **Tables** collection, and you can reference an individual table by using an index.

```
DataTable firstTable = myDataSet.Tables[0];
```

Using rows and columns in a DataSet

You can access individual rows in the DataTable by using the **Rows** collection. You can access columns by using the **Columns** collection.

The following code accesses the **Customers** table from the **Tables** collection. It then retrieves the number of rows in the table by accessing the **Count** property of the **Rows** collection. Finally, it retrieves the name of the first column in the table by accessing the **Columns** collection.

```
using System;
using System.Data;
using System.Data.SqlClient;

namespace LearningCSharp {
  class SampleSqlADO {
      static void Main(string[] args) {
          string connectionString = @"data source=localhost;
Initial catalog=Northwind; integrated security=SSPI";
          string commandString = @"SELECT * FROM Customers";
          SqlDataAdapter dataAdapter = new SqlDataAdapter(
commandString, connectionString );

          DataSet myDataSet = new DataSet();
          dataAdapter.Fill( myDataSet, "Customers" );

          DataTable myTable = myDataSet.Tables["Customers"];

          int numberRows = myTable.Rows.Count;
          Console.WriteLine("Rows: {0} ", numberRows);

          DataColumn c = myTable.Columns[0];
          Console.WriteLine("Column one: {0}", c.ColumnName);
      }
    }
}
```

This sample produces the following output:

```
Rows: 91
Column one: CustomerID
```

This sample is available on the Student Materials compact disc, in the Samples\Mod07\RowColumn folder.

Row and column names

You can reference the tables, rows and columns in a DataSet by name and by index.

The mapping between tables and names allows you to use names with the tables, rows and columns in your DataSet rather than having to reference them by their index. For example, in the code sample above, instead of writing:

```
DataColumn c = table.Columns[0];
```

you can write:

```
DataColumn c = table.Columns["CustomerID"];
```

CustomerID is the name of the column in the database. If you want to use a different name, you can create a mapping between the name used in the database and the one you choose yourself by using the **DataTableMapping** object in the **System.Data.Common** namespace.

Example

The following code creates a **DataTableMapping** object for the **Customers** table. The table mapping is maintained in the Data Adapter.

The **DataTableMapping** object maps the string **NWCustomers** to the **Customers** table. Note that the **Fill** method now uses **NWCustomers** as the name of the source table.

The **DataTableMapping** object maintains a collection named **ColumnMappings** that is used here to map two columns from the **Customers** table to a set of names specified by the programmer. For columns that are not mapped, the name of the column from the data source is used.

The new name of the column is then used to access the column.

```
using System;
using System.Data;
using System.Data.Common;
using System.Data.SqlClient;

namespace Samples {
  class DataTableMappingExample {
      static void Main(string[] args) {
          string connectionString = @"data source=localhost;
Initial catalog=Northwind; integrated security=SSPI";
          string commandString = @"SELECT * FROM Customers";
          SqlDataAdapter dataAdapter = new SqlDataAdapter(
commandString, connectionString );

          DataTableMapping dtm =
dataAdapter.TableMappings.Add("Customers", "NWCustomers");
          dtm.ColumnMappings.Add("CompanyName", "Company");

          DataSet myDataSet = new DataSet();
          dataAdapter.Fill( myDataSet, "NWCustomers" );

          DataTable myTable =myDataSet.Tables["NWCustomers"];

          DataColumn coColumn =myTable.Columns["CompanyName"];
      }
  }
}
```

Using DataRelation object

Usually when a DataSet contains multiple tables, there is a relationship between the data stored in the tables. You can express this relationship in ADO.NET by using the **DataRelation** object.

Example

In this example, the **Suppliers** tables and **Products** table are read into the **DataSet**. These tables are related in the database—the **SupplierID** from the **Suppliers** table identifies the supplier for the products that are listed in the **Products** table. In database terminology, **SupplierID** is the primary key for the **Supplier** table, meaning that it is unique and identifies each record in that table. Each supplier can provide multiple products, so the list of products may reference the same supplier ID more than once.

The following code uses the **DataSet.Relations.Add** method to create a relationship between the **SupplierID** in the **Suppliers** table and the **SupplierID** in the **Products** table. When this small application is run, the **foreach** loop prints a list with each company name (**CompanyName**) followed by the various products that they supply (**ProductNames**).

```csharp
using System;
using System.Data;
using System.Data.Common;
using System.Data.SqlClient;

namespace LearningCSharp {
    class SuppliersProducts {
        static void Main(string[] args) {
            DataSet myDataSet = new DataSet();

            // Products Table
            string connectionString = @"data source=localhost; Initial
catalog=Northwind; integrated security=SSPI";
            string commandString = @"SELECT * FROM Suppliers";

            SqlDataAdapter dataAdapter =
                new SqlDataAdapter(commandString, connectionString);

            // Suppliers Table
            connectionString = @"data source=localhost; Initial catalog=Northwind;
integrated security=SSPI";
            commandString = @"SELECT * FROM Products";

            SqlDataAdapter dataAdapter2 =
                new SqlDataAdapter(commandString, connectionString);

            dataAdapter.Fill( myDataSet, "Suppliers" );
            dataAdapter2.Fill( myDataSet, "Products" );

            int tableCount = myDataSet.Tables.Count;

            DataRelation dr = myDataSet.Relations.Add( "ProductSuppliers",
                    myDataSet.Tables["Suppliers"].Columns["SupplierID"],
                    myDataSet.Tables["Products"].Columns["SupplierID"]
                );

            foreach (DataRow pRow in myDataSet.Tables["Suppliers"].Rows) {
                Console.WriteLine(pRow["CompanyName"]);
                foreach (DataRow cRow in pRow.GetChildRows(dr)) {
                    Console.WriteLine("\t" + cRow["ProductName"]);
                }
            }
        }
    }
}
```

Sample output follows:

```
Exotic Liquids
  Chai
  Chang
  Aniseed Syrup
New Orleans Cajun Delights
  Chef Anton's Cajun Seasoning
  Chef Anton's Gumbo Mix
  ...
```

This code sample is available on your Student Materials compact disc in the Samples\Mod07\DataRelation folder.

How to Update a Database in ADO.NET

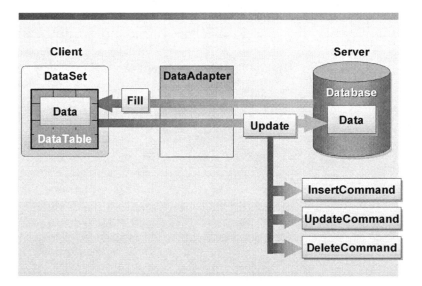

Introduction

After you populate the dataset with data, you must send it from the dataset to the database. The data adapter uses its **Update** method to send the data. The **Update** method examines every record in the specified data table in the dataset and, if a record has changed, sends the appropriate **Update**, **Insert**, or **Delete** command to the database.

Updating the database

Because a dataset is effectively a cache—an in-memory copy—of data, the process of updating the data in the dataset is separate from the process of updating the original data source.

Updating a database in ADO.NET involves three steps:

1. Update the data in the dataset.

2. Update the data in the database.

3. Notify the dataset that the database accepted the changes.

First step

The first step is to update the dataset with new information, which includes new records, changed records, and deleted records. The dataset marks the new information as **Modified**, and maintains a copy of the old information, so that it can restore the original data in the event of a problem updating the database.

Note In Windows Forms, the data-binding architecture takes sends changes from data-bound controls to the DataSet, so you do not have to explicitly update the DataSet with your own code.

Second step

Next, send the changes from the dataset to the original data source, by calling the **Update** method of the same data adapter that you used to populate the DataSet.

When you call the **Update** method, the **DataAdapter** analyzes the changes and then uses the **InsertCommand**, **UpdateCommand**, or **DeleteCommand** command to process the change. You must set the commands before calling the **Update** method. An exception is thrown if the **Update** method is called and the appropriate command does not exist for a particular update, for example, if no **DeleteCommand** exists for deleted rows.

Third step

After the **Update** method resolves your changes back to the data source, you must notify the DataSet that the database accepted the changes. You can do this by using the **AcceptChanges** method of the **DataSet**, or if the changes could not be made to the database, you can reject the changes and return to the last DataSet update by using the **RejectChanges** method. The **AcceptChanges** method removes the copy of the old row state, whereas the **RejectChanges** method restores the old row state and deletes the changes in the DataSet.

Other clients may have modified data at the data source since the last time you filled the **DataSet**. If you need to refresh your **DataSet** with current data, use the **DataAdapter** and **Fill** the **DataSet** again. New rows are added to the table and updated information is incorporated into existing rows.

Defining the Update commands

When you select **Update**, **Insert**, or **Delete**, the DataAdapter calls a **SqlCommand** object to execute the function. These **SqlCommand** objects are stored in the DataAdapter as the properties **SelectCommand**, **InsertCommand**, **UpdateCommand**, and **DeleteCommand**.

You must define, or build, these objects at either design time or run time.

- *Design time*. Use the DataAdapter Configuration Wizard.

- *Run time*. At run time or in code, use the **SqlCommandBuilder** object to create the necessary commands. After you define the commands, you can call **Update** to invoke the appropriate command and synchronize your DataSet with the database.

How to Create a Database Record

- **Create a new row that matches the table schema**

  ```
  DataRow myRow = dataTable.NewRow();
  ```

- **Add the new row to the dataset**

  ```
  dataTable.Rows.Add( myRow );
  ```

- **Update the database**

  ```
  sqlDataAdapter1.Update( dataSet );
  ```

Introduction

After you populate the dataset with data, you often manipulate the data before sending it back to the data source or to another process or application. Because each record in a dataset is represented by a **DataRow** object, changes to a dataset are accomplished by updating and deleting individual rows. You can also insert new records into the DataSet by adding new **DataRow** objects to the **Rows** collection of the **DataTable** object.

Creating a database record

To create a database record:

1. Create a new data row.

2. Add the new data row to the **DataRow** collection of a data table by using either the **NewRow** method or the **Add** method.

   - You can call the **NewRow** method on the data table object as shown in the following example:

     ```
     DataRow myRow = dataTable.NewRow();
     myRow[0] = …  // add data to the row
     dataTable.Rows.Add( myRow );
     ```

   - You can pass the row contents to the **Add** method of the **Rows** collection, as shown in the example at the end of this section.

3. Call the **Update** method on the **DataAdapter** as shown in the following example:

   ```
   sqlDataAdapter1.Update( dataSet );
   ```

4. Calling the update method invokes the **Insert** SqlCommand.

   Tell the DataSet to accept the changes:

   ```
   myDataSet.AcceptChanges();
   ```

Example

The following example creates a new row in the **Shippers** table of the Northwind database.

```csharp
using System;
using System.Data;
using System.Data.Common;
using System.Data.SqlClient;

namespace LearningCSharp {
    class AddToShippers {
        static void Main(string[] args) {
            string connectionString = @"data source=localhost;
Initial catalog=Northwind; integrated security=SSPI";
            string commandString = @"SELECT * FROM Shippers";

            SqlDataAdapter dataAdapter = new SqlDataAdapter(
commandString, connectionString );

            SqlCommandBuilder scb = new SqlCommandBuilder(
dataAdapter );

            DataSet myDataSet = new DataSet();
            dataAdapter.Fill( myDataSet, "Shippers" );

            DataTable sTable = myDataSet.Tables["Shippers"];

            // add data
            object[] o = { 0, "General", "555-1212" };
            sTable.Rows.Add( o );

            dataAdapter.Update(myDataSet, "Shippers");

            myDataSet.AcceptChanges();
        }
    }
}
```

How to Update a Database Record

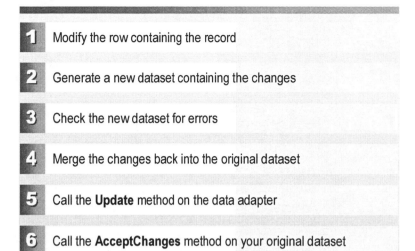

1 Modify the row containing the record

2 Generate a new dataset containing the changes

3 Check the new dataset for errors

4 Merge the changes back into the original dataset

5 Call the **Update** method on the data adapter

6 Call the **AcceptChanges** method on your original dataset

Introduction

When you modify a database record, you change the data in the row in the dataset and then call the **Update** method to merge the changes back into the database. However, because other users of the data may have changed the data while you were disconnected, you must also handle any errors that may be raised.

Modifying a database record

To modify a database record:

1. Make the desired modifications to the rows in the DataSet.

2. Generate a new dataset that contains only the changed records (rows).

3. Examine this dataset for errors, and then fix any errors that you can.

4. If you have fixed any changes, merge the new dataset back into the original dataset.

5. Call the **Update** method of the data adapter to merge the changes back into the database.

6. If the changes to the database were successful, accept them in the dataset by calling the **AcceptChanges** method. If they were unsuccessful, reject them by calling the **RejectChanges** method.

Handling an error

To handle an error that is raised because another user changed the data:

1. Use a **try...catch** block to handle exceptions that may be raised during the database update.

   The return value from the **Update** method tells you how many records were updated.

2. After the database update, call the DataSet **AcceptChanges** method to indicate that the changes are successful, or call the **RejectChanges** method to reject the changes.

Example

```csharp
using System;
using System.Data;
using System.Data.Common;
using System.Data.SqlClient;

namespace LearningCSharp {
    class SampleUpdate {
        static void Main(string[] args) {
              .
                .
                .
            // modify
            try {
                DataRow     targetRow = sTable.Rows[3];

                targetRow.BeginEdit();
                targetRow["CompanyName"] = "Standard";
                targetRow.EndEdit();

                DataSet changedSet;
                changedSet = myDataSet.GetChanges( DataRowState.Modified );
                if ( changedSet == null )
                    return;

                // check for errors
                bool fixed = false;
                if ( changedSet.HasErrors ) {
                    // Fix errors setting fixed=true
                    // or else return;
                    return;
                }

                if ( fixed ) {
                    myDataSet.Merge( changedSet );
                }
                int n = dataAdapter.Update(myDataSet, "Shippers" );

                if ( n > 0 ) {
                    myDataSet.AcceptChanges();
                }
            }
            catch {
                // handle error
                // attempt to fix changes
                // If not fixable, reject changes
                myDataSet.RejectChanges();
            }
        }
    }
}
```

How to Delete a Database Record

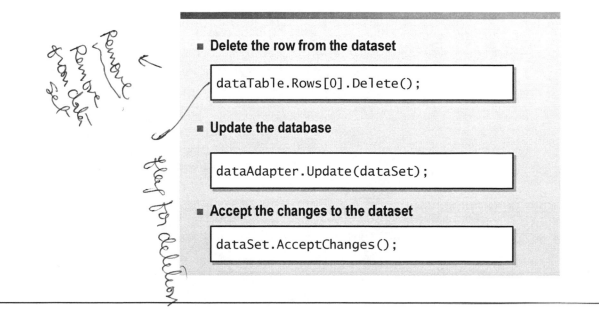

- **Delete the row from the dataset**

  ```
  dataTable.Rows[0].Delete();
  ```

- **Update the database**

  ```
  dataAdapter.Update(dataSet);
  ```

- **Accept the changes to the dataset**

  ```
  dataSet.AcceptChanges();
  ```

Introduction

To delete a **DataRow** object from a **DataTable** object, use the **Delete** method of the **DataRow** object.

Delete method

The **Delete** method marks the row for deletion. The actual removal occurs when the application calls the **AcceptChanges** method. By using **Delete**, you can programmatically check which rows are marked for deletion before actually removing them. When a row is marked for deletion, its **RowState** property is set to **Deleted**.

When using a **DataSet** or **DataTable** in conjunction with a **DataAdapter** and a relational data source, use the **Delete** method of the **DataRow** to remove the row. The **Delete** method marks the row as **Deleted** in the **DataSet** or **DataTable** but does not remove it. Instead, when the **DataAdapter** encounters a row marked as **Deleted**, it executes its **DeleteCommand** to delete the row at the data source. You can then permanently remove the row by using the **AcceptChanges** method.

Example

The following example demonstrates how to call the **Delete** method on a **DataRow** to change its **RowState** to **Deleted**:

```
DataTable sTable = myDataSet.Tables["Shippers"];
.
.
.
sTable.Rows[3].Delete();
int nRows = dataAdapter.Update(myDataSet, "Shippers" );
myDataSet.AcceptChanges();
```

Practice: Updating a Database Record

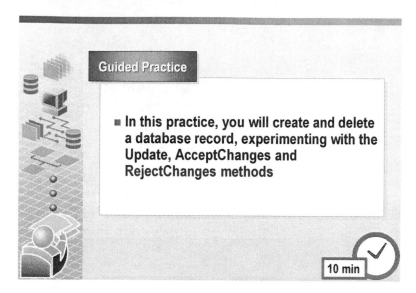

In this practice, you will use a simple application that adds and deletes a row of data to the **Shippers** table in the **Northwind** database. The application is shown in the following illustration:

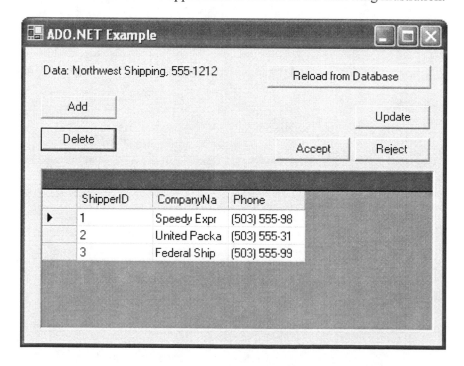

The application buttons perform the following functions:

- **Add**: Adds a row to the dataset (not the database table), with the data **Northwest Shipping** and **555-1212**.
- **Delete**: Deletes the fourth row from the dataset.
- **Reload from Database**: Reloads the table from the database into the dataset.
- **Update:** Updates the database, using *dataAdapter*.**Update()**.
- **Accept**: Accepts changes in the dataset, using *dataset*.**AcceptChanges()**.
- **Reject**: Rejects changes in the dataset, using *dataset*.**RejectChanges()**.

The DataGrid shows the current contents of the dataset.

The source code for the application used in this practice is located in *install_folder*\Practices\ Mod07\AddDelete\AddDelete.sln.

Tasks	Detailed steps
1. Using Windows Explorer, browse to *install_folder*\Practices \Mod07\AddDelete and double-click **AddDelete.exe**.	a. Using Windows Explorer, browse to *install_folder*\Practices\Mod07\AddDelete. b. Double-click **AddDelete.exe** to run the application.
2. Add a record to the dataset by clicking **Add**.	▪ In the application window, click **Add**. Note that a record is added to the dataset. This change is not yet committed to the database.
3. Refresh the dataset from the database by clicking **Reload from Database**.	▪ In the Application window, click **Reload from Database**. Note that the new record disappears. This is because the record was not added to the database.
4. Add a record to the dataset by clicking **Add** and then **Update**.	a. In the application window, click **Add** and then click **Update**. The **Update** button updates the dataset with the changes. b. Click **Reload from Database** to verify that the change was made to the **Shippers** table.
5. Delete the record from the dataset by clicking **Delete**.	▪ In the application window, click **Delete**.
6. Reject the deletion.	a. In the application window, click **Reject**. b. Verify that the deletion was rejected by clicking **Reload from Database** to reload the **Shippers** table.
7. When you are finished, close the application.	▪ When you have finished with the application, close it by clicking the **Close** button.

If time permits, experiment with the application, or examine the source code.

Review

- ADO.NET Architecture
- Creating an Application That Uses ADO.NET to Access Data
- Changing Database Records

1. Name two major parts of the ADO.NET object model.

2. What is the difference between a connected and disconnected environment?

3. What is the purpose of the **DataAdapter** object?

4. What is the name of the Windows Forms control that you can use to display multiple records that are retrieved from a data source?

5. Which method is used to populate a **DataSet** with results of a query?

Fill

Lab 7.1: Creating a Data Access Application with ADO.NET

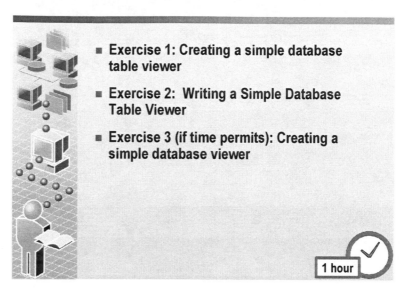

- Exercise 1: Creating a simple database table viewer
- Exercise 2: Writing a Simple Database Table Viewer
- Exercise 3 (if time permits): Creating a simple database viewer

1 hour

Objectives

After completing this lab, you will be able to:

- Use the Visual Studio .NET development environment database wizards and tools to create an ADO.NET application.

- Write an ADO.NET application in C#.

Note   This lab focuses on the concepts in this module and as a result may not comply with Microsoft security recommendations.

Prerequisites

Before working on this lab, you must have:

- The ability to create a Windows application in C#.

- The ability to use Server Explorer to access database tables.

Estimated time to complete this lab: 30 minutes

Exercise 0
Lab Setup

The Lab Setup section lists the tasks that you must perform before you begin the lab.

Task	Detailed steps
■ Log on to Windows by using your Student account.	■ Log on to Windows by using the following account information: • User name: **Student** • Password: **P@ssw0rd** Note that the 0 in the password is a zero.

Note that by default the *install_folder* is C:\Program Files\Msdntrain\2609.

Exercise 1
Creating a Simple Database Table Viewer

In this exercise, you will use the Visual Studio development environment database wizards and tools to build a simple application that reads, displays, and allows you to view and edit a specific table in a database.

Use the following information to build your connection string and your command statement.

- **Server**: *your computer* (or **localhost**)
- **Database**: 2609
- **Table**: BankCustomers

When you are finished, your solution should appear as shown in the following illustration:

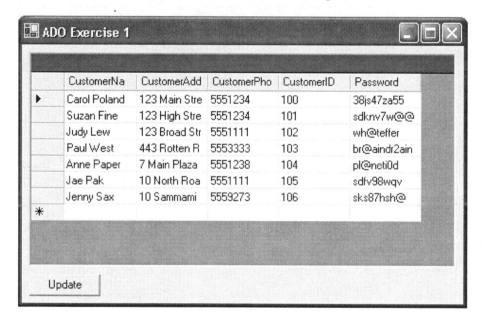

The solution for this lab is located in *install_folder*\Labfiles\Lab07_1\Exercise1\
Solution_Code\LabADO.sln. Start a new instance of Visual Studio .NET before opening the
solution.

Tasks	Detailed steps
1. Create a new Windows application and use Server Explorer to add a **SqlDataAdapter** object to your application. The data adapter should read all information from the **BankCustomers** table in the **2609** database on your computer.	a. Create a new Windows application. b. Use Server Explorer to locate the **2609** database and the **BankCustomers** table on your computer. c. Use Server Explorer to add the **BankCustomers** table to your application. By default, the **SqlDataAdapter** object created by Server Explorer reads all of the data in the table. This object is named **sqlDataAdapter1** by default; this is the name that we will use to refer to the object throughout this lab.
❓ What ADO.NET objects are created when you use Server Explorer to add the **BankCustomers** table to your application? _____ _____	
2. Create a **DataSet** object and fill it with the data from the **BankCustomers** table.	a. In the Designer window, select **sqlDataAdapter1** and on the **Data** menu, click **Generate Dataset**. b. Use the dialog box to add the **DataSet** object to your application. c. Write code to fill the **DataSet** object with the data that is read by **sqlDataAdapter1** by using **sqlDataAdapter1.Fill**. You can place this line of code in the Form1 constructor, after the call to **InitializeComponent**.
3. Add a **DataGrid** to your form, and bind its **DataSource** to the **BankCustomers** table in the **DataSet** object.	a. Use the Toolbox to add a **DataGrid** to your form. b. Use the Properties window to set the DataGrid **DataSource** property to the **BankCustomers** table in the **DataSet** object.

Tasks	Detailed steps
4. Add a button to your form, label it **Update**, and then add a **Click** event handler that will call the data adapter **Update** method.	a. Add a button to the form, changing its **Text** property to **Update**. b. Double-click the **Update** button and note that a new method is added. By default, this method is called **button1_Click**, and it is called when the Update button is clicked. c. In **button1_Click**, call the **Update** method of the **SqlDataAdapter** object. For example: `sqlDataAdapter1.Update( dataSet11 );`
5. Compile, run, and test your application.	a. Press F5 to compile and run your application. b. You can edit existing database entries and then click **Update** to commit these changes to the database. c. Use Server Explorer to verify that your changes have been made to the database. d. You can also add new records if you specify a unique **CustomerID**.
6. Save your application and quit Visual Studio .NET.	a. Save your application. b. Quit Visual Studio .NET.

Exercise 2
Writing a Simple Database Table Viewer

In this exercise, you will write code that creates a simple Windows-based application that reads information from the **BankCustomers** table in the **2609** database on your computer, and displays the Customer name and ID. This action will be performed when the user clicks the **Load** button on the form.

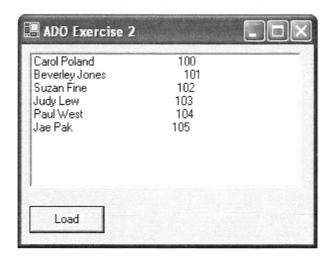

Do not use the Designer to add any ADO.NET components to your form.

The solution for this lab is located in *install_folder*\Labfiles\Lab07_1\Exercise2\ Solution_Code\LabADO2.sln. Start a new instance of Visual Studio .NET before opening the solution.

Tasks	Detailed steps
1. Start Visual Studio .NET and then open *install_folder* \Labfiles\Lab07_1\Exercise2 \LabADO2.sln.	a. Start a new instance of Visual Studio .NET. b. On the **Start Page**, click **Open Project**. c. In the **Open Project** dialog box, browse to the folder *install_folder*\Labfiles\Lab07_1\Exercise2, click **LabADO2.sln**, and then click **Open**.
2. In the **loadData_Click** method, write code to connect to the **BankCustomers** table in the **2609** database, and read the contents of the table into a **DataSet** object.	a. Create a connect string that connects to a data source on your computer, with an initial catalog of **2609**. b. Create a command string that selects everything from the **BankCustomers** table. c. Create a **SqlDataAdapter** object, using the connect string and the command string. d. Create a **DataSet** object. e. Use the **Fill** method of the **SqlDataAdapter** to fill the **DataSet** object.

Tasks	Detailed steps

3. Write code to write the contents of the **DataSet** table to the **ListBox** control.	a. Use a **foreach** loop to iterate over the **Rows** collection in the **DataSet** table.
	
	Each element of the **Rows** collection is of type **DataRow**.
	
	b. Within the **foreach** loop, create a string that contains the customer name and customer ID for each customer in the table.
	
	For example, if the row for an individual customer is called **customerRecord**, you can access the customer name by using the following code:
	
	`string name = customerRecord["CustomerName"];`
	
	c. Within the foreach loop, use the following code to add items to the ListBox, where the ListBox is named **listBox1**:
	
	`listBox1.Items.Add( name );`

4. Compile, run, and test your application.	a. Press F5 to compile and run your application. b. Compare your output to that shown in the graphic at the start of this exercise.
5. Save your application and quit Visual Studio .NET.	a. Save your application. b. Quit Visual Studio .NET.

If Time Permits
Creating a Simple Database Table Viewer

Modify the database query to view more than one table. For example, the **BankAccounts** table is related to the **BankCustomer** table by **CustomerID**.

Lab 7.2 (optional): Creating a Windows Application That Uses ADO.NET

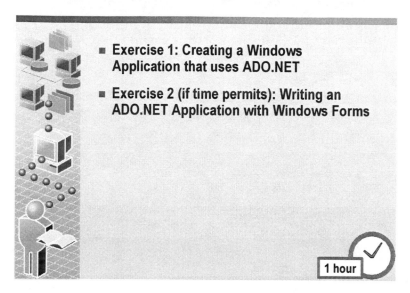

- Exercise 1: Creating a Windows Application that uses ADO.NET

- Exercise 2 (if time permits): Writing an ADO.NET Application with Windows Forms

1 hour

Objectives

After completing this lab, you will be able to create a Windows-based application that uses ADO.NET to add, delete, and modify database information.

Note This lab focuses on the concepts in this module and, as a result, may not comply with Microsoft security recommendations.

Prerequisites

Before working on this lab, you must be able to:

- Describe ADO.NET.

- Create a Windows-based application that uses ADO.NET.

- Connect to a database.

- Create a query.

- Use a **DataSet** object to manage data.

- Bind a **DataGrid** object to a data source.

Estimated time to complete this lab: 60 minutes

Exercise 0
Lab Setup

The Lab Setup section lists the tasks that you must perform before you begin the lab.

Task	Detailed steps
▪ Log on to Windows by using your Student account.	▪ Log on to Windows by using the following account information: • User name: **Student** • Password: **P@ssw0rd** Note that the 0 in the password is a zero.

Note that by default the *install_folder* is C:\Program Files\Msdntrain\2609.

Exercise 1
Creating a Windows Application That Uses ADO.NET

In this exercise, you will write a Windows application that reads information from a database table and provides users with the ability to add new records, delete records, and modify records.

When you are finished, your solution should appear as shown in the following illustration:

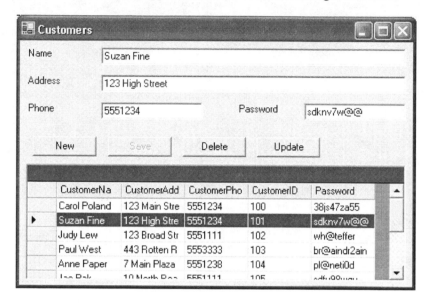

Starter code is provided for the user interface. In this lab, you will implement the **Save**, **Delete**, and **Update** button functionality.

The solution for this lab is located in *install_folder*\Labfiles\Lab07_2\Solution_Code\LabADO.sln. Start a new instance of Visual Studio .NET before opening the solution.

Tasks	Detailed steps
1. Start Visual Studio.NET and then open *install_folder* \Labfiles\Lab07_2 \LabADO.sln.	a. Start a new instance of Visual Studio.NET. b. On the **Start Page**, click **Open Project**. c. In the **Open Project** dialog box, browse to *install_folder*\Labfiles \Lab07_2, click **LabADO.sln**, and then click **Open**. d. In Solution Explorer, click **Form1.cs**, and then press **F7** to open the Code Editor.
2. Build and run the application, and familiarize yourself with the intended purpose of the **New**, **Save**, **Delete**, and **Update** buttons.	a. In Visual Studio .NET, press F5. b. Examine the Customers application and set breakpoints so that you can follow the execution sequence. c. Click **New**. Notice that the TextBoxes are cleared and that the **Save** button is active. Users can now enter new customer information in the text boxes and it will be saved to the database when they click **Save**. d. Click **Save**, and notice that the **Save** button is disabled. The **Save** function will place the new customer information in the database. e. The **Update** button will allow the user to change an existing record. f. The **Delete** button will allow the user to delete the currently selected record from the database. g. Close the Customers window.
3. Implement the **Save** function.	a. In Visual Studio .NET, on the **View** menu, point to **Show Tasks**, and then click **All**. b. In the Task List, double-click **TODO 1: Add the customer to the database**. Note that the code that reads the customer information from the form is supplied to you. The new customer information is placed in a new **DataRow** object called **newRow**. c. Write code to complete the **buttonSave_Click** method by adding the new row to the dataset, updating the database, and accepting the changes in the dataset. Note that the dataset is called **customerDS**.

Tasks	Detailed steps
4. Implement the **Delete** function.	a. In Visual Studio .NET, on the **View** menu, point to **Show Tasks** and then click **All**.
	b. In the Task List, double-click **TODO 2: Delete the selected customer from the database.**
	c. Use the following method provided in the **Form1** class to identify the currently selected row:
	`this.SelectedRow()`
	d. Delete the selected row from the dataset, and update the database. If the update is successful, accept the dataset changes, otherwise reject the changes.
	e. Use the following method to update the User Interface when you have finished the deletion:
	`this.UpdateTextBoxes()`
5. Implement the **Update** function.	a. In Visual Studio .NET, on the **View** menu, point to **Show Tasks** and then click **All**.
	b. In the Task List, double-click **TODO 3: Update the customer record.**
	c. Use the **GetChanges** method to get the changed dataset.
	d. If the changed dataset does not exist, has no changes, or has errors, then simply reject the changes and return.
	e. Update the database with the changed set, and if the update was successful, accept the changes.
	*Note: Do not use the **Merge** method of the dataset. The **Update** command that is auto-generated by **SqlCommandBuilder** is not intended to work with merged datasets and will cause the **Update** method to throw a **DBConcurencyException**.*
6. Save your solution and quit Visual Studio .NET.	a. On the **File** menu, click **Save All**.
	b. On the **File** menu, click **Exit**.

If Time Permits
Writing an ADO.NET Application with Windows Forms

Some areas of the **ValidCustomer** method in this sample application should be developed.

The sample application copies the input directly from the user and saves it to the database. In a real application, this action is a security risk because the user can enter SQL commands instead of data, and thereby attempt to access the database in unexpected ways. Although the database security should limit access so that users can access only what they really need, the application must also ensure that only valid data is sent to the database.

The **ValidCustomer** method should check that the values sent to the database are valid data. For example, the telephone number must contain only digits, a name must contain only the set of characters A to Z and a to z plus a period. Regular expressions are a good way to validate data in this way. The .NET Framework provides a regular expression class named **Regex**. If time permits, read about this class in the .NET Framework documentation.

msdn training

Module 8: Creating Windows–based Applications

Contents

Overview

- Creating the Main Menu
- Creating and Using Common Dialog Boxes
- Creating and Using Custom Dialog Boxes
- Creating and Using Toolbars
- Creating the Status Bar
- Creating and Using Combo Boxes

Introduction

Menus, dialog boxes, status bars, and toolbars are tools that enable you to expose functionality to your users or alert them to important information in your application. Menus contain commands that are grouped by a common theme. You can use dialog boxes to interact with the user and retrieve user input. Status bars indicate application state or provide information about the entity in the application that has focus, such as a menu command. Toolbars provide buttons that make frequently used commands available.

This module describes how to create menus, common and custom dialog boxes, status bars, and toolbars to enhance the usability of your application.

Objectives

After completing this module, you will be able to:

- Create the main menu.
- Create and use common dialog boxes.
- Create and use custom dialog boxes.
- Create and use toolbars.
- Create the status bar.
- Create and use combo boxes.

Lesson: Creating the Main Menu

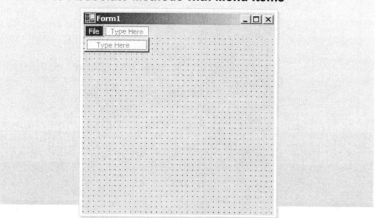

- How to Create the Main Menu
- How to Associate Methods with Menu Items

Introduction

This lesson explains how to create the main window menu, add items to the menu, and associate methods with menu items.

Lesson objectives

After completing this lesson, you will be able to:

- Create the main menu.
- Add items to the menu.
- Associate methods with menu items.

Lesson agenda

This lesson includes the following topics and activities:

- Demonstration: Creating the Main Menu
- How to Create the Main Menu
- How to Associate Methods with Menu Items
- Practice: Creating the Main Menu

Demonstration: Creating the Main Menu

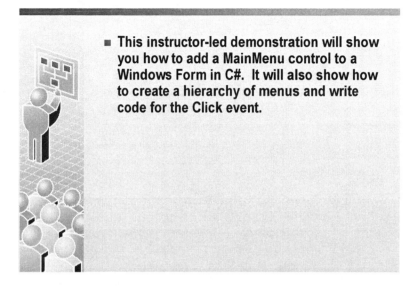

- This instructor-led demonstration will show you how to add a MainMenu control to a Windows Form in C#. It will also show how to create a hierarchy of menus and write code for the Click event.

This instructor-led demonstration will show you how to add a **MainMenu** control to a Microsoft® Windows® Form in C#. It will also show how to create a hierarchy of menus and write code for the **Click** event. The instructor will:

1. Open Microsoft Visual Studio® .NET and create a new Windows Application project named **MyForm**.

2. Add a **MainMenu** control to the form.

3. Add some menu items, for example **File**, **Edit**, and **View**.

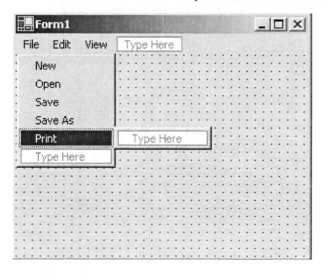

4. Add some submenus, for example, **New**, **Open**, **Save**, **Save As**, and **Print**.

5. Add an event handler to a menu item.

How to Create the Main Menu

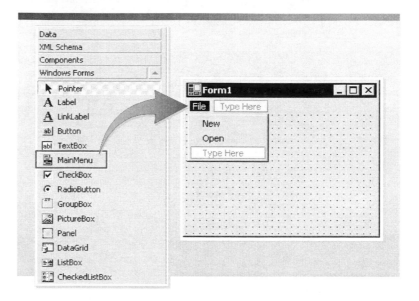

Introduction

The purpose of a menu is to make using your application easy and intuitive for the user. You can create a menu in Windows Forms by adding a **MainMenu** object from the Toolbox to the form at design time. You can then create the menu items and submenus for your menu by using the Menu Designer.

Creating a menu, menu items, and submenus

To add a menu and menu items to a form:

1. In the Windows Forms Designer, open the form to which you want to add a menu.

2. In the Toolbox, double-click the **MainMenu** control.

   A menu is added to the form. The menu displays the text "Type Here."

3. Click the text **Type Here**, and then type the name of the desired menu item to add it to the menu.

4. To provide access to the built-in keyboard shortcut feature of Microsoft Windows, type an ampersand (&) in front of the letter that will be the shortcut. These shortcuts are indicated by an underlined letter, and can be activated by pressing ALT plus the underlined letter.

   For example, enter the string **&File** to place <u>F</u>ile on the menu, or **E&xit** for E<u>x</u>it. If you need to place an ampersand in a menu, type **&&**

5. The name you type is listed as the **Text** property of the menu item.

   Note By default, the **MainMenu** object contains no menu items, so the first menu item that you add to the menu becomes the menu heading.

6. To add another menu item, click another "Type Here" area in the Menu Designer.

    a. To add a submenu, click the area to the right of the current menu item. You cannot add a submenu to a menu heading.

    b. To add another item to the same menu, click the area below the current menu item.

7. Change the **Name** property of the menu item to something meaningful. For example, if you added a menu item labeled **Open** to the **File** menu, name the item **fileOpen**.

8. You can insert a horizontal line into a menu by setting the text property to the minus symbol (–).

How to Associate Methods with Menu Items

- **Double-click the menu item to open the event handler**
- **Write code for the event handler**

```
this.menuItemFilePrint.Index = 4;

this.menuItemFilePrint.Text = "Print...";

this.menuItemFilePrint.Click += new
  System.EventHandler(this.menuItemFilePrint_Click);


public void menuItemFilePrint_Click( Object sender,
                                EventArgs e ) {

  // code that runs when the event occurs

}
```

Introduction

After you create the menu, you can add functionality to the menu by associating methods with the menu items.

Associating methods with menu items

You can add functionality to menu items by associating methods with the **Click** event of the menu item. The **Click** event occurs when the user clicks the menu item, when the user selects the item by using the keyboard and presses ENTER, or when the user clicks an access key or shortcut key that is associated with the menu item.

To associate methods, and therefore functionality, with a menu item:

1. In the Menu Designer, click the menu item you want to add functionality to.

2. In the Properties window, rename the **Name** property of the item by using the naming convention that you will use for all items on the menu. For example, name the **Open** menu item **OpenItem**.

3. Double-click the menu item to open an event handler for its **Click** event.

4. Write the code for the event handler.

Practice: Creating the Main Menu

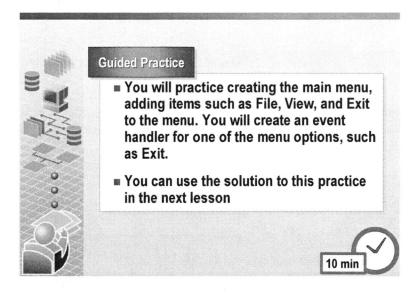

In this practice, you will open an application, add a main menu to it, and then implement menu functions.

The existing application reads animal information from an XML file and displays it in a simple Windows-based application. Currently, the application appears as follows:

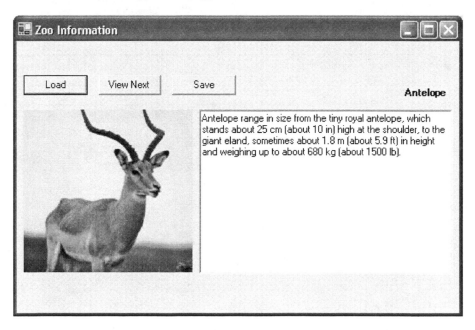

The solution for this practice is located in *install_folder*\Practices\Mod08\MainMenu_Solution. Start a new instance of Visual Studio .NET before opening the solution.

Your task is to use menu functions to replace the buttons.

Note that the solution contains the following three C# files:

- Animals.cs—contains the definitions for the animal types. You will not need to change anything in this file.

- Form1.cs—the Windows interface code. You will write your code in this file.

- Zoo.cs—the class that contains the collection of animals. You will not need to change anything in this file.

The application expects to find the data files in the solution folder.

The solution for this practice is in *install_folder*\Practices\Mod08\MainMenu_Solution \Animals.sln. Start a new instance of Visual Studio .NET before opening the solution.

Tasks	Detailed steps
1. Start Visual Studio .NET, and then open *install_folder*\Practices \Mod08\MainMenu\Animals.sln.	a. Start a new instance of Visual Studio .NET. b. On the **Start Page**, click **Open Project**. c. In the **Open Project** dialog box, browse to *install_folder* \Practices\Mod08\MainMenu, click **Animals.sln**, and then click **Open**. d. In Solution Explorer, click **Form1.cs**, and then press F7 to open the Code Editor.
2. Build and run the solution, and familiarize yourself with it.	a. In Visual Studio .NET, press F5. b. In the Zoo Information window, click **Load**, and then click **View Next**. c. Close the Zoo Information window.
3. Add a **MainMenu** control to the Form.	▪ For detailed information on how to complete this task, see How to Create the Main Menu in this lesson.
4. Add the following menu items, and create event handlers for them as specified in the following tables:	▪ For detailed information on how to complete this task, see How to Create the Main Menu and How to Associate Methods with Menu Items in this lesson.

Menu	Action
File	None
Open	Same as **Load** button: call the **Zoo.Load** method and Initialize the form
Save	Same as **Save** button: call the **Save** method in the **Zoo** class
-	Insert a horizontal line
Exit	(Optional: use **Application.Exit()** to exit the application.)
View	None
Next	Same as View Next button: display the next animal
-	Insert a horizontal line
Options	Do nothing in the event handler

Tasks	Detailed steps
5. Build and test your solution.	a. On the **Build** menu, click **Build Solution**.
	b. If necessary, use breakpoints and the debugging tool to check your application.
6. Delete the **Load**, **View Next**, and **Save** buttons, and their event handlers, and test your application again.	▪ After you load the data, your application should appear as follows:
7. Save your solution.	▪ On the **File** menu, click **Save All**.

Lesson: Creating and Using Common Dialog Boxes

- How to Create and Use a Common Dialog Box
- How to Set Common Dialog Box Properties
- How to Read Information from a Common Dialog Box

Introduction

This lesson examines some of the most common dialog boxes that are provided in the **Forms** namespace and explains how to use them in a Windows-based application.

Lesson objectives

After completing this lesson, you will be able to:

- Use the **OpenFileDialog** control.
- Use the **SaveFileDialog** control.
- Use the **PrintDialog** control.
- Use the **FontDialog** control.

Lesson agenda

This lesson includes the following topics and activities:

- Demonstration: Creating and Using a Common Dialog Box
- How to Create and Use a Common Dialog Box
- How to Set Common Dialog Box Properties
- How to Read Information from a Common Dialog Box
- Practice: Using a Common Dialog Box

Demonstration: Creating and Using a Common Dialog Box

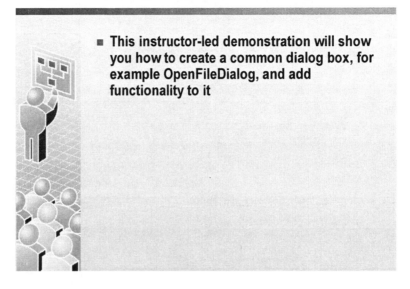

- **This instructor-led demonstration will show you how to create a common dialog box, for example OpenFileDialog, and add functionality to it**

This instructor-led demonstration will show you how to create a common dialog box, for instance **OpenFileDialog**, and add functionality to it. The instructor will:

1. Open Visual Studio .NET and create a new Windows Application project named **MyForm**.

2. Create an instance of any one of the common dialog boxes, such as **OpenFileDialog**, **SaveFileDialog**, **FontDialog**, or **PrintDialog**.

3. Set the properties of the common dialog box. The following table shows properties of an **OpenFileDialog** dialog box.

Property	Description
Filter	The file filters to display in the dialog box, for example, C# files (*.cs); all files (*.*)
Multiselect	Controls whether multiple files can be selected in the dialog box
ShowHelp	Enables the **Help** button.

4. Add an event handler to open the dialog box.

5. Use the **ShowDialog( )** method to display the dialog box.

6. Test the application.

How to Create and Use a Common Dialog Box

To create a dialog box in an application:

- **Drag a common dialog box to your form**

- **Browse to the event handler with which you want to open the dialog box**

- **In the event handler, add the code to open the dialog box**

```
private void OpenMenuItem_Click(object sender,
                                System.EventArgs e) {
    openFileDialog1.ShowDialog();

}
```

Introduction

In this topic, you will learn how to add a common dialog box to a form, how to configure it, and how to write code to display it.

The Microsoft .NET Framework provides six classes that provide the common user interface functions of opening files, saving files, selecting fonts, setting page printing values, printing, and selecting a color. These classes, **OpenFileDialog**, **SaveFileDialog**, **FontDialog**, **PageSetupDialog**, **PrintDialog**, and **ColorDialog**, are implemented as dialog boxes.

Creating and displaying a dialog box

To add a common dialog box to an application, you select it from the Toolbox and drag it onto your form. To display a dialog box, you must create the object and then invoke the **ShowDialog** method on the object.

It is normal to display the dialog box in response to an event, such as a menu selection or a button click from the user of the application.

To display a dialog box:

1. Create an instance of the common dialog box.

2. Browse to the event handler within which you want to open the dialog box.

3. Use the **ShowDialog()** method to show the dialog box.

Example

For example, Visual Studio .NET inserts the following line of code when you add an **OpenFileDialog** control to your project:

```
private System.Windows.Forms.OpenFileDialog openFileDialog1;
```

OpenMenuItem_Click, an event handler that is called when the user clicks **Open** on the **File** menu, is shown in the following example. This method displays the common Windows **Open File** dialog box.

```
private void OpenMenuItem_Click( object sender,
                                 System.EventArgs e) {
    openFileDialog1.ShowDialog();
}
```

How to Set Common Dialog Box Properties

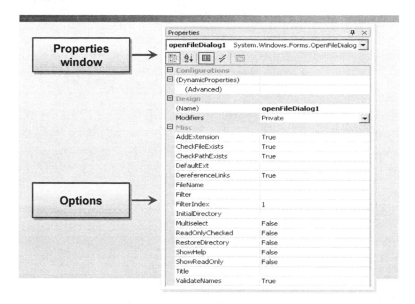

Introduction

Visual Studio .NET includes a set of preconfigured dialog boxes, which you can adapt for your own applications. By relying on standard Windows dialog boxes, you create applications whose basic functionality is immediately familiar to users.

Common dialog boxes

The following table shows some of the most common dialog boxes, their functions, and some of their associated properties.

Options	Description	Properties
OpenFileDialog	Allows users to open files by using a preconfigured dialog box.	**Multiselect:** You can enable users to multi-select files to be opened with the **Multiselect** property
		Filter property sets the current file name filter string, which determines the options that appear in the **Files of type** box in the dialog box.
SaveFileDialog	Selects files to save and the location where they are saved.	**FileName:** The file first shown in the dialog box, or the last one selected by the user
		Filter: The file filters to display in the dialog box
FontDialog	Exposes the fonts that are currently installed on the system.	**Font:** The font selected by the user
		MaxSize: The maximum size that can be selected (or zero to disable)
		MinSize: The minimum size that can be selected (or zero to disable)
PrintDialog	Displays a document as it would appear when it is printed.	**AllowPrintToFile:** Enables and disables the **Print To File** check box

Example

The **OpenFile** and **SaveFile** dialog boxes show all types of files unless the **Filter** property is set. To set this property, you pass a properly formatted string to the property. The string consists of pairs of labels and filters, separated by the vertical bar (|) character. The first pair is the default value.

For example, a graphics program may allow the user to browse for TIF files and JPEG files, expecting file extensions of .tif and .jpg. The Filter string could be "TIF files (*.tif) | *.tif | JPEG files (*.jpg) |*.jpg".

If you want to use more than one file extension filter with a label, separate the filters with a semicolon as shown in the following example:

```
openFileDialog1.Filter = @"C Sharp files|*.cs;*.csproj|XML
Files|*.xml|All files (*.*)|*.*";
```

When this dialog box is opened, it appears as follows:

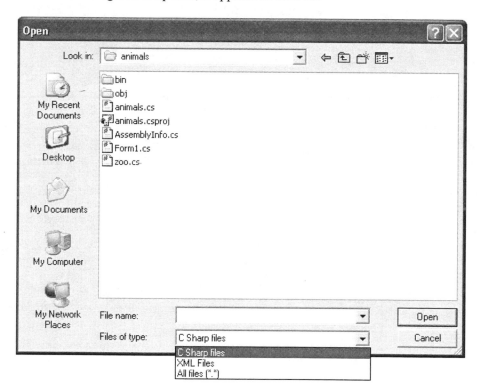

How to Read Information from a Common Dialog Box

DialogResultProperty

Use the value returned by this property to determine what action the user has taken

Reading the results from a dialog box

Determine the DialogResult
OK, Cancel, Abort, Retry, Ignore, Yes, No, (or None)

```
if (openFileDialog1.ShowDialog() == DialogResult.OK) {
    MessageBox.Show(openFileDialog1.FileName);
}
```

Introduction

When you display a dialog box in an application, it is very important to know what action the user took. For example, if you display a dialog box that prompts users to dismiss the dialog box, you must know whether the user clicked the **OK** button or the **Cancel** button.

Retrieving a result from a dialog box

When the user closes a dialog box, the **ShowDialog** method returns a **DialogResult** value to the calling method. The object that displayed the dialog box can check the **DialogResult** to determine if the user clicked **OK**, **Cancel**, or some other value.

For example:

```
if ( openFileDialog1.ShowDialog() == DialogResult.OK ) {
    MessageBox.Show( "You selected " +
                             openFileDialog1.FileName );
}
```

Possible **DialogResult** values are **OK**, **Cancel**, **Abort**, **Retry**, **Ignore**, **Yes**, and **No** (or **None**).

Reading the user information

The dialog box object maintains information about user selections and makes that information available through properties. For example, you can use the **Font** property of the **FontDialog** object to determine the font that the user selected. In the preceding examples, the **FileName** property of the **OpenFileDialog** object is used to determine the name of the file that the user selected.

Reading user information from a dialog box

To read user information from a dialog box:

1. Browse to the event handler or the method for which you want to set the **DialogResult** property.

2. Add code to retrieve the **DialogResult** value.

The following examples illustrate how user input is derived from a **FontDialog** object:

```
fontDialog1 = new FontDialog();
if ( fontDialog1.ShowDialog() == DialogResult.OK ) {
  string fontInfo = fontDialog1.Font.Name + " -- ems:"
                         + fontDialog1.Font.Size.ToString();
  MessageBox.Show("You selected: " + fontInfo );
}
```

The preceding code shows how to read the name of the selected font and the size of the font in ems. This code produces the following output:

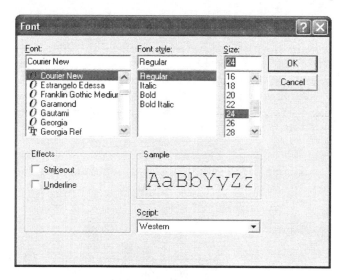

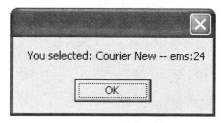

Setting the owner of the dialog box

The **Form.ShowDialog** method has an optional argument, *owner*, that you can use to specify a parent-child relationship for a form. Usually, you want the owner of the dialog box to be the object that created and uses the dialog box. When you specify that a dialog box is a child of your form, that dialog box always appears in front of the form, which is the correct Windows behavior for dialog boxes.

In your form code, you can use the **this** keyword to specify the calling object as the owner of the dialog box, as shown in the following code:

```
public class Form1 : System.Windows.Forms.Form {
  // . . .
  openFile_Click( object sender, EventArgs e ) {
      OpenfileDialog openFile = new OpenFileDialog();
      if ( openFile.ShowDialog( this ) == DialogResult.OK ) {
          // open the file
      }
   }
}
```

Practice: Using a Common Dialog Box

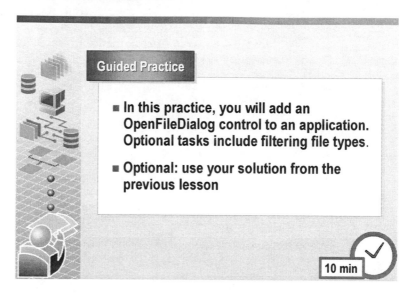

In this practice, you will add an **OpenFileDialog** control to the Zoo Information application.

If you have a working solution from the Creating the Main Menu lesson in this module and you want to build upon that, open that solution and skip steps 1 and 2 in this practice.

The solution for this practice is located in *install_folder*\Practices\Mod08 \CommonDialog _Solution\Animals.sln. Start a new instance of Visual Studio .NET before opening the solution.

Tasks	Detailed steps
1. Start Visual Studio .NET, and then open *install_folder* \Practices\Mod08\CommonDialog \Animals.sln.	**a.** Start a new instance of Visual Studio .NET. **b.** On the **Start Page**, click **Open Project**. **c.** In the **Open Project** dialog box, browse to *install_folder*\Practices\Mod08\CommonDialog, click **Animals.sln**, and then click **Open**. **d.** In Solution Explorer, click **Form1.cs**, and then press F7 to open the Code Editor.
2. *(Optional)* Build and run the solution, and familiarize yourself with it.	**a.** In Visual Studio .NET, press F5. **b.** Examine the Zoo Information application. **c.** Close the Zoo Information window.
3. Add an **OpenFileDialog** control to your project.	▪ Drag an **OpenFileDialog** control from the Toolbox onto your Form. By default, this is called **openFileDialog1**.

Tasks	Detailed steps

4. In the event handler for the **loadItem** menu item, add code so that the **OpenFileDialog** object shows XML files by default.	**a.** In Design view, on the **File** menu, double-click **Open**.
	
	b. In the **loadItem_Click** method, use the **Filter** property of **openFileDialog** to show XML files and all files:
	
	`openFileDialog1.Filter = @"XML Files`
	`(*.xml)|*.xml|All files (*.*)|*.*";`

5. Show the **OpenFileDialog** object, retrieve the filename selected by the user, and then load the file.	Note that the provided **LoadZoo** method loads the file that is specified in the **zooFile** string.
	
	a. Use the **ShowDialog** method to display **openFileDialog1**.
	
	b. If **ShowDialog** returns **DialogResult.OK**, then execute the following code:
	
	`zooFile = openFileDialog1.FileName;`
	
	`this.LoadZoo();`
	
	`InitializeDisplay();`
	
	c. An alternative solution to this task is to call the **Zoo.Load** method directly. If you do this, remember to handle any exceptions that may be thrown.

6. Test your application by loading the XML data file **AnimalData.xml**.	**a.** On the **Build** menu, click **Build Solution**. **b.** If necessary, use breakpoints and the debugger to check your application.
7. Save your solution.	▪ On the **File** menu, click **Save All**.

Lesson: Creating and Using Custom Dialog Boxes

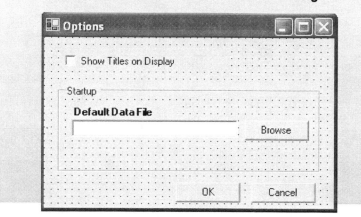

- How to Create and Use a Custom Dialog Box
- How to Create and Use a Custom Tabbed Dialog Box

Introduction

This lesson explains how to work with tabbed dialog boxes by using the development environment.

Lesson objectives

After completing this lesson, you will be able to:

- Create and use a dialog box.
- Create and use a tabbed dialog box.

Lesson agenda

This lesson includes the following topics and activities:

- Demonstration: Creating and Using a Custom Dialog Box
- How to Create and Use a Custom Dialog Box
- Demonstration: Creating a Custom Tabbed Dialog Box
- How to Create and Use a Custom Tabbed Dialog Box
- Practice: Creating a Custom Dialog Box

Demonstration: Creating and Using a Custom Dialog Box

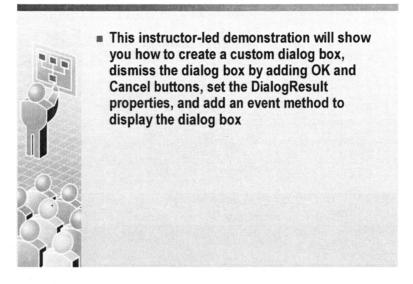

■ This instructor-led demonstration will show you how to create a custom dialog box, dismiss the dialog box by adding OK and Cancel buttons, set the DialogResult properties, and add an event method to display the dialog box

This instructor-led demonstration will show you how to create a custom dialog box, dismiss the dialog box by adding **OK** and **Cancel** buttons, set the **DialogResult** properties, and add an event method to display the dialog box. The instructor will:

1. Open Visual Studio .NET and create a new Windows Application project named **MyForm**.

2. Add a dialog box to the project by right-clicking the project in Solution Explorer. *form*

3. Set the dialog box properties, as shown in the following table:

Property	Setting
FormBorderStyle	FixedDialog
ControlBox	False
MinimizeBox	False
MaximizeBox	False
ShowInTaskbar	False

4. Provide a way for users to dismiss the dialog box by adding two buttons to the form. Change the **Text** property of one button to **OK** and the other button to **Cancel** as follows:

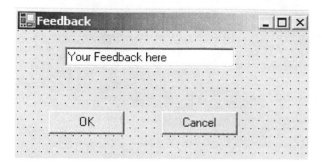

5. Set the **DialogResult** property of the **OK** and **Cancel** buttons to **OK** and **Cancel** respectively.

6. Instantiate and display the dialog box from the event handler of any menu item by using the **ShowDialog** method.

How to Create and Use a Custom Dialog Box

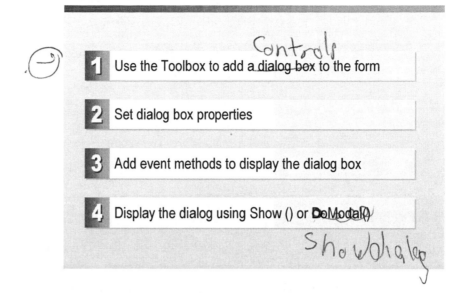

1 Use the Toolbox to add a dialog box to the form   *Controls*

2 Set dialog box properties

3 Add event methods to display the dialog box

4 Display the dialog using Show () or DoModal()   *ShowDialog*

Introduction

A dialog box is a form, **System.Windows.Forms.Form**, whose **FormBorderStyle Enumeration** property is set to **FixedDialog**. Dialog boxes are often used to provide or collect information from the user.

A dialog box is usually, but not always, characterized by a modal style of interaction with the user. (*Modal* means that the user is not able to use the rest of the software application while the modal dialog box is open.)

Dialog boxes are derived from the **System.Windows.Forms.Form** class, so when you create a new dialog box, you must inherit this class. You can do this easily by using the Visual Studio .NET Windows Forms Designer. The Windows Forms Designer automatically creates a new class for your dialog box that is derived from **System.Windows.Forms.Form**, and you can place controls on it just as you would on the main form.

Modal or modeless dialog boxes

A dialog box is either modal or modeless.

A *modal* dialog box, the most common type, must be explicitly closed before you can continue working with the rest of the application. To close the dialog box, you usually click **OK**, **Cancel**, or an equivalent. A *modeless* dialog box allows you to keep it open while you work in another window in the same application.

Use modal dialog boxes when you must obtain some information from the user before the program can proceed. For example, if the user wants to save a file, you must get a filename before you can create or open the file. So, you create a modal dialog box to obtain this information.

Use a modeless dialog boxes when an application must have multiple windows open at once. For example, a painting program may have a modeless dialog box that you can keep open so that you can adjust paintbrush properties.

Example

Any dialog box can be displayed in either manner.

To display a modal dialog box, use the following code:

```
userOptions.ShowDialog()
```

To display a modeless dialog box, use the following code:

```
userOptions.Show();
```

Show and **ShowDialog** take an optional parameter that allows you to specify the owner of the dialog box. Dialog boxes always layer on top of their owner. Normally, you can easily pass a reference to the main form by using **this** keyword.

```
printDialog.ShowDialog(this);
```

Adding a custom dialog box

To add a custom dialog box to your application from the Toolbox:

1. Add a form to your project by right-clicking the project in Solution Explorer, pointing to **Add**, and then clicking **Windows Form**.

2. Right-click the form in Solution Explorer, and then click **Rename** to rename the dialog box to something meaningful for your application.

3. In the Properties window, change the **FormBorderStyle** property to **FixedDialog**.

4. Set the **ControlBox**, **MinimizeBox**, and **MaximizeBox** properties to **false**. Dialog boxes do not usually include menu bars, window scroll bars, **Minimize** and **Maximize** buttons, status bars, or sizable borders.

5. Set the **ShowInTaskbar** property to **false**, because dialog boxes should not show in the Windows taskbar.

Dismissing the dialog box

Because a dialog box does not have a **Close** box, you must provide a way for users to dismiss the dialog box. Normally, you do this by add **OK** and **Cancel** buttons.

To add an **OK** button and a **Cancel** button:

1. Add two buttons to the form.

2. Change the **Text** property of one button to **OK** and change the **Name** property to something meaningful, for example **ok**.

3. Change the **Text** property of the other button to **Cancel**, and change the **Name** property to something meaningful, such as **cancel**.

Setting the DialogResult property of a button

Your dialog box must return a **DialogResult** property to the calling method so that the application can determine if the dialog box was accepted or canceled. Because buttons are used to perform this function, they have a **DialogResult** property that you can set to determine the value that is returned to the calling method. For example:

```
Button ok;
...
ok.DialogResult = DialogResult.OK;
```

Setting accept and cancel behavior

The dialog box must know which buttons provide **accept** and **cancel** types of behavior, so it can provide normal Windows behaviors, such as being dismissed when the user presses the **Escape** key. You set these behaviors with the **AcceptButton** and **CancelButton** properties.

- Set the dialog box properties **AcceptButton** and **CancelButton** to the **okOptions** and **cancelOptions** button objects.

Now you can add controls and code to the dialog box to implement the required functionality.

Adding an event method

You display custom dialog boxes in an application the same way you display a common dialog box or any other form, by using the **ShowDialog** method. Usually this is done in response to a user request, in an event handler.

For example, the following event handler is called when the user selects an **Options** menu item. It creates a custom dialog box **OptionsDialog** and calls the **ShowDialog** method to display the form.

```
private void OptionsItem_Click(object sender,
                                System.EventArgs e) {
  OptionsDialog userOptions = new OptionsDialog();
  if ( userOptions.ShowDialog() == DialogResult.OK ) {
      // User clicked OK
  }
}
```

The return value from the **ShowDialog** method is checked to discover whether the user clicked **OK** or **Cancel**.

Obtaining selections

The reason for using a dialog box is to allow the user to provide information or to change application settings. When the user clicks **OK** and closes the dialog box, your application needs a way to examine the settings of the dialog box. To do this, you create public properties for the dialog box form.

For example, if you have a **TextBox** called **myName** in a dialog box, you can encapsulate **myName.Text** in a public property called **Name**, as shown in the following code:

```
public class OptionsDialog : System.Windows.Forms.Form {
...
public string Name {
  get {
      return myName.Text;
  }
}
...
}
```

You can use the following code from the main form:

```
if ( userOptions.ShowDialog() == DialogResult.OK ) {
    string username = userOptions.Name;
}
```

Setting the tab order of a form or dialog box

The tab order is the order in which a user moves focus from one control to another on a form by pressing the TAB key. Each form has its own tab order. By default, the tab order is the same as the order in which you created the controls. Tab-order numbering begins with zero.

Setting the tab order using the View menu

To set the tab order by using the **View** menu:

1. On the **View** menu, click **Tab Order**.

2. Click the controls sequentially to establish the tab order that you want.

3. When you are finished, on the **View** menu, click **Tab Order** again.

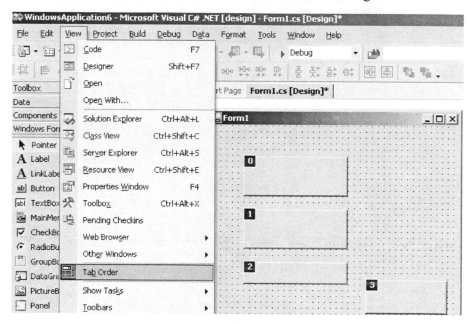

Alternatively, you can set tab order in the Properties window by using the **TabIndex** property. The **TabIndex** property of a control determines where it is positioned in the tab order. By default, the first control drawn has a TabIndex value of **0**; the second has a TabIndex of **1**, and so on.

Setting the tab order using the TabIndex property

To set the tab order using the **TabIndex** property:

1. Select the control.

2. Set the **TabIndex** property to the required value.

3. Set the **TabStop** property to **True**.

   If you set the **TabStop** property to **False**, the control is passed over in the tab order of the form. A control whose **TabStop** property has been set to **False** still maintains its position in the tab order, even though the control is skipped when you cycle through the controls by using the TAB key.

Demonstration: Creating a Custom Tabbed Dialog Box

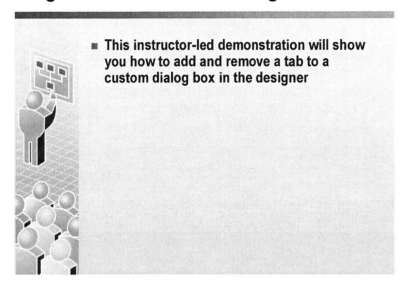

This instructor-led demonstration will show you how to add and remove a tab to a custom dialog box in the designer. The instructor will:

1. Open Visual Studio .NET and create a new **Windows Application** project named **MyForm**.

2. Add a dialog box to the project by right-clicking the project in Solution Explorer.

3. Add a **TabControl** to the dialog box.

4. Add or remove tabs by using the TabPage Collection Editor.

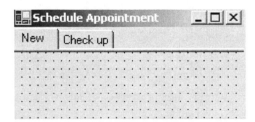

How to Create and Use a Custom Tabbed Dialog Box

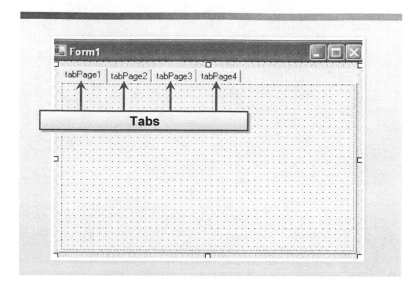

Introduction

The .NET Framework provides many controls that you can add to your application so that it provides a standard Windows user interface. Most of these are simple to use, but others have some unique features. Some of the more interesting controls are described in this topic.

TabControl object

You can customize a dialog box by adding a Windows Forms **TabControl** object. The **TabControl** object displays multiple tabs, like dividers in a notebook or labels in a set of folders in a filing cabinet. The tabs can contain pictures and other controls. You can use the **TabControl** object to produce the kind of multiple-page dialog box that appears many places in the Windows operating system, such as the Display control panel.

TabControl properties

The most important property of the **TabControl** object is the **TabPages** collection, which contains the individual tabs. Each individual tab is a **TabPage** object. Clicking a tab raises the **Click** event for that **TabPage** object.

You can change the appearance of tabs in Windows Forms by using the properties of the **TabControl** and the **TabPage** objects that make up the individual tabs on the control. By setting these properties, you can display images on tabs, display tabs vertically instead of horizontally, have multiple rows of tabs, and enable or disable tabs programmatically.

Adding and removing a tab in the designer

To add a tab in the designer:

1. Drag a **TabControl** from the **Windows Forms** tab of the Toolbox to the designer.

2. In the Properties window, click the **Add Tab** link.

   - Or -

   In the Properties window, click the **Ellipsis** button ... next to the **TabPages** property to open the TabPage Collection Editor, and then click the **Add** button.

To remove a tab in the designer:

1. In the Properties window, click the **Ellipsis** button ⋯ next to the **TabPages** property to open the TabPage Collection Editor.

2. In the left window, under **Members:**, select the tab to remove, and then click the **Remove** button.

Adding, removing, enabling, and disabling tabs programmatically

To add a tab programmatically:

- Use the **Add** method of the **TabPages** property.

```
TabPage myTabPage = new TabPage("Print Options");
tabControl1.TabPages.Add(myTabPage);
```

To remove a tab programmatically:

- To remove selected tabs, use the **Remove** method of the **TabPages** property. To remove all tabs, use the **Clear** method of the **TabPages** property.

```
tabControl1.TabPages.Remove(tabControl1.SelectedTab);
 // Removes all the tabs:
tabControl1.TabPages.Clear( );
```

To enable or disable tabs programmatically:

```
tabPage1.Enabled = false;
```

Practice: Creating a Custom Dialog Box

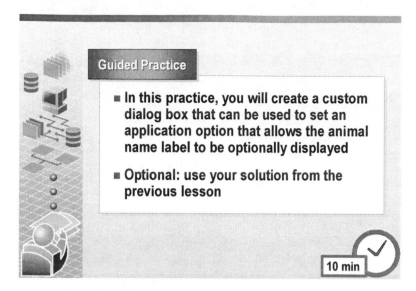

In this practice, you will create a custom dialog box that can be used to set an application option that allows the animal name label to be optionally displayed. The **Options** dialog box is launched from the **Options** item on the **View** menu.

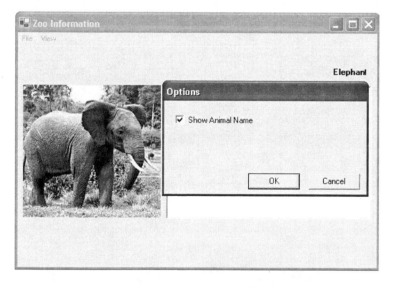

If you have a working solution from the Using a Common Dialog Box lesson in this module and you want to build on that, open that solution and skip steps 1 and 2 in this practice.

The solution for this practice is located in *install_folder*\Practices\Mod08\Custom_Solution \Animals.sln. Start a new instance of Visual Studio .NET before opening the solution.

Tasks	Detailed steps
1. Start Visual Studio .NET and then open *install_folder*\Practices \Mod08\Custom\Animals.sln.	a. Start a new instance of Visual Studio .NET. b. On the **Start Page**, click **Open Project**. c. In the **Open Project** dialog box, browse to *install_folder* \Practices\Mod08\Custom folder, click **Animals.sln**, and then click **Open**. d. In Solution Explorer, click **Form1.cs**, and then press F7 to open the Code Editor.
2. *(Optional)* Build and run the solution, and familiarize yourself with it.	a. In Visual Studio .NET, press F5. b. Examine the Zoo Information application. c. Close the Zoo Information window.
3. Add a new custom dialog box to your project.	a. In Solution Explorer, use the **Add New Item** option on the **Add** menu to add a new Window Form to your project. • Name the form **Options.cs**. b. Set the following property values: • FormBorderStyle: **FixedDialog** • ControlBox, MinimizeBox, MaximizeBox and ShowInTaskbar: **false** **Note:** • **FormBorderStyle** is located under **Appearance** in the Properties window. • **ControlBox**, **MinimizeBox**, **MaximizeBox,** and **ShowInTaskbar** are located under **Window Style** in the Properties window.
4. Add **OK** and **Cancel** buttons to your dialog box.	▪ Drag two buttons from the Toolbox to the **Options** form. • Name the **OK** button **ok**, and change the **Text** property to **OK**. • Name the **Cancel** button **cancel**, and change the **Text** property to **Cancel**. • Set the **DialogResult** properties for the buttons to the correct values.
5. Add a **CheckBox** control to your Options form, and set the following properties: • Name: **showLabel** • Text: **Show animal name** • Checked: **true**	a. Drag a **CheckBox** control from the Toolbox to the **Options.cs** form. b. Change the **Name, Text,** and **Checked** properties to the values shown in the left column.

Tasks	Detailed steps
6. Write a Property **bool Options.ShowLabel** that returns **true** when the CheckBox is checked. This value is retrieved from the **CheckBox.Checked** property.	a. Switch to the Code Editor for the Options form. b. Write a property named **ShowLabel** that returns the value of **CheckBox.Checked**. Place this code between the class member variable declarations and the **Options** constructor. Example code: ```csharp\npublic bool ShowLabel {\n get {\n return showLabel.Checked;\n }\n}\n```
7. In the event handler for the **Options** menu item, write code to create and display your new dialog box.	a. If necessary, create an event handler for the **Options** menu item by switching to Design view and double-clicking the **Options** menu item. b. In the event handler, create your dialog box by using the following code: ```csharp\nOptions zooOptions = new Options();\n``` c. Use the **ShowDialog** method to display the dialog box.
8. In the **Options** event handler, set **animalName.Visible** to **false** if the user cleared the **Show animal name** check box on your dialog box, and clicked **OK**.	▪ In the **Options** event handler, write code that sets the **animalName.Visible** property to the value of the **showLabel** property on your custom dialog box if the **DialogResult** is **DialogResult.OK**: ```csharp\nanimalName.Visible = zooOptions.ShowLabel;\n```
9. Test your application by loading the XML data file **AnimalData.xml**, and changing the **Show Animal Name** option.	a. On the **Build** menu, click **Build Solution**. b. If necessary, use breakpoints and the debugger to check your application.
10. Save your solution.	▪ On the **File** menu, click **Save All**.

Lesson: Creating and Using Toolbars

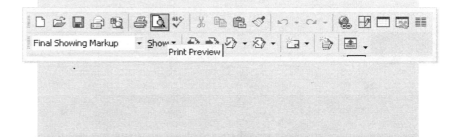

- How to Create a Toolbar
- How to Use Toolbar Properties
- How to Write Code for the ButtonClick Event

Introduction

The toolbar is a standard feature in many Windows-based applications. Toolbars display a row of buttons and drop-down menus that activate commands. Typically, the buttons and drop-down menus correspond to items in the menu structure of an application, providing a graphical interface through which the user has quick access to the application's most frequently used functions and commands.

Lesson objectives

After completing this lesson, you will be able to:

- Create a toolbar.
- Set toolbar icons and docking options.
- Write an event handler for the **ButtonClick**.event.

Lesson agenda

This lesson includes the following topics and activities:

- Demonstration: Creating a Toolbar
- How to Create a Toolbar
- How to Use Toolbar Properties
- How to Write Code for the **ButtonClick** Event
- Practice: Creating and Using a Toolbar

Demonstration: Creating a Toolbar

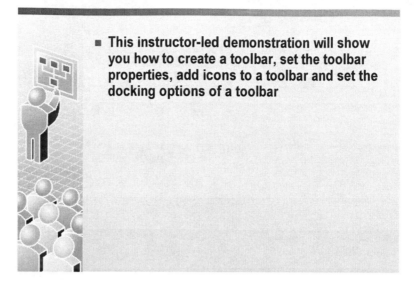

■ **This instructor-led demonstration will show you how to create a toolbar, set the toolbar properties, add icons to a toolbar and set the docking options of a toolbar**

This instructor-led demonstration will show you how to create a toolbar, set the toolbar properties, add icons to a toolbar, and set the docking options of a toolbar.

The instructor will:

1. Open Visual Studio .NET and create a new **Windows Application** project named **MyForm**.

2. Add a **Toolbar** control to the form.

3. Set toolbar properties.

Property	Description
Appearance	Controls the appearance of the **ToolBar** control: **Normal** for a three-dimensional and raised view **Flat** for a flat button that rises to a three-dimensional view
Button size	Suggests the size of buttons of the toolbar
Buttons	**(Collection)** editor allows adding and removing tool bar buttons
Cursor	The cursor that appears when the mouse passes over the control
ImageList	The imageList from which this tool bar will get all of the button images
Dock	Determines the docking location of the tool bar

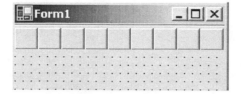

4. Add icons to the toolbar.

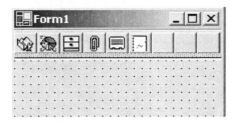

Tip   Visual Studio .NET provides a library of icons in the
Program_Files\Visual Studio.NET\Common7\Graphics\icons\ folder.

---

5. Set docking options for a toolbar.

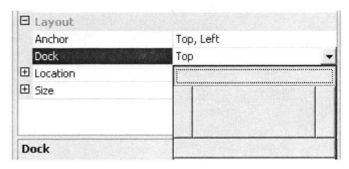

How to Create a Toolbar

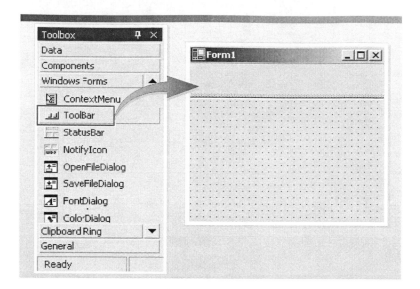

Introduction

To create a toolbar for an application, you use the Windows Forms **ToolBar** control.

Creating a toolbar

To create and add a toolbar to a form:

1. In the Windows Forms Designer, open the form to which you want to add a toolbar.

2. In the Toolbox, double-click the **Toolbar** control. A toolbar is added to the form.

When you want to add a toolbar that uses images to your application, you must:

- Add a **ToolBar** control to the form.

- Add **ToolBarButton** objects to the **Buttons** collection of the toolbar.

- Add an **ImageList** control to the form.

- Load icon images into the **Images** collection of the **ImageList** object.

- Assign an index to the **Images** collection of the **ImageIndex** property of each **ToolBarButtons** object.

- Set docking options.

- Write an event handler for the toolbar.

Toolbar properties

The following table shows **ToolBar** properties that you will frequently use.

Property	Description
Appearance	Affects the appearance of the buttons that are assigned to the toolbar.
	Normal: The toolbar buttons appear three-dimensional and raised.
	Flat: The toolbar buttons have a flat appearance. As the mouse pointer moves over the flat buttons, they appear raised and three-dimensional.
Buttons	Holds all the **ToolBarButton** controls that are assigned to the toolbar. The **Buttons** property is a zero-based indexed collection. Use this property to add buttons to or remove buttons from the toolbar.
ButtonSize	Sets the size of the **ToolBarButton** controls on the toolbar. If the **ButtonSize** property is not set, it will either be set to a default size or large enough to accommodate the image and text, whichever is greater.
ImageList	If you instantiate an **ImageList** object and assign it to the **ImageList** property, you can assign an image from the list to the **ToolBarButton** controls.
ShowToolTips	Determines whether ToolTips will be visible to the user. ToolTips allow you to provide help to users when they rest the mouse pointer on a **ToolBarButton** control. The default value is **True**.

How to Use Toolbar Properties

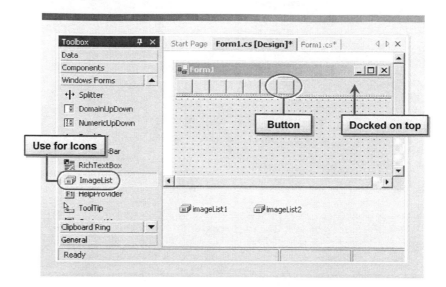

Introduction

After you add a **ToolBar** control to your form, you must add buttons to it. You can add icons to the buttons to represent various functions, and set docking options for the toolbar.

Adding buttons to a toolbar

To add buttons to a toolbar:

1. In Visual Studio .NET, open the Properties window for the **ToolBar** control.

2. Click the **Buttons** property to select it, and then click the **Ellipsis** button **...** to open the ToolBarButton Collection Editor.

3. Use the **Add** and **Remove** buttons to add buttons to and remove buttons from the **ToolBar** control.

4. Set the properties of the individual buttons in the Properties window that appears in the pane to the right of the editor.

5. Click **OK** to close the dialog box and create the buttons that you specified.

Button properties

The following table shows toolbar button properties that you will frequently use.

Property	Description
DropDownMenu	Sets the menu that is to appear in the drop-down toolbar button. The **Style** property of the toolbar button must be set to **DropDownButton**.
Pushed	Sets whether a toggle-style toolbar button is currently in the pushed state. The **Style** property of the toolbar button must be set to **ToggleButton** or **PushButton**.
Style	Sets the style of the toolbar button. **DropDownButton:** A drop-down control that displays a menu or other window when clicked. **PushButton:** A standard three-dimensional button. **Separator:** A space or line between toolbar buttons. **ToggleButton:** A toggle button that appears sunken when clicked and retains the sunken appearance until it is clicked again.
Text	Specifies the text string displayed by the button.
ToolTipText	Specifies the text that appears as a ToolTip for the button. ToolTips allow you to provide help to users when they rest the mouse pointer on a toolbar button.

Adding icons to toolbar buttons

Toolbars usually have buttons that use icons to represent a function of the application. The icons provide easy identification for users. For example, an icon of a floppy disk is commonly used to represent a **File Save** function. Each button should have text or an image assigned to it; you can also assign both.

To display images on your toolbar, you must first add the images to the **ImageList** component and then associate the **ImageList** component with the **ToolBar** control.

To add an icon for a toolbar button at design time:

1. Add an **ImageList** control from the Toolbox to your form.

2. In the Properties window for the **ImageList** component, click the **Images** property to select it, and then click the **Ellipsis** button ... to open the Image Collection Editor.

3. Use the **Add** button to add images to the **ImageList** component, and then click **OK** to close the Image Collection Editor.

Tip   Visual Studio .NET provides a library of icons in the Program_Files\Visual Studio.NET\Common7\Graphics\icons\ folder.

---

4. In the Properties window for of the **ToolBar**, set the **ImageList** property to the **ImageList** component that you added earlier.

5. Click the **Buttons** property of the **ToolBar** control to select it, and then click the **Ellipsis** button ••• to open the ToolBarButton Collection Editor.

6. Select and click a button. Then, in the Properties window that appears in the pane to the right of the ToolBarButton Collection Editor, set the **ImageIndex** property of each toolbar button to one of the values in the list, which is drawn from the images that you added to the **ImageList** component. Click **OK** to close the ToolBarButton Collection Editor.

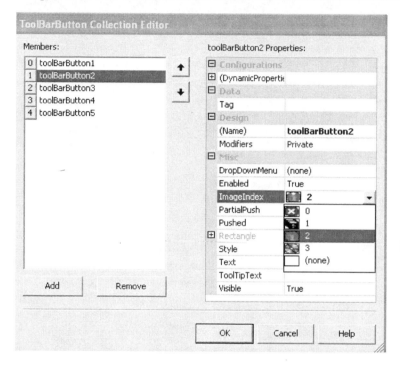

Docking the toolbar

You can dock toolbars to the edges of your form, either on the top, bottom, right, or left.

Setting docking options for a toolbar

To set docking options for a toolbar on a form:

1. Drag a **Toolbar** control onto your form.

2. In the Properties window, click the arrow to the right of the **Dock** property.

   An editor is displayed that shows a series of boxes representing the edges and the center of the form.

3. Click the button that represents the edge of the form where you want to dock the toolbar. In the Properties window, click the arrow to the right of the **Dock** property.

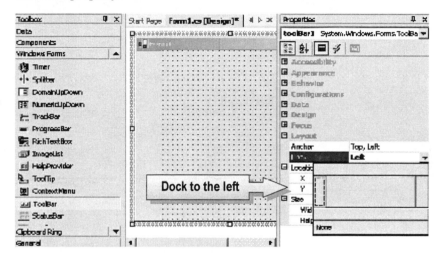

How to Write Code for the ButtonClick Event

- **All buttons on a toolbar share a single Click event**

- **Use the Tag property of the button to define the action**

- **Add an event handler for the ButtonClick event of the Toolbar control**

- **Determine the button the user clicks**

- **Call the action defined in the Tag property**

Introduction

All buttons on a toolbar share a single **Click** event. To add functionality to your toolbar, you must know which button the user clicks.

Determining which button is clicked

Toolbar buttons normally duplicate events that can be raised in some other manner, usually from menu items. Therefore, when you handle an event on the toolbar, you identify the button that was pressed and then call the event handler that it is associated with that button.

Tag property

The **ToolBarButton** class provides a **Tag** property that makes this task easy. When you create the **ToolBarButton** object, set the **Tag** property to the object whose behavior you are duplicating. When the toolbar event handler is called, you can use this property to send a **Click** event to the original object.

Example

For example, if the user clicks the icon to open a file, you call the same event handler that you would call in response to the user selecting **Open** on the **File** menu. The following code, which assumes that you have a menu item, **openFile**, illustrates this example.

```
MenuItem openFile = new MenuItem();
openFile.Click += new EventHandler(openFile_Click);
...
// create the ToolBar and ToolBarButton objects
...
ToolBarButton openButton = new ToolBarButton();
openButton.Tag = openFile;
```

The event handler for the toolbar can handle any button with the following code:

```
private void toolBar1_ButtonClick(
                    object sender,
                    ToolBarButtonClickEventArgs e) {
    ToolBarButton tbb = e.Button;
    MenuItem mItem = (MenuItem) tbb.Tag;
    mItem.PerformClick();
}
```

From the *ToolBarButtonClickEventArgs* parameters, the event handler for the toolbar retrieves a reference to the button that was clicked. The button uses the **Tag** property to reference the menu item that has the duplicate functionality, so the event handler can call the **PerformClick** method of the menu item, similar to a click. The **PerformClick** method causes the event handler for the menu item to be called.

The advantage of this technique is that the event handler can handle any button.

Note that although the code in the example is broken onto three lines, it normally would be written as follows:

```
((MenuItem)(e.Button.Tag)).PerformClick();
```

Practice: Creating and Using a ToolBar

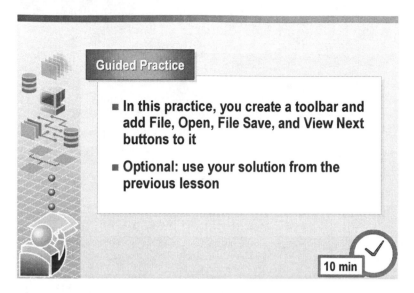

In this practice, you will create a toolbar and add **File Open**, **File Save** and **View Next** buttons to it. At the end of this practice, your solution should appear similar to the following illustration:

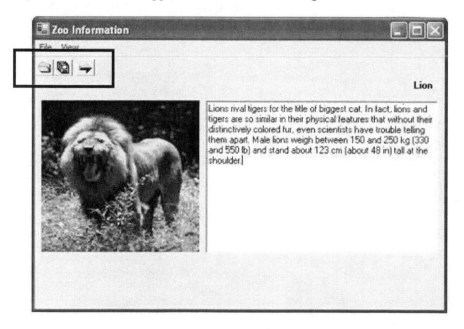

If you have a working solution from the Creating a Custom Dialog Box lesson in this module and you want to build upon that, open that solution and skip steps 1 and 2 in this practice.

The solution for this practice is located at *install_folder*\Practices\Mod08\ ToolBar_Solution\Animals.sln. Start a new instance of Visual Studio .NET before opening the solution.

Tasks	Detailed steps
1. Start Visual Studio .NET and then open *install_folder*\Practices \Mod08\ToolBar\Animals.sln.	a. Start a new instance of Visual Studio .NET. b. On the **Start Page**, click **Open Project**. c. In the **Open Project** dialog box, browse to *install_folder* \Practices\Mod08\ToolBar, click **Animals.sln**, and then click **Open**. d. In Solution Explorer, click **Form1.cs**, and then press F7 to open the Code Editor.
2. *(Optional)* Build and run the solution, and familiarize yourself with it.	a. In Visual Studio .NET, press F5. b. Examine the Zoo Information application. c. Close the Zoo Information window.
3. Load icons for buttons by adding an **ImageList** control to the form and then loading three appropriate images from Program Files \Microsoft Visual Studio .NET \Common7\Graphics\icons.	a. Press SHIFT+F7 to switch to Design view and then drag an **ImageList** control from the Toolbox to **Form1**. b. Use the **Images** collection and the **Image Collection Editor** to add 3 images to the **ImageList**. Samples images can be found in the folders under Program Files \Microsoft Visual Studio .NET\Common7\Graphics\icons.
4. Add a **ToolBar** control to your form, and set the ImageList property to the ImageList that you created in the previous task.	a. Drag the **ToolBar** control from the **Toolbox** to your form. b. Set the **ImageList** property to the **ImageList** that you created earlier. By default, this will be **imageList1**.
5. Add four buttons to the Toolbar, using the information in the following table.	▪ Use the **Buttons** collection and the **ToolBarButton Collection Editor** to add the buttons.

Button	Style	Name	ImageIndex
First button	PushButton	openFile	Select an icon
Second button	PushButton	saveFile	Select an icon
Third button	Separator	default	none
Fourth button	PushButton	viewNext	Select an icon

Tasks	Detailed steps
6. Write code to set the **Tag** property of each **PushButton** to reference the menu item that the button is equivalent to, using the table to the right.	▪ Place the code in the main form constructor, after the **InitializeComponents()** method. **Button name** **Set the tag property value to:** openFile Name of the **File Load** menu item saveFile Name of the **File Save** menu item viewNext Name of the **View Next** menu item For example: `openFile.Tag = loadItem;`

7. Create an event handler for the **ToolBar** control that calls the **PerformClick** method on the menu item associated with the button.	a. In Design view, double-click the toolbar.
	b. Use the following code to invoke the desired method:
	
	`ToolBarButton anyButton = e.Button;`
	`MenuItem anyMenuItem =`
	`  (MenuItem) anyButton.Tag;`
	`anyMenuItem.PerformClick();`

8. Test your application by clicking the **ToolBar** button that loads the XML data file **AnimalData.xml**.	a. On the **Build** menu, click **Build Solution**. b. If necessary, use breakpoints and the debugger to check your application.
9. Save your solution.	▪ On the **File** menu, click **Save All**.

Lesson: Creating the Status Bar

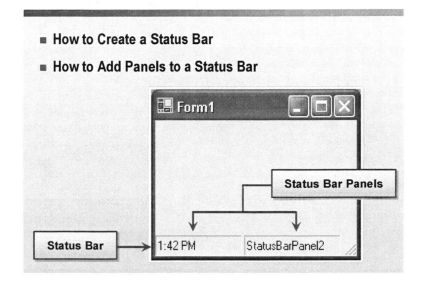

- How to Create a Status Bar
- How to Add Panels to a Status Bar

Introduction

A **StatusBar** control can be added to a form and customized to provide useful information, such as the name of a file that is currently open, the current date or time, or the status of certain keys on the keyboard. In this lesson, you will learn how to enhance the interface of an application by using the **StatusBar** control.

Lesson objectives

After completing this lesson, you will be able to:

- Create the status bar.
- Set the status bar properties.

Lesson agenda

This lesson includes the following topics and activities:

- Demonstration: Creating a Status Bar
- How to Create a Status Bar
- How to Add Panels to a Status Bar
- Practice: Creating a Status Bar

Demonstration: Creating a Status Bar

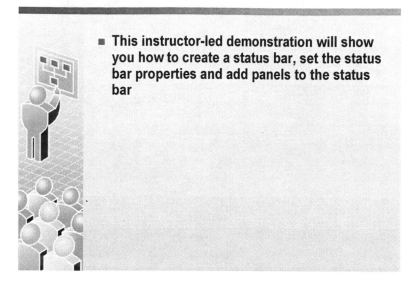

This instructor-led demonstration will show you how to create a status bar, add panels to it, and set the panel properties. The instructor will:

1. Open Visual Studio .NET and create a new **Windows Application** project named **MyForm**.

2. Add a **StatusBar** control to the form.

3. Set the status bar properties, as shown in the following table:

Properties	Description
ShowPanel	Determines if a status bar displays panels, or if it displays a single line of text.
Panels	**(Collection) Editor** allows adding and removing panels to the status bar.

4. Add panels to a status bar at design time.

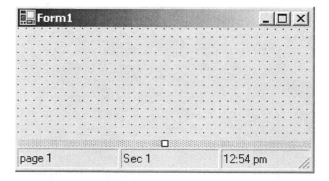

How to Create a Status Bar

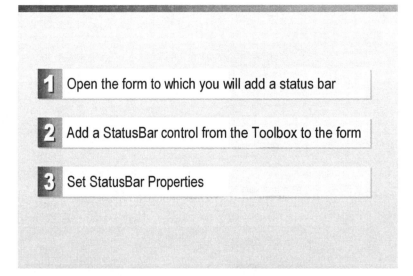

1 Open the form to which you will add a status bar

2 Add a StatusBar control from the Toolbox to the form

3 Set StatusBar Properties

Introduction

You can add a **StatusBar** control to a form and customize the control to provide useful information, such as the name of a file that is currently open, the current date or time, or the status of certain keys on the keyboard. The Windows Forms **StatusBar** control appears on forms as an area, usually displayed at the bottom of a window, in which an application can display various kinds of status information.

Adding a status bar

To add a status bar to your form:

1. Open the form to which you want to add a status bar.

2. Use the Toolbox to add a **StatusBar** control to the form.

3. Set the appropriate **StatusBar** properties, including **ShowPanels**.

StatusBar properties

The following table shows **StatusBar** properties that you will frequently use.

Property	Description
Panels	By default, a status bar has no panels. Use the **Panels** property to add panels to or remove panels from the StatusBarPanels collection.
ShowPanels	If set to **False** (default), displays only the value of the **Text** property of the control. If set to **True**, enables you to display panels in your status bar.
SizingGrip	Displays a sizing grip on the lower right corner of the form to indicate to users that the form can be resized. Use only on a form that can be resized.
Text	Contains the text string displayed in the status bar.

If you will not add panels to the status bar, set the **ShowPanels** property to **False** (the default), and then set the **Text** property to the text that you want to appear in the status bar.

To display more than one type of information in the status bar, set the **ShowPanels** property to **True**, and then add the desired number of **StatusBarPanel** objects to the **Panels** collection.

How to Add Panels to a Status Bar

1	Open the Properties window for the StatusBar control
2	Set the ShowPanels property to True
3	In the Panels property, open the StatusBarPanel Collection Editor
4	Use the Add and Remove buttons to add and remove status bar panels
5	Set the panel properties
6	Close the StatusBarPanel Collection Editor

Introduction

The programmable area in a **StatusBar** control consists of instances of the **StatusBarPanel** class. You can display more than one type of information in the status bar by setting the **ShowPanels** property to **True** and adding panels to the status bar.

You can use status bar panels to display text or icons to indicate state, or to display a series of icons in an animation to indicate that a process is working. For example, a status bar panel in Microsoft Word displays a small icon to indicate when a document is being saved.

Adding panels to a status bar

To add panels to a status bar at design time:

1. Open the Properties window for the StatusBar control.

2. In the Properties window for the status bar, set the **ShowPanels** property to **True**.

3. Click the **Panels** property to select it, and then click the **Ellipsis** button ... to open the StatusBarPanel Collection Editor.

4. Use the **Add** and **Remove** buttons to add panels to and remove panels from the **StatusBar** control.

5. Configure the properties of the individual panels in the Properties window that appears in the pane to the right of the editor.

6. Click **OK** to close the dialog box and create the panels that you specified.

Panel properties

The following table shows **StatusBar** panel properties that you will frequently use.

Property	Description
AutoSize	Sets the resizing behavior of the panel.
	Contents: The width of the panel is determined by its contents.
	None: The panel does not change size when the status bar control is resized.
	Spring: The panel shares the available space on the status bar with other panels that have their **AutoSize** property set to **Spring**.
Alignment	Sets the alignment of the panel in the **StatusBar** control. Options include **Center**, **Left**, and **Right**.
BorderStyle	Sets the type of border that is displayed at the edges of the panel.
	None: No border is displayed.
	Raised: The panel is displayed with a three-dimensional raised border.
	Sunken: The panel is displayed with a three-dimensional sunken border.
Icon	Sets the icon (.ico file) that is displayed in the panel.
MinWidth	Sets the minimum width of the panel in the status bar.
Style	Sets the style of the panel.
	OwnerDraw: Supports the display of images or the use of a different font than the rest of the panel objects on a status bar.
	Text: The panel displays text in the standard font.
Text	Sets the text string displayed in the panel.
Width	Sets the width of the panel, in pixels. This property may change when the form is resized, depending on the setting of the **AutoSize** property.

Practice: Creating the Status Bar

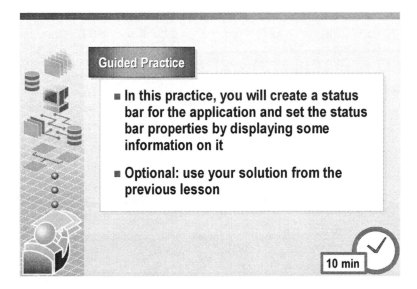

In this practice, you will create a status bar that shows the name of the file that is loaded. When you are finished, your solution should look similar to the following illustration:

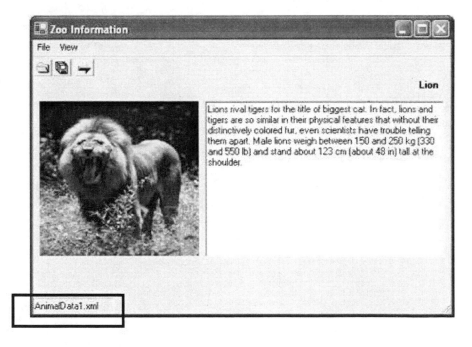

If you have a working solution from the Creating and Using ToolBars lesson in this module that you want to develop, open that solution and skip steps 1 and 2 in this practice.

The solution for this practice is located in *install_folder*\Practices\Mod08\ StatusBar_Solution \Animals.sln. Start a new instance of Visual Studio .NET before opening the solution.

Tasks	Detailed steps
1. Start Visual Studio .NET and then open *install_folder*\Practices \Mod08\StatusBar\Animals.sln.	a. Start a new instance of Visual Studio .NET. b. On the **Start Page**, click **Open Project**. c. In the **Open Project** dialog box, browse to *install_folder* \Practices\Mod08\StatusBar\, click **Animals.sln**, and then click **Open**. d. In Solution Explorer, click **Form1.cs**, and then press F7 to open the Code Editor.
2. *(Optional)* Build and run the solution, and familiarize yourself with it.	a. In Visual Studio .NET, press F5. b. Examine the Zoo Information application. c. Close the Zoo Information window.
3. Add a **StatusBar** control to your application, and set the **ShowPanels** property to true.	a. Press SHIFT+F7 to switch to Design view. b. Use the Toolbox to add a **StatusBar** control to your form. c. Set the **ShowPanels** property to **true**.
4. Add a panel to the **StatusBar** object, naming it **filePanel**.	a. Use the **Panels** property and the StatusBarPanel Collection Editor to add a panel to the status bar. b. Set the **Name** property of the panel to **filePanel**.
5. Write code to assign the filename to **filePanel.Text** when a file is loaded.	a. Locate the **LoadZoo** method in Form1, and then under the call to **Zoo.Load**, assign the name of the file being loaded to the **filePanel.Text** property. b. **zooFile** holds the full path and file name of the file being loaded. Use the following code to extract the file name.
<code>int lastFilemarkerIndex = zooFile.LastIndexOf('\\');</code> <code>filePanel.Text = zooFile.Substring(lastFilemarkerIndex + 1);</code>	
6. Test your application by loading the XML data file **AnimalData.xml**.	a. Press F5 to build and run your application. b. If necessary, use breakpoints and the debugger to check your application.
7. Save your solution.	▪ On the **File** menu, click **Save All**.

Lesson: Creating and Using Combo Boxes

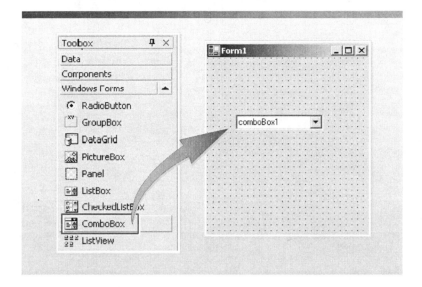

Introduction

The Windows Forms **ComboBox** control is used to display data in a drop-down combo box. This lesson explains how to create a combo box, and how to associate objects with it.

Lesson objectives

After completing this lesson, you will be able to:

- Use a **ComboBox** control.
- Associate objects with the combo box.
- Add an event handler for the combo box.

Lesson agenda

This lesson includes the following topic and activities:

- Demonstration: Creating and Using a Combo Box
- How to Use a Combo Box
- Practice: Using a **ComboBox** Control

Demonstration: Creating and Using a Combo Box

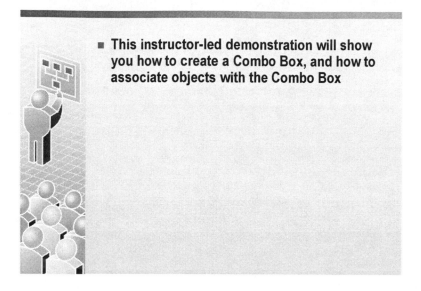

This instructor-led demonstration will show you how to create a combo box , and how to associate objects with the **ComboBox** control. The instructor will:

1. Open Visual Studio .NET and create a new **Windows Application** project named **MyForm**.

2. Add a **ComboBox** control to the form.

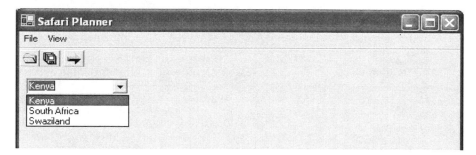

3. Add strings to the **items** collection using the **Add** and **AddRange** method.

How to Use a Combo Box

- **Create the combo box**

```
ComboBox cb = new ComboBox()
```

- **Add items to the combo box**

```
object[] cbItems = {"Lion", "Elephant", "Duck"};
ComboBox.Items.Add(cbItems);
```

- **Write an event handler**

```
comboBox1_SelectedIndexChanged(object sender,
System.EventArgs e) {
        ComboBox c = (ComboBox) sender;
        MessageBox.Show( c.SelectedItem );
}
```

Introduction

Generally, a combo box is appropriate when there is a list of *suggested* selection. A combo box contains a text box field, so users can type selections that are not on the list. Also, combo boxes save space on a form. Because the full list is not displayed until the user clicks the down arrow, a combo box can easily fit in a small space. By default, the **ComboBox** control contains two parts:

- A text box at the top that allows the user to type a list item.

- A list box on the bottom that displays a list of items that the user can select from.

After you create a combo box, you can add to and remove items from it, write an event handler for it, and associate methods with it.

Creating a combo box

As with other controls, you can create a **Combobox** control by dragging the control from the Toolbox onto your form. You can also create it with code as shown in the following example:

```
ComboBox cb = new ComboBox();
```

Adding items to a combo box

You can add items to a combo box in a variety of ways, because these controls can be bound to a variety of data sources. The simplest way to add items to a combo box is to add strings to the **Items** collection by using the **Add** or **AddRange** method, as shown in the following code:

```
string[] animalNames = { "Antelope", "Bear", "Elephant",
"Lion" };
comboBox1.Items.AddRange( animalNames );
```

A much more useful way to add items to a combo box is to add the objects themselves, as shown in the following code:

```
animalList = new object[] {
                new Antelope(),
                new Bear(),
                new Elephant(),
                new Lion() };
comboBox1.Items.AddRange( animalList );
```

Or:

```
for (int i = 0; i < object.Length; i++ ) {
  comboBox1.Items.Add( animalist[i] );
}
```

The advantage of adding an object is that when you retrieve the user's selection, you can get a reference to the selected object rather than a string.

The combo box uses the **ToString** method to generate the label for the drop-down list, so you must often override the **ToString** method.

Finally, you can bind a combo box to a data source, as shown in the following code:

```
comboBox1.DataSource = animalist;
```

Writing an event handler

Because a combo box has a test entry element and a menu element, you normally must write event handlers for both of these components. The most useful events for the menu are **SelectedIndexChanged** and **SelectionChangeCommitted**. The **SelectedIndexChanged** event is sent when the index changes, including when the user scrolls through the menu. The **SelectionChangeCommitted** event is sent when the selection is made, such as when the user closes the menu.

For example, to show the selected item in a message box, you can use the following code:

```
private void comboBox1_SelectionChangeCommitted (object
sender, System.EventArgs e) {
  // cast the object sender parameter to a combo box
  ComboBox c = (ComboBox) sender;
  MessageBox.Show(c.SelectedItem);
}
```

The text box component of the combo box generates a **TextChanged** event when the user types in the text box. You can use this event to retrieve the **Text** property from the combo box and, for example, match it against the contents of the menu.

```
private void comboBox1_TextChanged(object sender,
                             System.EventArgs e) {
  ComboBox c = (ComboBox) sender;
  MessageBox.Show(this, "You typed " + c.Text );
}
```

Note Often you will want a combo box to use the menu items to automatically complete the text typed into the text box. This is achieved by using the **FindString** method of the combo box. A working sample is provided on the Student Materials compact disc, in the file Samples\Mod08\ComboBoxSample\ComboBoxSample.sln.

Example

The following example shows how to associate objects with the combo box. In this example, the combo box holds a collection of objects that are derived from the **Animal** class.

```
public abstract class Animal { }

public class Elephant : Animal {
  public override string ToString() { return "Elephant"; }
}

public class Lion : Animal {
  public override string ToString() { return "Lion"; }
}

public class Bear : Animal {
  public override string ToString() { return "Bear"; }
}

public class Antelope : Animal {
  public override string ToString() { return "Antelope"; }
}

// ...create a combobox, name it comboBox1...
```

The preceding code is written as an array. Under normal circumstances, this code is created somewhere else in the program and copied into an array, as shown in the following code:

```
object[] animalList = {
            new Antelope(),
            new Bear(),
            new Elephant(),
            new Lion()
        };
```

You can then add these items to the **ComboBox** object. To improve performance when you use the **Add** method to add the objects, call the **BeginUpdate()** method before you add and the **EndUpdate()** method after you add.

```
comboBox1.Items.AddRange( animalList );
```

The event handler for this is shown in the following code:

```
private void comboBox1_SelectionChangeCommitted (
                        object sender, System.EventArgs e) {
    ComboBox c = (ComboBox) sender;
    Animal a = (Animal) c.SelectedItem;
    MessageBox.Show(this, "You selected " + a.ToString() );
}
```

Note that the event handler is able to get a reference to the **Animal** object.

Practice: Using a ComboBox Control

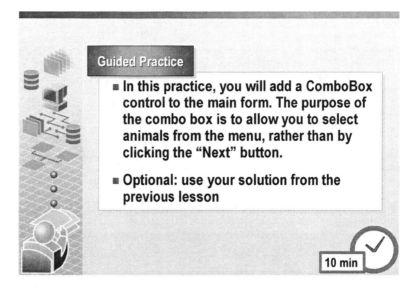

Guided Practice

- In this practice, you will add a ComboBox control to the main form. The purpose of the combo box is to allow you to select animals from the menu, rather than by clicking the "Next" button.

- Optional: use your solution from the previous lesson

10 min

In this practice, you will add a combo box to the main form. The purpose of the combo box is to allow the user to select animals from the menu, rather than by clicking the **Next** button.

If you have a working solution from the Creating the Status Bar lesson in this module that you want to develop, open that solution and skip steps 1 and 2 in this practice.

Your solution should appear as shown in the following illustration:

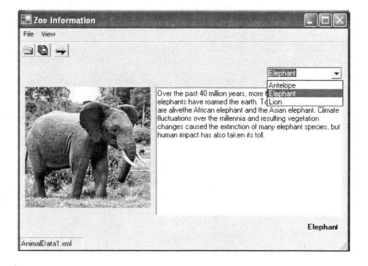

The solution for this practice is located in *install_folder*\Practices\Mod08\ComboBox_Solution\Animals.sln. Start a new instance of Visual Studio .NET before opening the solution.

Tasks	Detailed steps
1. Start Visual Studio .NET and then open *install_folder*\Practices\Mod08\ComboBox\Animals.sln.	a. Start a new instance of Visual Studio .NET. b. On the **Start Page**, click **Open Project**. c. In the **Open Project** dialog box, browse to *install_folder*\Practices\Mod08\ComboBox , click **Animals.sln**, and then click **Open**. d. In Solution Explorer, click **Form1.cs**, and then press F7 to open the Code Editor.
2. (Optional) Build and run the solution, and familiarize yourself with it.	a. In Visual Studio .NET, press F5. b. Examine the Zoo Information application. c. Close the Zoo Information window.
3. Add a **ComboBox** control to Form1, and name it **animalSelection**.	a. Press SHIFT+F7 to enter Designer mode. b. Drag the **ComboBox** control from the **Toolbox** onto **Form1**. c. Change the **Name** property to **animalSelection**.
4. In Form1, write a method named **InitializeAnimalSelection**. The purpose of this method is to add the **Animal** objects to the **Items** collection in the **animalSelection** object.	a. In the **Form1** class, write a method named **InitializeAnimalSelection**. This method does not return a value and takes no parameters. b. The method adds the **Animal** objects to the **Items** collection in the combo box. Sample code is provided below. The **for** loop checks **myZoo.Count** and adds a reference to each animal in the **Zoo** to the **Items** collection in the **animalSelection** object. Note that **myZoo** has an indexer.

``
public void InitializeAnimalSelection() {
   for (int i = 0; i < myZoo.Count; i++) {
        animalSelection.Items.Add((object) myZoo[i]);
   }
}
``	

5. Ensure that **InitializeAnimalSelection** is called after the data file is loaded.	▪ Insert a call to **InitializeAnimalSelection** in the **loadItem_Click** event handler, after the call to the **Zoo.Load()** method.

Tasks	Detailed steps
6. Write an event handler for the **SelectionChangeCommitted** event that gets the reference to the selected animal from the sender parameter, and calls **DisplayAnimal** to display it.	a. Press SHIFT+F7 to switch to Design view. b. Click the **ComboBox** control, click the **Events** button (shown to the left) in the **Properties** window, and then double-click **SelectionChangeCommitted**. c. Write code that converts the sender parameter to a **ComboBox**, then convert the **SelectedItem** in the **ComboBox** object to an **Animal**. d. Call **DisplayAnimal** with the **Animal** object.

```
ComboBox c = (ComboBox) sender;
Animal a = (Animal) c.SelectedItem;
DisplayAnimal( a );
```

Tasks	Detailed steps
7. Test your application by loading the XML data file **AnimalData.xml**.	a. On the **Build** menu, click **Build Solution**. b. If necessary, use breakpoints and the debugger to check your application.
8. Save your solution and quit Visual Studio .NET.	a. On the **File** menu, click **Save All**. b. Quit Visual Studio .NET.

Review

- Creating the Main Menu
- Creating and Using Common Dialog Boxes
- Creating and Using Custom Dialog Boxes
- Creating and Using Toolbars
- Creating the Status Bar
- Creating and Using Combo Boxes

1. What namespace contains menus, dialog boxes, status bars, and toolbars?

2. What is the difference between a form and a dialog box?

3. Which of the following statements are true?

    Images for a toolbar's buttons are:

    a. Assigned an index number in the Image Collection Editor.

    b. Automatically attached to the toolbar button based on function.

    c. Maintained in the ToolBarButton Image Collection Editor.

    d. Maintained in a separate **ImageList** control.

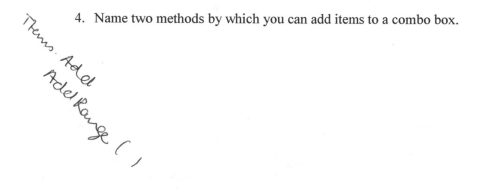

4. Name two methods by which you can add items to a combo box.

Lab 8.1: Building Windows Applications

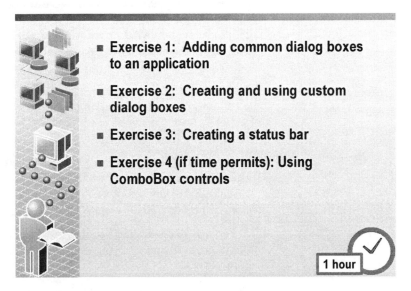

- **Exercise 1: Adding common dialog boxes to an application**

- **Exercise 2: Creating and using custom dialog boxes**

- **Exercise 3: Creating a status bar**

- **Exercise 4 (if time permits): Using ComboBox controls**

1 hour

Objectives

After completing this lab, you will be able to create an application that uses standard Windows controls to create a user interface.

Note This lab focuses on the concepts in this module and, as a result, may not comply with Microsoft security recommendations.

Prerequisites

Before working on this lab, you must have the ability to add Windows controls to an application.

Scenario

In this lab, you will add typical Windows functionality to an existing bank teller application.

The existing application is a very simple example, so that you can quickly understand it in this lab.

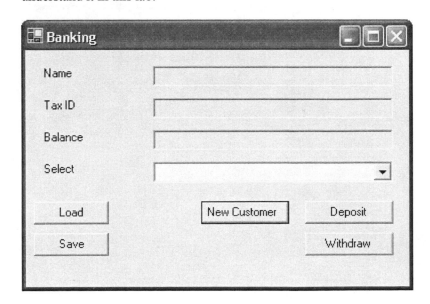

The provided application has the following files:

- *Account.cs*. Contains **CheckingAccount** and **SavingAccount** classes, both derived from **BankAccount**. These have properties, such as **Balance**, and methods, such as **Withdraw** and **Deposit**. This class is complete and you will not need to change the code in this file to complete the lab.

- *Customer.cs*. Contains the **Customer** class. Each customer contains a list of bank accounts, although this example creates only one bank account per customer. Customers have properties, such as **Name**, and methods, such as **AddAccount**. This class is complete and you will not need to change the code in this file to complete the lab.

- *Bank.cs*. Contains the list of bank customers. Important methods in the Bank class are **Load** and **Save**, which load and save the bank data, and **Add**, which adds a new customer to the bank. This class is complete and you will not need to change the code in this file to complete the lab.

- *Form1.cs*. The main application window, shown in the preceding illustration. In this lab, you will modify this class so that it uses Windows controls.

- *NewCustomer.cs*. A dialog box that allows the user to create a new customer account. This class is complete and you will not need to change the code in this file to complete the lab.

In the starter code:

- The **Load** button loads the bank data from a file.

- The **Save** button saves the bank data to the same file.

- The **New Customer** button opens a dialog box that allows the user to enter new customer information.

- The **Deposit** and **Withdraw** buttons do nothing.

Estimated time to complete this lab: 60 minutes

Exercise 0
Lab Setup

The Lab Setup section lists the tasks that you must perform before you begin the lab.

Task	Detailed steps
▪ Log on to Windows using your Student account.	▪ Log on to Windows using the following account information: • User name: **Student** • Password: **P@ssw0rd** Note that the 0 in the password is a zero.

Note that by default the *install_folder* is C:\Program Files\Msdntrain\2609.

The solution code for this lab is located in *install_folder*\Labfiles\Lab08_1\Exercise1 \Solution_Code\Bank.sln. Start a new instance of Visual Studio .NET before opening the solution.

Note that exercises 2 and 3 do not have separate starter code. If necessary, you can use the starter code listed in exercise 1, step 1, to start these exercises.

Exercise 1
Adding Common Dialog Boxes to an Application

In this exercise, you will modify the bank teller application so that it uses the **OpenFileDialog** and **SaveFileDialog** controls instead of the current **Load** and **Save** buttons.

The application uses a data file to store all the information. By default, this is called bankdata.bnk and is located in the same folder as the starter code.

Allow users of the application to use a typical **File Open** menu selection to browse to any file location, and load the file. Also, allow them to use a typical **File Save** menu selection to save the file to any location.

Tasks	Detailed steps
1. Start Visual Studio.NET and then open *install_folder* \Labfiles\Lab08_1\Exercise1 \Bank.sln.	**a.** Start a new instance of Visual Studio.NET. **b.** On the **Start Page**, click **Open Project**. **c.** In the **Open Project** dialog box, browse to *install_folder*\ Labfiles\ Lab08_1\Exercise1, click **Bank.sln**, and then click **Open**.
2. Add a main menu to the application, with a **File** menu that contains an **Open** option.	**a.** Add a main menu to the application. **b.** Add a **File** menu to the main menu. **c.** Add an **Open** menu item to the **File** menu. Remember to change the name properties of the menu items to meaningful values.
3. Add an **OpenFileDialog** control, display it when the user selects **Open** from the **File** menu, and then load the selected data file.	**a.** Add an **OpenFileDialog** control to your application. **b.** Add an event handler to the **Open** menu item by double-clicking it in the design window. **c.** In the event handler, write code that uses the **OpenFileDialog** to locate a data file, and then load it. The data file is called **bankdata.bnk**, and it located in *install_folder*\ Labfiles\ Lab08_1\Exercise1. **d.** If the result returned from the **OpenFileDialog** is **DialogResult.OK**, then use the method **Load** in the **Bank** class to load the data file specified in the **FileName** property of the **OpenFileDialog** object.

Tasks	Detailed steps
4. Add a **Save** option to the **File** menu. Implement the expected functionality for this option.	a. Add a **Save** item to the **File** menu. b. Add a **SaveFileDialog** control to your application. c. Add an event handler to the Save menu item, and write code that uses the **SaveFileDialog** to define a file name, and then save the data. The method **Save** in the **Bank** class saves a data file. Remember to delete the **Load** and **Save** buttons from the form.
5. Test your code.	a. Copy the data file **bankdata.bnk** to your desktop. b. Press F5 to compile your application and then locate the copy of the data file that is on your desktop, and load it. c. Add a new customer record. d. Save the data, and exit your application. e. Restart your application and load the data file, to ensure that the new customer record is loaded.

Exercise 2
Creating and Using Custom Dialog Boxes

In this exercise, you will invoke the **New Customer** dialog box, and create custom dialog boxes that allow the user of the application to withdraw and deposit amounts of money into the selected account.

The **New Customer** dialog box appears as follows:

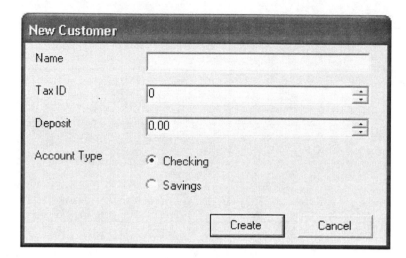

The **Withdraw** and **Deposit** dialog boxes appear as follows:

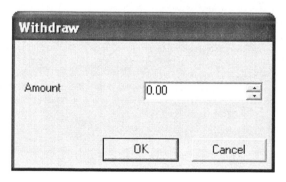

Tasks	Detailed steps
1. Create a new menu labeled **Customers** with an item labeled **New**. Invoke the **New Customer** dialog box when this item is selected.	a. On the main menu, add a menu labeled **Customers** and a menu item labeled **New**. The purpose of this item is to allow the user to choose to create a new customer account. b. Add an event handler to the menu item and in the event handler, create a **NewCustomer** object, and then display it by using the **ShowDialog** method.
2. Create a new customer account and a bank account for that customer.	a. If the dialog box is closed by clicking the **Create** button, create a new customer record and a new bank account. Note that the value of the **DialogResult** property for the **Create** button is **DialogResult.OK**. Look in the **newCustomer_Click** method in the **Form1** class for sample code. b. Delete the **New Customer** button from **Form1**.
3. Add menu items that will invoke the **Withdraw** and **Deposit** dialog boxes.	a. Add a **Withdraw** menu item. b. Add a **Deposit** menu item. c. Create event handlers for these menu items.
4. Create a **Withdraw** dialog box.	a. Using Solution Explorer, add a new Windows form to the project, name it **Withdraw**, and configure it as a dialog box by setting the **FormBorderStyle** property to **FixedDialog**, and the **ControlBox**, **MaximizeBox**, **MinimizeBox**, and **ShowInTaskBar** properties to **false**. b. Add a **NumericUpDown** control to the **Withdraw** form. c. Create a public property called **WithdrawalAmount** that returns the value in the **Value** property of the **NumericUpDown** object. d. Add **OK** and **Cancel** buttons to the form.

Tasks	Detailed steps
5. Write code to open the **Withdraw** dialog box from the application menu.	**a.** In the **Withdraw** menu item event handler in **Form1**, write code to create and display the **Withdraw** dialog box.
	b. If the **Withdraw form** object returns a **DialogResult** of **DialogResult.OK**, then read the value in the **WithdrawalAmount** property, and perform the withdrawal from the currently selected customer's account.
	The currently selected customer is always referenced from the **currentCustomer** member of **Form1**.
	The currently selected customer's bank account can be accessed by using the following code:
| | ```
BankAccount thisAccount = (BankAccount)
currentCustomer.Accounts[0];
``` |
	c. Use the **Withdraw** method of the **BankAccount** object to remove the correct amount from the currently selected account.
	For the purposes of this lab, you can assume that every customer has one bank account.
	d. Use the **SetCurrentCustomer** method to update the display on the main form after you have withdrawn the money.
6. Implement a **Deposit** dialog box.	**a.** Following the steps outlined in the previous two tasks, create a **Deposit** dialog box.
	b. Use the **BankAccount.Deposit** method to add the correct amount of money in the currently selected account.
7. Test your code.	**a.** Press F5 to compile your application.
	b. Withdraw money and deposit money to ensure that your application is working as expected.
8. Save your application and quit Visual Studio .NET.	**a.** Save your application.
	b. Quit Visual Studio .NET.
```

Exercise 3
Creating a Status Bar

In this exercise, you will add a status bar to the application.

Tasks	Detailed steps
1. Add a status bar to the application, with one status pane.	a. Add a status bar control to your application. b. Use the **Panels** property and the **StatusBarPanel Collection Editor** to add one panel to the status bar. c. Remember to set the **ShowPanels** property to **true**.
2. Display the total number of customers in the status bar pane.	▪ Write code that displays the total number of customers in the status bar. The following code returns the total number of customers: `theBank.Customers.Count.ToString();` The **SetCurrentCustomer** method is called every time a change is made to the data, so this is a good place to add the code that updates the contents of the status bar panel.
3. Test your application.	a. Press F5 to compile your application. b. Add a new customer to the list and make sure that the status bar updates correctly.
4. Save your application and quit Visual Studio .NET.	a. Save your application. b. Quit Visual Studio .NET.

If Time Permits
Using ComboBox Controls

Write a dialog box that transfers money from one account to another. Use a combo box on the transfer dialog box to select destination customer accounts.

training

Module 9: Using XML Web Services in a C# Application

Contents

Microsoft

Overview

- **Consuming an XML Web Service**
- **Building an XML Web Service**

Introduction

This module introduces the **System.Web.Services** namespace and the process of building and using XML Web services in a C# application.

Objectives

After completing this module, you will be able to:

- Request data from an XML Web service from within a C# application.
- Build an XML Web service.

Lesson: Consuming an XML Web Service

- **What Is an XML Web Service?**
- **How to Locate the URL of an XML Web Service**
- **How to Add a Web Reference to an XML Web Service**
- **How to Call an XML Web Service Method in Code**

Introduction

This lesson presents XML Web services and explains how to request data from an XML Web service from within a C# application.

Lesson objectives

After completing this lesson, you will be able to:

- Add an XML Web service reference to a C# project.
- Invoke methods and properties of an XML Web service.

Lesson agenda

This lesson includes the following topics and activity:

- What Is an XML Web Service?
- How to Locate the URL of an XML Web Service
- How to Add a Web Reference to an XML Web Service
- How to Call an XML Web Service Method in Code
- Practice: Using an XML Web Service from Within C#

What Is an XML Web Service?

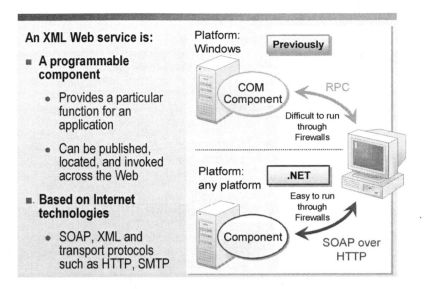

An XML Web service is:

- **A programmable component**
  - Provides a particular function for an application
  - Can be published, located, and invoked across the Web
- **Based on Internet technologies**
  - SOAP, XML and transport protocols such as HTTP, SMTP

Platform: Windows — Previously

COM Component ← RPC

Difficult to run through Firewalls

Platform: any platform — .NET

Easy to run through Firewalls

Component ← SOAP over HTTP

Introduction

Applications consist of components. Like components, XML Web services are black boxes. XML Web services encapsulate their functionality and provide an interface for using this functionality. Therefore, you can use XML Web services as building blocks for applications.

Definition

An XML Web service is a programmable component that provides a particular function for an application, such as application logic. Because XML Web services communicate by using Hypertext Transport Protocol (HTTP) and XML, any network node that supports these technologies can both host and access XML Web services. This means that an XML Web service is one component that you can use to build services and applications.

Examples

Examples of XML Web services follow:

- An airline company can provide an XML Web service that accepts a flight number and returns the status of the flight.

- A raw material supply company can provide an XML Web service that allows customers to place orders.

- An online calendar service provider can provide an XML Web service that allows users to update and query their online calendars.

XML Web services protocols

The foundations for XML Web services are XML, SOAP, and commonly supported Internet transport protocols such as HTTP and Simple Mail Transport Protocol (SMTP). This kind of support makes it simple for heterogeneous systems to communicate. For example, a component written in C# and exported as an XML Web service can be used by any application capable of sending and reading XML over the applicable transport.

SOAP is a lightweight XML-based protocol that is used for information exchange. SOAP is transport protocol independent and can be exchanged between a server and a client over transport protocols such as HTTP and SMTP, although it is most commonly implemented over HTTP.

> **Note** The development of these technologies is governed by the World Wide Web Consortium (W3C).

When is an XML Web service an appropriate solution?

Scenarios that may require XML Web services can be categorized as follows:

- Simple services that provide a fundamental piece of functionality for your clients to use.

- Application integration services that expose the functionality and data of existing disparate applications as an XML Web service.

- Workflow services that enable applications that constitute end-to-end workflow solutions to be created. Such solutions are appropriate for long-running scenarios such as those found in business-to-business transactions.

Examples of scenarios that may require such services are described in the following table.

Service type	Example application	Details
Simple	An e-commerce application that calculates charges for an assortment of shipping options.	Such an application requires current shipping cost tables from each shipping company to use in these calculations.
Simple	An application that sends a simple XML-based message over the Internet, where the message provides the weight and dimensions of the package, ship-from and ship-to locations, and other parameters, such as class of service.	Such an application can send a simple XML-based message over the Internet, using a standard transport protocol such as HTTP, to the shipper's cost calculation XML Web service. The shipper's XML Web service can then calculate the shipping charge, using the latest cost table and return, in a simple XML-based response message, this amount to the calling application for use in calculating the total charge to the customer.
Application integration	By using XML-based messages, applications running on different operating systems and/or hardware platforms can be integrated.	Earlier systems are a good example of systems that may need to be integrated into other system. However, often the platforms on which these earlier systems run make it difficult to integrate into other systems. XML-based messages can provide a common communication mechanism.
Workflow solution	Some organizations depend on integrating business information into the systems of their partners and customers.	Microsoft BizTalk® provides the framework, and technology for business document routing, transformation, and tracking so that you can define mechanisms for identifying and addressing messages, define the message lifetime, package the message with attachments, deliver the message reliably, and secure message contents for authentication, integrity, and privacy.

How to Locate the URL of an XML Web Service

1 On the **Start** page click **XML Web Services**

2 On the **Find a Service** tab, click either **UDDI Production Environment** or **UDDI Test Environment**

3 In the **Search For** box, enter a keyword of the XML Web service you want to locate

4 Click **Go** to start the search

5 Use the results to display more information about an XML Web service, or you can just click **Add as web reference to current project**

Introduction

If you are developing an application that uses data from a business partner, it is likely that the partner will give you the Uniform Resource Locator (URL) for the XML Web service. However, you may want your application to use other XML Web services that provide special services and data that you do not have the URL for. The advantages of XML Web services are limited if you cannot locate the service that you need. To allow you to easily locate XML Web services, Universal Description Discovery and Integration (UDDI) was created.

UDDI definition

UDDI is a comprehensive industry initiative that allows businesses to:

- Define their business.

- Discover other businesses.

- Share information about how they interact in a global registry.

UDDI is the building block that allows businesses to quickly, easily, and dynamically find and transact business with one another by using their preferred applications.

UDDI also contains standards-based specifications for service description and discovery. The UDDI standard takes advantage of W3C and Internet Engineering Task Force (IETF) standards such as XML, HTTP, and Domain Name System (DNS) protocols.

Locating XML Web service information

You can use UDDI to locate an XML Web service. Microsoft Visual Studio® .NET allows you to search for an XML Web service and then add a suitable XML Web service to your project.

To locate information about XML Web services, perform the following procedure:

1. On the Visual Studio .NET **Start** page, click **XML Web Services**.

   If the **Start** page is not visible, click **Help**, and then click **Show Start Page**.

2. On the **Find a Service** tab, click either **UDDI Production Environment** or **UDDI Test Environment**.

Note The **UDDI Production Environment** option is selected by default. If you are developing your application, click **UDDI Test Environment**.

---

3. In the **Search For** box, enter a keyword of the XML Web service that you want to locate.

4. Click **Go** to start the search.

5. The results of the search are displayed under the search criteria. You can use the results to display more information about an XML Web service, or you can just click **Add as web reference to current project**.

Note This procedure does not work in an environment that is not connected to the Internet.

How to Add a Web Reference to an XML Web Service

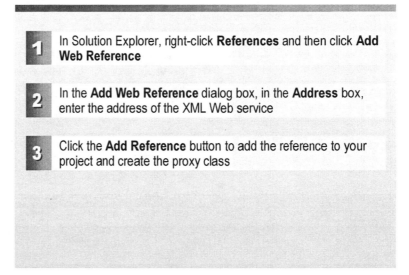

Introduction

The functionality necessary to use an XML Web service is integrated into the .NET Framework. In the .NET Framework, this functionality is provided by a *proxy class*.

Proxy class

To access an XML Web service from a client application, you first add a Web reference, which is a reference to an XML Web service. When you create a Web reference, Visual Studio .NET creates an XML Web service proxy class automatically and adds it to your project. This proxy class exposes the methods of the XML Web service, bundles client requests into SOAP messages that are sent on to the server, and retrieves the responses that contain the result.

You can then create an instance of the proxy class in your code so that you can use the methods of the XML Web service as if they were methods of a class that is held locally on your computer.

Adding a Web reference

To add a Web reference to an XML Web service, perform the following procedure:

1. In Solution Explorer, right-click **References**, and then click **Add Web Reference**.

2. In the **Add Web Reference** dialog box, in the **Address** box, enter the address of the XML Web service, such as http://advworks.msft/webservices/testservice.asmx.

3. Click the **Add Reference** button to add the reference to your project and create the proxy class.

Note This procedure requires that a connection using the transport protocol indicated is possible.

How to Call an XML Web Service Method in Code

■ After you add the XML Web service to your project you can write the code necessary to call the methods of that service, just as you would write code to call the methods of a class that is installed on your computer

```
com.Advwks.TempConv testwebservice = new
    com.advwks.TempConv();

MessageBox.Show(testwebservice.CToF(100)
    .ToString());
```

Introduction

After you add the XML Web service to your project, you can write the code necessary to call the methods of that service, just as you would write code to call the methods of a class that is installed on your computer.

Example

For example, if you add the XML Web service that is defined at http://advwks.com/TempConv, the full name of the class created is:

```
<application name space>.com.advwks.TempConv
```

An example of calling the **CToF** method of this XML Web service is:

```
com.Advwks.TempConv testwebservice = new
    com.advwks.TempConv();
MessageBox.Show(testwebservice.CToF(100).ToString());
```

The first line of the preceding code creates an instance of the **TempConv** class. The last line uses the static method of the **MessageBox** class **Show** to display a message box that shows the result of **TempConv** class method **CToF**.

Note After the reference to the XML Web service is made, the class is treated in code as a local class, and the details of SOAP and HTTP are abstracted.

Practice: Using an XML Web Service from Within C#

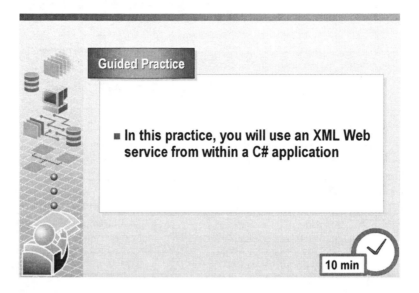

In this practice, you will use an XML Web service from within a C# application. The provided XML Web service will run on your computer. The XML Web service provides four basic math functions: add, subtract, divide, and multiply.

The solution for this practice is in *install_folder*\Practices\Mod09\Consume_Solution. Start a new instance of Visual Studio .NET before opening the solution.

Tasks	Detailed steps
1. Install the Math Web Service by using the Setup.exe in *install_folder*\Practices \Mod09\MathWebService.	a. Click **Start**, and then click **Run**. b. In the **Run** dialog box, in the **Open** box, type *install_folder***Practices\Mod09\MathWebService \Setup.exe** and then click **OK**. c. In the **Math Web Service** setup wizard, on the **Welcome to the Math Web Services Setup Wizard** page, click **Next**. d. On the **Select Installation Address** page, click **Next**. e. On the **Confirm Installation** page, click **Next**. f. On the **Installation Complete** page, click **Close**.
2. Start Visual Studio .NET, and create a new project. Name: **Consume** Project Type: **Visual C# projects** Template: **Windows Application** Location: *install_folder***Practices\Mod09**	a. Start Visual Studio .NET. b. On the **File** menu, point to **New**, and then click **Project**. c. In the **New Project** dialog box, under **Project Types**, click **Visual C# Projects**. d. Under **Templates**, click **Windows Application**. e. In the **Name** box, type **Consume** f. In the **Location** box, type *install_folder***Practices\Mod09** and then click **OK**.

Tasks	Detailed steps
3. Add a Web reference to the project URL: http://localhost/MathWebService/ Math.asmx	a. In Solution Explorer, right-click **References**, and then click **Add Web Reference**. b. In the **Add Web Reference** dialog box, in the **Address** box, type **http://localhost/MathWebService/Math.asmx** and then click the **Go (↱)** button. c. When the download is complete, click **Add Reference**.
4. Add two text boxes to the form.	▪ Add two text boxes to the form.
5. Add a button with a caption **Add**.	▪ Add a button with a caption **Add**.
6. Add a button with a caption **Subtract**.	▪ Add a button with a caption **Subtract**.
7. Add a button with a caption **Multiply**.	▪ Add a button with a caption **Multiply**.
8. Add a button with a caption **Divide**.	▪ Add a button with a caption **Divide**.
9. Write code into each button click event that uses the appropriate Web method of the Math Web service. Use the data held in textbox1 and textbox2 as parameters for the method. Use the **MessageBox** class to display the result.	▪ Refer to the code example earlier in this module to help you write the code that satisfies the task on the left.
10. Run, debug if necessary, and then test your application.	▪ Run, debug if necessary, and then test your application.

Lesson: Building an XML Web Service

- How to Create an XML Web Service by Using Visual Studio .NET
- How to Test an XML Web Service by Using Visual Studio .NET

Introduction

This lesson explains how to build and test an XML Web service.

Lesson objectives

After completing this lesson, you will be able to:

- Create XML Web services by using Visual Studio .NET.
- Test an XML Web service.

Lesson agenda

This lesson includes the following topics and activity:

- How to Create an XML Web Service by Using Visual Studio .NET
- How to Test an XML Web Service by Using Visual Studio .NET
- Practice: Creating an XML Web Service

How to Create an XML Web Service by Using Visual Studio .NET

- **Start with an ASP.NET Web service solution**

```
[WebService(Namespace="http://advwks.msft/TempConv
    /", Description="A temperature conversion
    service.")]
public class Service1 :
    System.Web.Services.WebService
```

- **Add the methods necessary for your Web service**

```
[WebMethod]
public string ReturnXYZ(){
    return "XYZ";
}
public string ReturnABC() {
    return "ABC";
}
```

Introduction

The .NET Framework and Visual Studio NET provide all the functionality that is necessary to implement an XML Web service. Visual Studio .NET provides a project template for developing an XML Web service.

Creating an XML Web service

Visual Studio .NET provides an ASP.NET Web Service project template to help you create XML Web services in Microsoft Visual C#®.

To create an XML Web service by using Visual Studio .NET, perform the following procedure:

1. On the **File** menu, point to **New**, and then click **Project**.

2. In the **New Project** dialog box, select the Visual C# Projects folder.

3. Click the **ASP.NET Web Service** icon.

4. Enter the location of the XML Web service, for example http://localhost/webservice.

5. Click **OK** to create the project.

6. In Solution Explorer, right-click **Service1.asmx**, and then click **Rename**. Enter a suitable name for the XML Web service, for example **TempConv**.

7. In Solution Explorer, right-click the service, for example **TempConv**, and then click **View Code**.

8. It is important to provide a unique namespace for your XML Web service. To do this, add a **WebService** attribute on the line above the class definition as shown in the following example:

```
[WebService(Namespace="http://advwks.msft/TempConv/",
Description="A temperature conversion service.")]
public class Service1 : System.Web.Services.WebService
```

Important If you do not provide a namespace for your XML Web service, when you test your XML Web service, you will see a warning message stating that the service is using the namespace http://tempuri.org as its namespace.

---

9. After adding the XML Web service attribute, you can scroll through the code to the EXAMPLE WEB METHOD section. Here, you add the methods that are necessary for your XML Web service. Each Web method must be defined as public and marked with a special attribute, **WebMethod**, or the method will not be available in the XML Web service. For example, only the **ReturnXYZ** method shown in the following example will be available as an XML Web service method, because the second method is not marked with the **WebMethod** attribute.

```
[WebMethod]
public string ReturnXYZ(){
    return "XYZ";
}

public string ReturnABC() {
    return "ABC";
}
```

10. Compile the project.

How to Test an XML Web Service by Using Visual Studio .NET

1 In Visual Studio, click **Start** on the **Standard** toolbar

2 In the browser window, click the name of the Web method you want to test

3 On the next page, complete the parameter fields as necessary to test the XML Web service method and then click **Invoke**

4 Another browser window opens displaying the SOAP response message (XML). Verify that the contents of this message are what you expect.

Introduction

Because messages are protocol independent, a message can be used with HTTP-GET/POST, SOAP, or any other protocol that an XML Web service provider supports. If you use SOAP, the message element corresponds to the payload of the SOAP request or response. An XML Web service created by using the .NET Framework and Visual Studio .NET can receive requests in three different formats:

- HTTP GET
- HTTP POST
- SOAP (over HTTP)

The first way to test a new XML Web service is by using the HTTP GET format. Visual Studio .NET provides access to this method.

Testing an XML Web service

To test your XML Web service, perform the following procedure:

1. In Visual Studio .NET, click **Start** on the **Standard** toolbar.

   The project compiles and then launches a browser window to the XML Web service address. This browser window allows you to test the XML Web service by completing a Web form.

2. In the browser window, click the name of the Web method that you want to test.

3. On the next page, complete the parameter fields as necessary to test the XML Web service method, and then click **Invoke**.

4. Another browser window opens displaying the SOAP response message in XML. Verify that the contents of this message are what you expect.

After the responses to the HTTP GET tests are correct, you should plan to test the Web service from a test application using SOAP over HTTP.

Practice: Creating an XML Web Service

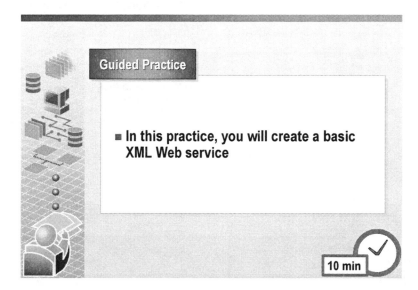

In this practice, you will create a basic XML Web service. This XML Web service will accept an array of decimal values and will calculate the average value from the array of decimal values.

The solution for this practice is in *install_folder*\Practices\Mod09\Create_Solution. To open the solution, follow the instructions in the Readme.txt file located in the folder.

Tasks	Detailed steps
1. Start Visual Studio .NET and create a new project. Name: **Create** Project Type: **Visual C# projects** Template: **ASP.NET Web Service** Location: **http://localhost/Create**	a. Start Visual Studio .NET. b. On the **File** menu, point to **New**, and then click **Project**. c. In the **New Project** dialog box, under **Project Types**, click **Visual C# Projects**. d. Under **Templates**, click **ASP.NET Web Service**. e. In the **Location** box, type **http://localhost/Create** and then click **OK**.
2. Rename Service1.asmx to **Stats.asmx**	a. In Solution Explorer, right-click **Service1.asmx**, and then click **Rename**. b. Type **Stats.asmx**
3. Display the code view of **Stats.asmx**.	▪ In Solution Explorer, right-click **Stats.asmx**, and then click **View Code**.
4. Find and replace all occurrences of **Service1** with **Stats**.	a. On the **Edit** menu, point to **Find and Replace**, and then click **Replace**. b. In the **Replace** dialog box, in the **Find What** box, type **Service1** c. In the **Replace with** box, type **Stats** and then click **Replace All**. Three replacements are made.

Tasks	Detailed steps
5. Add a public method to the **Stats** class named **Analyze**. This method should accept an array of decimal types and return the average as type **decimal**.	**a.** Add a public method to the **Stats** class named **Analyze.** This method should accept an array of decimal values and return a decimal (the average of the values passed into the procedure). **b.** Write code to loop through the array, summing the values contained in the array. Finally, divide the total by the number of values contained in the array and return this value as the result of the Web method.

6. Add the **WebService** attribute to the **Stats** class. Set the Namespace for the Web service to **http://advworks.msft /webservices/**	▪ Above the line
	
	```public class stats : System.Web.Services.WebService```
	
	Add the following line:
	
	```[WebService(Namespace="http://advworks.msft /webservices/")]```

7. Add the **WebMethod** attribute to the **Analyze** method.	▪ Above the line:
	
	```public decimal Analyze(decimal[] values)```
	
	Add the following line:
	
	```[WebMethod]```

8. Compile the Web service.	▪ In the Solution Explorer window, right-click **Create**, and then click **Build**.

> **Note:** Because this Web service takes an array as a parameter it is not possible to test this Web service using the browser interface. You must create a test application to call the Web service with an array of values.

Tasks	Detailed steps
9. Start another instance of Visual Studio .NET. Create a C# Windows application to test the Web service created above.	**a.** Start a new instance of Visual Studio .NET. **b.** Create a new C# Windows Application project. **c.** Add a Web reference to **http://localhost/Create/stats.asmx** **d.** Add a button to the form. **e.** In the button's click event, create an array of decimal values **100, 20.2, 34.5, 42.3, 103**. **f.** Create an instance of the Web service proxy class (**localhost.Stats**). **g.** Call the **Analyze** method of the proxy class passing the array of decimal values. **h.** Use a **MessageBox** to display the average returned. The average of the decimal values is **60**.

Review

- Consuming an XML Web Service
- Building an XML Web Service

1. How do you declare a method as a Web method?

2. How do you define a class as an XML Web service?

3. When would you use an XML Web service?

4. Why would you use an XML Web service in an internal network?

Lab 9.1: Using XML Web Services

Exercise 1: Writing the Office Building Estimation Application

1 hour

Objectives

After completing this lab, you will be able to:

- Use an XML Web Service.

Prerequisites

Before working on this lab, you must have:

- Completed Module 9.

Scenario

This lab demonstrates how an application can use multiple XML Web Services to provide a solution. You will write a basic Windows application that prompts the user to enter the quantities for different components that make up an office building and then responds by providing the cost estimates from different suppliers for the raw materials. Each materials supplier has implemented an XML Web service to allow you to convert quantities into a cost.

The solution for this lab is provided in *install_folder*\Labfiles\ Lab09_1\MaterialApplication_Solution. To open the solution, follow the instructions in the Readme.txt file located in the folder.

**Complete this lab:
60 minutes**

Exercise 0
Lab Setup

The Lab Setup section lists the tasks that you must perform before you begin the lab.

Tasks	Detailed steps
1. Log on to Windows as **Student** with a password of **P@ssw0rd**.	▪ Log on to Windows with the following account: • User name: **Student** • Password: **P@ssw0rd**
2. Install the Material Web Services using the Setup.exe found in *install_folder***Lab09_1\\WebService.**	a. Click **Start**, and then click **Run**. b. In the **Run** dialog box, in the **Open** box, type *install_folder***Lab09_1\\WebService\\Setup.exe** and then click **OK**. c. In the **Material Web Services** setup wizard, on the **Welcome to the Material Web Services Setup Wizard** page, click **Next**. d. On the **Select Installation Address** page, click **Next**. e. On the **Confirm Installation** page click **Next**. f. On the **Installation Complete** page, click **Close**.

Exercise 1
Writing the Office Building Estimation Application

In this exercise, you will create a Windows Application by using C#.

Your instructor will have on display a list of the names of the servers in the room. Each server in the room has a Web service with methods to calculate the cost and shipping cost for each of six raw materials.

Select a server (not your own). The URL you need for the Web service on that server is provided below.

http://*servername*/materialwebservices/estimate.asmx

Tasks	Detailed steps
1. Start Visual Studio .NET, and create a new Visual C# Project based on the Windows Application template.	a. Start a new instance of Visual Studio .NET. b. On the **Start Page**, click **New Project**. c. In the **New Project** dialog box, under **Project Types**, click **Visual C# Projects**, under **Templates**, click **Windows Application**. d. In the **Name** box, type **MaterialApplication** e. In the **Location** box, type *install_folder***Lab09_1\\MaterialApplication** and then click **OK**.
2. Add a Web Reference to the Web service specified by the URL above this table.	a. In the Solution Explorer window, right-click **References**, and then click **Add Web Reference**. b. In the **Add Web Reference** dialog box, in the **Address** box, type **http://*servername*/materialwebservices/estimate.asmx** and then press Enter. c. Click **Add Reference**.

 Note: You must now select 3 of the following raw materials. You will implement controls on the form to accept the quantities for these raw materials.

- Concrete (cubic meters)
- Steel Bars (meters)
- Windows
- Doors
- Carpet (square meters)
- Paint (cubic meters)

Tasks	Detailed steps
3. Add to the form a label and text box pair for each of the three selected raw materials.	**a.** Add a label to the form and change **Text** property of the label to match the name of the first raw material.
	b. Add a text box to the form, next to the first label. You may wish to change the name of the text box to the name of your first raw material.
	c. Add a label to the form and change **Text** property of the label to match the name of the second raw material.
	d. Add a text box to the form, next to the second label. You may wish to change the name of the textbox to the name of your second raw material.
	e. Add a label to the form and change **Text** property of the label to match the name of the third raw material.
	f. Add a text box to the form, next to the third label. You may wish to change the name of the textbox to the name of your third raw material.

Note: If you select Windows as a raw material, you must add a check box control to your form, under the label and window quantity text box, that allows you to specify double-glazed windows. In Step 5, add checkBox1.Checked as the second parameter of the call to the Web service.

Tasks	Detailed steps
4. Add a button to the form and change the caption of the button to **Calculate**.	▪ Add a button to the form and change the **Text** property of the button to **Calculate**.
5. Add code to the click event of the **Calculate** button to call the appropriate Web service method for each raw material passing the quantities from the related text box on the form.	▪ Add code to the click event of the **Calculate** button to call the appropriate Web service method for the three raw materials your application is using. The code in the note below can be modified and used for each raw material. You need to add additional code to calculate the total cost and total delivery charges and display this information in a message box.

Note: Example code for calling the Concrete raw material Web service method.

```
Servername.Estimate EstimateWebService = new
        Servername.Estimate();
Servername.Result result = EstimateWebService.Concrete(
        System.Convert.ToDecimal(Concrete.Text));
\\result.Cost now contains the cost of the concrete
\\result.Delivery now contains the delivery charge
```

Tasks	Detailed steps
6. Run and test the application.	▪ Run and test the application.

msdn training

Module 10: Creating a Web Application with Web Forms

Contents

Microsoft

Overview

- **Creating a Web Forms Application**
- **Accessing Data by Using a Web Form Application**
- **Configuring ASP.NET Application Settings**

Introduction

Microsoft® Visual Studio® .NET allows you to create applications that take advantage of the important features of the World Wide Web. These features include traditional Web sites that use HTML pages, fully-featured business applications that run on an intranet or the Internet, and sophisticated business-to-business applications that provide Web-based components that can exchange data by using Extensible Markup Language (XML).

In Visual Studio .NET, you can use Web Forms to create powerful, programmable Web pages. These Web pages serve as the user interface for your Web application. This module introduces the **System.Web.UI** namespace and describes how to create a Web application with a Web Form. The module also explains how to add controls to a Web Form and then use the Web Form to submit data and respond to events. The module also covers Microsoft ASP.NET state management, security, and configuration settings.

Objectives

After completing this module, you will be able to:

- Create a Web Forms application.
- Handle events on a Web Form application.
- Access data from a Web Forms application.
- Configure ASP.NET application settings.

Lesson: Creating a Web Forms Application

- **What Is ASP.NET?**
- **What Is a Web Forms Application?**
- **How to Create a Web Forms Application**
- **What Are the Components of a Web Forms Application?**
- **What Is the Life Cycle of a Web Forms Application?**
- **How to Add Controls to a Web Forms Application**
- **How to Add an Event Handler for the Control**

Introduction	This lesson introduces Web Forms and describes how to create a Web Form, add controls to it, and add event handlers for the controls.
Lesson objectives	After completing this lesson, you will be able to:

- Explain ASP.NET.
- Create a Web Form and add controls.
- Write event handlers for the controls.

Lesson agenda This lesson includes the following topics and activity:

- What Is ASP.NET?
- What Is a Web Forms Application?
- How to Create a Web Forms Application
- What Are the Components of a Web Forms Application?
- What Is the Life Cycle of a Web Forms Application?
- How to Add Controls to a Web Forms Application
- How to Add an Event Handler for the Control
- Practice: Creating a Web Forms Application

What Is ASP.NET?

- **Evolutionary, more flexible successor to Active Server Pages (ASP)**

- **Dynamic Web pages that can access server resources**

- **Server-side processing of Web forms**

- **Language independent**

- **Browser independent**

- **XML Web services let you create distributed Web applications**

Introduction

For many years, developers have used Active Server Pages (ASP) technology to build dynamic Web pages. ASP.NET is the logical development of ASP; it runs on a Web server and provides a way for you to develop content-rich, dynamic, personalized Web sites by using the power of Microsoft .NET.

Definition

ASP.NET is a Web run-time environment that is built on top of .NET. ASP technology mixed HTML and script together in the same document. In ASP.NET, the code, which can be any .NET-compatible language, is held separately from the HTML page.

A new component of ASP.NET is the Web Form. As the user interface to an application based on Microsoft Windows® is made up of Windows Forms, an ASP.NET Web application user interface is made up of Web Forms. An ASP.NET Web application includes one or more Web Forms.

XML Web services

The ASP.NET technology provides the platform for running XML Web services. XML Web services allow distributed applications to transfer information between clients, applications, and other XML Web services. It is also possible from within an ASP.NET application to consume XML Web services from other servers.

What Is a Web Forms Application?

- **Based on ASP.NET technology to create powerful programmable Web pages**
- **Compatible with any browser or mobile device**
- **Compatible with any language supported by common language runtime**
- **Allow for separation between code and content on a page**
- **Support a rich set of controls**
- **Provide a set of state management features that preserve the view state of a Web page between requests**

Introduction

Just as you use Windows Forms to create Windows-based applications, you can use Web Forms to build powerful programmable Web pages dynamically. Web Forms pages are built with ASP.NET technology. You can add Web Forms pages to several types of Visual Studio .NET projects. Most often, when you want to work with Web Forms pages, you will use the project template for the ASP.NET Web Application.

Definition

A Web Form is a dynamic Web page, which users view in a browser that can access server resources.

Features

Web Forms Applications:

- Are based on ASP.NET technology to create powerful programmable Web pages.

- Run on any browser and automatically render the correct, browser-compliant HTML code for features such as styles and layout.

- Are programmable in any language that the common language runtime supports, including C#, Microsoft Visual Basic®, and Microsoft JScript® .NET.

- Support WYSIWYG (what you see is what you get) editing tools and powerful rapid application development (RAD) tools, such as Visual Studio .NET, for designing and programming your forms.

- Provide a rich set of controls that allow you to encapsulate page logic into reusable components and declaratively handle page events.

State management

Web Forms provide a set of state management features that automatically preserve the view state of a page between requests. *State* refers to the information that an application must maintain about a Web page.

When a Web server receives a request for a page, it finds the page, processes it, sends it to the browser, and then discards all page information. If the user requests the same page again, the server repeats the entire sequence, reprocessing the page from the beginning. Servers have no memory of the pages that they have processed. Therefore, if an application must maintain information about a page, you must provide for it in application code. Web Forms automatically handle the task of maintaining the state of your form and its controls, and provides you with explicit ways to maintain the state of application-specific information.

How to Create a Web Forms Application

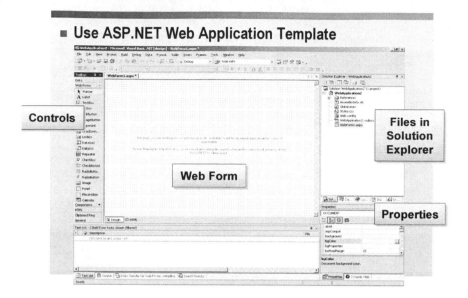

■ Use ASP.NET Web Application Template

Controls

Files in Solution Explorer

Web Form

Properties

Introduction

The first step in creating a Web Form is to create an ASP.NET Web Application project.

Creating a Web Application project

To create an ASP.NET Web Application project:

1. On the **File** menu, point to **New**, and then click **Project**.

2. In the **New Project** dialog box, perform the following steps:

   a. In the Project Types pane, click **Visual C# Projects**.

   b. In the Templates pane, click **ASP.NET Web Application**.

   c. In the **Location** box, enter the complete Uniform Resource Locator (URL) for your application, including http://, the name of the server, and the name of your project.

   d. Click **OK**.

      When you click **OK**, a new project is created at the root of the Web server that you specified. Also, a new Web Forms page named WebForm1.aspx is displayed, in Design view, in the Web Forms Designer.

Project files created

When you create an ASP.NET Web Application project by using Microsoft Visual C#™, Visual Studio .NET creates several files on your local computer. The following table lists and describes some of these files.

File Created	Description
WebForm1.aspx and WebForm1.aspx.cs files	These two files make up a single Web Forms page. The .aspx file contains the visual elements of the Web Forms page, for example the HTML elements and Web Forms controls. The WebForm1.aspx.cs class file is a dependent file of WebForm1.aspx. It contains the code-behind class for the Web Forms page, which contains event-handler code.
AssemblyInfo.cs	A project information file (AssemblyInfo.vb or AssemblyInfo.cs file) that contains metadata about the assemblies in a project, such as name, version, and culture information.
Web.config	An XML-based file that contains configuration data about each unique URL resource that is used in the project.
Global.asax and Global.asax.cs files	Global.asax is an optional file for handling application-level events. This file resides in the root directory of an ASP.NET application. The Global.asax.cs class file is a hidden, dependent file of Global.asax. It contains the code for handling application events, such as the Application_OnError event. At run time, this file is parsed and compiled.
.vsdisco (project discovery) file	An XML-based file that contains links (URLs) to resources providing discovery information for an XML Web service.

Viewing the files

To view all of the files in a project, click the **Show All Files** button in the toolbar of Solution Explorer.

What Are the Components of a Web Forms Application?

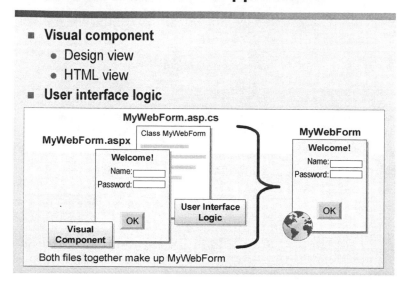

Introduction

Web Forms pages provide a distinction between the visual component, the visible portion of the form, and user interface logic, the code that interacts with the form.

Visual component views

When you work with Web Forms, you must understand the two views that Visual Studio .NET provides. These views are the Design view and the HTML view.

You can work in either view. When you switch between them, each view is updated with the changes that you make in the other view.

Design view

The **Design** tab is located at the bottom of the Web Forms Designer.

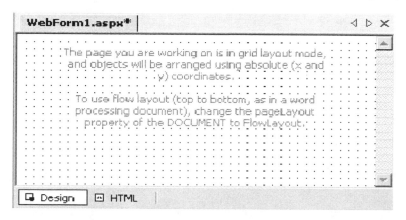

The Design view shows you the WYSIWYG view of the .aspx file that you are working with. In the Design view, you can drag controls from the Toolbox and use the Properties window to configure the controls.

HTML view   The **HTML** tab is located at the bottom of the Web Forms Designer.

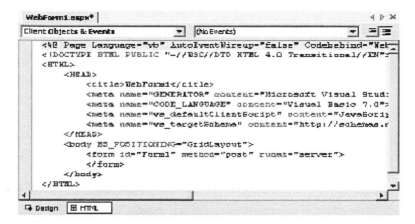

The HTML view shows you the HTML format of the .aspx file that you are working with. As in other code editor views, the Web Forms Designer supports Microsoft IntelliSense® for elements in HTML view.

User interface logic   A Web Forms page code model consists of two files:

■   WebForm.aspx

    The WebForm1.aspx file is referred to as the *page*. This file contains Hypertext Markup Language (HTML), static text, and the server controls that make up the visual components of the page. HTML is the computer language that is used to create documents for the Web. The page works as a container for the text and controls that you want to display.

■   WebForm.aspx.cs

    This file, which is also referred to as the code-behind file, contains code that you create to interact with the form. The extension for this file is language specific. For example, the extension is vb if you use Visual Basic .NET and cs if you are using C#.

What Is the Life Cycle of a Web Forms Application?

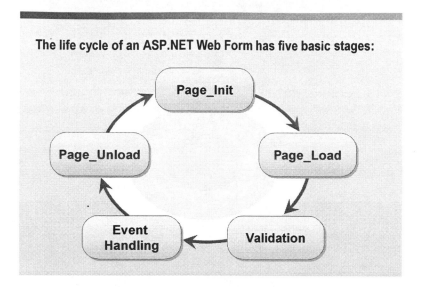

The life cycle of an ASP.NET Web Form has five basic stages:

Page_Init → Page_Load → Validation → Event Handling → Page_Unload → (Page_Init)

Introduction

It is helpful to understand some fundamental characteristics of how Web Forms pages work in Web applications before you examine the details of what occurs inside a page when it is processed.

Round trips

It is important to understand the division of labor on a Web Forms page. The browser presents the user with a form, and the user interacts with the form, causing the form to post back to the server. However, because all processing that interacts with server components must occur on the server, for each action that requires processing, the form must be posted to the server, processed, and returned to the browser. This sequence of events is referred to as a *round trip*.

In Web Forms, most user actions—such as clicking a button—result in a round trip. For that reason, the events that are available in ASP.NET server controls are usually limited to click-type events.

Recreating the page

In any Web scenario, pages are re-created with every round trip. As soon as the server finishes processing and sending the page to the browser, it discards the page information. By freeing server resources after each request, a Web application can scale to support hundreds or thousands of simultaneous users. The next time the page is posted, the server starts over in creating and processing it, and for this reason, Web pages are said to be stateless.

The life cycle of an ASP.NET Web Form

The life cycle of an ASP.NET Web Form has five basic stages:

1. *Page_Init*. The ASP.NET page framework uses this event to restore control properties and postback data, which is data that the user entered in controls before the form was submitted.

2. *Page_Load*. The developer uses this event either to perform some initial processing, if this is the first visit to the page, or to restore control values, if this is a postback.

3. *Validation*. The **Validate** method of ASP.NET server controls is called to perform validation for the controls.

4. *Other event handling*. Various controls expose many events. For example, the **Calendar** control exposes a **SelectionChanged event**. If the page contains validation controls, you should check the **IsValid** property of the page and individual validation controls to determine whether validation has been passed.

5. *Page_Unload*. This event is called as the page finishes rendering.

Tip It is at this last stage where you clean up any resources that were allocated, especially expensive resources such as the file handlers and database connections.

How to Add Controls to a Web Forms Application

■ **To add a Web server control**

- In Design view, drag Web Server control object from the Toolbox Web Forms tab

■ **To add an HTML server control**

- Drag an HTML element onto the page from the HTML tab of the Toolbox

- Right-click the element and choose Run As Server Control to convert it to a control

Introduction

After you create the Web Form, you can add controls to build the user interface. Visual Studio .NET provides Forms Designer, an editor, controls, and debugging tools, which together allow you to build programmable user interfaces for the Web.

Server controls

Controls for Web Forms are called server controls because when the page runs, the controls are instantiated in server code as part of the page class. When users interact with a control, the code that is associated with the control runs on the server after the page is posted. For example, when a user clicks a **Web Forms** button control, the code for the button runs on the server after the page is displayed. You can set properties and write event handlers in the server code.

There are two types of server controls:

■ Web server controls

These are controls specific to Web Forms that provide more features than HTML server controls and do not map directly to HTML elements.

■ HTML server controls

These are HTML elements that are marked to be programmable in server code. Typically, you convert HTML elements to HTML server controls only if you want to program them from server code.

Converting client controls to run as server controls

Not every element on the Web Forms page is a server control. For example, by default, static HTML text is not a server control, and you cannot control it from server code. Even standard HTML controls, such as an HTML button, are not server controls by default. You can program the HTML elements in the client code. Therefore, to work with controls on a Web Forms page, you must add them as server controls.

Adding an HTML server control by using Web Forms Designer

Adding an HTML server control to a Web Forms page is a two-step process.

To add an HTML control to a Web Forms page and convert it to a server control:

1. From the **HTML** tab of the Toolbox, drag an HTML element onto the page.

2. Convert the element to a server control by right-clicking it, and then clicking **Run As Server Control**.

The Web Forms Designer adds the attribute **runat="server"** to the element, which alerts the server to treat the element as a server control. A symbol appears on the control in Design view to indicate that it is a server-based control.

By default, the Web Forms page uses Grid layout, and you place controls at absolute positions on the page by using x and y coordinates. If you want to use linear layout, in which the page elements flow in the same manner as in a word processing document, you can change the **pageLayout** property or include a **Flow Layout Panel** HTML server control.

How to Add an Event Handler for the Control

- **Many events are triggered by user action in the browser**

- **Code to handle raised event is executed on the server**

- **When code completes execution, the resulting Web page is sent back to the browser**

```
private void Button1_Click(object
    sender,System.EventArgs e) {
    //(..........)
}
```

Introduction

After you create the project and add controls, you can add event handlers to the controls. Web Forms bring to Web applications the model of writing event-handling methods for events that occur in either the client or server. The Web Forms framework abstracts this model in such a way that the underlying mechanism of capturing an event on the client, transmitting it to the server, and calling the appropriate handler is automatic and invisible. The result is a clear, easily written code structure.

Adding events

Interacting with users is one of the primary reasons for creating ASP.NET Web Forms. You program various events to handle these interactions. The Web page itself can execute code, and so can the many events that are raised by various objects, including all of the server controls.

You can add events to individual controls, to a page, to an application, or to a session.

Controls have a default event, which is the event that is most commonly associated with that control. For example, the default event for a button is the **Click** event. You can create event handlers for both the default event and other events, but the procedure is different for each type of event.

Creating an event handler for a non-default event

To create an event handler for non-default events:

1. In Design view, select the control, and then press F4 to display the Properties window.

2. In the Properties window, click the **Events** button ( ).

   The Properties window displays a list of the events for the control, with boxes to the right that display the names of the event handlers that are bound to those events.

3. Locate the event that you want to create a handler for, and then, in the event name box, type the name of an event handler.

Creating the event handler for a default event

To create the event handler for a default event:

- In Design view of the Web Forms Designer, double-click the control or page. The Code Editor opens with the insertion point in the event handler.

Example

A **Button** Web server control can raise a **Click** event when a user clicks a button on the page.

The code to handle the raised event is executed on the server. When the user clicks a button, the page is posted back to the server. The framework for the ASP.NET page parses the event information, and if you have an event handler corresponding to the event, your code is called automatically. When your code finishes, the page is sent back to the browser with any changes that the event handler code made.

To create an event handler for the Button **Web** server control:

- Double-click the **Button** Web server control.

  The designer opens the class file for the current form and creates a skeleton event handler for the **Click** event of the button control. The code is as follows:

```
private void button1_Click(object sender, System.EventArgs
e) {
}
```

Note For more information about recommendations for ASP.NET server controls, see the Visual Studio. NET documentation. Use the Help index and search for ASP.NET Server Control.

Practice: Creating a Web Forms Application

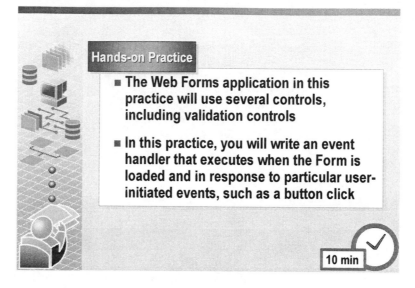

In this practice, you will develop a simple Web Forms application that calculates the sum of two values that are entered into the form. The form will validate that the first number entered is in the range of 1 to 1000 and that the second number entered is in the range of 1 to 500.

The solution for this practice is in *install_folder*\Practices\Mod10\WebFormPractice_Solution. To open the solution, follow the instructions in the Readme.txt file located in the folder.

Tasks	Detailed steps
1. Start Visual Studio .NET.	▪ Start a new instance of Visual Studio .NET.
2. Create a new project: Project Type: Visual C# Project Template: ASP.NET Web Application. Location: http://localhost/WebFormPractice	a. On the **Start** page, click **New Project**. b. In the **New Project** dialog box, under **Project Types**, click **Visual C# Projects**. c. Under **Templates**, click **ASP.NET Web Application**. d. In the **Location** box, type **http://localhost/WebFormPractice** and then click **OK**.
3. From the **Web Forms** tab of the Toolbox, add the following controls to the form: 2 TextBox controls 1 Label control 1 Button control	a. Point to the Toolbox, and then drag a **TextBox** control onto the form. b. Point to the Toolbox, and then drag another **TextBox** control onto the form. c. Point to the Toolbox, and then drag a **Label** control onto the form. d. Point to the Toolbox, and then drag a **Button** control onto the form.

Tasks	Detailed steps
4. (*Optional*) From the **Web Forms** tab of the Toolbox add the following controls to the form: 2 **RangeValidator** controls	a. Point to the Toolbox, and then drag a **RangeValidator** control onto the form. b. Point to the Toolbox, and then drag another **RangeValidator** control onto the form.
5. Lay out the controls on the form to match the following illustration.	▪ Lay out the controls on the form to match the following illustration.
Note: Lay out your form to match the illustration, **RangeValidator** controls are optional.	
6. Set the Text property of the button to **Calculate**.	a. In the WebForm1.aspx form editor, click the button. b. In the Properties window, click **Text**, and then type **Calculate**
7. (*Optional*) Change the following properties of the **RangeValidator** located at the top of the form. Errormessage: **The number entered must be in the range 1-1000**. ControlToValidate: **TextBox1** MaximumValue: **1000** MinimumValue: **1** Type: **Integer**	a. In the WebForm1.aspx form editor, click the **RangeValidator** control located at the top of the form. b. In the Properties window, click **Errormessage**, and then type **The number entered must be in the range 1-1000** c. In the **ControlToValidate** list, click **TextBox1**. d. Click **MaximumValue**, and then type **1000** e. Click **MinimumValue**, and then type **1** f. In the **Type** list, click **Integer**.
8. (*Optional*) Change the following properties of the **RangeValidator** located beneath the other **RangeValidator**. Errormessage: **The number entered must be in the range 1-500**. ControlToValidate: **TextBox2** MaximumValue: **500** MinimumValue: **1** Type: **Integer**	a. In the WebForm1.aspx form editor window, click the **RangeValidator** control located beneath the other **RangeValidator** control. b. In the Properties window, click **Errormessage**, and then type **The number entered must be in the range 1-500** c. In the **ControlToValidate** list, click **TextBox2**. d. Click **MaximumValue**, and then enter **500** e. Click **MinimumValue**, and then enter **1** f. In the **Type** list, click **Integer**.

Tasks	Detailed steps
9. Add code into the Button click event to calculate the sum of the two text boxes and place the result into the label.	a. Double-click **Calculate** on the form to open WebForm1.aspx.cs in the Code Editor. The cursor is placed in the **Button1_Click** event. b. Type the following code: ``` Label1.Text = (System.Convert.ToInt32(TextBox1.Text) + System.Convert.ToInt32(TextBox2.Text)) .ToString(); ```
10. Run the application, enter various values into the textboxes displayed and examine the behavior of the application.	a. On the standard toolbar, click **Start**. b. Enter various values into the text boxes that are displayed, and examine the behavior of the application.
11. Quit Microsoft Internet Explorer.	▪ Quit Internet Explorer.
12. Save any changes to the project, and then quit Visual Studio .NET.	a. On the **File** menu, click **Save All**. b. On the **File** menu, click **Exit**.

Lesson: Accessing Data by Using a Web Forms Application

- **How to Access Data by Using a Web Forms Application**
- **How to Display Data on a Web Forms Application**

Introduction

This lesson explains how use Microsoft ADO.NET to access data by using a Web Forms application.

Lesson objectives

After completing this lesson, you will be able to:

- Use ADO.NET from a Web Forms application.
- Display data on a Web Forms application.

Lesson agenda

This lesson includes the following topics:

- How to Access Data by Using a Web Forms Application
- How to Display Data on a Web Forms Application
- Practice: Displaying Data from a Database on a Web Forms Application

How to Access Data by Using a Web Forms Application

- **Fundamental principles**
  - Using a disconnected model
  - Reading data more often than updating it
  - Minimizing server resource requirements
  - Accessing data using remote processes
- **Data sources for Web Forms pages**
  - Database access, ADO.NET
  - XML data
  - Other sources

Introduction

Many Web Forms pages involve data access, displaying data and, in some cases, allowing users to edit and update data. Knowledge of data access technology in Web Forms pages helps you create efficient Web applications.

Principles

Data access in Web Forms pages is built around the following fundamental principles:

- Using a disconnected model

  Web Forms pages are disconnected. Each time a Web Forms page is requested, it is built, processed, sent to the browser, and discarded from server memory. By extension, the same process applies to data access in a Web Forms page. Data is read or updated while the page is processed on the server. After the page is processed and sent to the browser, data is discarded along with other page elements.

- Reading data more often than updating it

  The Web Forms data model presumes that most data access by Web pages is read-only. Typical examples are catalog or search listings that display data items. In most cases, the user does not enter data that is written back to the data source.

- Minimizing server resource requirements

  Data access in Web Forms pages therefore requires careful attention to how you use resources.

- Accessing data by using remote processes

  Web Forms pages are the presentation tier of your Web application. You can build data access into your pages, but it is also common to separate data access logic from the user interface by building it into another component, such as an XML Web service, that interacts with the data source.

Data sources for Web Forms

The Web Forms page architecture provides a very flexible notion of data. This includes everything from traditional database access, to using XML documents as a data source, to generating data at run time and storing it in an array:

- Database access

  To read and write database data, you use ADO.NET. ADO.NET includes managed data providers (connection and command objects) to communicate with Microsoft SQL Server™ or OLE DB–compatible databases. ADO.NET also includes support for disconnected data access by means of a dataset, which is an in-memory cache into which you can read records to work with.

  Alternatively, you can use ADO.NET objects to execute SQL commands or stored procedures directly. This allows you to read data straight from the database and send updates back.

- XML data

  Another possible source of data in a Web Forms page is an XML document or stream. You can work with XML data in two ways:

  - If the XML data is structured—that is, if it can be represented as relational data—you can convert the XML data into a dataset and use ADO.NET data functions to read and update the data. This feature allows you to take advantage of the comparatively sophisticated and simple data-processing functionality of datasets. You can then convert the data back to XML to share with other processes.

  - If the XML data cannot be represented as relational data, you can use XML parsing and processing functions from the **System.Xml** namespace to manipulate the data. In Web Forms pages, you can do this by using the XML Web server control. Alternatively, you can work directly with XML documents in code.

- Other data sources

  Web Forms pages allow you to work with virtually any other type of data also.

  The data-binding architecture of Web Forms pages allows you to bind a control to any structure. In practice, this means you can bind to any arrays or collections that are available in the page, as well as to properties of the page or of other controls.

How to Display Data on a Web Forms Application

① Create the Web Application project and a Web Form page

② Create and configure the dataset you will bind the grid to

③ Add the DataGrid control to the form and bind it to the data

④ Add code to fill the dataset, and test

```
private void Page_Load(object sender,
System.EventArgs e) {
   if ( !IsPostBack)  {
        SqlDataAdapter1.Fill(customerDS1);
        DataGrid1.DataSource = customerDS1;
        DataGrid1.DataBind();
   }
}
```

Introduction

Web Forms pages often must display information that is derived from a database, an XML document or stream, or some other data source. The architecture of Web Forms pages provides you with ways to incorporate data sources, or references to them, in the page, to bind controls to data, and to manipulate data in various ways.

Note Displaying data in Web Forms is similar to displaying data in Windows Forms.

Displaying data

To display data on a Web Form:

1. Create the Web application project and a Web Forms page.

2. Create and configure the dataset that you will bind the grid to. This includes creating a query that populates the dataset from the database.

3. Add the **DataGrid** control to the form and bind it to data.

4. Add code to fill the dataset, and test.

This procedure is described in detail in the following steps.

Step 1

To create a Web application project and a Web Forms page:

1. On the **File** menu, point to **New**, and then click **Project**.

2. In the **New Project** dialog box, do the following:

   a. In the Project Types pane, click **Visual C# Projects**.

   b. In the Templates pane, click **ASP.NET Web Application**.

   c. In the **Location** box, enter the complete URL for your application, including **http://**, the name of the server, and the name of your project.

   d. Click **OK**. A new Web Forms project is created at the root of the Web server that you specified. Also, a new Web Forms page named WebForm1.aspx is displayed in the Web Forms Designer in Design view.

Step 2

The second step is to create the data connection and data adapter.

1. From the **Data** tab of the Toolbox, drag a **SqlDataAdapter** object onto the form. The Data Adapter Configuration Wizard starts which helps you create both the connection and the adapter. In the wizard, do the following:

2. Click **Next**. On **Choose Your Data Connection**, create or select a connection pointing to the **SQL Server Northwind** database.

3. Click **Next**. On **Choose a Query Type**, specify that you want to use a SQL statement to access the database.

4. On **Generate the SQL Statements**, create the SQL statements, or to build the SQL statement click **Query Builder** to launch the **Query Builder** dialog box.

5. Click **Finish**. The wizard creates a connection, **sqlConnection1**, containing information about how to access your database. The wizard also creates a data adapter, **sqlDataAdapter1**, that contains a query specifying the table and columns in the database that you want to access.

Step 3

The next step is to create and configure the dataset.

After you establish the connection to the database and specify the information you want to access by means of the SQL command in the data adapter, you can have Visual Studio .NET create a dataset. The dataset is an instance of the **DataSet** class based on a corresponding schema, .xsd file, that describes the elements of the class, such as the table, columns, and constraints. Visual Studio .NET can generate the dataset automatically based on the query that you specified for the data adapter.

1. On the **Data** menu, click **Generate DataSet**.

   Tip   If you do not see the **Data** menu, make sure that the focus is on the form, and then click the form. The **Generate Dataset** dialog box appears.
   ---

2. Click **New** and name the dataset (CustomerDS in this example). In the list under **Choose which table(s) to add to the dataset**, make sure that the table you want to display is selected.

3. Select the **Add this dataset to the designer** check box, and then click **OK**. Visual Studio .NET generates a typed dataset class and a schema that defines the dataset. The new schema, **CustomerDS.xsd**, is displayed in Solution Explorer.

At this point, you have set up everything you need in order to get information out of a database and into a dataset.

Step 4

Next, add a DataGrid to display data.

1. From the **Web Forms** tab of the Toolbox, drag a **DataGrid** control onto the page.

2. In the **DataSource** property, select **customerDS1** (this is the instance of the CustomerDS class) as the data source. This binds the grid to the dataset as a whole.

3. In the **DataMember** property, select the table specified in your SQL query from Step 2. If a data source contains more than one bindable object, you can use the **DataMember** property to specify which object to bind to. Setting these two properties binds the specified data table in the **customerDS1** dataset to the grid.

Step 5

The next step is to fill the dataset and display data in the **DataGrid** control.

Although the grid is bound to the dataset that you created, the dataset itself is not automatically filled in. Instead, you must fill the dataset yourself by calling a data-adapter method.

1. Double-click the page to display the class file of the page in the Code Editor.

2. In the **Page_Load** event handler, call the **Fill** method of the adapter, passing it the dataset that you want to populate:

```
sqlDataAdapter1.Fill(customerDS1);
```

3. Call the **DataBind** method of the **DataGrid** control (DataGrid1) to bind the control to the dataset.

Tip You do not need to refill the dataset and bind the grid with each round trip. After the **DataGrid** control is populated with data, its values are preserved in view state each time the page is posted. Therefore, you must fill the dataset and bind the grid only the first time that the page is called. You can test for this by using the **IsPostBack** property of the page.

The following code shows the complete handler:

```
private void Page_Load(object sender, System.EventArgs e) {
// Put user code to initialize the page here
if ( !IsPostBack ) {
    sqlDataAdapter1.Fill(customerDS1);
    DataGrid1.DataBind( );
    }
}
```

The final step is to test the Web Forms page.

1. Save the page.

2. In Solution Explorer, right-click the page, and then click **Build and Browse**.

3. Confirm that a list of categories is displayed in the grid.

Practice: Displaying Data from a Database on a Web Forms Application

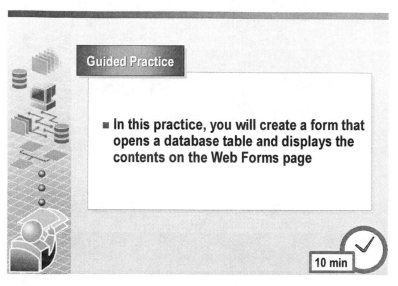

In this practice, you will develop a simple Web Forms application that contains a **DataGrid** control. The **DataGrid** control will be used to display the contents of the SQL Server table **BankCustomers**.

The solution for this practice is in *install_folder*\Practices\Mod10\DataGridPractice_Solution. To open the solution, follow the instructions in the Readme.txt file located in the folder.

Tasks	Detailed steps
1. Start Visual Studio .NET.	▪ Start a new instance of Visual Studio .NET.
2. Create a new project: Project Type: Visual C# Project Template: ASP.NET Web Application. Location: http://localhost/DataGridPractice	a. On the **Start** page, click **New Project**. b. In the **New Project** dialog box, under **Project Types**, click **Visual C# Projects**. c. Under **Templates**, click **ASP.NET Web Application**. d. In the **Location** box, type **http://localhost/DataGridPractice** and then click **OK**.
3. Drop a **DataGrid** control onto the form.	▪ Point to the Toolbox, and then drag a **DataGrid** control onto the form.
4. Position the **DataGrid** control in the upper-left corner of the form.	▪ Drag the **DataGrid** control to the upper-left of the form.
5. Drop a **SqlDataAdapter** control onto the form. This control is held under the **Data** tab of the Toolbox.	▪ Point to the Toolbox, click the **Data** tab, and then drag a **SqlDataAdapter** control onto the form.

Tasks	Detailed steps
6. Step through the Data Adapter Configuration Wizard. Create a new connection to your local server; use Microsoft Windows NT® Integrated Security and database 2609. Use SQL statements for the query type. Enter a SQL statement of **Select * from BankCustomers**.	**a.** In the Data Adapter Configuration Wizard, on the **Welcome to the Data Adapter Configuration Wizard** page, click **Next**. **b.** On the **Choose Your Data Connection** page, click **New Connection**. **c.** In the **Data Link Properties** dialog box, in the **Select or enter a server name** box, type *your_server_name* **d.** Under **Enter information to log on to the server**, click **Use Windows NT Integrated security**. **e.** Under **Select the database on the server**, click **2609**, and then click **OK**. **f.** On the **Choose Your Data Connection** page, click **Next**. **g.** On the **Choose A Query Type** page, click **Use SQL Statements**, and then click **Next**. **h.** Under **What data should the data adapter load into the dataset**, type **SELECT * from BankCustomers** and then click **Next**. **i.** On the **View Wizard Results** page, click **Finish**.

ⓘ **Note:** Your form now has two hidden controls. A **sqlDataAdapter1** control and a **sqlConnection1** object. The connection object is generated automatically by the wizard.

Tasks	Detailed steps
7. Use the **Generate Dataset** option on the **Data** menu to create a dataset named **Customers**. Add the **BankCustomers** table to this dataset.	**a.** On the **Data** menu, click **Generate Dataset**. **b.** In the **Generate Dataset** dialog box, under **Choose a dataset**, click **New**, replace DataSet1 with **Customers** and then click **OK**.
8. Set the **DataSource** property of the **DataGrid** control to **customers1**.	**a.** In the **WebForm1.aspx** form editor, click the **DataGrid** control. **b.** In the Properties window, in the **DataSource** list, click **customers1**.
9. Use the **Auto Format** URL at the bottom of the Properties window to set the format to **Colorful 2**.	**a.** In the Properties window, click the **Auto Format** link. **b.** In the **Auto Format** dialog box, under **Select a scheme**, click **Colorful 2**, and then click **OK**.
10. Add the following code to the **Form_Load** event of the form.	**a.** Double-click an area of the form that is not covered by the **DataGrid** control. **b.** Add the following code to the **Page_Load** event procedure.

```
if (!IsPostBack) {
  sqlDataAdapter1.Fill(customers1);
  DataGrid1.DataBind();
}
```

Tasks	Detailed steps
11. Run the application and view the contents of the data grid.	▪ On the standard toolbar, click **Start**.
ℹ **Note:** The **DataGrid** control contains all the columns of data held in the dataset. The following steps show how the columns of the dataset can be modified.	
12. Close the browser window.	▪ Close the browser window.
13. Change the **AutoGenerateColumns** property to **False**.	a. In the editor, click the **WebForm1.aspx** tab. b. Click the **DataGrid** control on the form. c. In the Properties window, change AutoGenerateColumns from **True** to **False**.
14. Use the Property Builder feature of the **DataGrid** control to add the following columns to the DataGrid. **CustomerID** **CustomerName** **CustomerAddress** **CustomerPhone**	a. Right-click the **DataGrid** control, and then click **Property Builder**. b. In the DataGrid1 Properties window, click **Columns**. c. Under **Available Columns**, click **CustomerID**, and then click >. d. Under **Available Columns**, click **CustomerName**, and then click >. e. Under **Available Columns**, click **CustomerAddress**, and then click >. f. Under **Available Columns**, click **CustomerPhone**, click > and then click **OK**.
15. Run the application and view the contents of the DataGrid.	▪ On the standard toolbar, click **Start**.
ℹ **Note:** The DataGrid now contains only the required columns.	
16. Close the browser window.	▪ Close the browser window.
17. Save the changes to the project, and then quit Visual Studio .NET.	a. On the **File** menu, click **Save All**. b. On the **File** menu, click **Exit**.

Lesson: Configuring ASP.NET Application Settings

- **ASP.NET State Management**
- **ASP.NET Security**
- **How to Configure an ASP.NET Application Setting**

Introduction

This lesson introduces ASP.NET technology, as it relates to developing Web applications.

Lesson objectives

After completing this lesson, you will be able to:

- Explain ASP.NET state management.
- Explain ASP.NET security.
- Configure an ASP.NET application setting.

Lesson agenda

This lesson includes the following topics and activities:

- Multimedia: ASP.NET Execution Model
- ASP.NET State Management
- ASP.NET Security
- How to Configure an ASP.NET Application Setting
- Practice: Configuring a Web Application Using Web.Config

Multimedia: ASP.NET Execution Model

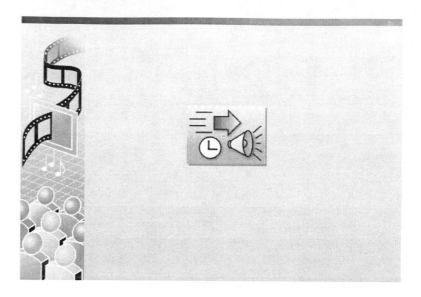

Introduction   In this animation, you will see how ASP.NET works to send information to a requesting client.

ASP.NET State Management

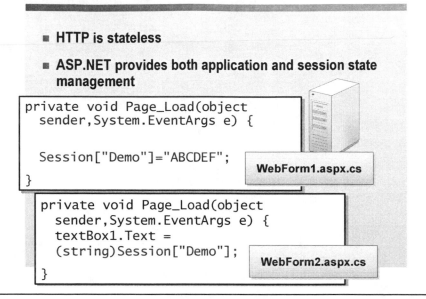

- HTTP is stateless
- ASP.NET provides both application and session state management

```
private void Page_Load(object
    sender,System.EventArgs e) {

    Session["Demo"]="ABCDEF";
}
```
WebForm1.aspx.cs

```
private void Page_Load(object
    sender,System.EventArgs e) {
    textBox1.Text =
    (string)Session["Demo"];
}
```
WebForm2.aspx.cs

Introduction

HTTP is a stateless protocol. A browser requests a page from a Web server; the Web server receives that request, fetches the page from the hard disk, and then returns that page to the browser.

However, if the browser requests another page from the same Web server, the Web server has no knowledge of the fact that the browser recently requested a page. In the early days of the Internet, when much of the available content was static, this process was not a problem.

The fact that the Internet is currently being used for more than just the casual browsing of static Web pages presents the Web application developer with a problem. How can the developer maintain information between requests to different pages while the user browses the developer's Web application? This problem is solved by ASP.NET state management.

ASP.NET state management

ASP.NET improves on the state management mechanism provided by the earlier versions of ASP.NET, Active Server Pages. ASP.NET provides two objects: **Application** and **Session**. You use the **Application** object to hold information that is common to all users of a particular Web application. You use the **Session** object to store information on a user-by-user basis.

Example

As shown in the following code, the string ABCDEF is placed into the **Session** object for storage between pages. As you keep track of variables by using different names, this string is held in the **Session** object against the name Demo. When a user accesses this page, ASP.NET creates a **Session** object for the user and stores the string against the name Demo. When the user accesses the second page in the example, ASP.NET retrieves the object from the **Session** object by the name Demo.

```
private void Page_Load(object sender,System.EventArgs e){
    Session["Demo"]="ABCDEF";
}
```

Notice the cast from Session["Demo"], which is type **object**, to string.

```
private void Page_Load(object sender,System.EventArgs e) {
    textBox1.Text = (string)Session["Demo"];
}
```

Note   In ASP.NET, the previous implementation of state management was enhanced to allow it to scale better for large installations and to be more reliable.

ASP.NET Security

- **Authentication**
  - None
  - Windows
  - Forms
  - Passport
- **Authorization**
- **Impersonation**

Introduction

Developing dynamic and interactive Web sites typically involves some element of security.

Authentication

Allowing users of a Web site to save their preferred airlines for future use requires an ability to validate the user who is accessing the Web site so that the correct information can be retrieved. This type of security is called *authentication*.

Authorization

You may want to restrict some pages of your Web site to particular users. After your Web application authenticates the user, access to specific pages can be allowed or denied. This type of security is called *authorization*.

Impersonation

Finally, you may want your Web application to interact with other applications, such as a database. You also may want it to appear to other applications that it is being accessed by the user of the Web site, or possibly by a different, fixed user account. This type of security is called *impersonation*.

To enable an authentication provider

To enable an authentication provider for an ASP.NET application, you need only create an entry for the application configuration file as shown in the following code:

```
// web.config file
<authentication mode= "[Windows/Forms/Passport/None]">
</authentication>

ASP.Net Authorization
<authentication mode="Forms">
  <forms name="Test Application Logon Page"
loginURL="logonform.aspx" />
</authentication>
<authorization>
  <deny users="?">
</authorization>
```

How to Configure an ASP.NET Application Setting

■ Using Web.CONFIG

```xml
<?xml version="1.0" encoding="utf-8" ?>
  <configuration>
      <system.web>
      <compilation defaultLanguage="c#"
                  debug="true"/>
      <identity impersonate="true"
                  userName="DOMAIN\User"
                  password="123dfget252"/>
      <authentication mode="Forms">
          <forms name="AdvWorks"
loginUrl="logon.aspx"/>
      </authentication>
      <authorization>
          <deny users="?"/>
      </authorization>
```

Introduction

The configuration file for an ASP.NET application is contained in the file Web.config. Configuration files in ASP.NET applications inherit the settings of configuration files in the URL path.

For example, given the URL www.microsoft.com/aaa/bbb, where www.microsoft.com/aaa is the Web application, the configuration file that is associated with the application is located at www.microsoft.com/aaa. ASP.NET pages that are in the subdirectory /bbb use both the settings that are in the configuration file at the application level and the settings in the configuration file that is in /bbb.

Hierarchical configuration architecture

ASP.NET applies configuration settings to resources in a hierarchical manner. Web.config files supply configuration information to the directories in which they are located and to all child directories. The configuration settings for a Web resource are supplied by the configuration file that is located in the same directory as the resource and by all configuration files in all parent directories.

Using Visual Studio .NET to change Web.Config

Web.Config should be listed as a file in your project in Solution Explorer. Double-click **Web.Config** to open an editing window to make changes to the file.

Example

In the following example, the ASP.NET application impersonates the identity DOMAIN/User. Authentication for the application uses the **Forms** method and specifically the Web page **logon.aspx** to validate logon requests. Users must be authenticated as anonymous users ("?") or will otherwise be denied access.

```xml
<?xml version="1.0" encoding="utf-8" ?>
<configuration>
  <system.web>
  <compilation defaultLanguage="c#"
          debug="true"/>
  <identity impersonate="true"
          userName="DOMAIN\User"
          password="123dfget252"/>
  <authentication mode="Forms">
      <forms name="AdvWorks" loginUrl="logon.aspx"/>
  </authentication>
  <authorization>
      <deny users="?"/>
  </authorization>
….
```

Practice: Configuring a Web Application Using Web.Config

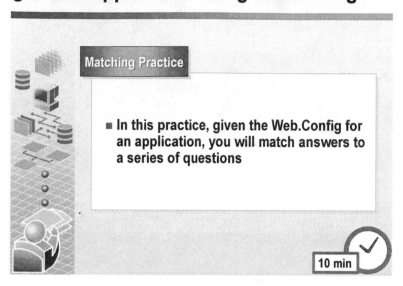

In this practice, you will match answers to a series of questions about the following Web.Config file for an application:

```xml
<?xml version="1.0" encoding="utf-8" ?>
<configuration>
  <system.web>
    <compilation defaultLanguage="c#" debug="true" />
    <!--  AUTHENTICATION
        This section sets the authentication policies of the
application. Possible modes are "Windows", "Forms",
        "Passport" and "None"
        -->
    <authentication mode="windows" />
    <authorization>
        <deny users="?" />
    </authorization>
    <trace enabled="false" requestLimit="10"
pageOutput="false" traceMode="SortByTime" localOnly="true" />
    <sessionState mode="InProc"
stateConnectionString="tcpip=127.0.0.1:42424"
sqlConnectionString="data source=127.0.0.1;user
id=sa;password=" cookieless="true" timeout="20" />
    <!--  GLOBALIZATION
        This section sets the globalization settings of the
application.
    -->
    <globalization requestEncoding="utf-8"
responseEncoding="utf-8" />
  </system.web>
</configuration>
```

With reference to the preceding Web.Config file, answer the following questions:

1. What kind of authentication mechanism is specified by this Web.Config file?

2. Are un-authenticated users allowed access to this Web application?

3. What is the default language of this Web application?

Review

- **Creating a Web Forms Application**
- **Accessing Data by Using a Web Form Application**
- **Configuring ASP.NET Application Settings**

1. How can you view all of the files that Visual Studio .NET creates for a new ASP.NET Web application?

2. What are the extensions for the two files that make up a Web Forms page?

3. What are the three components, not visible on a Web page, that are required to display the contents of a SQL Server table in a **DataGrid** control?

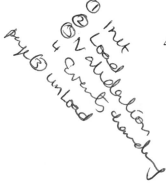

4. Name the five basic stages of a Web Forms page life cycle.

5. Name the five steps that are necessary to display data on a Web Forms page.

6. What browsers are supported by ASP.NET?

7. Can you have more than one Web.Config applications settings?

Lab 10.1: Developing an ASP.NET Web Application

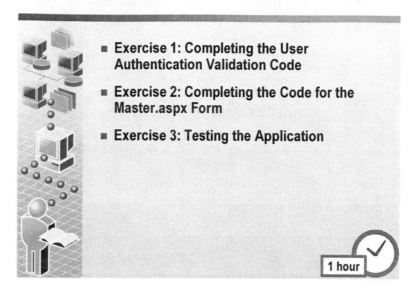

- Exercise 1: Completing the User Authentication Validation Code
- Exercise 2: Completing the Code for the Master.aspx Form
- Exercise 3: Testing the Application

1 hour

Objectives

After completing this lab, you will be able to:

- Develop an ASP.NET Web application.
- Use Forms based authentication.

Prerequisites

Before working on this lab, you must have the ability to:

- Create a Web Form.
- Handle events on a Web Form.
- Access data from Web Form applications.
- Configure ASP.NET application settings.

Scenario

In this lab, you will complete the code development of a basic Web interface to the AdventureWorks bank. This Web application allows users to view their accounts, display the transactions against an account, change their logon password, transfer money between accounts, and request traveler's checks in various currencies.

This lab consists of two exercises. In the first exercise, you will write the code to validate the user's logon. In the second exercise, you will complete the code in the event procedures for the main form, master.aspx. The code for the main form is provided. However, you must examine each code block, and then copy and paste it into the appropriate event procedure because this information is not given to you.

The solution for this lab is provided in install_folder\Labfiles\Lab10_1\ AdvWorksBank_Solution. To open the solution, follow the instructions in the Readme.txt file located in the folder.

Estimated time to complete this lab: 60 minutes

Exercise 0
Lab Setup

The Lab Setup section lists the tasks that you must perform before you begin the lab. The ASP.NET application calls a local XML Web service. This Web service must be installed before you complete the lab.

Tasks	Detailed steps

1. Log on to Windows as **Student** with a password of **P@ssw0rd**.	▪ Log on to Windows with the following account:
	  • User name: **Student**
	  • Password: **P@ssw0rd**.

2. Install the Travelers Checks Web Service using the Setup.exe located in *install_folder*\Labfiles\Lab10_1\Web Service.	a. Click **Start**, and then click **Run**. b. In the **Run** dialog box, in the **Open** box, type *install_folder***Labfiles\Lab10_1\WebService\Setup.exe** and then click **OK**. c. In the **Travelers Checks Web Service** setup wizard, on the **Welcome to the Travelers Checks Web Service Setup Wizard** page, click **Next**. d. On the **Select Installation Address** page, click **Next**. e. On the **Confirm Installation** page click **Next**. f. On the **Installation Complete** page, click **Close**.

Exercise 1

Completing the User Authentication Validation Code

Because this ASP.NET Web Application uses Forms-based authentication, the first exercise involves writing the code that authenticates the user's logon attempt.

When the user attempts to access the Web site, ASP.NET will test the user for the presence of an encrypted session cookie. If the session cookie is not present on the client computer, ASP.NET automatically redirects the user to the logonform.aspx page. This redirection is accomplished by the authentication element that is contained in the Web.Config file. The logonform.aspx page contains two text boxes: a label to display any error messages, and a button. Users enter their customer number in one text box and then enter their password in the second text box. You must add code to the button click event that tests whether the password entered on the form matches the password stored in the database. If the passwords match, the user is issued a session cookie and redirected to the main page of the application.

Tasks	Detailed steps
1. Copy the folder *install_folder*\Labfiles\Lab10_1\ AdvWorksBank to C:\Inetpub\wwwroot.	a. Click **Start**, point to **All Programs**, point to **Accessories**, and then click **Windows Explorer**. b. Click *install_folder***labfiles\Lab10_1,** in the list of items in this folder right-click **AdvWorksBank**, and then click **Copy**. c. In the left pane of Windows Explorer, right-click **C:\Inetpub\wwwroot**, and then click **Paste**. d. Close the **Windows Explorer** window.
2. Using the Microsoft Internet Information Services application, change the virtual folder **AdvWorksBank** from the default application to standalone application named **AdvWorksBank**. Execute Permissions: **Scripts only**. Application Protection: **Medium (Pooled)**.	a. Click **Start**, and then click **Control Panel**. b. In Control Panel, double-click **Performance and Maintenance**, and then double-click **Administrative Tools**. c. In the **Administrative Tools** dialog box, double-click **Internet Information Services**. d. Expand *your_servername*. e. Expand **Web Sites**. f. Click **Default Web Site** g. In the content list of the **Default Web Site**, right-click **AdvWorksBank**, and then click **Properties**. h. In the AdvWorksBank Properties window, under **Application Settings**, click **Create** (this gives the Web site the default Execute Permissions of Scripts only and the Application Protection of Medium), and then click **OK**. i. Close **Internet Information Services**. j. Close **Administrative Tools**. k. Close **Control Panel**.

Tasks	Detailed steps
3. Open the AdvWorksBank solution in the folder C:\Inetpub\wwwroot\AdvWorksBank	a. Start Visual Studio .NET. b. On the **File** menu, click **Open Solution**. c. In the **Open Solution** dialog box, select the AdvWorksBank folder in the **Look In** folder (under C:\Inetpub\wwwroot). d. If it is not already selected, click **AdvWorksBank.sln**, and then click **Open**.
4. View the code for the file logonform.aspx.	■ In Solution Explorer, right-click **logonform.aspx**, and then click **View Code**.
5. Scroll down and locate the Button1_Click procedure. Add code to this procedure as directed by the comments included.	■ Scroll down and locate the Button1_Click procedure. Using the comments included in the procedure, write the code necessary to authenticate the user logon.

Exercise 2
Completing the Code for the Master.aspx Form

In this exercise, you will complete the code for the main form, master.aspx.   Five event procedures in the form have no code. You are provided with five (5) code blocks in a text file called (Code Blocks.txt). These code blocks contain no comments to indicate which event procedure they should be copied to. You must examine each code block, determine what the code does, and then paste the code into the correct event procedure. In the file master.aspx.cs, you will find 5 procedures with a comment indicating that the procedure needs one of the code blocks from the code block text file.

Tasks	Detailed steps
1. Open the Code Editor for master.aspx.	▪ In Solution Explorer, right-click **master.aspx**, and then click **View Code**.
2. Open the text file **Code Blocks.txt**.	▪ In Solution Explorer, right-click **Code Blocks.txt**, and then click **Open**.
3. Read each code block and determine its functionality. Paste the code block into the correct event procedure in master.aspx. Repeat for each code block.	a. Read the first code block and determine its functionality. b. Highlight the lines of code for the code block, and then on the **Edit** menu, click **Copy**. c. In the Code Editor, click the **master.aspx.cs** tab. d. Scroll down the code to the area where the event procedures contain the comment **Code block required here**. Click inside the correct event procedure. e. Press ENTER to start a new line. f. On the **Edit** menu, click **Paste**. g. Repeat steps **a** through **f** until all event procedures in master.aspx.cs have code.

Exercise 3
Testing the Application

In this exercise, you will test that the application functions correctly.

Tasks	Detailed steps
1. Run the application. If prompted to set the initial Web page, select **master.aspx.**	▪ On the standard toolbar, click **Start**. If prompted to set the initial Web page, select **master.aspx.**
2. Log on to the application using Customer Number: 100 Password: Password	a. In the AdventureWorks Internet Banking form, in the **Customer number** box, enter **100** b. In the **Password** box, type **Password** and then click **Logon**.
ⓘ Note: If you entered the customer number and password correctly, the page displays the accounts that are held by this customer. If you failed to log on, try logging on again. If you still cannot log on or your application generates an error, you must debug the application.	
3. Display the transactions for account 1000.	▪ In the list of accounts, in the row for account 1000, click **View**.
4. Request $1000 of traveler's checks in British Pounds Sterling.	a. Click **Request Travelers Checks**. b. In the **Amount of Travelers Checks in USD** box, type **1000** c. In the **Check Currency** list, click **British Pounds Sterling**, and then click **Order**.
ⓘ Note: A message should appear on the page stating "**Order reference is *nn* for 720.00 British Pounds Sterling Made up of 1 500s 4 50s 2 10s. Total cost $1,1014.08**".	

Course Evaluation

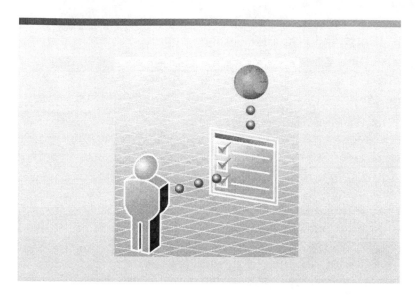

Your evaluation of this course will help Microsoft understand the quality of your learning experience.

At a convenient time between now and the end of the course, please complete a course evaluation, which is available at http://www.metricsthatmatter.com/survey.

Microsoft will keep your evaluation strictly confidential and will use your responses to improve your future learning experience.

msdn® training

Module 11: Application Settings and Deployment

Contents

Overview

- **Working with Application Settings**
- **Deploying Applications**

Introduction

This module describes how to store user preferences and configure application settings. It also introduces the procedures that are involved in deploying a C# application by using Microsoft® Visual Studio® .NET. It explains how to deploy both Web-based applications and applications that are based on Microsoft Windows®.

Objectives

After completing this module, you will be able to:

- Work with application settings.
- Deploy an application.

Lesson: Working with Application Settings

- **How to Work With User Preferences and Application Settings**

- **How to Save Application Settings by Using XML Serialization**

- **How to Save Application Settings to a Database**

- **How to Save Application Settings to the Windows Registry**

Introduction

This lesson explains how to manage application configuration in a Windows-based application.

Lesson objectives

After completing this lesson, you will be able to store application settings by:

- Using XML serialization.
- Using a database.
- Using the Windows registry.

Lesson agenda

This lesson includes the following topics:

- How to Work with User Preferences and Application Settings
- How to Save Application Settings by Using XML Serialization
- How to Save Application Settings to a Database
- How to Save Application Settings to the Windows Registry
- Practice: Using the Windows Registry

How to Work with User Preferences and Application Settings

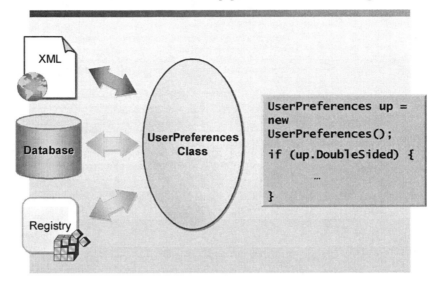

Introduction

When developing an application, you may establish application or user settings that you want to be persisted between sessions of the application. For example, you may want to store a color scheme or maintain the size of a window. These preferences must be stored somewhere so that they can be used the next time the application is run.

Options

The Microsoft .NET Framework provides several mechanisms for storing information about an application, its users, and default system settings. Depending upon the type of application that you are deploying, there are three primary ways that you can save settings and preferences:

- XML files

  For a Web application, an XML file may be a good choice for persisting information. XML files are also useful for persisting settings while an application is offline and therefore unable to connect to and set or retrieve settings from a database or other storage mechanism.

- Database files

  If your application depends upon data that is stored in a database, to the point where it will not function if a connection to the database is not established, then storing user preferences in the database is an appropriate decision.

- Windows registry

  For a Windows-based application, storing application settings in the Windows registry is often the preferred method.

An object-oriented solution to storing preferences

Regardless of where user preferences and application settings are stored, it is recommended that you create a class to access and manipulate this data. Using an object-oriented approach provides many benefits:

- *Encapsulation.* Because objects encapsulate both data and functionality together, only the data and methods that a user must access are made public, and not all the internal information about the object.

- *Scalability.* There is no limitation to the number and type of user preferences that you can save.

- *Portability.* If the application must store user preferences somewhere other than its current location, you can update the **UserPreferences** object without affecting any other code.

How to Save Application Settings by Using XML Serialization

```xml
<?xml version="1.0" ?>

    <UserPreferences
    xmlns:xsd="http://www.w3.org/2001/XMLSchema"
    xmlns:xsi="http://www.w3.org/2001/XMLSchema-
    instance">

      <pageOrientation>false</pageOrientation>

      <doubleSided>true</doubleSided>

      <addPageNumbers>true</addPageNumbers>

    </UserPreferences>
```

Introduction

The .NET Framework provides classes that you can use to serialize an object. When you store your application or user settings in a class, serializing the class is straightforward.

Definition

XML serialization is the process of converting the public properties and fields of an object to an XML serial format for storage or transport. *Deserialization* re-creates the object in its original state from the XML output.

Note For more information about XML serialization, see Module 6, "Building .NET-based Applications with C#," in Course 2069, *Introduction to C# Programming with Microsoft .NET.*

Syntax

To serialize an object to a file, you must instantiate a new **XmlSerializer** object and then call the **Serialize** method, as shown in the following code:

```csharp
MySerializableClass myObject = new MySerializableClass( );
XmlSerializer mySerializer = new
  XmlSerializer(typeof(MySerializableClass));
StreamWriter myWriter = new StreamWriter("myFileName.xml");
mySerializer.Serialize(myWriter, myObject);
```

To deserialize an object, you call the **Deserialize** method.

Example

The following code shows a class named **UserPreferences** that contains three properties, **pageOrientation**, **doubleSided**, and **addPageNumbers**. An instance of the class is created by calling the **UserPreferences.Load** static method. This method returns an instance of the class with the settings loaded from an XML file. The name of the XML file is the user domain and user name, which are available through the **System.Environment.UserDomainName** and **System.Environment.UserName** static properties.

```csharp
public class UserPreferences {
  private bool pageorientation;
  private bool doublesided;
  private bool addpagenumbers;

  public bool pageOrientation {
      get {
          return pageorientation;
      }
      set {
          pageorientation=value;
      }
  }

  public bool doubleSided {
      get {
          return doublesided;
      }
      set {
          doublesided=value;
      }
  }

  public bool addPageNumbers {
      get{
          return addpagenumbers;
      }
      set {
          addpagenumbers=value;
      }
  }

  public UserPreferences() {
  }

  public static UserPreferences Load() {
      UserPreferences up;
      XmlSerializer myXmlSerializer = new
          XmlSerializer(typeof(UserPreferences));
      string filename = System.Environment.CurrentDirectory+
          "\\"+System.Environment.UserDomainName+
          System.Environment.UserName+".xml";
      if (File.Exists(filename)) {
          FileStream fs = new
              FileStream(filename,FileMode.Open);
          up=(UserPreferences)myXmlSerializer.Deserialize(fs);
          fs.Close();
      }
      else {
          up = new UserPreferences();
      }
      return up;
  }
```

Code continued on the following page.

```
public void Save() {
    XmlSerializer myXmlSerializer = new
        XmlSerializer(typeof(UserPreferences));
    string filename =
        System.Environment.CurrentDirectory+
        "\\"+System.Environment.UserDomainName+
    System.Environment.UserName+".xml";
    FileStream fs = new FileStream(filename,
        FileMode.Create);
    myXmlSerializer.Serialize(fs,this);
    fs.Close();
  }
}
```

The **UserPreferences** object is created for the current user by using the static method of the **UserPreferences** class, as shown in the following code:

```
UserPreferences up = UserPreferences.Load();
```

The following XML code is created:

```
<?xml version="1.0" ?>
- <UserPreferences
xmlns:xsd="http://www.w3.org/2001/XMLSchema"
xmlns:xsi="http://www.w3.org/2001/XMLSchema-instance">
        <pageOrientation>false</pageOrientation>
        <doubleSided>true</doubleSided>
        <addPageNumbers>true</addPageNumbers>
</UserPreferences>
```

How to Save Application Settings to a Database

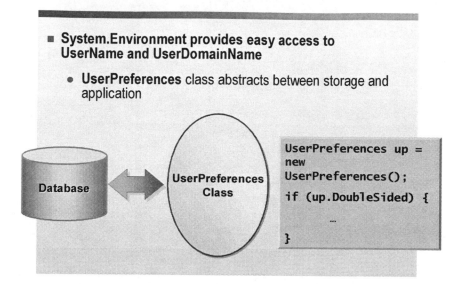

- **System.Environment provides easy access to UserName and UserDomainName**

    - **UserPreferences** class abstracts between storage and application

```
Database  ⟷  UserPreferences
              Class
```

```
UserPreferences up =
new
UserPreferences();
if (up.DoubleSided) {
    …
}
```

Introduction

If the application that you develop depends upon data that is stored in a database, to the point where it will not function if a connection to the database is not established, then an appropriate place to store your user preferences is in the database.

In object-oriented programming, a good way to manage user preferences is to create a class that encapsulates the specific functions of retrieving and updating the user preferences.

Benefits of using a database

There are several benefits of using a database to store settings:

- *Central location.* When all user settings are saved in a database, administrative changes must be made in only one location instead of at each user's computer.

- *Global preferences.* User preferences are available to users on any computer that they use to run your application.

- *Regular backups.* User preferences are backed up with the database backup.

Example

In the following example, three user preferences are held as properties of a class and stored in a database. Notice the use of the **System.Environment** class, which is provided by the .NET Framework class library, to retrieve the user name and domain name for the currently logged-on user.

The class definition is shown in the following code:

```csharp
public class UserPreferences {
  private bool pageorientation;
  private bool doublesided;
  private bool addpagenumbers;

  public bool pageOrientation {
      get {
          return pageorientation;
      } .
      set {
          pageorientation=value;
      }
  }

  public bool doubleSided {
      get {
          return doublesided;
      }
      set {
          doublesided=value;
      }
  }

  public bool addPageNumbers {
      get {
          return addpagenumbers;
      }
      set {
          addpagenumbers=value;
      }
  }
}
```

The default constructor for the class

Notice in the remainder of the code how the default constructor for the **UserPreferences** class uses information from the **System.Environment** class to query the Microsoft SQL Server™ database for the user preferences for the logged-in user.

```
public UserPreferences() {
    SqlConnection sqlcon = new SqlConnection(
        "Data Source=localhost; Integrated "+
        "Security=SSPI;Initial Catalog=2609");
    sqlcon.Open();
    string sqlcomtext="SELECT * FROM  UserPreferences "+
        "WHERE UserName = N'" +
        System.Environment.UserDomainName + "\\" +
        System.Environment.UserName.ToString() + "')";
    SqlCommand sqlcom = new SqlCommand(sqlcomtext,sqlcon);
    SqlDataReader sqldr=sqlcom.ExecuteReader();
    while (sqldr.Read()) {
        pageorientation=System.Convert.ToBoolean
            (sqldr.GetInt32(1));
        doublesided=System.Convert.ToBoolean
            (sqldr.GetInt32(2));
        addpagenumbers=System.Convert.ToBoolean
            (sqldr.GetInt32(3));
    }
    sqldr.Close();
    sqlcon.Close();
}
```

The save method

The **UserPreferences** class has only one public method, **Save**. In the remainder of the code, the preferences for this user are updated in the **UserPreferences** table in the database.

```
public void Save() {
    SqlConnection sqlcon = new SqlConnection(
        "Data source=localhost;Integrated "+
        "Security=SSPI;Initial Catalog=2609");
    sqlcon.Open();
    string sqlcomtext="UPDATE UserPreferences SET "+
        "DoubleSide=" + System.Convert.ToInt32
        (doublesided).ToString() + " ,AddPageNumbers=" +
        System.Convert.ToInt32(addpagenumbers).ToString()+
        ",PrintPageOrientation="+System.Convert.ToInt32
        (pageorientation).ToString()+" WHERE ("+
        "UserName = N'" + System.Environment.UserDomainName
        + "\\" + System.Environment.UserName.ToString() +
        "')";
    SqlCommand sqlcom = new SqlCommand(sqlcomtext,sqlcon);
    sqlcom.ExecuteNonQuery();
    sqlcon.Close();
    }
}
```

The following illustration shows how the User Preferences table looks in the database:

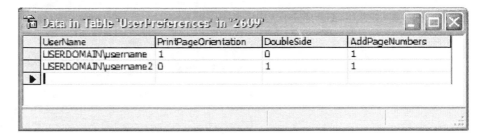

Example using the class

The following code uses the **UserPreferences** class defined above:

```
UserPreferences up = new UserPreferences();
If (up.AddPageNumbers) {
  // add page numbers code
}
```

How to Save Application Settings to the Windows Registry

■ **Registry Key Base Class**

Common Static Fields	Common Methods
HKEY_CLASSES_ROOT	CreateSubKey
HKEY_CURRENT_USER	OpenSubKey
HKEY_LOCAL_MACHINE	SetValue
HKEY_USERS	GetValue
	Close

Introduction

The Windows registry is a general-purpose mechanism for storing program information that must be maintained when a Windows-based application terminates.

Accessing the registry

The .NET Framework class library makes accessing the registry straightforward.

Registry static fields

The static read-only base keys that are exposed by the **Registry** class are shown in the following table.

Base key	Stores information about
HKEY_CLASSES_ROOT	Types and classes and their properties
HKEY_CURRENT_USER	User preferences
HKEY_LOCAL_MACHINE	Configuration of local computer
HKEY_USERS	Default user configuration

RegistryKey methods

The most common methods used to manipulate the **RegistryKey** class are shown in the following table.

RegistryKey method	Used for
CreateSubKey	Creating your own key for your application
OpenSubKey	Opening a key for reading and writing to the registry
SetValue	Modifying and storing an integer or a string to the registry
GetValue	Retrieving current values from the registry
Close	Exiting the registry

Example

The following code uses the **Registry.CurrentUser** static field to access the **HKEY_CURRENT_USER** registry base key. The **OpenSubKey** method of the **RegistryKey** class is then used to open the appropriate lower-level key.

Notice the use of the **GetValue** and **SetValue** methods to read and write values in the registry, respectively. Also, notice the use of the **CreateSubKey** method to create a new subkey.

```
public class UserPreferences {
  private bool pageorientation;
  private bool doublesided;
  private bool addpagenumbers;

  public bool pageOrientation {
      get {
          return pageorientation;
      }
      set {
          pageorientation=value;
      }
  }

  public bool doubleSided {
      get {
          return doublesided;
      }
      set {
          doublesided=value;
      }

  }

  public bool addPageNumbers {
      get {
          return addpagenumbers;
      }
      set {
          addpagenumbers=value;
      }
  }

  public UserPreferences() {
      RegistryKey uprk=Registry.CurrentUser.OpenSubKey
          ("SOFTWARE\\Microsoft\\Demo");
      if (uprk!=null) {
          pageorientation=System.Convert.ToBoolean
              (uprk.GetValue("PageOrientation"));
          doublesided=System.Convert.ToBoolean
              (uprk.GetValue("DoubleSided"));
          addpagenumbers=System.Convert.ToBoolean
              (uprk.GetValue("AddPageNumbers"));
      }
      else {
          pageorientation    =false;
          doublesided        =false;
          addpagenumbers     =false;
      }
  }
```

Code continued on the following page.

```
public void Save() {
    RegistryKey uprk=Registry.CurrentUser.OpenSubKey
        ("SOFTWARE\\Microsoft\\Demo",true);
    if (uprk==null) {
        RegistryKey msrk=Registry.CurrentUser.OpenSubKey
            ("SOFTWARE\\Microsoft",true);
        uprk=msrk.CreateSubKey("Demo");
    }
    uprk.SetValue("PageOrientation",pageorientation);
    uprk.SetValue("DoubleSided",doublesided);
    uprk.SetValue("AddPageNumbers",addpagenumbers);
}
}
```

Example using the class   The following code creates a user preferences object tests the AddPageNumbers property:

```
UserPreferences up = new UserPreferences();
If (up.AddPageNumbers) {
  // add page numbers code
}
```

Notice that the preceding code is the same as the example for storing data in the database.

Practice: Using the Windows Registry

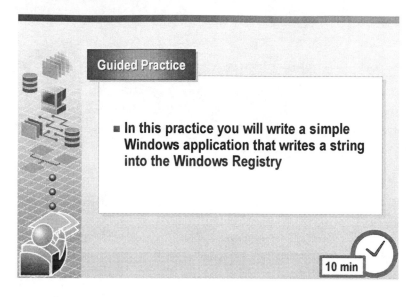

In this practice, you will write a simple Windows application that writes a string into the Windows Registry.

The solution for this practice is located at *install_folder*\Practices\Mod11\ Registry_Solution\Registry_Solution.sln. Start a new instance of Visual Studio .NET before opening the solution.

Tasks	Detailed steps
1. Start Visual Studio and create a new project. Name: **Registry** Project Type: **Visual C# projects** Template: **Windows Application** Location: *install_folder***Practices\ Mod11**	a. Start Visual Studio.NET. b. On the **File** menu, point to **New**, and then click **Project**. c. In the New Project window, under **Project Types**, click **Visual C# Projects**. d. Under **Templates**, click **Windows Application**. e. In the **Name** box, type **Registry** f. In the **Location** box, type *install_folder***Practices\Mod11** and then click **OK**.
2. Add a button to the form. Set the Text property of the button to **Add Info to the Registry**.	a. Hover over the toolbox, drag a button control from the toolbox and drop it onto the form. b. In the **Properties** window, click **Text** and then type **Add Info to the Registry**.

Tasks	Detailed steps
3. Add the code below into the button click event.	a. Double-click the button. b. In the **button1_Click** event procedure, add the code below.

ℹ **Add the following code into the button1_Click event procedure**.

```
Microsoft.Win32.RegistryKey key = Microsoft.Win32.Registry.
  CurrentUser.CreateSubKey("SOFTWARE\\MSDNTraining");
key.SetValue("TestData","ABCDEF");
key.Close();
```

Tasks	Detailed steps
4. Run the application and click the button. Close the window.	a. Click **Start** on the standard toolbar. b. Click the button on the form. c. Close the window.
5. Open RegEdit and verify that the key **HKEY_CURRENT_USER \Software\MSDNTraining** contains a value for **TestData** of **ABCDEF**. Close the Registry Editor window, close Visual Studio.	a. Click **Start**, and then click **Run**. b. In the **Run** dialog box, in the **Open** box, type **RegEdit** and then click **OK**. c. In the **Registry Editor** window, expand **HKEY_CURRENT_USER**, expand **SOFTWARE**, and then click **MSDNTraining**. d. Verify that the string value **TestData** contains **ABCDEF**. e. Close the **Registry Editor** window. f. Close Visual Studio.

? The first line of the code added into the button click event could be shortened. How would you accomplish this?

_____

_____

Lesson: Deploying Applications

- **What Are the .NET Packaging and Deployment Options?**

- **How to Package and Deploy an Application Using Windows Installer**

- **How to Deploy a Web Application by Using XCOPY**

Introduction

This lesson explains how to package and deploy Windows-based and Web-based applications in the .NET environment.

Lesson objectives

After completing this lesson, you will be able to:

- Package and deploy a Windows-based application.
- Deploy a Web application.

Lesson agenda

This lesson includes the following topics:

- What Are the .NET Packaging and Deployment Options?
- How to Package and Deploy an Application Using Windows Installer
- How to Deploy a Web Application by Using XCOPY

What Are the .NET Packaging and Deployment Options?

- **Packaging Options**
  - As a set of executables and DLLs
  - Microsoft Windows Installer project
  - Cabinet files
- **Deployment Options Using Windows Installer**
  - **Merge Module Project**: packages files/components into a single module
  - **Setup Project**: builds an installer for a Windows-based application
  - **Web Setup Project**: builds an installer for Web application
  - **Cab Project**: creates a cabinet file for downloading to legacy

Introduction

This lesson explores the packaging and deployment options that are available for applications that you develop on the .NET Framework. Your choices depend primarily upon whether you are deploying a Web server application or a Windows-based desktop application.

Packaging

Packaging is the act of creating a package that can install your application on the user's computer.

There are several methods that you can use to package .NET Framework applications:

- As copied files.
- The easiest way to package your application is simply to copy the files directly. For example, you can put all the files on a CD-ROM and write a batch file to copy the files to a directory on the user's hard disk. The user can then just run the application. To uninstall the application, you simply delete the files.
- As cabinet (.cab) files.

   This option is typically used for Internet download scenarios to compress files and reduce download time.
- As a Microsoft Windows Installer 2.0 package.

   With this option, you create .msi files for use with Windows Installer.

Deployment

Deployment is the act of distributing a finished application to the computer and setting up the application so it will run correctly.

Deployment in the .NET Framework differs from traditional setup and deployment in many respects. The .NET Framework provides the following options for deploying applications:

- Use XCOPY or FTP.

  Because common language runtime applications are self-describing and require no registry entries, you can use XCOPY or FTP to simply copy the application to an appropriate directory. The application can then be run from that directory. For all but the simplest cases, it is recommended that you deploy your project rather than use XCOPY.

- Use code download.

  If you distribute your application over the Internet or through a corporate intranet, you can simply download the code to a computer and run the application there.

- Use no-touch deployment.

  Windows Forms allow no-touch deployment, in which applications can be downloaded, installed, and run directly on the user's computer without any alteration of the registry. The application removes itself from the user's computer when the application is closed.

- Use an installer program, such as Windows Installer 2.0.

  The Microsoft Windows Installer that is provided with Visual Studio .NET includes templates for four types of deployment projects and a Setup wizard that guides you through the process of creating a deployment project.

  The following four templates are available for your deployment project:

  - *Merge Module Project*. Packages components that may be shared by multiple applications. Merge Module projects allow you to package files or components into a single module to facilitate sharing. You can use the resulting .msm files in any other deployment project.

  - *Setup Project*. Builds an installer for a Windows-based application.

  - *Web Setup Project*. Builds an installer for a Web application.

  - *Cab Project*. Creates a cabinet file for downloading to an earlier version of a Web browser.

  The distinction between the Setup and Web Setup projects is where the installer deploys the files:

  - For a Setup project, the installer installs files into a Program Files directory on a target computer.

  - For a Web Setup project, the installer installs files into a virtual root directory on a Web server.

How to Package and Deploy an Application Using Windows Installer

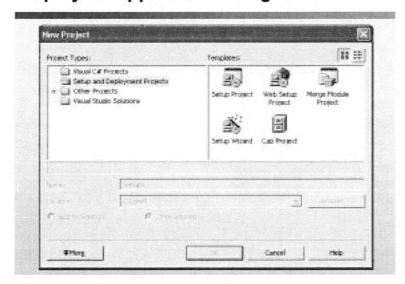

Introduction

This lesson explains how to use the Windows Installer Setup Project template to customize and deploy an application. In addition to using Windows Installer to package your application as an .msi file and copy the file to the target computer's hard disk, you can also use the installer to add information in the registry, add shortcuts to the application, and create uninstall files.

Components of a Windows Installer Setup project

The following table describes the uses for the various components of a Windows Installer Setup project.

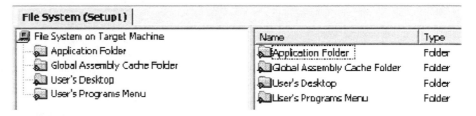

Setup component	Description
Application Folder	Used to store the application itself
Global Assembly Cache Folder	Used to install shared assemblies
User's Desktop	Used to install shortcuts on the desktop
User's Programs Menu	Used to install a shortcut in the **Programs** menu

A note about the bootstrapping application

When you deploy a Windows-based application on a version of Windows earlier than Microsoft Windows XP, you must include a *bootstrapping* application, which will execute Windows Installer on your target system before installing the application. To do this, on the **Visual Studio .NET** menu, click **Project**, click **Properties**, and then on the **Bootstrapper** menu, click **Windows Installer Bootstrapper**.

Note For more information about deploying applications in the .NET Framework and including a bootstrapping application, see the MSDN® article, *.NET Framework Deployment Guide*.

Procedure: Using a Windows Installer Setup Project

To use the Setup Project template to create a Windows Installer package:

1. Start Visual Studio .NET, and then click **New Project**.

2. In the **New Project** dialog box, under **Project Types**, click **Setup and Deployment Projects**, and then under **Templates**, double-click **Setup Project**.

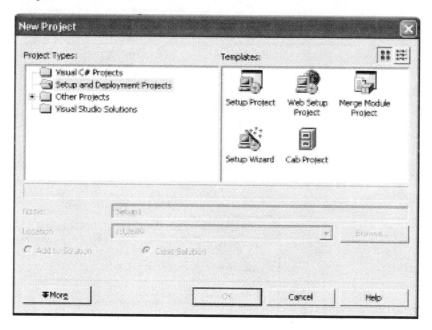

3. In the Properties window, set project properties such as **Author**, **Description**, **Manufacturer**, **ManufacturerUrl**, **ProductName**, **Title**, and **Version**.

4. To add the application files to be installed in the application folder, right-click the **Application Folder** in the left pane, click **Add**, and then click **Folder** or **File**, as appropriate.

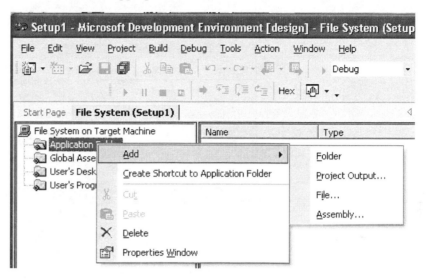

5. If you want to change the location where the contents of the Application folder will be installed, change the **DefaultLocation** property of the Application Folder.

6. To add the icons for your application to the setup project, in the left pane, right-click **User's Desktop** or **User's Program Menu**, and then click **Create Shortcut to User's Desktop** or **Create Shortcut to User's Programs Menu**, as appropriate.

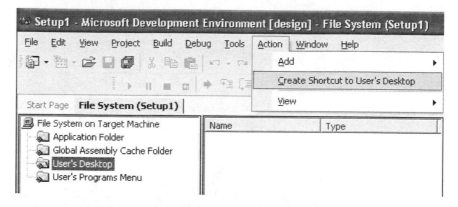

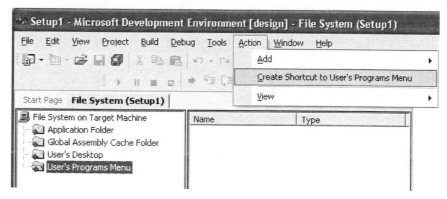

7. Build the setup project.

   The output is an .msi file.

8. Using Windows Explorer, locate and double-click the .msi file to install the application on your computer.

How to Deploy a Web Application by Using XCOPY

- **Copy command**
  - On the **Project** menu, click **Copy Project**.
  - Select the destination project folder.
  - Select the Web access method.
  - Select the files to be copied.
- **XCOPY command**
  - Type **xcopy/?** in a command prompt window

Introduction

In the .NET Framework, you can deploy Web applications by using the **Copy Project** or **XCOPY** commands. The **Copy Project** command is available on the **Project** menu of Visual Studio .NET. To use the **XCOPY** command, type **xcopy/?** in a command prompt window.

Pros and cons

Copying a project, rather than deploying it, is the simpler way to move the content of your project to a target Web server. Copying does not automatically configure the directory settings of Microsoft Internet Information Services (IIS). Therefore, it is recommended that you deploy your project in most cases, because it allows you to take advantage of extensive deployment project management features, such as registration and IIS configuration.

There are three major steps that are required to move your application from the development environment to a production server. You must first build the application, then you remove all unnecessary files, and finally you copy the files to the production environment.

Build the application

The first step is to build (compile) your Web application. This process creates the dynamic-link libraries (DLLs) that contain the code for the Web application.

Remove unnecessary files

The second step in deploying a Web application is to remove all unnecessary files from the directory that contains the Web application. This increases the security of your production site by not exposing uncompiled code.

The files that are not needed on the production server include:

- C# solution files (.csproj, and so on)
- Resource (.resx) files
- Code-behind pages (.cs)

The files that are required on the production server include:

- The \bin directory and the DLL files within it
- All Web form, user control, and XML Web service files (.aspx, .ascx, .asmx)
- Configuration files, including Web.config and global.asax
- Any additional support files that are in the directory, such as XML files

After you compile the Web application and remove all unnecessary files, you simply copy all of the remaining Web application files in the development directory to the production directory.

Using Copy Project

These are the typical steps for copying a project to a server:

1. On the **Project** menu, click **Copy Project**.
2. Select the destination project folder.
3. Select the Web access method.
4. Select the files to be copied.

By default, the **Copy Project** command creates a new Web application on the target server and copies only the files that are required to run to the application. Alternatively, you can deploy all project files or all files in the project folder. Note that Microsoft FrontPage® Server Extensions must be installed on the target server to use the **Copy Project** command.

Using XCOPY

The **XCOPY** command copies both files and directories, including subdirectories, to the target computer. Use the following syntax:

XCOPY *source* [*destination*] *options*

The source specifies the location and names of the files that you want to copy and must include either a drive or a path.

The destination specifies the location where you want to copy the files to. The destination parameter can include a drive letter, a directory name, a file name, or a combination of these. If you omit a destination, the **XCOPY** command copies the files to the current directory.

XCOPY options

The following table lists a few of the options that you can use when deploying an assembly by using the **XCOPY** command.

Option	Description
/p	Prompts you to confirm whether you want to create each destination file.
/q	Suppresses display of XCOPY messages.
/e	Copies all subdirectories, even if they are empty.
/s	Copies directories and subdirectories, unless they are empty. If you omit this option, XCOPY works within a single directory.

If you save Web application-specific information in the Machine.config file and transfer the Web application to a different server, you may need to edit the new Machine.config file. Deploying an application by using XCOPY or FTP will not copy the settings in the Machine.config file.

Securing Web servers

When you use the **Copy Project** or **XCOPY** commands, securing your servers is critical. As with any server, it is imperative that you keep up with the latest security updates from Microsoft at http://www.microsoft.com/security. Also, it is recommended that you turn off or disable all services on your Web servers that are not used, particularly those services that allow you to access the file system, such as File Transfer Protocol (FTP) and Web-based Distributed Authoring and Versioning (WebDAV).

Review

- **Working with Application Settings**
- **Deploying Applications**

1. What are some benefits of storing user preferences in a database?

2. What are the four deployment templates that are available in Visual Studio .NET?

Lab 11.1: Deploying an Application

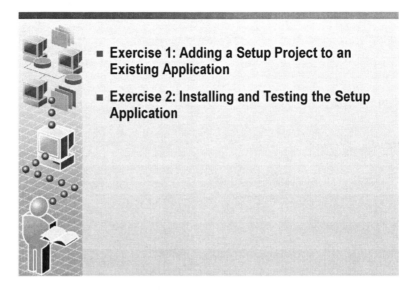

- ■ Exercise 1: Adding a Setup Project to an Existing Application
- ■ Exercise 2: Installing and Testing the Setup Application

Objectives

After completing this lab, you will be able to:

- ■ Add a deployment project to an existing solution.
- ■ Set registry settings during the setup of an application.
- ■ Under **All Programs** on the **Start** menu, create a shortcut to the installed application.

Prerequisites

Before working on this lab, you must have:

- • Knowledge of deploying an application with Visual Studio.NET.

Scenario

In this lab, you will create a setup application to deploy the Zoo Information application. You will customize the setup project created to set some registry settings and add a shortcut under **All Programs** on the **Start** menu for the installed application.

Estimated time to complete this lab: 60 minutes

Exercise 0
Lab Setup

Task	Detailed steps
▪ Log on to Windows as **Student** with a password of **P@ssw0rd**.	▪ Log on to Windows with the following account: • User name: **Student** • Password: **P@ssw0rd**

Exercise 1
Adding a Setup Project to an Existing Application

In this exercise, you will use the Setup Wizard to add a Setup project to the existing Zoo Information application.

Tasks	Detailed steps
1. Start Visual Studio .NET, and then open the project in the *install_folder*\Labfiles\Lab11_1 folder .	a. Start a new instance of Visual Studio .NET. b. On the **Start Page**, click **Open Project**. c. In the Open Project window, browse to *install_folder*\Labfiles\Lab11_1, click **animals.sln**, and then click **Open**.
2. Use Solution Explorer to add a Setup Wizard template project to the existing solution. Name: **Setup** Location: *install_folder***Labfiles\Lab11_1**	a. In Solution Explorer, right-click **Solution 'animals'**, point to **Add**, and then click **New Project**. b. In the Add New Project window, under **Project Types**, click **Setup and Deployment Projects**. c. Under Templates, click Setup Wizard. d. In the **Name** box, type **Setup** e. In the **Location** box, type *install_folder***Labfiles\Lab11_1** and then click **OK**.
3. Complete the setup wizard using the following information: Project Type: **Create a setup for a Windows application**. Include: **Primary output from animals**. Additional Files: **AnimalData.xml, Antelope.jpg, Elephant.jpg, Lion.jpg** from the folder *install_folder***Labfiles\Lab11_1**	a. In the Setup Wizard, on the **Welcome to the Setup Project Wizard** page, click **Next**. b. On the **Choose a project type** page, click **Next**. c. On the **Choose project outputs to include** page, under **Which project output groups do you want to include?** Click **Primary output from animals**, and then click **Next**. d. On the **Choose files to include** page, click **Add**. e. In the **Add Files** dialog box, change **Look In** to *install_path***Labfiles\Lab11_1**. f. Press and hold the CTRL key, and then click **AnimalData.xml**. With the CTRL key still held down, click **Antelope.jpg**, click **Elephant.jpg**, click **Lion.jpg**, and then click **Open**. g. On the **Choose files to include** page, click **Next**. h. On the **Create Project** page, click **Finish**.
4. Set the following properties of the Setup project: Author: **AdventureWorks** Manufacturer: **AdventureWorks** Title: **Zoo Information** ProductName: **Zoo Information**	a. In Solution Explorer, click **Setup**. b. In the Properties window, click **Author**, and then type **AdventureWorks** c. Click **Manufacturer**, and then type **AdventureWorks** d. Click **Title**, and then type **Zoo Information** e. Click **ProductName**, and then type **Zoo Information**

Tasks	Detailed steps
5. Create a shortcut to the primary output, and then move this shortcut to a folder under the users Programs Menu. Program Sub-menu name: **Zoo Applications**.	a. In the File System (Setup) editor window, under **File System on Target Machine**, right-click **User's Programs Menu**, point to **Add**, and then click **Folder**. b. Type **Zoo Applications** c. Under **File System on Target Machine**, click **Application Folder**. d. In the contents of the **Application Folder**, right-click **Primary output from animals**, and then click **Create Shortcut to Primary output from animals (Active)**. e. Type **Zoo Information** f. Drag this new shortcut icon from the Application Folder to the Zoo Applications folder under **User's Programs Menu**.
6. Use the Registry editor of the Setup project to create a sub-key under **HKEY_CURRENT_USER\Software\[Manufacturer]** called **ZooInformation**. Add two string values to this key: AutoLoad = **False** ShowTitle = **True**	a. In Solution Explorer, right-click **Setup**, point to **View**, and then click **Registry**. b. In the **Registry (Setup)** editor window, under **Registry on Target Machine**, under **HKEY_CURRENT_USER**, under **Software**, right-click **[Manufacturer]**, point to **New**, and then click **Key**. c. Type **ZooInformation** d. Right-click **ZooInformation**, point to **New**, and then click **String Value**. e. Type **AutoLoad** f. In the Properties window, click **Value**, and then enter **False**. g. Right-click **ZooInformation**, point to **New**, and then click **String Value**. h. Type **ShowTitle** i. In the Properties window, click **Value**, and then enter **True**.
7. Build the Setup project.	▪ In Solution Explorer, right-click **Setup**, and then click **Build**.

Exercise 2

Installing and Testing the Setup Application

In this exercise, you will install the application on your computer. You will then run the application.

Tasks	Detailed steps
1. Install the setup.	a. In Solution Explorer, right-click **Setup**, and then click **Install**. b. Accept the defaults provided by the setup wizard.
2. Run the Zoo Information application.	a. Click **Start**, point to **All Programs**, point to **Zoo Applications**, and then click **Zoo Information**. b. In the Zoo Information window, click **File**, and then click **Open**. c. In the **Open** dialog box, click **AnimalData.xml**, and then click **Open**.
3. Close the application, save changes to your solution, and then quit Visual Studio .NET.	a. Close the Zoo Information window. b. In Visual Studio .NET, on the **File** menu, click **Save All**. c. On the **File** menu, click **Exit**.

Lab 11.2 (optional): Working with Application Settings

- Exercise 1: Adding the UserPreferences Class
- Exercise 2: Adding User Preferences to the Form Load Event
- Exercise 3: Adding User Preferences to the loadItem_Click Event
- Exercise 4: Declaring an Instance of the UserPreferences Class in the Options Form
- Exercise 5: Setting the Checkbox Controls to the Values Contained in the Registry
- Exercise 6: Save the Checkbox Controls Values to the Registry
- Exercise 7: Testing the Zoo Information Application

Objectives

After completing this lab, you will be able to:

- Read data from the registry.
- Write data to the registry.

Prerequisites

Before working on this lab, you must have:

- Knowledge of working with application settings including the **RegistryKey** class of the .Net Framework Class Library.

Scenario

In this lab, you will enhance the existing code of the Zoo Information application, which is already written, to store the following simple user preferences in the Windows registry:

- *ShowTitle preference.* Controls whether to display the name of the animal above the text in the user interface.

- *AutoLoad preference.* Controls whether the application automatically attempts to open the data file that it last opened. The AutoLoad functionality requires that the last file opened by the application is stored in the registry.

The solution for this lab is provided in install_folder\Labfiles\Lab11_1\ Solution_Code\Animals.sln. Start a new instance of Visual Studio .NET before opening the solution.

Estimated time to complete this lab: 30 minutes

Exercise 0
Lab Setup

Task	Detailed steps

■ Log on to Windows as **Student** with a password of **P@ssw0rd**.	■ Log on to Windows with the following account:
	   • User name: **Student**
	   • Password: **P@ssw0rd**

Exercise 1
Adding the UserPreferences Class

The first step in modifying the application is adding the **UserPreferences** class definition to the application. The **UserPreferences** class has three public fields: *showtitle*, *autoload*, and *lastfilename*. Information is retrieved from the registry during the execution of the class constructor and saved to the registry in a method called **Save**.

Tasks	Detailed steps
1. Start Visual Studio .NET, and the open *install_folder*\Labfiles \Lab11_2\animals.sln.	a. Start a new instance of Visual Studio .NET. b. On the **Start Page**, click **Open Project**. c. In the **Open Project** dialog box, browse to *install_folder*\Labfiles\Lab11_2, click **animals.sln**, and then click **Open**.
2. View the code of Form1.cs.	▪ In Solution Explorer, right-click **Form1.cs**, and then click **View Code**.

3. Add the **UserPreferences** class definition at the bottom of the existing code in Form1.cs.	a. Scroll to the bottom of Form1.cs.
	
	b. On the line before the last brace, **}**, add the following class definition:
	
	`public class UserPreferences{`
	
	`}`

4. In the **UserPreferences** class, create three public fields: • showtitle (Boolean) • autoload (Boolean) • lastfilename (String)	▪ In the class definition that you created in the preceding step, add the following three public fields: • showtitle (Boolean) • autoload (Boolean) • lastfilename (String)

Tasks	Detailed steps
5. Add a default constructor to the **UserPreferences** class. You should be able to modify the code examples in this module to solve this problem.	a. In this constructor, open the registry key **HKEY_CURRENT_USER\Software\AdventureWorks\ ZooInformation**. **Note:** If this key does not exist, your application should default the values of the fields shown in the following step. b. Set the public fields that you created in the preceding step from the values held in the key: **ShowTitle** (default true) **AutoLoad** (default false) **LastFileName** (default "")
6. Add a **Save** method to the **UserPreference** class. You should be able to modify the code examples in this module to solve this problem.	a. In this method, open the registry key **HKEY_CURRENT_USER\Software\AdventureWorks\ ZooInformation** for writing. **Note:** If this key does not exist, your application should create it. b. Store the public fields in the registry values: **ShowTitle** **AutoLoad** **LastFileName**

Exercise 2

Adding User Preferences to the Form Load Event

In this exercise, you will use the **UserPreferences** class to read the user preferences and determine if the application should automatically load the last file opened.

Task	Detailed steps
▪ Locate the **Form1_Load** event in Form1.cs. Complete the instructions in the comments for Lab11.2 Exercise 2.	a. Locate the **Form1_Load** event. b. Add the required code as described in the comments titled Lab11.2 Exercise 2.

Exercise 3
Adding User Preferences to the loadItem_Click Event

In this exercise, you will use the **UserPreferences** class to update the **LastFileName** value held in the registry after a user selects a file to open.

Task	Detailed steps
▪ Locate the **loadItem_Click** event in Form1.cs. Scroll through the code in this event until you locate the Exercise 3 instructions. Complete the instructions.	a. Locate the loadItem_Click event. b. Scroll through the code until you locate the Exercise 3 instructions. c. Add the code as described in the instructions.

Exercise 4

Declaring an Instance of the UserPreferences Class in the Options Form

In this exercise, you will declare an instance of the **UserPreferences** class as private for use in the Options form.

Tasks	Detailed steps
1. Open the Options.cs code editor.	▪ In Solution Explorer, right-click **Options.cs**, and then click **View Code**.
2. Within the definition of the class Options, locate and then follow the Lab11.2 Exercise 4 instructions.	a. Locate the **Options** class within the code. b. Locate and then follow the Lab11.2 Exercise 4 instructions.

Exercise 5

Setting the Checkbox Controls to the Values Contained in the Registry

In this exercise, you will create an instance of the **UserPreferences** class and use the properties of the class to set the check boxes on the form. You will place this code into the **Options_Load** event.

Task	Detailed step
▪ Locate the **Options_Load** event, and then follow the Lab11.2 Exercise 5 instructions.	▪ Locate the **Options_Load** event, and then follow the Lab11.2 Exercise 5 instructions.

Exercise 6

Save the Checkbox Controls Values to the Registry

In this exercise, you will set the values of the check boxes on the form into the properties of the **UserPreferences** instance that you created in Exercise 5, and then call the **Save** method.

Task	Detailed step
▪ Locate the **ok_Click** event, and then follow the Lab11.2 Exercise 6 instructions.	▪ Locate the **ok_Click** event, and then follow the Lab11.2 Exercise 6 instructions.

Exercise 7

Testing the Zoo Information Application

In this exercise, you will run the Zoo Information application and test that the user preferences are stored correctly in the registry.

Tasks	Detailed steps
1. Run the Zoo Information application.	▪ On the Standard toolbar, click **Start**.
2. In the Zoo Information window, open the file AnimalData.xml.	a. In the Zoo Information window, on the **File** menu, click **Open**. b. In the **Open** dialog box, click **AnimalData.xml**, and then click **Open**.
3. On the **View** menu, click **Options**, and then click **Autoload Last File on Startup**.	a. On the **View** menu, click **Options**. b. In the **Options** window, click **Autoload Last File on Startup**, and then click **Open**.
4. Close the Zoo Information window.	▪ Close the Zoo Information window.
5. Run the application.	▪ On the Standard toolbar, click **Start**.
ℹ **Note:** The application should automatically load the AnimalData.xml file and display the Antelope information page. If the application displays an error or this functionality does not appear, debug your application.	
6. Close the Zoo Information window.	▪ Close the Zoo Information window.
7. Save the changes to the solution, and then quit Visual Studio .NET.	a. In Visual Studio .NET, on the **File** menu, click **Save All**. b. On the **File** menu, click **Exit**.

msdn training

Module 12: Exploring Future Learning

Contents

Overview

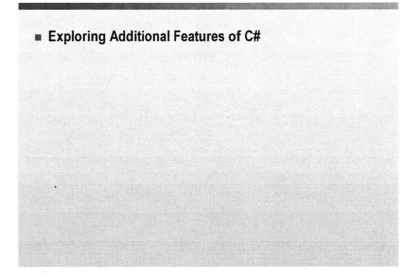

- **Exploring Additional Features of C#**

Introduction

This module provides an opportunity for you to explore some of the more advanced capabilities of C#, to practice the knowledge and skills that you acquired during the course, and to discuss your questions as a group.

Objectives

After completing this module, you will be able to:

- Locate resources for information about additional C# features.

- Use those resources to further develop any of the projects that you started earlier in this course.

Lesson: Exploring Additional Features of C#

- **The C# Preprocessor**
- **Structs**
- **C# Threads and Threading**
- **Attributes and Reflection**
- **.NET Framework Security**
- **Interoperability**
- **.NET Remoting**

Introduction

This lesson presents some additional features of C# that may interest you as you further develop your Microsoft® .NET-based projects. These advanced features are covered only briefly in this lesson. The focus of this lesson is to identify resources that you can use for further study and to provide an opportunity for you to develop a project that you started earlier in this course.

Lesson objectives

After completing this lesson, you will be able to:

- Locate resources for information about advanced features of C#.
- Use those resources to further develop any of the projects that you started in the practices or labs of this course.

Lesson agenda

This lesson includes the following topics:

- The C# Preprocessor
- Structs
- C# Threads and Threading
- Attributes and Reflection
- .NET Framework Security
- Interoperability
- .NET Remoting

The C# Preprocessor

- **You can use the preprocessing directives to provide instructions to the compiler**

- **Examples of preprocessing directives are # if, #else, #define**

```
#define DEBUG
...
public void Calculate() {
#if DEBUG
    // write debug messages
    WriteToLogfile("Entering method");
#endif

    . . .

}
```

Introduction

Before your code is actually compiled, a *preprocessor* runs, examines, and prepares your program for the compiler. You can use the preprocessor to control the code that the compiler receives. In some circumstances, such as debugging, you may want to compile extra debugging statements into your program. However, you do not want these statements in your finished application. You can use preprocessing directives to cause the preprocessor to compile sections of code only under certain circumstances. This is called *conditional compilation*.

Preprocessing directives

Preprocessing directives provide the ability to conditionally skip sections of source files, to report error and warning conditions, and to delineate distinct regions of source code.

Preprocessing in C#

C# is designed to avoid the need for include files, because classes do not require a separate definition file. For this reason, the C# preprocessor is less important than it is in C or C++. Items that typically occur in header files, such as macros, are also eliminated to provide for simpler code maintenance and speedy compilation.

A main function of the preprocessor in C# is to enable conditional compilation.

Directive syntax

A preprocessing directive always occupies a separate line of source code and always begins with a pound sign (#) character and a preprocessing directive name. White space may occur before the # character and between the # character and the directive name.

Commonly used directives

The following table describes some of the preprocessing directives that are available for C#:

Directive	Description
#if...#endif	The **#if** directive allows you to begin a conditional directive, test a symbol or symbols to see if they evaluate to **true**. If they do evaluate to **true**, the compiler evaluates all of the code between the **#if** and the next directive. The **#endif** directive terminates the scope of the **#if** directive.
#else	The **#else** directive allows you to create a compound conditional directive, so that if none of the expressions in the preceding **#if** or (optional) **#elif** directives evaluate to **true**, the compiler evaluates all code between **#else** and the subsequent **#endif**.
#define	The **#define** directive allows you to define a symbol, such that, by using the symbol as the expression passed to the **#if** directive, the expression evaluates to **true**.
#region...#endregion	The #**region** and #**endregion** directives allow you to define areas of code that can be collapsed and hidden under a label. The development environment uses this directive to hide the code that it generates automatically.

Example

In the following example, the call to the **WriteToLogfile** method is compiled only when "#define DEBUG" appears as a line in the code.

```
#define DEBUG
...
public void Calculate() {
#if DEBUG
  // write debug messages
  WriteToLogfile("Entering method");
#endif
  . . .
}
```

Resources

For further information about the C# preprocessor, see "2.5 Preprocessing Directives" in the *Microsoft .NET Framework Software Development Kit (SDK)*.

Structs

- A *struct* is a value type that can contain constructors, constants, fields, methods, properties, indexers, operators, and nested types
- Data structures suitable for use with structs
  - Contain a small number of data members
  - Do not require use of inheritance
  - Can be implemented using value semantics
- Structs vs classes
  - *Classes* are reference types
  - *Structs* are value types

Introduction

When you create a class, you create a new reference type. You can also create new value types called structs, which are similar to classes but do not support class functionality such as inheritance, although they can implement interfaces.

Definition

A *struct* type is a value type that can contain constructors, constants, fields, methods, properties, indexers, operators, and nested types. Examples of structs are complex numbers, points in a coordinate system, or key-value pairs in a dictionary.

Data structures suitable for use with structs

Structs are particularly useful for small data structures that have value semantics. You should use structs for types that:

- Contain a small number of data members.
- Do not require the use of inheritance.
- Use value semantics, for example, where you expect an assignment to copy a value instead of a reference.

Structs vs. classes

Structs are similar to classes in that they are types that can contain properties and methods. Unlike classes, structs are value types and do not require heap allocation. An instance of a struct directly contains the data of the struct, whereas an instance of a class contains a reference to the data.

- Structs are value types.
- Classes are reference types.

Resources

For further information about structs, see the following resources:

- "Structs Tutorial" in the *C# Programmers Reference* in the online Help.
- "**System.Data.SqlTypes** namespace" in the *.NET Framework SDK*, which includes an excellent example of data types that are implemented as structs in the .NET Framework.

C# Threads and Threading

- *Threads* are the basic unit to which an operating system allocates processor time
- **Advantages**
  - Multiple threads increase responsiveness to the user and simultaneously process the data necessary to complete the task
- **Disadvantages**
  - Use as few threads as possible to minimize the use of operating-system resources and improve performance
- **Threading features**
  - The C# language provides the **lock** statement
  - The .NET Framework provides classes in the **System.Threading** namespace

---

Introduction

Sometimes you may want to run parts of your application in a different process, or thread.

Definition

A *thread* is the basic unit to which an operating system allocates processor time. More than one thread at a time can execute code inside that process.

Advantages and disadvantages

There are both advantages and disadvantages to using threading:

- Advantages

  Using more than one thread is the most powerful technique available to simultaneously increase responsiveness to the user and process the data necessary to complete the job.

- Disadvantages

  It is recommended that you use as few threads as possible, thereby minimizing the use of operating-system resources and improving performance. Threading also has resource requirements and potential conflicts that you must consider when you design your application.

Example

For example, when you print a large document, you do not want your application to stop responding to the user as it processes the print job. So, you create a new thread that handles the printing work while your main application continues to be available to the user.

Threading features

C# and the .NET Framework provide features that allow different threads in a program to start and to communicate with each other.

- The C# language provides the **lock** statement that allows you to manage resource conflicts.

- The .NET Framework provides classes in the **System.Threading** namespace that support threading and interthread communication.

Resources

For more information about threads and threading, see the following:

Books

If you are new to threads and threading, it is recommended that you complete an advanced course or read an appropriate book.

- "Assemblies, Threads and AppDomains" in *C# and the .NET Platform*, by Andrew Troelsen, Apress, 2001.

- "Multithreaded Programming" in *Inside C#*, by Tom Archer, Microsoft Press®, 2001.

Online seminars

- "How to Build Multi-Threaded Application in .NET" online seminars, which are available under **Developer Resources** at http://www.microsoft.com/net/develop/. Eight seminars are available.

SDK

- The *.NET Framework SDK*. The SDK is a useful source of information and tutorials about threads and threading.

Attributes and Reflection

- **Use attributes and reflection to:**
  - Write a program that displays information about an application
  - Dynamically write new code at run time
  - Create applications called *type browsers*
  - Example: classes in the **System.Runtime.Serialization** namespace use reflection to access data and to determine which fields to persist
- **Reflection methods**
  - The **System.Reflection.MemberInfo** class discovers the attributes of a member and provides access to member metadata

Introduction

You use attributes to add metadata to your application, and you use reflection to read the metadata. Metadata in this context means data about the application. You can think of attributes as annotations that you insert into your application and reflection as the process that reads these annotations at run time.

Uses for attributes and reflection

You can use attributes and reflection to:

- Write a program that displays information about other applications, for example, for purposes of documenting those applications.

  The **Reflection** namespace contains the classes and interfaces that support this functionality.

- Dynamically write new code at run time, and then call that code.

  The classes of the **System.Reflection.Emit** namespace provide a specialized form of reflection that enables you to build types at run time.

- Create applications called *type browsers*, which enable users to select types and then view the information about those types.

- The classes in the **System.Runtime.Serialization** namespace use reflection to access data and to determine which fields to persist.

Reflection methods

The main reflection methods to query attributes are contained in the **System.Reflection.MemberInfo** class, which discovers the attributes of a member and provides access to member metadata.

The following example demonstrates the basic way of using reflection to obtain access to attributes:

```
class MainClass {
  public static void Main() {
      System.Reflection.MemberInfo info = typeof(SomeClass);
      object[] attributes = info.GetCustomAttributes(true);
      for (int i = 0; i < attributes.Length; i ++) {
          System.Console.WriteLine(attributes[i]);
      }
  }
}
```

Resources

For more information about attributes and reflection, see:

- Any C# language book, most of which discuss this topic. For example, *Inside C#*, by Tom Archer, Microsoft Press, 2001.

- "Attributes Tutorial" in the *.NET Framework SDK.*

.NET Framework Security

- **Common language runtime security**
  - Code access security
  - Role-based security
  - Cryptographic services
- **Command-line security tools**
  - Caspol.exe
  - Signcode.exe

Introduction

As a programmer, you must consider the security of the data that you manage. You are at risk when you open a database, and Web-based applications are a clear target for malicious users. Security checks ensure that a piece of code has the credentials to access certain resources.

Common language runtime security

Although it is unnecessary for most application developers to do any special work to gain the advantages of the .NET Framework security system, it is useful to have knowledge of the classes and services that the .NET Framework provides.

The classes and services that the common language runtime and .NET Framework provide also enable system administrators to customize the access that code has to protected resources. Additionally, the runtime and the .NET Framework provide classes and services that facilitate the use of cryptography and role-based security.

Code access security

The .NET Framework provides a security mechanism called *code access security*. All managed code that targets the common language runtime receives the benefits of code access security, even if that code does not make a single code access security call.

The code access security mechanism:

- Protects computer systems from malicious mobile code.
- Allows code from unknown origins to run safely.

Tip For more information about .NET Framework code access security, see "Code Access Security" in the *.NET Framework Developer's Guide*.

Role-based security

The runtime provides support for role-based authorization based on a Microsoft Windows® account or a custom identity. After you define identity (the user) and principal objects (the security context for that user), you can perform various security checks against them.

Tip For more information about .NET Framework role-based security, see "Role-Based Security" in the *.NET Framework Developer's Guide*.

Cryptographic services

The classes in the .NET Framework **Cryptography** namespace manage many details of cryptography for you. You do not need to be an expert in cryptography to use these classes. When you create a new instance of one of the encryption algorithm classes, keys are auto-generated for ease of use, and default properties are always as safe and secure as possible.

Tip For more information about .NET Framework cryptographic services, see "Cryptographic Services" in *the .NET Framework Developer's Guide*.

Command-line security tools

The .NET Framework SDK supplies command-line tools that help you perform security-related tasks and test your components and applications before you deploy them. Some of those tools include:

- *Caspol.exe*. The policy tool for code access security enables you to view and configure security policy.

- *Signcode.exe*. This file-signing tool signs a portable executable (PE) file with requested permissions, giving you more control over the security restrictions that are placed on your components.

Tip For more information about .NET Framework security tools, see "Security Tools" in the *.NET Framework Developer's Guide*.

Resources

For more information about making your code secure, see the following:

- Course 2350, *Securing and Deploying Microsoft .NET Assemblies.*

- *Writing Secure Code*, by Michael Howard and David LeBlanc. Microsoft Press, 2001.

- The *.NET Framework SDK*, which provides a tutorial on security. For further information, see the C# Programmer's reference section for the security tutorial.

Interoperability

- The .NET Framework supports interaction with COM components, COM+ services, external type libraries, and many operating system services

- **Marshaling service**

  The Interop marshaler maps between managed and unmanaged types

- **Platform invocation service**

  Platform invoke service uses attributes to locate exported functions and pass them arguments at run time

- **COM components**

  Marshals method calls between COM components and managed code

---

Introduction

The .NET Framework supports interaction with unmanaged code, such as COM components, COM+ services, external type libraries, and many operating system services. Data types, method signatures, and error-handling mechanisms vary between managed and unmanaged object models. To simplify interoperation between the .NET Framework components and unmanaged code, the common language runtime conceals the differences in these object models from both clients and servers.

Marshaling service

Most data types have common representations in both managed and unmanaged memory. The interop marshaler handles these types for you. Other types can be ambiguous or not represented at all in managed memory. Marshaling occurs whenever the caller and recipient cannot operate on the same instance of data. The interop marshaler makes it possible for both the caller and recipient to appear to be operating on the same data even though the caller and recipient have their own copy of the data. You can supply explicit instructions to the interop marshaler about how it is to marshal an ambiguous type.

Platform invocation service

You can call C functions in dynamic-link libraries (DLLs) through a feature called Platform invoke. *Platform invoke* is a service that uses attributes to locate exported functions and pass arguments to them at run time. This service enables managed code to call unmanaged functions that are implemented in DLLs, such as those in the Microsoft Win32® application programming interface (API). The Platform invoke feature uses interop marshaling to pass method parameters and return values between managed code and the unmanaged library.

COM components

A .NET Framework application that must support a COM component cannot directly consume the functionality that is exposed by that component. Instead, it must access the functionality by using a proxy class, sometimes called a *wrapper*. Although a utility (Tlbimp.exe) is provided to help create this class, this utility does not remove the requirement for manual coding when you require detailed control of the component.

Resources

For more information about interoperability, see the following:

- Course 2571: *Application Upgrade and Interoperability Using Microsoft Visual Studio® .NET.*

- Any C# language book that discusses this topic. For example, *Inside C#*, by Tom Archer, Microsoft Press, 2001.

.NET Remoting

- **Supports distributed applications**
- **Communicate with applications:**
  - On the same computer
  - On a different computer on the same network
  - On a different computer at a remote location
- **Improves scalability**
- **Similarities to XML Web services**

Introduction

You can use .NET Remoting to enable different applications to communicate with one another, whether those applications reside on the same computer, on different computers in the same local area network, or across the world in very different networks; even if the computers run different operating systems.

The **System.Runtime.Remoting** namespace provides classes to activate remote objects, send messages to and receive messages from remote objects, and much more.

You can use remoting to create distributed applications and to make your applications more scalable.

.NET Remoting vs. XML Web services

On the surface, .NET Remoting and XML Web services appear very similar to each other. In fact, XML Web services are built on the .NET Remoting infrastructure. However, as a general rule:

- .NET Remoting tends to be more appropriate for applications where the implementation of the applications at both ends of the conversation is under the control the same organization.

- XML Web services are more appropriate for applications where the client side of the service is likely to be outside the control of a particular organization, for example, a trading partner.

Resources

For more information about .NET Remoting, see Course 2349, *Programming the Microsoft .NET Framework with C#.*

Course Evaluation

Your evaluation of this course will help Microsoft understand the quality of your learning experience.

To complete a course evaluation, go to http://www.microsoft.com/traincert/coursesurvey.

Microsoft will keep your evaluation strictly confidential and will use your responses to improve your future learning experience.

msdn training

Appendix A: Key Concepts Guide

Microsoft

Concept	Module	Topic title
Debugging tool	5	How to Initialize and Access Array Members
Definition	5	What Is an Array?
Index	5	How to Index an Object
Iterate through an array	5	How to Iterate Through an Array Using the foreach Statement
Jagged	5	What Is an Array?
Methods	5	What Is an Array?
Multidimensional	5	What Is an Array?
Using as method parameters	5	How to Use Arrays as Method Parameters
ArrayList	5	How to Use the ArrayList Class
Methods	5	How to Use the ArrayList Class
ASP.NET	10	What Is ASP.NET?
Application setting	10	How to Configure an ASP.NET Application Setting
Authentication	10	ASP.NET Security
Authorization	10	ASP.NET Security
Definition	10	What Is ASP.NET?
Impersonation	10	ASP.NET Security
State management	10	ASP.NET State Management

B

Concept	Module	Topic title
Base	4	What Are Abstract Methods and Classes?
Scope	3	How to Define Accessibility and Scope

C

Concept	Module	Topic title
C# Types		
Constants	2	How to Create and Use Constants
Converting between types	2	How to Convert Between Types
Enumerations	2	How to Create and Use Enumeration Types
Strings	2	How to Declare and Initialize Strings
Value types and reference types	3	How to Pass Parameters by Reference
	3	What Are Value Types and Reference Types?
Variables	2	How to Declare and Initialize Variables
	2	What Are Predefined Types?
Class		
Constructors	4	How to Call a Base Constructor from a Derived Class
	3	How to Initialize a Class
	3	How to Overload a Constructor
Derived	4	How to Create a Derived Class
	4	How to Use Base Class Members from a Derived Class
	4	How to Use a Sealed Class
	4	What Is Inheritance?
Collections	5	What Are Lists, Queues, Stacks, and Hash Tables?

Concept	Module	Topic title
F		
File I/O		
Definition	6	What Is File I/O?
Enumerations	6	What Is File I/O?
Files		
Binary files	6	How to Read and Write Binary Files
Windows File System	6	How to Traverse the Windows File System
H		
Hash tables	5	What Are Lists, Queues, Stacks, and Hash Tables?
Using	5	How to Use Hash Tables
I		
Interfaces	5	What Is an Interface?
Declaring	5	How to Use an Interface
Definition	5	What Is an Interface?
Design considerations	5	What Is an Interface?
Implementing	5	How to Use an Interface
	5	How to Work with Objects That Implement Interfaces
Interface invariance	5	What Is an Interface?
Purpose	5	What Is an Interface?
L		
Lists	5	What Are Lists, Queues, Stacks, and Hash Tables?
M		
Main Menu	8	How to Create the Main Menu
Associating methods	8	How to Associate Methods with Menu Items
Method		
Abstract	4	What Are Abstract Methods and Classes?
Overloading	3	How to Overload a Method
Passing parameters	3	How to Pass Parameters to a Method
	3	How to Pass Parameters by Reference
	3	How to Pass a Reference Type
Virtual	4	How to Write Virtual Methods
Writing methods	3	How to Write a Method
MSIL (Microsoft Intermediate Language)		
Definition	1	How the .NET Framework Works
N		
Namespaces	3	How to Organize Classes Using Namespaces

Concept	Module	Topic title
W		
Web Forms	10	What Is a Web Forms Application?
Accessing data	10	How to Access Data by Using a Web Forms Application
Adding controls	10	How to Add Controls to a Web Forms Application
Components	10	What Are the Components of a Web Forms Application?
Creating	10	How to Create a Web Forms Application
Definition	10	What Is a Web Forms Application?
Displaying data	10	How to Display Data on a Web Forms Application
Event handler	10	How to Add an Event Handler for the Control
Features	10	What Is a Web Forms Application?
Life cycle	10	What Is the Life Cycle of a Web Forms Application?
State management	10	What Is a Web Forms Application?
Windows Forms Designer		
Function	1	How to Use the Windows Forms Designer
X		
XML		
XMLTextReader class	6	How to Read and Write Text Files
XMLTextWriter class	6	How to Read and Write Text Files
XML Web services		
Building	9	How to Create an XML Web Service by Using Visual Studio .NET
Calling in code	9	How to Call an XML Web Service Method in Code
Definition	9	What Is an XML Web Service?
Locating	9	How to Locate the URL of an XML Web Service
Referencing	9	How to Add a Web Reference to an XML Web Service
Testing	9	How to Test an XML Web Service by Using Visual Studio .NET
vs. .NET remoting	12	.NET Remoting

msdn training

Appendix B: Advanced Topics

Contents

How to Use Multidimensional Arrays

■ **Declare an array**

```
int[,] myArray = new int [4,2];
```

■ **Initialize when declaring**

```
int[,] myArray = { {1,2}, {3,4}, {5,6}, {7,8} };
```

● Use *new* operator when declaring without initialization

■ **Assign a value to an array element**

```
myArray[2,1] = 25;
```

Introduction

You can use a multidimensional array to store values that naturally fall into a grid-like or rectangular structure. For example, to keep track of each pixel on your computer screen, you can refer to its X coordinates in one dimension and its Y coordinates in a second dimension.

Declaring

To declare a multidimensional array, use the following syntax:

```
int[,] myArray;
```

Multidimensional arrays can have any number of dimensions. The following declaration creates an array of three dimensions, 4, 2, and 3:

```
int[,,] myArray = new int [4,2,3];
```

If a two-dimensional array is like a rectangle, you can visualize a three-dimensional array as being like a cube, with the dimensions corresponding to height, width, and depth.

Initializing

You can initialize the array upon declaration, as shown in the following example:

```
int[,] myArray;
myArray = new int[,] { {1,2}, {3,4}, {5,6}, {7,8}};
```

Or more simply:

```
int[,] myArray = new int[,] {{1,2}, {3,4}, {5,6}, {7,8}};
```

Or even more simply:

```
int[,] myArray = {{1,2}, {3,4}, {5,6}, {7,8}};

string[,] siblings = new string[,] { {"Mike","Amy"},
                                     {"Mary","Ray"} };
```

Assigning a value to an array element

You can also assign a value to an array element, for example:

```
myArray[2,1] = 25;
```

Note   The total storage that the array requires increases dramatically when you start adding dimensions to an array. Declare the smallest array that you can.

How to Use Jagged Arrays

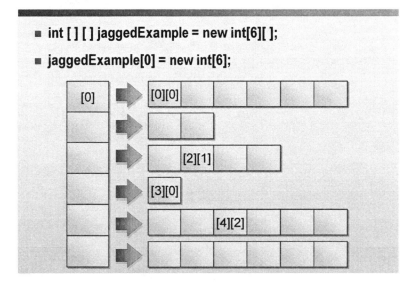

- int [ ] [ ] jaggedExample = new int[6][ ];
- jaggedExample[0] = new int[6];

| | Introduction | A *jagged array* is an array whose elements are arrays. The elements of a jagged array can be of different dimensions and sizes. A jagged array is sometimes called an array of arrays. |

Introduction

A *jagged array* is an array whose elements are arrays. The elements of a jagged array can be of different dimensions and sizes. A jagged array is sometimes called an array of arrays.

Declaring

The following code declares a two-dimensional jagged array that is made up of a single-dimensional array that has six elements, each of which is another single-dimensional array of integers:

```
int[ ][ ] myJaggedArray = new int[6][ ];
```

Initializing

Before you can use **myJaggedArray**, you must initialize its elements. You can initialize the elements as shown in the following example:

```
myJaggedArray[0] = new int[6];
myJaggedArray[1] = new int[2];
myJaggedArray[2] = new int[4];
myJaggedArray[3] = new int[1];
myJaggedArray[4] = new int[6];
myJaggedArray[5] = new int[6];
```

Each of the elements of the first array is a single-dimensional array of integers. The first element is an array of 6 integers, the second is an array of 2 integers, the third is an array of 4 integers, and so on.

Examples

You can use initializers to fill the array elements with values, in which case, you do not need the array size as shown in the following example:

```
myJaggedArray[0] = new int[] {1,3,5,7,9,11};
myJaggedArray[1] = new int[] {0,2};
myJaggedArray[2] = new int[] {11,22,33,44};
```

You can also initialize the array upon declaration as shown in the following example:

```
int[ ][ ] myJaggedArray = new int [ ][ ]
                    {
                        new int[ ] {1,3,5,7,9},
                        new int[ ] {0,2,4,6},
                        new int[ ] {11,22}
                    };
```

You can also mix jagged and multidimensional arrays. The following example shows a declaration and initialization of a single-dimensional jagged array that contains two-dimensional array elements of different sizes:

```
int[ ][,] myJaggedArray = new int [3][,]
                    {
                        new int[,] { {1,3}, {5,7} },
                        new int[,] { {0,2}, {4,6}, {8,10} },
                        new int[,] { {11,22}, {99,88}, {0,9} }
                    };
```

Accessing array elements

You can access individual array elements, as shown in the following examples:

```
// Assign 33 to the second element of the first array:
myJaggedArray[0][1] = 33;
// Assign 44 to the second element of the third array:
myJaggedArray[2][1] = 44;
```

How to Use XML with a DataSet

- **Read data from a DataSet object in XML format**

- **Fill a DataSet object with XML data**

- **Create an XML Schema for the XML representation of the data in a DataSet**

- **Load XML data into a Document Object Model (DOM) tree, from a stream or file. You can then manipulate the data as XML or as a DataSet**

- **Create typed DataSets**

Introduction

Microsoft® ADO.NET is tightly integrated with XML. The ADO.NET object model was designed with XML at its core. As a result, ADO.NET makes it easy to convert relational data into XML format. You can also convert data from XML into tables and relations.

Benefit of using XML

XML is a rich, platform-independent, and portable way of representing data. An important characteristic of XML data is that it is text-based. Using text-based data makes it easier to pass XML data between applications and services, even if they are running on different platforms. XML also enables organizations to exchange data without further customization of each organization's proprietary software.

Scenario

You must write an application that processes XML data. That XML data may come from an external business through an XML Web service, e-mail, Microsoft BizTalk® Server, or many other sources.

XML support

The ADO.NET object model includes extensive support for XML. Consider the following facts and guidelines when you use the XML support in ADO.NET:

- You can write data from a **DataSet** object in XML format. The XML format is useful if you want to pass data between applications or services in a distributed environment.

- You can fill a **DataSet** object with XML data. This is useful if you receive XML data from another application or service, and want to update a database by using this data.

- You can create an XML Schema for the XML representation of the data in a DataSet. You can use the XML Schema to perform tasks such as serializing the XML data to a stream or file.

- You can load XML data into a Document Object Model (DOM) tree from a stream or file. You can then manipulate the data as XML or as a DataSet. To do this, you must have an XML Schema to describe the structure of the data to the DataSet.

- You can create typed DataSets. A typed DataSet is a subclass of DataSet, with added properties and methods to expose the structure of the **DataSet**. To describe the XML representation of the DataSet, Microsoft Visual Studio® .NET generates an equivalent XML Schema definition for the typed DataSet.

Example

The following code loads the **Customer** table from the **Northwind Traders** database, saves it as XML to a temporary file, creates a new DataSet, and then loads the XML representation of the Customers table from the temporary file. The **System.IO** namespace is included for the **Path** class.

```
using System;
using System.Data;
using System.Data.SqlClient;
using System.IO; // included to get the temp path

namespace Samples {
    class DataSetXMLExample {
        static void Main(string[] args) {

            string tempfile = Path.GetTempFileName();

            string connectionString = @"data source=localhost;
Initial catalog=Northwind; integrated security=SSPI";
            string commandString = @"SELECT * FROM Customers";
            SqlDataAdapter dataAdapter = new SqlDataAdapter(
commandString, connectionString );

            DataSet myDataSet = new DataSet();
            dataAdapter.Fill( myDataSet, "Customers" );

            myDataSet.WriteXml( tempfile );
        Console.WriteLine( "Wrote Customer table to XML file
{0}", tempfile );

            DataSet data2 = new DataSet();
            data2.ReadXml( tempfile );

            int nRows = data2.Tables["Customers"].Rows.Count;
        Console.WriteLine( "Read {0} records from XML file
{1}", nRows, tempfile );
            // nRows is 91
        }
    }
}
```

This code sample is available on the Student Materials compact disc in the Samples\ModXB\XML folder.

Note For more information about how to fill a **DataSet** with an XML stream, see "DataSet class, XML" in the Visual Studio .NET online documentation.

For more information about obtaining data as XML from SQL Server, see "SQL Server .NET Data Provider, XML" in the Visual Studio .NET online documentation.

How to Change or Filter the View of the Data in the DataGrid

- **Bind to DataViewManager to specify single or multiple column sort orders, including ascending and descending parameters**

- **ApplyDefaultSort to automatically create a sort order**

- **RowFilter to specify subsets of rows based on their column values**

- **RowStateFilter to specify which row versions to view**

- **DataGridTableStyle**

Introduction

A **DataView** object provides a method for creating a customizable view for a single DataTable. You can sort and filter the view and specify what editing operations can be performed on the view's data.

You use a **DataViewManager** object to manage view settings for all the tables in a DataSet. The **DataViewManager** provides you with a convenient way to manage default view settings for each table. When you must bind a control to more than one table of a **DataSet**, binding to a **DataViewManager** is the ideal choice.

Sorting and filtering data using a DataView

The **DataView** provides several ways to sort and filter data in a **DataTable**, as shown in the following table.

Use the:	To:
Sort property	Specify single or multiple column sort orders and include **ASC** (ascending) and **DESC** (descending) parameters
ApplyDefaultSort property	Automatically create a sort order, in ascending order, based on the primary key column or columns of the table
RowFilter property	Specify subsets of rows based on their column values
Find or **FindRows** methods of the **DataView**	Return the results of a particular query on the data rather than provide a dynamic view of a subset of the data
RowStateFilter property	Specify which row versions to view

Example

For example, the following code snippet sorts items in the **Customers** table by Country.

```
string connectionString = @"data source=localhost; Initial
catalog=Northwind; integrated security=SSPI";
string commandString = @"SELECT * FROM Customers";
dataAdapter = new SqlDataAdapter( commandString,
connectionString );

myDataSet = new DataSet();
dataAdapter.Fill( myDataSet, "Customers" );

DataViewManager dvm = new DataViewManager( myDataSet );

dvm.DataViewSettings["Customers"].Sort = "Country";

dataGrid1.SetDataBinding( dvm, "Customers");
```

How to Overload Operators

- ■ **Overload operators such as == or + when you want your class to exhibit value-type semantics**

```
Measurement m1 = new Measurement(100,MeasurementUnit.CM);
Measurement m2 = new Measurement(1,MeasurementUnit.M);
```

```
if (m1==m2) {
   MessageBox.Show("Lengths are equal");
}
     Not overriden                              ✖
```

```
if (m1==m2) {
   MessageBox.Show("Lengths are equal");
}
     Overriden                                 ✓
```

Introduction

You override operators such as == or + when you want your class to use value-type semantics. The following code demonstrates when you may want your class to display value-type semantics.

Overloading the == operator

```
public class Measurement {
  public decimal Length;
  public MeasurementUnit Unit;
  public Measurement(decimal len, MeasurementUnit t) {
     Length=len;
     Unit=t;
  }
}

public enum MeasurementUnit {
  M,
  CM,
  MM,
}
```

The preceding code contains a simple class, **Measurement**. Each instance of the class should store a **Length** and **Unit** value. Consider the following code:

```
Measurement m1 = new Measurement(100,MeasurementUnit.CM);
Measurement m2 = new Measurement(1,MeasurementUnit.M);
if (m1==m2) {
  MessageBox.Show("Measurements are the same");
}
else {
  MessageBox.Show("Measurements are not the same");
}
```

Although the two lengths are actually the same, the preceding test is testing for the instances referenced by the two measurement variables being the same, which in this case they are not.

For the preceding code to work, it is necessary to override the == operator. Overriding the == operator allows the class to behave more like a value type. In the following code, the class overrides the == operator:

```csharp
public class Measurement {
  public decimal Length;
  public MeasurementUnit Unit;
  public Measurement(decimal len, MeasurementUnit t) {
      Length=len;
      Unit=t;
  }

  public static bool operator==(Measurement m1,
    Measurement m2) {
      decimal meters1 = 0;
      decimal meters2 = 0;
      switch (m1.Unit) {
          case MeasurementUnit.M:
              meters1 = m1.Length;
              break;
          case MeasurementUnit.CM:
              meters1 = m1.Length / 100;
              break;
          case MeasurementUnit.MM:
              meters1 = m1.Length / 1000;
              break;
      }
      switch (m2.Unit) {
          case MeasurementUnit.M:
              meters2 = m2.Length;
              break;
          case MeasurementUnit.CM:
              meters2 = m2.Length / 100;
              break;
          case MeasurementUnit.MM:
              meters2 = m2.Length / 1000;
              break;
      }
      if (meters1 == meters2) {
          return true;
      }
      else {
          return false;
      }
  }
}
```

The code in the overridden $==$ operator converts each length to a length specified as a meter. The lengths can then be compared correctly. Notice how the overridden operator must be static; references to the two objects to be compared are passed as parameters.

When overriding the $==$ operator, it is necessary to also override the $!=$ operator. This is accomplished by adding the following code:

```
public static bool operator !=(Measurement m1,
    Measurement m2) {
        return !(m1 == m2);
}
```

Best practices

It is strongly recommended that you also override the **Equals** and **GetHashCode** methods when overriding the $==$ and $!=$ operators. Failure to override **Equals** and **GetHashCode** can generate confusion by those who develop with the class because the logic is not consistent.

How to Override and Implement Equals

- **If a class overrides the operators == and != then the Equals method should be overridden to match the logic of the == operator.**

```
public override bool Equals(object o) {
    return (this==(Measurement)o);
}
```

Introduction

If your class must override the ==operator and != operator, you should also override the **Equals** method. You should use the == operator in the overridden **Equals** method to ensure that implemented logic is consistent between the == operator and **Equals** method.

Overriding the Equals method

Expanding on the **Measurement** class example in the How to Overload Operators topic, it is good practice to override the **Equals** method, because the == operator and != operator are already overridden.

```
public class Measurement {
  public decimal Length;
  public MeasurementUnit Unit;
  public Measurement(decimal len, MeasurementUnit t) {
      Length=len;
      Unit=t;
  }

  public override bool Equals(object o) {
      return (this==(Measurement)o);
  }

  public static bool operator==(Measurement m1,
    Measurement m2) {
    decimal meters1=0;
    decimal meters2=0;
    switch (m1.Unit) {
        case MeasurementUnit.M:
            meters1=m1.Length;
            break;
        case MeasurementUnit.CM:
            meters1=m1.Length / 100;
            break;
        case MeasurementUnit.MM:
            meters1=m1.Length / 1000;
            break;
    }
    switch (m2.Unit) {
        case MeasurementUnit.M:
            meters2=m2.Length;
            break;
        case MeasurementUnit.CM:
            meters2=m2.Length / 100;
            break;
        case MeasurementUnit.MM:
            meters2=m2.Length / 1000;
            break;
    }
    if (meters1==meters2) {
        return true;
    }
    else {
        return false;
    }
  }

  public static bool operator !=(Measurement m1,
    Measurement m2) {
    return !(m1==m2);
  }
}
```

Best Practices

It is strongly recommended that you override **GetHashCode** methods when overriding the **==**, **!=** and **Equals** operators.

How to Override GetHashCode

- The .NET Framework uses hash tables to store objects

- The value returned by GetHashCode should be related to the value returned by Equals

- If you override Equals, override GetHashCode

- Try to return a value unique to your object

```
public override int GetHashCode() {
    return this.Length.GetHashCode();
}
```

Introduction

You use hashing to efficiently find objects in lookup tables. A *hash table* is a method for speeding up a lookup process by producing a hash key for the objects in the table. You use a *hash key* to locate the area in the lookup table where you will most likely find the object, reducing the time spent looking for the object. For example, when executing a **switch** statement, C# uses the **Hashtable** class to quickly determine which branch to execute.

GetHashCode method

You can store any object in a hash table. To store an object, use the **GetHashCode** method to calculate the object's hash key.

Hash function properties

A hash function must have the following properties:

- If two objects of the same type represent the same value, the hash function must return the same constant value for either object.

- For the best performance, a hash function should generate a random distribution for all of the input.

- A hash function should be based on an immutable data member. *Immutable* means the data member, or string, and so on, does not change. The hash function should return exactly the same value regardless of any changes that are made to the object.

Caution Basing the hash function on a mutable data member can cause serious problems, including never being able to access that object in a hash table if the data member changes.

Using the Equals method with the GetHashCode method

If the **Equals** method determines that two objects are equal, the **GetHashCode** method must return the same integer for both objects. If a class overrides the **Equals** method, it should override the **GetHashCode** method.

For example, in the **Measurement** class example in the How to Override and Implement Equals topic and in the How to Overload Operators topic, to complete the implementation, you must override **GetHashCode**. This is accomplished by using the **GetHashCode** method of the data that is used in the == operator (Length).

```csharp
public class Measurement {
  public decimal Length;
  public MeasurementUnit Unit;

  public Measurement(decimal len, MeasurementUnit t) {
      Length=len;
      Unit=t;
  }

  public override bool Equals(object o) {
      return (this==(Measurement)o);
  }

  public override int GetHashCode() {
      return this.Length.GetHashCode();
  }

  public static bool operator==(Measurement m1,
    Measurement m2) {
      decimal meters1=0;
      decimal meters2=0;
      switch (m1.Unit) {
          case MeasurementUnit.M:
              meters1=m1.Length;
              break;
          case MeasurementUnit.CM:
              meters1=m1.Length / 100;
              break;
          case MeasurementUnit.MM:
              meters1=m1.Length / 1000;
              break;
      }
      switch (m2.Unit) {
          case MeasurementUnit.M:
              meters2=m2.Length;
              break;
          case MeasurementUnit.CM:
              meters2=m2.Length / 100;
              break;
          case MeasurementUnit.MM:
              meters2=m2.Length / 1000;
              break;
      }
      if (meters1==meters2) {
          return true;
      }
      else {
          return false;
      }
  }

  public static bool operator !=(Measurement m1,
    Measurement m2) {
      return !(m1==m2);
  }
}
```

What Is Serialization?

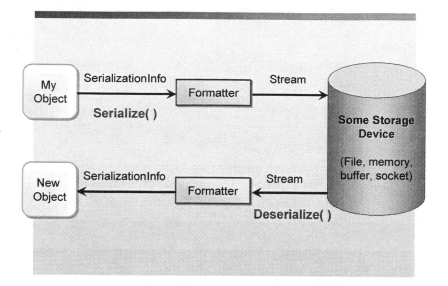

Introduction

When you create an application, the ability to save information between user sessions is imperative. Occasionally, you will find it necessary to save the state of your component. You may do this to save personal information about users of your component, or to change the default configuration of a custom control.

Definitions and terms

Serialization is the term describing the process of converting the state of an object into a form (a linear sequence of bytes) that can be persisted or transported. The byte stream contains all of the necessary information to reconstruct or *deserialize* the state of the object for use later.

Example

When you serialize an object to a stream, you also serialize any additional object references that are required by the root object. After you save a set of objects to a stream, you can relocate the byte pattern as necessary.

For example, if you serialize a stream of objects to a memory stream, you can forward this stream to a remote computer or the Microsoft Windows® Clipboard, save it to a compact disc (CD), or simply store it in a file. It does not matter where the byte stream itself is stored. What matters is that this stream of 1s and 0s correctly represents the state of serialized objects.

.NET Framework serialization

The Microsoft .NET Framework provides two formatters for serialization: the **BinaryFormatter** class and **SoapFormatter** class. These classes convert an in-memory representation of your object to a stream of data.

- *Binary serialization* is accomplished by using **BinaryFormatter**, which converts the object graph to a binary stream, which is most useful for desktop applications.

- *XML serialization* is accomplished by using the **SoapFormatter**, which converts the object graph to SOAP format, which is most useful for Internet applications.

You can save these streams as files that you can deserialize and convert back to objects when needed.

Using serialization

Why would you want to use serialization? The two most important reasons are:

- To persist the state of an object to a storage medium so that you can re-create an exact copy at a later stage.

  It is often necessary to store the value of fields of an object to disk and then retrieve this data at a later stage. Although storing data and retrieving it later is easy to achieve without relying on serialization, this approach is often cumbersome and error prone, and becomes progressively more complex when you must track a hierarchy of objects.

  For example, if you write a large business application containing many thousands of objects and you must write code to save and restore the fields and properties to and from a disk for each object, serialization provides a convenient mechanism for achieving this objective with minimal effort.

- To send the object by value from one application domain to another.

Reflection

The common language runtime manages how objects are laid out in memory and provides an automated serialization mechanism by using *reflection*. When an object is serialized, the name of the class, the assembly, and all of the data members of the class instance are written to storage. Objects often store references to other instances in member variables. When the class is serialized, the serialization engine keeps track of all referenced objects already serialized to ensure that the same object is not serialized more than once.

When the serialized class is *deserialized*, the class is re-created and the values of all the data members are automatically restored.

Tip For more about serialization guidelines, see the Visual Studio .NET documentation.

How to Use Binary Serialization

- **Mark the class with the Serializable attribute**

```
[Serializable]
public class MyObject {
  public int    n1 = 0;
  public int    n2 = 0;
  public string str = null;
}
```

Introduction

The **BinaryFormatter** class defines two core methods that read and write an object to a stream:

- *Serialize ( )*. Serializes an object to a stream.

- *Deserialize ( )*. Deserializes a stream of bytes to an object.

The default configuration of **BinaryFormatter** also defines a number of properties that configure specific details regarding the serialization or deserialization process.

Example

Mark each class that you wish to persist to a stream with the **Serializable** attribute as follows:

```
[Serializable]
public class MyObject {
  public int n1 = 0;
  public int n2 = 0;
  public string  str = null;
}
```

The following code demonstrates how to serialize an instance of this class to a file:

```
MyObject obj = new MyObject( );
obj.n1 = 1;
obj.n2 = 24;
obj.str = "Some String";
IFormatter formatter = new BinaryFormatter( );
Stream stream = new FileStream("MyFile.bin", FileMode.Create,
    FileAccess.Write, FileShare.None);
formatter.Serialize(stream, obj);
stream.Close( );
```

This example uses a binary formatter to perform the serialization. All you must do is create an instance of the stream and the formatter that you intend to use, and then call the **Serialize** method on the formatter.

Restoring the object state

Restoring the object to its former state is just as simple. First, create a stream for reading and a formatter, and then instruct the formatter to deserialize the object. The following code snippet demonstrates all of the above:

```
IFormatter formatter = new BinaryFormatter( );
Stream stream = new FileStream("MyFile.bin", FileMode.Open,
  FileAccess.Read, FileShare.Read);
MyObject obj = (MyObject) formatter.Deserialize(fromStream);
stream.Close( );

Console.WriteLine("n1: {0}", obj.n1);
Console.WriteLine("n2: {0}", obj.n2);
Console.WriteLine("str: {0}", obj.str);
```

Tip   All objects that are serialized with this formatter can also be deserialized with it.

How to Use XML Serialization

- **To serialize and deserialize an object**
  - Create the object
  - Construct an **XMLSerializer**
  - Call the Serialize/Deserialize methods

```
StreamWriter mySWriter = new StreamWriter(
    @"C:\myFileName.xml" );
try {
    // Serialize the customerList object
    XmlSerializer serializer = new XmlSerializer(
        typeof ( CustomerList ) );
    serializer.Serialize( mySWriter, customerList );
}
finally {
    mySWriter.Close( );
}
```

Introduction

XML serialization serializes only the public fields and property values of an object into an XML stream, and does not include type information. Because XML is an open standard, any application can process the XML stream, as needed, regardless of platform.

Note   XML serialization does not convert methods, indexers, private fields, or read-only properties, except read-only collections. To serialize all of an object's fields and properties, both public and private, use the **BinaryFormatter** class instead of XML serialization.

XmlSerializer class

You can use the **XmlSerializer** class to serialize the following items.

- Public read/write properties and fields of public classes
- Classes that implement the **ICollection** interface or the **IEnumerable** interface.

  Note   Only collections are serialized, not public properties.

- **XmlElement** objects
- **XmlNode** objects
- **DataSet** objects

SoapFormatter class

You can also use XML serialization to serialize objects into XML streams that conform to the SOAP specification. The other available formatter for serializing your types is the **SoapFormatter** class. The **SoapFormatter** class represents your object as a SOAP message, which is expressed in XML format. Use the **SoapFormatter** if portability is a requirement. Simply replace the formatter in the code that is used in the following example with **SoapFormatter**, and call the **Serialize** and **Deserialize** methods.

Serialize and Deserialize methods

To serialize an object, first create the object that is to be serialized and set its public properties and fields. To set the properties and fields, you must determine the transport format in which the XML stream is to be stored—either as a stream or as a file. For example, if the XML stream must be saved in a permanent form, create a **FileStream** object. When you deserialize an object, the transport format determines whether you will create a stream or file object. After you have determined the transport format, you can call the **Serialize** or **Deserialize** methods, as required.

Serializing an object

To serialize an object, complete the following tasks:

1. Create the object and set its public fields and properties.

2. Construct an **XmlSerializer** class by using the type of the object.

3. Call the **Serialize** method to generate either an XML stream or a file representation of the object's public properties and fields. The following example creates a file.

Example

```
MySerializableClass myObject = new MySerializableClass( );
XmlSerializer mySerializer = new
  XmlSerializer(typeof(MySerializableClass));
StreamWriter myWriter = new StreamWriter("myFileName.xml");
mySerializer.Serialize(myWriter, myObject);
```

Deserializing an object

To deserialize an object, complete the following tasks:

1. Construct an **XmlSerializer** class by using the type of the object to deserialize.

2. Call the **Deserialize** method to produce a replica of the object. When deserializing, you must convert the returned object to the type of the original, as shown in the following example. The following example deserializes the object into a file; however, it could also be deserialized into a stream.

```
MySerializableClass myObject;
XmlSerializer mySerializer = new
XmlSerializer(typeof(MySerializableClass));
FileStream myFileStream = new FileStream("myFileName.xml",
    FileMode.Open);
myObject = (MySerializableClass)
mySerializer.Deserialize(myFileStream)
```

Lab B.1: Using Serialization

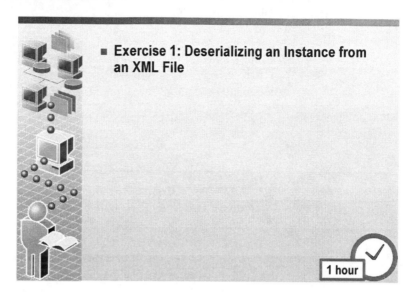

Objectives

After completing this lab, you will be able to:

- Serialize an object into an XML file.
- Deserialize an object from an XML file.

Prerequisites

Before working on this lab, you must have:

- Knowledge of the .NET Framework class library **XmlSerializer** class.
- Knowledge of the **Serializable** attribute.

Scenario

In this lab, you will add code to the Zoo Animal Information Display application that will add code to the **Zoo.Load** method that will deserialize the XML file and return an instance of the **Zoo** class.

The solution for this lab is provided in install_folder\Labfiles\LabXB_1\ Solution_Code\Animals.sln. Start a new instance of Visual Studio .NET before opening the solution.

Estimated time to complete this lab: 60 minutes

Exercise 1
Deserializing an Instance from an XML File

In this exercise, you will complete the code in the **Zoo.Load** method to deserialize an XML file into an instance of the **Zoo** class.

Tasks	Detailed steps
1. Start Visual Studio .NET, and then open the *install_folder*\Labfiles \LabXB_1\animals.sln.	a. Start a new instance of Visual Studio .NET. b. On the **Start** Page, click **Open Project**. c. In the **Open Project** dialog box, browse to *install_folder* \Labfiles\LabXB_1, click **animals.sln**, and then click **Open**.
2. Locate the method **Zoo.Load** contained in the file zoo.cs.	a. In Solution Explorer, right-click **zoo.cs**, and then click **View Code**. b. Scroll through the code until you locate the method **public static Zoo Load(string filename);**.
3. To the **Zoo.Load** method, add code that creates a **FileStream** object that uses the filename passed to the method. Create an **XmlSerializer** object, and then use this object to deserialize the file stream.	▪ Refer to the content in this module for code samples of deserializing an object. You must modify this code to suit the application used in this lab. Note that the method returns a value of **True** if the method was successful.
4. Run the application. Open the file install_*folder***Labs\LabXB_1\Anim alData.xml**. Browse through the text that describes the animals.	a. On the standard toolbar, click **Start**. b. In the Zoo information window, click **File**, and then click **Open**. c. In the **Open** dialog box, click **AnimalData.xml**, and then click **Open**. At this point, your de-serialization code is being executed. If your code fails, attempt to debug your code and repeat this step. d. On the **View** menu, click **Next**.
5. Close the application. Save changes to your solution and then quit Visual Studio .NET.	a. Close the Zoo Information window. b. In Visual Studio .NET, on the **File** menu, click **Save All**. c. On the **File** menu, click **Exit**.

C# Statements

Statement	Example
Statement lists and block statements	```static void Main() {` ` F();` ` G(); {` ` H();` ` I();` ` }` `}```
Labeled statements and goto statements	```static void Main(string[] args) {` ` if (args.Length == 0)` ` goto done;` ` Console.WriteLine(args.Length);` `done:` ` Console.WriteLine("Done");` `}```
Local constant declarations	```static void Main() {` ` const float pi = 3.14f;` ` const int r = 123;` ` Console.WriteLine(pi * r * r);` `}```
Local variable declarations	```static void Main() {` ` int a;` ` int b = 2, c = 3;` ` a = 1;` ` Console.WriteLine(a + b + c);` `}```
Expression statements	```static int F(int a, int b) {` ` return a + b;` `}` `static void Main() {` ` F(1, 2); // Expression statement` `}```
if statements	```static void Main(string[] args) {` ` if (args.Length == 0)` ` Console.WriteLine("No args");` ` else` ` Console.WriteLine("Args");` `}```
switch statements	```static void Main(string[] args) {` ` switch (args.Length) {` `case 0:` ` Console.WriteLine("No args");` ` break;` `case 1:` ` Console.WriteLine("One arg ");` ` break;` `default:` ` int n = args.Length;` ` Console.WriteLine("{0} args", n);` ` break;` ` }` `}```
while statements	```static void Main(string[] args) {` ` int i = 0;` ` while (i < args.Length) {` ` Console.WriteLine(args[i]);` ` i++;` ` }` `}```
do statements	```static void Main() {` ` string s;` ` do {` ` s = Console.ReadLine();` ` } while (s != "Exit");` `}```

SOURCE: ECMA Standard ECMA-334, December 2001

Statement	Example
| for statements | ```csharp
static void Main(string[] args) {
    for (int i = 0; i < args.Length; i++)
        Console.WriteLine(args[i]);
}
``` |
| foreach statements | ```csharp
static void Main(string[] args) {
    foreach (string s in args)
        Console.WriteLine(s);
}
``` |
| break statements | ```csharp
static void Main(string[] args) {
    int i = 0;
    while (true) {
        if (i == args.Length)
            break;
        Console.WriteLine(args[i++]);
    }
}
``` |
| continue statements | ```csharp
static void Main(string[] args) {
    int i = 0;
    while (true) {
        Console.WriteLine(args[i++]);
        if (i < args.Length)
            continue;
        break;
    }
}
``` |
| return statements | ```csharp
static int F(int a, int b) {
    return a + b;
}
static void Main() {
    Console.WriteLine(F(1, 2));
    return;
}
``` |
| throw statements and try statements | ```csharp
static int F(int a, int b) {
    if (b == 0)
        throw new Exception("Divide by zero");
    return a / b;
}
static void Main() {
    try {
        Console.WriteLine(F(5, 0));
    }
    catch(Exception e) {
        Console.WriteLine("Error");
    }
}
``` |
| checked and unchecked statements | ```csharp
static void Main() {
    int x = Int32.MaxValue;
    Console.WriteLine(x + 1); // Overflow
    checked {
        Console.WriteLine(x + 1); // Exception
    }
    unchecked {
        Console.WriteLine(x + 1); // Overflow
    }
}
``` |
| lock statements | ```csharp
static void Main() {
    A a = foo;
    lock(a) {
        a.P = a.P + 1;
    }
}
``` |
| using statements | ```csharp
static void Main() {
    using (Resource r = new Resource()) {
        r.F();
    }
}
``` |
```

C# Predefined Types

Type	Description	Example
object	The ultimate base type of all other types	`object o = null;`
string	String type; a string is a sequence of Unicode characters	`string s = "hello";`
sbyte	8-bit signed integral type	`sbyte val = 12;`
short	16-bit signed integral type	`short val = 12;`
int	32-bit signed integral type	`int val = 12;`
long	64-bit signed integral type	`long val1 = 12;` `long val2 = 34L;`
byte	8-bit unsigned integral type	`byte val1 = 12;`
ushort	16-bit unsigned integral type	`ushort val1 = 12;`
uint	32-bit unsigned integral type	`uint val1 = 12;` `uint val2 = 34U;`

ulong	64-bit unsigned integral type	`ulong val1 = 12;`
		`ulong val2 = 34U;`
		`ulong val3 = 56L;`
		`ulong val4 = 78UL;`

float	Single-precision floating point type	`float val = 1.23F;`
double	Double-precision floating point type	`double val1 = 1.23;` `double val2 = 4.56D;`
bool	Boolean type; a bool value is either true or false	`bool val1 = true;` `bool val2 = false;`
char	Character type; a char value is a Unicode character	`char val = 'h';`
decimal	Precise decimal type with 28 significant digits	`decimal val = 1.23M;`

Each of the predefined types is shorthand for a system-provided type. For example, the keyword for `int` refers to the struct `System.Int32`. As a matter of style, the use of the keyword is favored over the use of the complete system type name.

The types `string` and `object` are reference types; the others are value types.

SOURCE: ECMA Standard ECMA-334, December 2001

Notes

Notes

Notes

Notes

Notes

Notes

Notes

Notes